June 30/22

Living Forever

Living Forever

Self-Presentation in Ancient Egypt

Edited by
Hussein Bassir

The American University in Cairo Press
Cairo New York

113 Sharia Kasr el Aini, Cairo, Egypt
200 Park Ave., Suite 1700, New York, NY 10166

Dar el Kutub No. 13059/18
ISBN 978 977 416 901 4

Dar el Kutub Cataloging-in-Publication Data

Bassir, Hussein
Living Forever: Self-representation in Ancient Egypt / Hussein Bassir.—Cairo: The American University in Cairo Press, 2019.
p. cm.
ISBN: 978 977 416 901 4
1- Egypt — Antiquities
I. Title
932

1 2 3 4 5 23 22 21 20 19

Designed by Sally Boylan
Printed in the United States of America

To my father

To my mother

To my wife

To my sons

Contents

Acknowledgments

First of all, I would like to thank Dr. Nigel Fletcher-Jones for welcoming the book to be published at the AUC Press. Moreover, I should thank his wonderful team at the AUC Press, especially Nadia Naqib, Neil Hewison, Nadine El-Hadi, Ælfwine Mischler, and Tarek Ghanem.

I would like to thank Dr. Zahi Hawass and Dr. Mostafa El Feki, Director of Bibliotheca Alexandrina, for their continuous encouragement and unlimited support.

Many scholars have served as reviewers of the book chapters. I would like to thank them all here, and they are listed alphabetically: Betsy M. Bryan, Rita Freed, David Klotz, Ronald Leprohon, Juan Carlos Moreno García, Joachim Friedrich Quack, and Joshua A. Roberson.

Many thanks are due to Aidan Dodson for providing me with the map of ancient Egypt. I would like to thank the following persons for providing me with photographs: Sandro Vanini, Arnulf Schlüter, Friederike Seyfried, Olivia Zorn, Sandra Steiß, Klaus Finneiser, Rondot Vincent, Audry Viger, Georges Poncet, Florence Gombert-Meurice, Patricia Rigault-Deon, Sabah Abdel Razek, Marwa Badr El Din, Sameh Abdel Mohsen, and Ahmed Amin.

I would like to thank all the contributors to this book. Working with them over the years has been a source of much fun and knowledge. I would like to thank my family, my wife Hend and my sons Abdallah, Adam, and Farris, for supporting me during the process of working on this book.

Illustrations

Map

Illustrations

Notes on Contributors

Damien Agut-Labordère

Damien Agut-Labordère (permanent Researcher in the CNRS) is at the head of the Achemenet Program and co-leader of the CNRS team ArScAn-HAROC based in Nanterre, France. He is a specialist of Egyptian history from the sixth to the fourth centuries BC, focusing on social and economic aspects. As demoticist, he works on the documentation discovered in the Kharga Oasis. Involved in the excavations of several archaeological sites, he tries to cross the textual data with those collected by the other archaeological disciplines.

James P. Allen

James P. Allen is the Charles Edwin Wilbour Professor of Egyptology at Brown University. He received his PhD from the University of Chicago and has served as epigrapher with the Oriental Institute's Epigraphic Survey, Cairo Director of the American Research Center in Egypt, and curator in the Metropolitan Museum of Art. His chief interests and Egyptological contributions are in ancient Egyptian language, literature, history, and thought.

Mariam Ayad

Mariam Ayad is an associate professor of Egyptology at the American University in Cairo (AUC). Prior to joining AUC, Ayad was a tenured associate professor of art history and Egyptology at the University of Memphis, in the United States, where she also served as an assistant director of the Institute of Egyptian Art and Archaeology from 2003 to 2010. She obtained a BA in Egyptology at AUC (1994), minoring in archaeological chemistry, and an MA in ancient Near Eastern civilizations, specializing in

Egyptian language and literature (with a minor in Egyptian archaeology) at the University of Toronto, Canada, before earning her PhD in Egyptology at Brown University. At Brown, Ayad's research focused on ancient Egyptian mortuary texts, the Third Intermediate Period, and the role of women in temple hierarchy. Her dissertation, "The Funerary Texts of Amenirdis I: Analysis of Their Layout and Purpose," successfully defended in December 2002, combined her three major areas of interest. She is the author of a monograph on the God's Wives of Amun of the Twenty-third to the Twenty-sixth Dynasties, *God's Wife, God's Servant* (Routledge, 2009), and the editor of two volumes on Coptic culture. At AUC, Ayad teaches a year-long course on Middle Egyptian grammar (Egyptian hieroglyphs) as well as graduate seminars on Egypt in the first millennium BC, Nubian cultures and society, and ancient Egyptian women in temple ritual. Ayad also teaches an introduction to Coptic class and has led classes focusing on ancient Egyptian literature and Late Egyptian historical texts (read in Hieratic). Ayad is the director of the Opening of the Mouth Epigraphic Project at the Tomb of Harwa (TT 37) in Luxor.

Hussein Bassir

Hussein Bassir, an Egyptian archaeologist and Egyptologist, received his MA and PhD from Johns Hopkins University. He has been the general director of the Giza Pyramids, the Grand Egyptian Museum, and the National Museum of Egyptian Civilization, and is currently director of the Antiquities Museum and Zahi Hawass Center of Egyptology, Bibliotheca Alexandria. He has taught in Egypt and the United States, and is the author of *Image and Voice in Saite Egypt* and *Malikat al-far'ana: drama al-hubb wa-l-sulta*, as well as two novels, *al-Bahth 'an Khnum* and *al-Ahmar al-'aguz*.

Juan Carlos Moreno García

Juan Carlos Moreno García (PhD in Egyptology, 1995; Habilitation, 2009) is a CNRS senior researcher at the University of Paris IV–Sorbonne. He has published extensively on pharaonic administration, socio-economic history, and landscape organization, usually in a comparative perspective with other civilizations of the ancient world, and has organized several conferences on these topics. Recent publications include *Dynamics of Production in the Ancient Near East, 1300–500 BC* (2016), *L'Égypte des pharaons. De Narmer à Dioclétien (3150 av. J.-C.–284 apr. J.-C.)* (2016), and *Ancient Egyptian Administration* (2013). He is also chief editor of *The Journal of Egyptian History* (Brill) and area editor (economy) of the *UCLA Encyclopedia of Egyptology*. He has also launched a new series of Egyptological books ("Elements") for Cambridge University Press in collaboration with Gianluca Miniaci and Anna Stevens.

Colleen Manassa Darnell

Colleen Manassa Darnell received her BA and PhD in Egyptology from Yale University, where she taught as the Marilyn M. and William K. Simpson Associate Professor of Egyptology. Her publications include monographs on Egyptian funerary texts (*The Late Egyptian Underworld: Sarcophagi and Related Texts from the Nectanebid Period* and *The Ancient Egyptian Netherworld Books*, with John Coleman Darnell), New Kingdom literature (*Imagining the Past: Historical Fiction in New Kingdom Egypt*), and military history (*The Great Karnak Inscription of Merneptah: Grand Strategy in the 13th Century BC* and *Tutankhamun's Armies: Battle and Conquest in Ancient Egypt's Eighteenth Dynasty*, with John Coleman Darnell). She curated an exhibit entitled "Echoes of Egypt: Conjuring the Land of the Pharaohs" and edited the accompanying museum catalog, which explored two thousand years of Egyptian revival activities. Since 2008 she has directed the Moalla Survey Project, which has made several archaeological discoveries within the northern portion of the Third Nome of Upper Egypt ranging in date from the Predynastic Period through the Late Roman era.

Christopher Eyre

Christopher Eyre, BA (Oxford, 1973) in Oriental Studies, Egyptian with Akkadian, and DPhil (Oxford, 1980), is professor of Egyptology in the University of Liverpool. He has worked frequently on epigraphic projects in Egypt, and has published widely on Egyptian economic and social history, focusing particularly on the interpretation of literary and documentary sources, and the use of texts in pharaonic Egypt.

Roberto B. Gozzoli

Roberto B. Gozzoli (PhD Birmingham, 2004), is lecturer at Mahidol University International College, Thailand. His research interests embrace ancient Egyptian historiography, first millennium BC royal ideology, Nubian culture, as well as politics of heritage management worldwide. He is the author of *The Writing of History in Ancient Egypt during the First Millennium BC (ca.1070–180 BC): Trends and Perspectives* (GHP Egyptology 5; London, 2006) and *Psammetichus II: Reign, Documents and Officials* (GHP Egyptology 25; London, 2017).

Renata Landgráfová

Renata Landgráfová studied Egyptology and general linguistics at the Faculty of Arts, Charles University, and received her PhD in Egyptology at the same university in 2008. She has worked as a postdoc at the Freie

Universität Berlin. Since 2008, she has been a member of the Faculty of Arts, Charles University in Prague (teaching Middle Egyptian, Late Egyptian, and Demotic), and has regularly participated at the archaeological exploration of the Late Period shaft tomb necropolis at Abusir (documentation, analysis, and interpretation of texts).

Ronald Leprohon

Ronald Leprohon served as Education Officer and Project Egyptologist for the *Treasures of Tutankhamun* exhibition in Toronto in 1978–79, and has done archaeological work in Egypt for both the Akhenaten Temple Project and the Dakhleh Oasis Project. In 1981 he became the first director of the Canadian Institute in Egypt, and is currently Professor of Egyptology in, and past Chair of, the Department of Near and Middle Eastern Civilizations at the University of Toronto. The recipient of a University of Toronto Faculty of Arts and Science Outstanding Teaching Award in 2002–2003, he has also published a two-volume study of the funerary stelae in the Boston Museum of Fine Arts as well as *The Great Name*, a comprehensive study of the three-thousand-year history of the titulary of the pharaohs.

Hana Navratilova

Hana Navratilova, with doctorates in both history and Egyptology, is a historian and Egyptologist interested in historical thought, interdisciplinary history, and the contribution of biographies to historiography. She studied at Charles University in Prague, where she wrote theses on the Egyptian revival in Bohemia (2002) and a study on Egyptian historical thought (2006). She has held research grants at the University of Vienna, the Griffith Institute (Oxford), and the Mellon Fellowship at the Metropolitan Museum of Arts. She is currently research associate at the University of Reading and a visiting scholar at Wolfson College, University of Oxford. Her present projects include the recording and publication of visitors' graffiti in the pyramid complex of Senwosret III, Dahshur, Egypt, for the Metropolitan Museum of Art, and work on a new biography of Jaroslav Černý.

Jeremy Pope

Jeremy Pope is associate professor in the Department of History at the College of William & Mary, where he is also a Faculty Affiliate in Classical Studies. Pope is a member of the editorial board of *African Archaeological Review* and is the author of *The Double Kingdom under Taharqo: Studies in the History of Kush and Egypt c. 690–664 BC* (Brill, 2014). He has participated in archaeological excavations at Gebel Barkal in Sudan and at Karnak's Mut Precinct in Egypt.

R. Gareth Roberts

R. Gareth Roberts gained his bachelor's degree from the University of Canterbury in Christchurch, New Zealand, taking a double major in Classics and history. He then took a master's degree in Egyptology from the University of Liverpool, in the UK, before going on to read for a DPhil in Egyptology at the University of Oxford. While at Oxford he was involved in the Online Digital Library Project, digitizing Ippolito Rosellini's *I monumenti dell'Egitto e della Nubia*, Jean-François Champollion's *Monuments de l'Égypte et de la Nubie* (plates and *Notices descriptives*), and the original artwork from Arthur Evans's excavations at Knossos. He has undertaken extensive fieldwork, notably in Turkey with the Neubauer Expedition to Zincirli, where he was Area Supervisor of Area 6, and with the Konya Regional Archaeological Survey Project, and in Libya with the Western Marmarica Coastal Survey. At the time of writing he was Co-ordinating Editor of the *Online Egyptological Bibliography* (http://oeb.griffith.ox.ac.uk/), managing its transition from the earlier *Annual Egyptological Bibliography* and its expansion to include the *Bibliographie Altägypten* and the *Aigyptos* database.

Hend Sherbiny

Hend Sherbiny is the general director of scientific research, Abu Rawash Antiquities Area, Giza, Egypt. Her PhD dissertation is on "Identity Change of Royal Monuments in the Second Half of the Eighteenth Dynasty (The Amarna Period)." Her MS, "Studies in Dendro-Egyptology," was on archaeology, Egyptology, and dendrochronology (College of Sciences, University of Arizona, 2015). She has received her MA in Egyptology from the Faculty of Archaeology, Cairo University in 2012. She has received BA in Egyptology Department of Egyptology, Faculty of Archaeology, Cairo University in 2000. She has published extensively on Egyptology, archaeology, and dendrochronology, and has excavated at Giza, Saqqara, and Bahariya Oasis. She has participated in the Fieldwork of Laboratory of Tree-Ring Research and School of Anthropology, University of Arizona, at Santa Fe, New Mexico. She was a member of Dr. Zahi Hawass's excavations at the Sheikh Sobi Cemetery (Saite Period), and at the Valley of the Golden Mummies (Greco–Roman Period), Bahariya Oasis. She is a member the American Research Center in Egypt.

Hana Vymazalová

Hana Vymazalová graduated in Egyptology and logic at the Faculty of Arts, Charles University in Prague, and acquired her PhD in Egyptology in 2005. Since 2016 she has been an associate professor of Egyptology. She specializes in the economy of the Old Kingdom royal funerary complexes and in Old Hieratic palaeography. She also studies ancient Egyptian science, especially mathematics and medicine. Since 2006 she has participated in the Czech archaeological excavation in Abusir and since 2015 she has been a member of the Egyptian mission in south Saqqara.

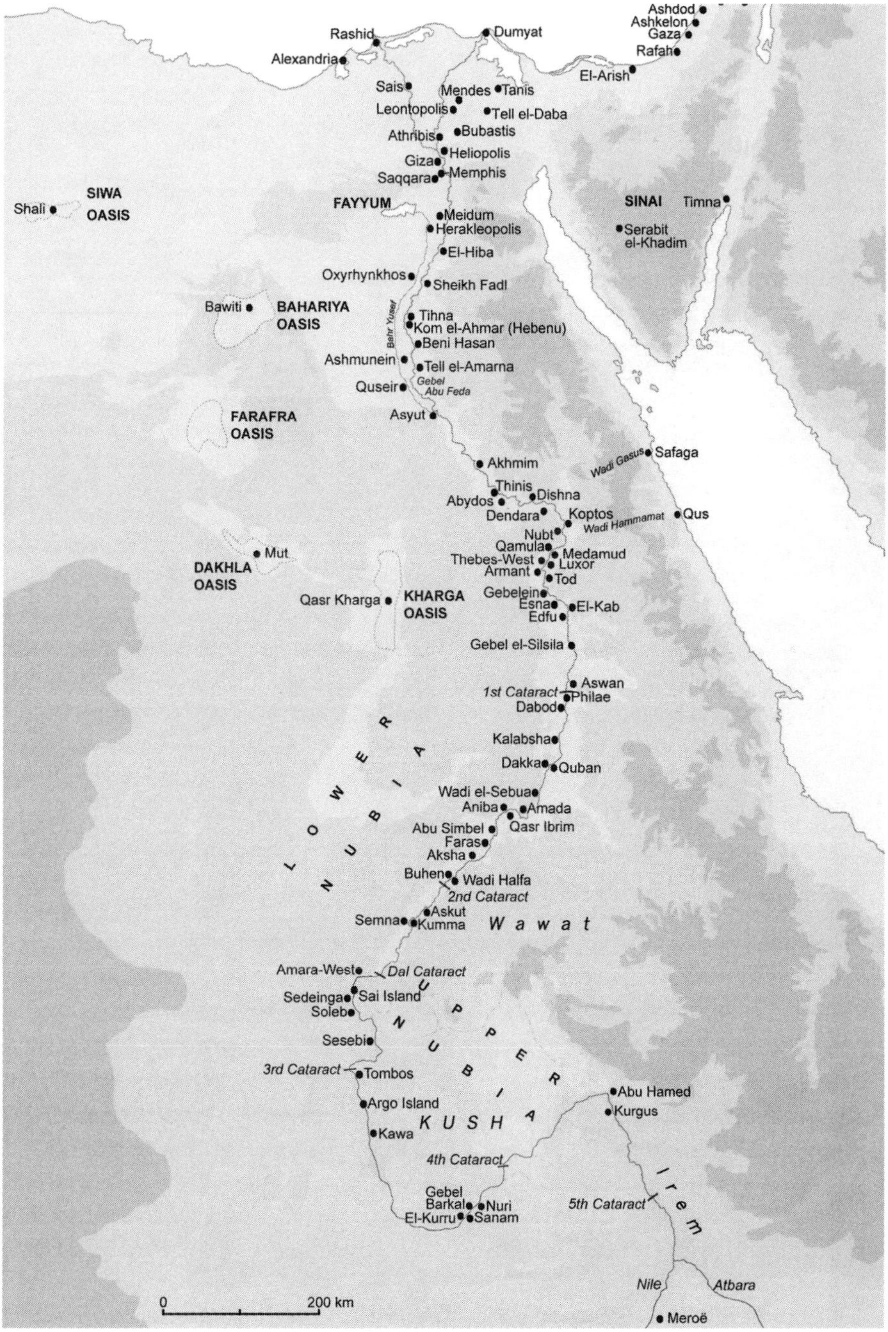

Ancient Egypt and Nubia (courtesy of Aidan Dodson)

Chronology

This chronolony of ancient Egypt is based on J. Baines and J. Malek, *Atlas of Ancient Egypt*, revised edition, Cairo, 2009, 36–37. All dates are BC. Dates from 664 BC on are precise to within a year.

Late Predynastic c. 3100
Early Dynastic Period c. 2950–2575
1st Dynasty c. 2950–2775
2nd Dynasty c. 2775–2650
3rd Dynasty c. 2650–2575

Old Kingdom c. 2575–2150
4th Dynasty c. 2575–2450
5th Dynasty c. 2450–2325
6th Dynasty c. 2325–2175
7th/8th Dynasty c. 2175–2125

1st Intermediate Period c. 2125–1975
9th Dynasty (Herakleopolitan) c. 2125–2080
10th Dynasty (Herakleopolitan) c. 2080–1975
11th Dynasty (Theban) c. 2080–1975

Middle Kingdom c. 1975–1640
11th Dynasty (all Egypt) c. 1975–1940
12th Dynasty c. 1938–1755
13th Dynasty c. 1755–1630
14th Dynasty contemporaneous with the 13th or 15th Dynasties

2nd Intermediate Period c. 1630–1520

15th Dynasty (Hyksos) c. 1630–1520
16th Dynasty contemporaneous with the 15th Dynasty
17th Dynasty c. 1630–1540

New Kingdom c.1539–1075

18th Dynasty c. 1539–1292
19th Dynasty c. 1292–1190
20th Dynasty c. 1190–1075

3rd Intermediate Period c. 1075–715

21st Dynasty c. 1075–945
22nd Dynasty c. 945–715
23rd Dynasty c. 830–715
24th Dynasty (Sais) c. 730–715
25th Dynasty (Nubia and Theban area) c. 770–715

Late Period c. 715–332

25th Dynasty (Nubia and all Egypt) c. 715–657
26th Dynasty 664–525
27th Dynasty (Persian) 525–404
28th Dynasty 404–399
29th Dynasty 399–380
30th Dynasty 380–343
2nd Persian Period 343–332

Abbreviations

AoF	*Altorientalische Forschungen*
Archéo-Nil	*Bulletin de la société pour l'étude des cultures prépharaoniques de la vallée du Nil*
ArOr	*Archív Orientální: Journal of African and Asian Studies*
ARYS	*Antiguëdad, Religiones y Sociedades*
ASAE	*Annales du Service des Antiquités de l'Égypte*
BES	*Bulletin of the Egyptological Seminar*
BIFAO	*Bulletin de l'Institut Français d'Archéologie Orientale*
BiOr	*Bibliotheca Orientalis*
BM	British Museum
BMA	Brooklyn Museum of Art
BMCR	*Bryn Mawr Classical Review*
BMMA	*Bulletin of the Metropolitan Museum of Art*
BMSAES	*British Museum Studies in Ancient Egypt and Sudan*
BSFE	*Bulletin de la Société Française d'Égyptologie*
CRAIBL	*Comptes rendus des séances de l'Académie des Inscriptions & Belles-Lettres*
CRIPEL	*Cahiers de Recherches de l'Institut de Papyrologie et d'Égyptologie de Lille*
DE	*Discussions in Egyptology*
GM	*Göttinger Miszellen*
JAOS	*Journal of the American Oriental Society*
JARCE	*Journal of the American Research Center in Egypt*

JEA	*Journal of Egyptian Archaeology*
JEOL	*Jaarbericht van het Vooraziatisch-Egyptisch Gezelschap Ex Oriente Lux*
JSA	*Journal of Social Archaeology*
JSSEA	*Journal of the Society of the Study of Egyptian Antiquities*
KRI	Kitchen, K.A. *Ramesside Inscriptions Historical and Biographical*, 8 vols. (Oxford), 1975–90.
LÄ	Helck, W. and E. Otto, eds., *Lexikon der Ägyptologie*, 7 vols. (Wiesbaden), 1972–92.
LAAA	*Liverpool Annals of Archaeology and Anthropology*
MAJA	Münchner Arbeitskreis Junge Aegyptologie
Man	1901–65: *Man: Journal of the Royal Anthropological Institute of Great Britain and Ireland* 1966–94: *Man: Journal of the Royal Anthropological Institute* (new series) (Continued from 1995 as *Journal of the Royal Anthropological Institute*)
MDAIK	*Mitteilungen des Deutschen Archäologischen Instituts Kairo*
MMA	Metropolitan Museum of Art
MMAB	*Metropolitan Museum of Art Bulletin*
MMJ	*Metropolitan Museum Journal*
MSGB	*Mitteilungen der Sudanarchäologischen Gesellschaft zu Berlin*
Origini	*Origini: preistoria e protostoria delle civiltà antiche*
PES	*Prague Egyptological Studies*
PM	Porter, B. and R.L.B. Moss, *Topographical Bibliography of Ancient Egyptian Hieroglyphic Texts, Reliefs, and Paintings*, 8 vols. (Oxford), 2003; 2004. [1927; 1964].
RdE	*Revue d'égyptologie*
RT	*Recueil de travaux relatifs à la philologie et à l'archéologie égyptiennes et assyriennes: pour servir de bulletin à la Mission Française du Caire*
SAK	*Studien zur Altägyptischen Kultur*
Urk. I	Sethe, K., *Urkunden des alten Reichs*, Leipzig, 1933.
Urk. IV	Sethe, K., *Urkunden der 18. Dynastie*, Leipzig, 1906.
Urk. VII	Sethe, K., *Historisch-biographische Urkunden des mittleren Reiches*, Leipzig, 1935.
VA	*Varia Aegyptiaca*
ZÄS	*Zeitschrift für ägyptische Sprache und Altertumskunde*

Foreword

James P. Allen

Self-presentation lies at the intersection of psychology and sociology, each area mirrored in one of the expression's two terms. On the one hand, self-presentation reveals what individuals want society to think of them, from the woman getting her nails done to the little boy dressing up as Batman. On the other, self-presentation reveals what a society values, or at least, what the self-presenter thinks it values.

The study of self-presentation in ancient Egyptian art and texts is significant for both these aspects. Comparison of the seated statue of Khafre in the Egyptian Museum, Cairo, with the statue of Nectanebo II in the Metropolitan Museum of Art, New York, for example, reveals much about the institution of kingship in the two eras in which they were created. In the Old Kingdom statue of Khafre, the falcon representing the god Horus, avatar of kingship, is almost imperceptible behind the head of the seated king who dominates the statue, whereas in the Late Period statue of Nectanebo, the falcon is the dominant figure, dwarfing the king standing beneath its breast. Self-presentation lies at the origin of both statues: among other things, supreme confidence in human ability in the Old Kingdom versus servile reliance on the gods in the Late Period. Both examples of self-presentation reveal much about the society in which they were created and how their subjects viewed that society.

Similar aspects underlie self-presentational inscriptions, the primary object of self-presentation studies. The statement of Nekhebu, "It was important how His Incarnation always blessed me for what he sent me to do, for my effort to do what His Incarnation sent me for" (*Urk*. I, 221, 4–5), in the Sixth Dynasty, reveals not only the writer's sense of self-importance but also what he based it on, his service to the king. In contrast, Ankhtifi's self-presentation, from the Tenth Dynasty, says nothing about the king, and his sense of self-worth comes solely from his own accomplishments. The two texts, separated by two hundred years, reflect both a change in the status of kingship in Egyptian eyes and in the criteria by which individuals judged their own merit.

The studies in this book, therefore, have a dual value: not merely as isolated analyses of data but also as windows into ancient Egyptian society at various points in its history. They show how individual inscriptions and works of art can be viewed not only in aesthetic and historical isolation but also as mirrors of the society in which they were created.

Preface

The presentation of nonroyal self in ancient Egypt represents a new window into its culture and historical periods. Self-presentation was the most ancient, common, and crucial component of ancient high culture, and existed from the Old Kingdom to the Greco-Roman Period. The nonroyal elite members of ancient Egyptian culture presented themselves through language and art. This edited and peer-reviewed book runs chronologically and aims to visualize precisely how and why the individuals of this culture represented themselves in literature, as well as how they depicted their positions in the history of the period and their relationships with the crown. Any historical aspect of the period that self-presentation reveals is discussed. One of the questions that this new book addresses is why the individuals of these ancient Egyptian historical periods represented themselves as such. A more thorough understanding of this question yields information about politics, culture change, religious change, and social change in ancient Egypt.

The primary focus of this book is an examination of how and why the individual presented himself or herself in literature, and how these have survived and have been interpreted in the cultural contexts of the various ancient Egyptian historical periods. The ancient Egyptian textual setting was utilized as a major tool to express and demonstrate the individual interacting with the self, deities, and society. The starting point is the premise that in ancient Egypt there were 'selves,' and a sense that these creations of 'selves' could be presented textually to other members of this ancient society. Different approaches are applied in this book, and various disciplines are engaged and focus on topics and themes on varied aspects from multiple ancient Egyptian historical periods.

This book employs an interdisciplinary and holistic approach to the topic, in order to examine how ancient Egyptian individuals expressed their 'selves.' Scholars, depending on the period, treat the various aspects of the selected texts of the individuals in question: the philological and historical issues, linguistic and literary notions, religious and moral values, and self-presentation features. In the philological treatment, contributors shed light on the main aspects of the texts, such as transliteration, translation, and lexigraphical and orthographical features. Contributors also cover the primary aspects of the texts such as dating, history, issues of cultural memory, the role of the individual (both within and relative to the royal sphere), and the relationship between the individual and deities. It is of particular interest that the elements of this book—varied as the ancient Egyptian protagonists are in titles, reign, professions, and overall background—all concentrate on the meanings of self in the telling of a life story. Contributors moreover uncover the close link between monumentality, identity, and ideology in the various periods represented.

Ultimately, this book explores the interdependency and interdisciplinary analysis and cross-cultural comparison of literature and history in the different periods, examined through texts. Study of the textual corpora of the individuals will analyze the emergence and rise of 'self' and 'individualism' as a historical phenomenon of ancient Egypt. Moreover, the elements of this book examine several cultural and political practices of a variety of periods, including but not limited to patronage and representations of authority, nobility, and royalty. The power of texts and representations to shape as well as to reflect history can be seen through the analyses. Text represents major components of shaping the overall self-presentations of the individuals in these periods; our understanding of self-presentation can thus also advance similar studies for several cultures and periods in the ancient world.

Introduction

Hussein Bassir

Living Forever: Self-Presentation in Ancient Egypt has been a great dream of my academic life and career. It has finally come into reality. As self-presentation differs from one period to another and from one person to another, the authors of this book's chapters differ in their approaches to the topic.

In Chapter 1, "Egyptian Self-Presentation Dynamics and Strategies," Christopher Eyre points out that Egyptian writing is more concerned with presenting the individual as the performer of a role than as a personality. Formal autobiography is a genre of self-praise, asking an audience to identify the speaker by his or her performance of a role within a social hierarchy. For a man this emphasizes relationship to the king and competence in function, enabling his role as patron of his family, and his roles to his subordinates and to his entire social milieu. In the rare female autobiographies, the social role is that of wife and mother: a narrative marginalization of women is normal. The target audience and purpose of the self-presentation are inseparable and deeply rooted in the broader history of writing and literature. Self-presentation and the behavior promulgated in wisdom literature both provide an incomplete picture of social reality: an idealized sociology of Pharaonic Egypt in which layers of social conformity mark appropriate discourse at different hierarchical levels. Both exemplify what we talk of as abstract by the specific event: any psychological self-presentation, or description of social attitudes, is presented through concrete behavior and specific actions. There is a strong tendency for presentation in terms of binary contrasts of ordered against disordered behavior, and not in nuanced ways. Emphasis on self-reliance reflects the autobiographer as the sole point of reference in his text, while the relationship with other genres of literature marks a social location for the autobiographer in a scribal cultured hierarchy.

In Chapter 2, "Self-Presentation in the Early Dynasties," Juan Carlos Moreno García confirms that the early dynasties witnessed the first attempts to materialize visual and written expressions of self-presentation in the private sphere. The advent of a unified monarchy in the Nile Valley was accompanied by the consolidation of a new, standardized imagery of the members of the elite where officials were firstly distinguished by their attitudes, position (often in registers, close to the king), and symbols of authority (sticks), and secondly by their titles and names. Such surprisingly limited use of writing contrasts with the importance of monumental architecture (private mastabas) to express the power and rank of their owners. Only gradually texts and a more elaborated iconography began playing a more important role as means for self-presentation, to the point that titles, honorable poses, and specific symbols of status crystallized in early codified forms called to prevail for centuries, and later expanded through elaborated biographies since the middle of the third millennium BC. Even then, continuous lengthy texts remained optional and were often reduced to lists of offerings and moral statements, more rarely to biographies and 'juridical' texts. Not by chance, some of the most creative, informative, and vivid biographies appeared in the provincial world, far from the royal court and its normative strict palatial codes. In any case, the continuity of basic poses and themes first developed during the Early Dynastic proves the existence of a visual tradition transmitted for centuries, whereas innovation, experiment, and withdrawal of previous dominant forms finally crystallized in potent icons of self-presentation during the Third Dynasty.

In Chapter 3, "Self-Presentation in the Fourth Dynasty," Hend Sherbiny presents the main features of self-presentations in the Fourth Dynasty, highlighting the relationship between the kings and the high officials of the dynasty. The Fourth Dynasty nonroyal self-presentations represent an early stage in the development of Egyptian self-presentation. They are good examples for understanding the status of the nonroyal elite members of the period. Although the surviving self-presentations are few, they do, nevertheless, reflect social hierarchies, political ideology, and the organization of the administration during the period. The relationship between the kings and nonroyal individuals of this dynasty is remarkable and passed through different stages. This dynasty presents the different aspects of the ancient Egyptian king's image as divine, half-divine, and human. Although the nonroyal elite members of this dynasty left magnificent monuments, they did not leave many self-presentational texts. This is one of the main characteristics of the nonroyal elite members' status in the period. Fourth Dynasty self-presentations come mainly from the Memphite necropolis, especially Giza. The content of these self-presentations is basic. They are ideal self-presentational phrases attached to other texts, such as appeals and warnings, while some self-presentations commemorate individual events. The self-presentations of the Fourth Dynasty are also short, mainly based on epithets and titles rather than consisting of long narratives, yet, nevertheless reveal the relationship between the nonroyal individual and the king. Furthermore, these nonroyal self-presentations introduce the nonroyal individual in perfect harmony with the ideals and expectations of the aristocracy of the period. These texts stress a total dependence upon the king. Although those self-presentations come from tomb contexts, mainly inscribed on tomb walls, they are condensed rather than elaborated, restricted in use of text, and do not correspond to the scenes on which they are inscribed. The nonroyal self-presentations of the period reflect more social history than political processes. They characterize high official individuals, summarize their professional careers, describe a few noteworthy episodes in their lives, and are linked to the social as well as the public lifestyle of the political and administrative nonroyal elites.

In Chapter 4, "Self-Presentation in the Late Old Kingdom," Hana Vymazalová explains that the social and administrative changes in the Fifth and Sixth Dynasties resulted in the increase in the number of administrative offices and the growing power of nonroyal officials. The highest-ranking officials presented themselves through the king, having their tombs built next to the royal funerary monument, imitating the royal architecture and decorative motifs, and narrating special favors from the king in their biographical inscriptions. Lower echelons of the Egyptian society seem to have highlighted family and professional ties, especially in the form of family tombs and clusters of associated tombs. Provinces became increasingly important in this period, as the officials lived and had themselves buried in their nomes. Their growing independence resulted in reforms on the part of the kings, which aimed to keep control over the country.

In Chapter 5, "Self-Presentation in the Eleventh Dynasty," Renata Landgráfová explores the nature of self-presentation in the Eleventh Dynasty, that is, at a time of the gradual recentralization of the Egyptian state following the First Intermediate Period. The image of the ideal official of the first half of the Eleventh Dynasty is a complex one: a powerful self-made man whom the king selected from among others for his excellent qualities, who gained an exclusive close access to the ruler and continued to excel in whatever task was entrusted to him, towering over his peers yet continuing to care for his nome or district, especially in the role of a provider in need. The main goal of self-presentation was to create for oneself a good reputation that was the source of social immortality. There were three sources of reputation: the primary source, that is, the inherent qualities and achievements of the text owner; the secondary source, that is, the proximity to and favored status by a highly prestigious individual; and the 'negative' source, the self-restraint, that is, the despicable deeds that the text owner may have had an opportunity to do but refrained from. While narrative segments are rare, the use of stock phrases that flourished fully in the later Middle Kingdom is only just beginning in the second half of the Eleventh Dynasty.

In Chapter 6, "Self-Presentation in the Twelfth Dynasty" Ronald Leprohon points out that Twelfth Dynasty self-presentations describe their owners' service to the crown, social standing, good qualities, and proper behavior toward their follow men. The suggestion of an oral component in their composition may be inferred from some of the texts themselves, which were actually requested to be read out loud to passersby, and the fact that many were introduced by the phrase *ḏd.f* (he says). The self-laudatory epithets can be found to convey complementary notions within pairings and show striking affinities to instructional literature, demonstrating the care with which they were compiled.

In Chapter 7, "Self-Presentation in the Second Intermediate Period," R. Gareth Roberts seeks to include the 'self' in a study of self-presentation by considering the role that memory, which is both personal and intrinsic to all people, played in Egyptian self-presentation material. He uses Second Intermediate Period data for this purpose, because in this period it was considered appropriate for personal elements to be included on commemorative monuments. After a précis of the most relevant memory states—working memory, declarative long-term memory, and episodic long-term memory—he identifies three non-mutually-exclusive modes of Egyptian self-presentation: probable autobiographical elements, which can be interpreted as containing memories *by* a person; elements that suggest others' memories *of* a person; and patterns that appear to be characteristic of a period or workshop, and which likely pertain to memories of a *sort* of person. He then uses Second Intermediate Period data to exemplify these three modes. The author's first conclusion is that it may be possible to determine whether the person commemorated on a given piece commissioned it and provided input as to its contents. In cases where this can be demonstrated, it might be considered autobiographical. Where it cannot, it is possible that the piece was constructed postmortem, either with the input of someone who knew the deceased, or by workers whose expertise supplied the elements that were considered suitable for the assignment. In these cases the material cannot truly be self-presentation. His second conclusion, implied in the first, is that many of the changes and evolutions now observed in self-presentation material came not from the dictates of elites, but from the experience—and memory—of ordinary workers.

In Chapter 8, "Self-Presentation in the Eighteenth Dynasty," Hana Navratilova reveals that the Eighteenth Dynasty offers rich archaeological and written sources for a study of the Egyptian personal and cultural identity. There were numerous venues for self-presentation, although the written representation of identity, and also of individuality, shown in the tomb contexts, appears as particularly well attested. At the risk of offering an unfocused paper, this contribution presents a text corpus that stretched over several centuries and addressed the process of self-fashioning that had underwritten different performances of self-representation. The elite identity in Eighteenth Dynasty Egypt was not preordained in a fixed pattern, although there were shared forms and shared principles, but there was also some flexibility in terms of how the social roles were carried out.

In Chapter 9, "Self-Presentation in the Ramesside Period," Colleen Manassa Darnell shows that during the Nineteenth and Twentieth Dynasties, the self-presentation of private individuals can be seen most markedly in three spheres of activity: funerary contexts (for example, tomb decoration and graffiti added to earlier tombs by Ramesside scribes), temple contexts (for example, the donation of statuary and votive surcharging of temple walls), and rock inscriptions. Hieroglyphic and hieratic texts within each of the three types of loci provide a starting point for the examination of self-presentation, while the larger context of each place indicates how those texts would function as intermediaries between an absent (or deceased) individual and the intended audience. Interaction with pre-existing funerary, sacral, or natural landscapes further enhances the significance of a text: a hieratic text on the wall of an earlier tomb may indicate appreciation for the past or literary knowledge; votive surcharging within a temple (from a hieroglyphic inscription to a simple sandal outline on a temple floor) denotes a level of priestly function; a rock inscription along a distant desert road (no matter how humble) can designate the administrative reach of a particular individual. One theme that runs through all three spheres of Ramesside self-presentation is the conscious link between an individual's career and life choices and his relationship to the divine, and during the Ramesside era in particular, the act of self-presentation could transform autobiographical statements into an act of devotion.

In Chapter 10, "Self-Presentation in the Third Intermediate Period," Roberto B. Gozzoli explains that with the collapse of the Egyptian New Kingdom, Egyptian self-representations during the Libyan Period (1069–712 BC) turned into a reflexive mood, and previous ecumenism disappeared in favor of a more personal introspection. People expressed their faith in the local gods as before, but instead of the pharaohs, they remarked family connections through long genealogical lists. Those genealogies boosted both illustrious ancestors as well as the continuity of earlier political and religious positions. And archaism—the revival of older artistic formats—made its appearance as well, as the past represented a bridge to the actual situation.

In Chapter 11, "Self-Presentation in the Twenty-fifth Dynasty," Jeremy Pope points out that within the long history of Egyptian self-presentation, the era of Kushite rule during the Twenty-fifth Dynasty is distinguished from preceding and succeeding periods by three enigmatic absences: the absence of royal names upon the great majority of nonroyal monuments in Egypt; the absence of pedigrees in the records of Kushite immigrants in Egypt; and the absence of private biographies and statuary for nonroyal individuals in Nubia. In this chapter he assesses multiple competing theories that might account for these phenomena and proposes an explanation for each.

In Chapter 12, "Self-Presentation in the Late Dynastic Period," Damien Agut-Labordère reveals that the Persian Period (526–332 BC) constitutes a deep rupture in the political and cultural history of Egypt: for the first time in its history, the crown is confiscated by a foreign imperial power for a long time. Egypt is then governed from the capitals located in Persia: Susa and Persepolis. For five generations, from 526 BC to 400 BC, the Egyptian elites are kept out of the power that is in the hands of the Persian elites headed by the satrap based in Memphis. At first, the author aims to show the way in which this profound transformation has marked the discourse that the Egyptian elites hold on themselves, their self-presentation. How can they present a career, a life itinerary, that now takes place outside the central power? The return to independence from 400 BC to 342 BC is characterized by a resurgence of classic form, that is Saite form, of self-presentation. However, the self-presentation of this period remains strongly marked by the themes that appeared or were highlighted during the Persian Period.

In Chapter 13, "Women's Self-Presentation in Pharaonic Egypt," Mariam Ayad analyzes women's titles, epithets, and particularly funerary biographical inscriptions that point to an association between periods of political and social upheaval and a woman's ability to appropriate and adapt stock biographical statements for her own use. In periods of greater political stability, the emphasis seems to be on a woman's more passive qualities of charm and beauty, her family connections, and her domestic, priestly, or courtly roles. Access to wealth, whatever the source, enabled women to present themselves as autonomous, moral characters whose ability to act on behalf of themselves and others ensured their salvation.

In Chapter 14, "Traditions of Egyptian Self-Presentation," I conclude with the main themes of ancient Egyptian self-presentations from the beginning of ancient Egyptian civilization to its pharaonic end. The traditions of Egyptian self-presentations were deeply rooted in ancient Egypt since the early Dynastic Period, and they varied in aspect, composition, and themes from the beginning of Egyptian history to the late Dynastic Period. Self-presentations display the lives of the elites and vividly represent their beliefs, culture, and expectations for the afterlife. They also display their wish to be remembered and not to be forgotten after death. They reveal their eagerness to be commemorated by the living to avoid the possibility of a miserable afterlife.

The relationship between royalty and nobility in self-presentations was changeable. In some periods, individuals witnessed a highly independent spirit, very visible in their self-presentations, when the power of elite members increased; and many cases reveal their king-like manner. Several examples reveal the rising power of the elite members. The actions of these nonroyal elite members are clear evidence for the prerogatives these officials probably received due to their rising power. Thus, Egyptian self-presentations were a reflection of kingship and a good indicator for the relationship between the king and his high officials. Nonroyal elite members showed appreciation to the ruling king, and as a result, the king appeared in an outstanding position in their texts when he was very strong. If the king was weak, some nonroyal elite members expressed themselves in a kingly manner and, in some cases, ignored the ruling king or mentioned him briefly in a remote place, revealing an increased sense of individualism of the nobles.

Individuals' presence is very rich especially when interacting with the formal presence of the royalty. Therefore, the relationship between royalty and nobility in self-presentations is unique and helps us to understand the periods and the circumstances that produced nonroyal self-presentations. The role of the individual within the formal sphere of the political realm is much increased. The three presences of individuality—the individual's presence, the deity's presence, and the king's presence—are well integrated in the individual's life, career, and afterlife. Their self-presentation and their concept of themselves, deities, and the king are intertwined in self-presentations.

There is an interplay of image and text in presenting the life and career of individuals' identities. The interdependency of literature and history through self-presentations is clear. The self-presentations and monuments of nonroyal individuals help us to understand the individuals' selves in any period. The cultural and political practices that formed the history of any period are patronage, representations of authority, nobility, and royalty. The shaping force of history on the status of individuals is revealed through self-presentations, which constitute as well as reflect history. History here is among the major components that shaped the overall self-presentations of nonroyal individuals. They highlight the distinctive characteristics of self-presentation, and place each text and its owner within the broad context of Egyptian self-presentation traditions. The well-documented self-presentations of elite members are among the most remarkable of their times.

1

Egyptian Self-Presentation Dynamics and Strategies

Christopher Eyre

Textual self-presentation lies at the beginning of social discourse as preserved from Egypt: to be addressed through its history and its target audiences.[1] In practice this means, at least initially, the tomb record. Modern knowledge of individual self-perception is dependent on the archaeological record—tombs, monuments, and their inscriptions—presenting the individual to an audience that was contemporary in its attitudes and preconceptions.[2] This self-presentation was purposeful, encapsulating a discourse with its specific audiences, although it may seem one-sided in the way it is articulated. The relationship to non-monumental genres—particularly those of wisdom literature and narrative—is thematically strong, but formally more elusive: the discourse only survives where formal genres of communication gelled into written form.

Characteristic of all textual material, to the modern mind, is the absence of any serious focus on the internal life of the individual, or his private and emotional life. Personality is subordinate to societal identity as the theme of public presentation, used to exemplify societal role and not internalized. This is, self-evidently, an issue of what was appropriate for public discourse: an issue of social acculturation and contemporary imperatives of honor and respect. This does not imply that the internal life of the individual was less intensively felt, but rather that it was not publically discussed. The surviving material provides an externalizing focus on the individual, into socially located norms, through what he chooses to discuss.

Autobiography is, for any society, rooted in cultural expectations and governed by topics with which its audience will engage and identify in the subject's social context. In that sense, content is as ideological in modern (auto)biography as it is in Egyptian self-presentation, where individuality as aberrant originality is not a focus of contemporary identification, and emotion is not a theme for publication or discourse. Such display of emotion broke with the cultural expectation of dignity, encapsulated in the 'silent man' (*gr*), whose self-control marked elite behavior, against the undignified display of emotion which marked low social behavior; but whose self-control was set off by his quality of *iḳr* (competence in action). Merit, attainment, and social leadership are the themes for identification, and not internal life.

Monuments as Self-Presentation

The history of Old Kingdom Egypt is very largely that of its tombs. The initial development of large, stone-built and decorated tombs is essentially restricted to Saqqara and Giza, close to the contemporary royal tombs, and seeming to reflect a restricted and central court culture,[3] replacing a broader geographical distribution in the Early Dynastic Period. The earliest major tombs are anepigraphic, asserting the importance of their owners in ways we cannot trace. Only gradually does pictorial, and more slowly textual decoration increase in importance. This record is not, however, to be understood purely as extravagance in burial practice, nor simply a complex but autonomous mode of preservation of the body, providing the material location and magical assurance of an afterlife. It has also to be understood as a mode of presentation to and integration with the living. The tomb was the place where the dead remain socialized with the living.

In the high Old Kingdom, endowed cult performance asserted a continuing association with the (now dead) court of the (now dead) king, as well as family continuity. It is in this context that self-presentation is first explicit in ways open to serious analysis: in the tomb as a whole, in the development of pictorial self-presentation—painting, relief decoration, and statuary—and then in textual address. This text belongs to the material record: part of the physical object, and not only words and sentences. Even at later periods, the textual self-presentation involves memorialization through monumental inscription and the performance of cult, asserting a social identity with both the living and the dead.[4]

At the core of modern evaluation lie the relationships between audience, functionality, and aesthetic. The issues are the same for both art and text, where the balance between individuation and presentation of role is central.[5] For instance, rare examples of textual self-presentation by women, which appear in the Late Period, are extremely limited in content and focused on a socially constrained set of themes: honor, beauty, family, marriage, husband, children, piety and divine service, early death.[6] This parallels the visual presentation of a woman in her husband's tomb. When, exceptionally, a woman had a tomb of her own, no husband was depicted in it: as tomb owner she was the sole point of reference, and not subordinated.

The obvious fact that both art and text are creations where a sophisticated aesthetic matters, in parallel to their functionality, is core to their discourse and their appeal to an audience.[7] Eloquence is central to the formal structure of textual self-presentation, located in social context where eloquence defined the contemporary aesthetic and carried social prestige.[8] The monumental record then targets the permanent reification of what is depicted or recounted—the reification of the tomb owner as individual through his core interests—parallel to the permanent physical reification of the dead in an afterlife, but it presents that as a continuing social interaction, and not an autonomous, magical reification.

Verbal self-presentation survives as an inscriptional genre, deeply integrated into its monumental context, but this is only a partial categorization. Its history[9] lies in a complex interaction with the development of the writing system, through greater complexity in what was written down, and the interrelationships between self-presentation and other literary genres, which do not appear in writing before the Middle Kingdom. One line of argument focuses, in a positivist way, on the monumental record as an autonomous body of evidence for the creation of a specifically inscriptional genre of literature: the beginning of an evolutionary history of Egyptian literature.[10] However, the act of inscription was itself purposeful, directly targeted at an audience and at a reciprocal discourse. The artistic structure was rooted in a performative style, although it is impossible directly to document ways in which monumental texts drew on genres of not-written self-presentation, and the use of performative literature more broadly in social rituals of this life. In practice, form and content provide the only evidence, beyond location, for hypothesis about purpose and audience.

Audience and Content

Textual self-presentation is first located in a central necropolis, where access to the necessary resources and craftsmen to build a tomb marked status within the court circle. Self-presentation begins as an expansion of the labeling of depictions of the tomb owner by titles and epithets,[11] as a discourse with the visitor develops, in the context of a direct address to the living by the dead, particularly at the tomb entrance. There is a focus on the justification of the speaker: his proper acquisition of and rights to both tomb and social role, with incidental evidence of royal favor, and threats against disrespectful behavior, providing self-justification in the request for performance of the offering ritual. The visitor behaves as a subordinate, showing respect and making an offering. The tomb owner will continue—in the social role of patron—to assist, punish, and seek retribution as a ghost: an *ꜣḫ* who is *iḳr ꜥpr* (effective and equipped) to intervene for good or evil. For those who provide food and service, he will provide assistance as a patron. The focus lies on meritorious, justified, and functional occupation of role and monument, while the memorialization is presented as continuity in social relationship between the living and the dead. But the address to the living, located at the most open point of contact, is explicit in its call on a literate audience.

Incidental narrative begins to appear in multiple ways: royal favors (related to the tomb provision), royal letters, the terms of mortuary endowments, apparently mixing the appeal for cult to a sort of archival documentation of rights. The social context of the tomb and its inscription was continuity within the court circle.[12] With the development of cemeteries at key sites in the provinces, broader description of service at a distance becomes an important theme for men whose power was not characterized by residence at court. Nekhebu, from a family of overseers of works, buried at Giza in the reign of Pepi I, stresses: "Whenever I came to the Residence, his Majesty praised (*ḥsi*) me over it."[13] Harkhuf, controller of the southern frontier, buried at Qubbet al-Hawa in the reign of Pepi II, provides a copy of the king's letter encouraging him to return quickly to the palace: "Indeed you pass the day and night thinking to do what your lord loves, praises and commands! His Majesty will carry out your many material (*iḳr*) requests (*sꜣr*), to the benefit (*ꜣḫ*) of your line (lit. 'son to son') forever, so that everybody will say, when they hear what My Majesty will do for you, 'Is there the like to that which was done for the Sole Companion Harkhuf, when he came down from Yam?'"[14]

Discourse is expected, about praise and reward. But Harkhuf's tomb reflects a change in social context for self-presentation. Participation in royal patronage runs in parallel to focus on a local identity,[15] marked by local control of, and so access to the material resources for building;[16] and a change in the balance of discourse, from royal presence to local responsibility and local role. This expansion of textual self-presentation—related to the construction of inscribed tombs in the provinces—does not focus only on incidental narrative, but broader changes in content. The clichéd claim to have fed the hungry, clothed the naked, and acted as local patron becomes important only in the early Sixth Dynasty, quickly becoming the core motif of the *Idealbiographie*.[17]

A balance between the formulaic and the individual is characteristic in self-presentations of all periods, parallel to the occasional appearance of individual detail in tomb decoration: from Nekhebu's claim, in the early Sixth Dynasty, that he never beat anybody to the point that he fell under his fingers,[18] to Inene, of the early Eighteenth Dynasty, recounting his innovative conduct in supervising (royal) tomb building, which he categorizes: "It was the craft of my mind, my example of knowledge; guidelines were not given me by an elder."[19] Or slightly later Amenemheb fighting an elephant in the sight of the king,[20] and depicting himself in his tomb encountering a hyena.[21] The extension of incidental narrative is not really a development of serious storytelling, but marks a love of the specific action, encapsulated in the New Kingdom assertion that "The name of hero (*ḳni*) is in what he has done, without perishing in this land forever," first appearing in the self-presentation of Ahmose son of Abana,[22] in the introduction to the Annals of Tuthmosis III,[23] and again[24] when he asserts the truthfulness of what he says: "To public knowledge" (*r rḫt b(w) nb*).[25] Emphasis lies on public reputation. Similarly, the Fifth Dynasty Nyankhsekhmet, receiving stonework for his tomb as a royal gift: "(I) gave praise (*i3w*) to the king greatly; (I) adored every god for Sahure—it being (publically) known—together with the entire (body) of followers."[26] His text calls on its audience to "adore every god for Sahure," finishing with the formulaic assertion: "Never did (I) do anything bad in respect of any person."

The target audience for self-presentation is never clear, because neither the social context of text, nor the monumental display—size, location, and visual effect—is itself unitary, in purpose or effect. Nor was the location of the text uniformly accessible, even for the limited number of people able to read it. Yet there was an expectation of a reading audience, and of a discourse about content. The assertion of truthfulness is a core theme,[27] in relation to both the formulaic and to the specific. It becomes common in royal inscriptions of the Eighteenth Dynasty, as a motif presenting the inscription as a subject for discourse, but is presented clearly in the Twelfth Dynasty stela of Montuwoser: "Then as for every person who will hear this stela, being among the living, they will say, 'It's the truth!' Their children will say to (their) children, 'It's the truth! There is no falsehood there.' And as for every scribe who will read this stela, all people—they will come up to him (*spr.sn ir.f*)."[28] The motif is then presented in its most complex form in the Ramesside autobiography of Nefersekheru: "I say to you, who are on earth, who will exist, *wꜥb*-priests and associates of the king, [. . . who decipher (?) the] texts in my tomb which is in the Oryx nome, your hearts shall ponder (? – seek?) in front of this writing, and you will say in firmness (?), in doing

(?) attention (?) to [. . .] so that the ignorant may know, like the skilled, all I have said on my chapel."[29] Nefersekheru then ends his text with a phrase formulaic to both letters and literature: "I speak so that you may know; it is good that you hear." The graffiti which record visitors' appreciation of the tomb provide the corollary to the appeals of the tomb owner to read. So, on the pylon-gateway of his tomb, Maya directly calls on the public who leave graffiti, in their vocabulary, to read: "He says to people who will come, desiring diversion on the West and walking about in the district [of eternity]."[30]

Individuation

Constraints on presentation of individuality are best understood as an overlap between cultural attitudes to what is appropriate for discussion and what was purposeful to the specific text: either as communication or reification. Text, like the decoration of the tomb, is entirely focused on the individual as self-sufficient: head of a family and patron of subordinates. He is the sole point of reference, only subordinate in relation to the king.[31] Within the tomb there is stress on the nuclear family. The role of son as continuation of the father is explicit, and marked when he is presented as dedicator of the monument. In tomb decoration, the owner is head of an extended household, although the labeling subordinates by name—priests,[32] functionaries, workers[33]—is uneven: individual choice or localized. Textual self-presentation is narrower, with only occasional naming of family members: education as a narrative theme and focus on genealogy only become important in the Ramesside Period as circumstantial context for social justification. The complexities of extended kinship and social circles are not part of the verbal presentation, and the presentation of the role of patron is depersonalized.

This deliberate separation from the immediate seems in strong contrast to the inclusion of individual deeds, presented as specific evidence to individualize the role played. The distinction drawn by Assmann between ideal(izing) biography *(Idealbiographie)* and event-biography *(Laufbahnbiographie* or *Ereignisbiographie)* has become a cliché in writing about Egyptian self-presentation,[34] as has his emphasis on "collective memory" as a core theme of idealization.[35] In reality, these distinctions oversimplify, where the nonformulaic is more an incidental expansion of the public self-characterization than the creation of a narrative. For instance, a stela of Antef son of Senet[36] provides an ideal(izing) biography as a sort of aretalogy: the text is presented in tabular form, each compartment containing a statement beginning with *ink* (I am).[37] As in his other texts, his actions are depersonalized in a way that comes over as idealizing, but it would be distorting to read his text as purely formulaic. It is not fictional, but generalizes his behavior in the social context of public address. His expectation is that "The magistrates who will pass by shall speak; then they will give to me (the quality of) *ꜣḫ*, that I may live from the breath that people give. They shall make my name live: they are the gods of the powerful after(wards), and the *bꜣ* is satisfied when they cause that it is remembered."[38]

When specific events are presented, these are entirely personal: individual but public acts, not involving other named individuals, exemplifying personal competence particular to the social context. In so far as a curriculum vitae is presented, it is done as assertion of meritocracy—recognized by the king, as the context for individual rank and role—but still a personalized role and not a full narrative of career. The role, or even existence of superiors in the hierarchy, simply does not form part of the narrative. Incidents of political reality are generally missing, except where (as in the case of Weni) they can be presented as individual actions. Political behavior is generalized as popularity, avoiding events, and evidenced, for instance, by the clichés of never accusing and never being accused.

The presentation is one of self-sufficiency within cultural norms. At the extreme this is seen in the First Intermediate Period stela of Uha: "I am a successful independent-man (*nḏs iḳr*), who lives on his (own) property (*išt*), who ploughs with (his own) team, who sails his (own) boat, and not from what (I) found from the hand of (my) father."[39] This self-sufficiency comes over to the modern reader as social integration—an idealization—but the role is neither colorless nor abstracted from reality, only restricted by contemporary expectations of appropriate and purposeful discourse. Individuality and personal charisma are not incompatible with hierarchy or social solidarity. Ideology is, in the end, only reality with gaps.

The more detailed the narrative—the more it approaches a curriculum vitae—the more one suspects a context of special pleading: asserting merit to explaining new status.[40] For instance, Ahmose son of Abana seems to have risen from a rather humble background, through military distinction, so that his self-presentation lists the lands and people comprising his new wealth assigned to him by royal patronage. Reading between the lines of the highly incidental narrative self-presentation of Anhermose,[41] it appears that he gained the office of local chief priest after marriage to the daughter of his predecessor. The claim to an exceptional career may suggest that the autobiographer was an outsider or parvenu, but does not provide reliable evidence for social mobility. For instance, Weni claims to have risen from a relatively low post to become overseer of Upper Egypt through personal service to Pepi I; he does not mention his family background, although he provides the most varied narrative of any Old Kingdom text. Yet his father was vizier, and he himself held that office at the end of his life.[42] The audience for such special pleading remains unclear: its reading from the tomb wall, its use as mortuary eulogy, or its use in some formal context of praise during life.

Genre

Textual self-presentation is most naturally understood as a genre rooted in otherwise unwritten genres of praise poetry: social situations where formalized praise provided a context for the artistic use of language in performance;[43] styles of unwritten literature, used in both secular and ritual contexts, singing the praise of the individual, or adoration of the deity in prayer and ritual. The Egyptian term for praise—*ḥsi*—is a root with the sense "sing," while the term for thank—*dwꜣ-nṯr n*, literally "adore god for"—similarly emphasizes public and oral performance. Characteristic of such praise is the use of an essentially listing format, presented in a poetic-hymnic, or at least recitational structure, to which a blending with linguistically narrative genres is secondary.

Explicit reference to formal praise is common, associated with reward for service to the king, but also as the formal acclaim of subordinates. Following a ceremony of royal praise, Nefersekheru says: "I go out at the gates of the king's house, and all people are acclaiming to the height of the sky; everyone who saw me (say)ing: 'It is fitting for him, Nefersekheru, true of heart.'"[44]

Royal eulogy survives as a literary genre on papyrus, for instance in the Middle Kingdom hymns praising the king,[45] and as self-presentation on the Semna Stela of Sesostris III.[46] Middle Kingdom nomarchs frequently assert that they were "praised" (*ḥsi*) by their town. Eulogy evidently belongs to social interaction between superior and subordinate at all levels,[47] mixing the generic, the formulaic, and the specific event within a performative genre: where titles and epithets of secular self-presentation parallel the typical hymn that celebrates the nature of god as an aretalogy. The art lies in the ability to hold the attention of an audience, while verbal dexterity, variations on a theme, and the engagement in discourse with the minds of the audience, provide the motifs for critical evaluation. Textual self-presentation does not, however, comprise a single genre, or even a single communicative purpose, but is inextricably linked to the full history of written and unwritten genres of Egyptian literature.[48] Broader literary contexts can only be addressed directly at later periods, as a wider range of literature is preserved in writing. This is not simply the chances of survival, but the history of use of writing for both documentary and literary genres, and a matter of contextualizing that history in social reality.

The key literary narrative found in the Story of Sinuhe is presented as if it were a tomb inscription—a self-presentation—although not in a manner found in actual tombs: exploiting genres of narrative inscription, letters, and praise poetry (to the king).[49] In contrast, the fragmentary text from the facade of the tomb of Khnumhotep at Lisht, of the reign of Sesostris III, seems to be presented in a comparably new narrative style and content,[50] while the self-presentation from the tomb of his father, Khnumhotep II, at Beni Hasan,[51] provides the finest piece of coherent narrative prose. There is so little clarity about the practical audience or readership of this Middle Kingdom literary narrative—mixed between inscription and papyrus—that one cannot hypothesize with confidence over generic priority, but only stress the depth of the intertextuality.

The didactic letter of Papyrus Anastasi I provides a variation on the theme of self-praise. The writer, Hori, introduces himself in an extended list of epithets, closely comparable in form to New Kingdom tomb self-presentations. It characterizes him as peculiarly literate, a model of learning, instructor of others, and fully socialized in royal function. He addresses his correspondent in even more flowery epithets, but then explores his colleague's (in)competence in detail.[52] Hori is here using self-presentation as extended justification for his literary presentation, going beyond extended politeness formulations.

Thematically there is a strong overlap between self-presentation and the presentation of proper conduct in wisdom literature.[53] Literary teachings are presented as the direct instruction of a father to a son, where the self-presentation presents the father as model, addressing a broader audience. The self-presentation of a nomarch (?) Montuhotep, of the reign of Sesostris I, ends: "The good character of a man is (more) for him than thousands of actions. The testimony of people is in that proverb (?) on the mouth of commoners (? *nḏs*): 'The monument of a man is his goodness. Forgotten is the one of bad character.'"[54] Self-presentation is, of its nature, didactic in its self-justification.

Lyric becomes an influence from the Ramesside Period. The Ramesside self-presentation of Samut Kyky[55] moves beyond traditional themes to focus on his religious experience. He expresses his devotion to Mut as patron, in emotional language and poetic structure, calling directly on his audience to follow his experience. Childless, and relying on the goddess for burial, he had dedicated everything to her, locating his social continuity with the deity rather than king and family. The late Ptolemaic inscription of Taimhotep—an exceptional self-presentation by a woman—incorporates genuine lyric, lamenting death and encouraging her husband to live a full life, in ways directly comparable to the harpers' songs of New Kingdom tombs.[56] It is difficult not to see her husband's voice, both thematically and in the sophisticated literary format.[57] The most striking examples of Ramesside self-presentation—like those of Nefersekheru (whose tomb wall includes a complex harper's song), or of Anhermose—similarly exploit strong literary-poetic formats, even if it is not possible to assert that they are the authors or primary editors of their own texts.

Literary creativity pervades the corpus of textual self-presentation. The formulaic incorporates the compositional technique of free variation on a theme, while the switching of genre or format from section to section—such as the Old Kingdom inclusion of (royal) letters and decrees—shows a different type of variation. Both are characteristic of the bricolage and intertextuality so typical of Egyptian literary composition,[58] reflecting literary and scribal sophistication as an important aspect of the individuality of the autobiographer. His social position is located among the users of papyri,[59] like the collector who included papyrus literature in his burial.

Self-Presentation as Rite of Passage

The address of self-justification to a living audience relates to that seen in rites of passage, associated with the funeral:[60] specifically the presentation of the dead to Osiris and the negative confession.[61] The performance of the tomb self-presentation within the funerary ritual cannot be demonstrated by specific evidence,[62] although the relationship of such texts to the justified afterlife becomes a clear theme by the New Kingdom. A self-presentation text appears on a votive shabti box of the Eighteenth Dynasty, dedicated by Qenamun and directly addressed to his mother,[63] but the theme is picked up when the occasional inscription of self-presentation on late sarcophagi seems to relate directly to the judgment of the dead: such material was not accessible to an audience in this world, apparently providing an ethical-moral self-presentation to divine rather than human judgment.[64] The problem remains, however, that the narrative of performance for funeral—or any other rite of passage—is fragmentary at all periods.

Summary

The genre of self-presentation is one in which the character and the role of an individual, evidenced by specific actions, are presented purposefully: published by inscription, to a contemporary audience and to a posterity. The problems for modern understanding lie in form, content, and purpose. But neither purpose nor audience can be limited to the monumental locations in which the texts survive. The texts involve a discourse about both role and individuality. Personal identity is focused on a social context, defined by role and social relationships, and exemplified by meritocracy within a social norm: a mixture of individual and public identity, with the balance reflecting the purpose and the context of the discourse. Eulogy must, however, reflect a social structure, where the imperatives are socially functional and not internalized. The search for reality then shows both the functional, which is normative, ideological or didactic, justifying status or reward; and the incidental, typically an event, which exemplifies the individuality of merit. Audience reaction is assumed, and purposefully targeted: identification of the audience, with which the individual text justifies social integration, is core to understanding.

Changes in form, content, and location provide a series of histories: a history of what was written, of literature, of institutions, of religious practice. However, it is continuities, rooted in socio-economic norms, attitudes, and behavior, that are most striking: patterns of face-to-face hierarchy, presented as a patriarchal role—head of house, provider, patron—that do not change because they are what made possible the very publication of such a text. The attractive fragment of personal event is what sometimes makes self-presentation seem closer to a modern vision of autobiography, but the real interest lies in breaking down the barriers structured by modern preconceptions of individuality, and modern preconceptions of the lack of individuality in the non-western world. The problem is to credit what the texts actually say as an incomplete but genuine picture of reality, and not to be distracted by what Douglas and Isherwood[65] define as "the falsely abstracted individual": the projection of the modern individual, and modern socio-economic reality, onto the different realities of a pre-modern social integration. Modern individuality is as much a role-based and partial ideology as is the different role-based core of Egyptian self-presentation.

Notes

1 A. Gnirs, "Die ägyptische Autobiographie," in A. Loprieno, ed., *Ancient Egyptian Literature: History and Forms* (Leiden, 1996), 191–241.

2 For a basic discussion of the relationship of monuments to reification of display and performance see J. Baines, "Public Ceremonial Performance in Ancient Egypt," in T. Inomata and L. Coben, eds., *Archaeology of Performance: Theatres of Power, Community, and Politics* (Lanham, 2006), 261–302.

3 M. Fitzenreiter, "Grabmonument und Gesellschaft: funeräre Kultur und soziale Dynamik im Alten Reich," *SAK* 40 (2011), 67–101, following D. Franke, "Arme und Geringe im Alten Reich Altägyptens: 'Ich gab Speise dem Hungernden, Kleider dem Nackten…'," *ZÄS* 133 (2006), 104–20.

4 D. Vischak, *Community and Identity in Ancient Egypt: The Old Kingdom Cemetery at Qubbet el-Hawa* (New York, 2015), 7–11, 208–209, exploiting the broader theoretical context of the archaeology of identity.

5 P. Vernus, "Comment l'élite se donne à voir dans le programme décoratif de ses chapelles funéraires: Stratégie d'épure, stratégie d'appogiature et le frémissement du littéraire," *CRIPEL* 28 (2009–2010), 67–113, for detail parallel to that of the event in self-presentation.

6 K. Jansen-Winkeln, "Bemerkungen zu den Frauenbiographien der Spätzeit," *AoF* 31/2 (2004), 358–73; cf. C. Eyre, "Women and Prayer in Pharaonic Egypt," in E. Frood and A. McDonald, eds., *Decorum and Experience: Essays in Ancient Culture for John Baines* (Oxford, 2013), 114.

7 J. Baines, "What is Art?" in M. Hartwig, ed., *A Companion to Egyptian Art* (Chichester, 2015), 1–21. Neither picture nor text can be treated as an autonomous category in a modern sense, but embedded in functional or performative context.

8 L. Coulon, "Célébrer l'élite, louer Pharaon: éloquence et cérémonial de cour au Nouvel Empire," *CRIPEL* 28 (2009–2010), 238.

9 J. Baines, "Forerunners of Narrative Biographies," in A. Leahy and J. Tait, eds., *Studies on Ancient Egypt in Honour of H.S. Smith* (London, 1999), 23–37.

10 J. Assmann, "Schrift, Tod und Identität: Das Grab als Vorschule der Literatur im alten Ägypten," in A. Assmann, J. Assmann, and C. Hardmeier, eds., *Schrift und Gedächtnis: Beiträge zur Archäologie der literarischen Kommunikation* (Munich, 1983), 64–93; J. Assmann, "Der literarische Aspekt des ägyptischen Grabes und seine Funktion im Rahmen des 'monumentalen Diskurses,'" in A. Loprieno, ed., *Ancient Egyptian Literature: History and Forms* (Leiden, 1996), 97–104.

11 S. Kubisch, *Lebensbilder der 2. Zwischenzeit: Biographische Inschriften der 13.–17. Dynastie* (Berlin, 2008), 20; Vischak, *Community and Identity*, 211–12.

12 Fitzenreiter, "Grabmonument und Gesellschaft," expanding on themes developed by Franke, "Arme und Geringe," to argue that the tomb record here reflects new social structures, which gave more room for individuality, and not just the expression of it. The argument is, however, strongly social-evolutionary: following Assmann's general evolutionary approach to the history of Egyptian culture, with a consistent hunt for causality against a more neutral observation of coincidence.

13 *Urk.* I, 215, 14; N. Strudwick, *Texts from the Pyramid Age* (Leiden, Atlanta, 2005), 266; cf. C. Eyre, "The Practice of Literature: The Relationship between Content, Form, Audience, and Performance," in R. Enmarch and V. Lepper, eds., *Ancient Egyptian Literature: Theory and Practice* (Oxford, 2013), 123.

14 *Urk.* I, 129, 6–12.

15 Vischak, *Community and Identity*; S. Seidlmeyer, "People at Beni Hassan: Contributions to a Model of Egyptian Rural Society," in Z. Hawass and J. Richards, eds., *The Archaeology and Art of Ancient Egypt: Essays in Honor of David B. O'Connor* (Cairo, 2007), II, 351–68.

16 C. Eyre, "Who Built the Great Temples of Egypt?" in B. Menu, ed., *L'Organisation du travail en Égypte ancienne et en Mésopotamie* (Cairo, 2010), 117–38.

17 Franke, "Arme und Geringe," a change from themes of royal provision of his officials to elite provision of their subordinates.
18 *Urk.* I, 217, 4.
19 *Urk.* IV, 57, 16–58, 1.
20 *Urk.* IV, 893, 114–894, 1.
21 H. Guksch, "Amenemheb und die Hyäne: Norm und Individualität in der Grabdekoration der 18. Dynastie," in H. Guksch, E. Hoffmann, and M. Bommas, eds., *Grab und Totenkult im Alten Ägypten* (Munich, 2003), 104–17.
22 *Urk.* IV, 2, 5–6.
23 *Urk.* IV 684, 9–10; also 780, 14–15, façade of the Seventh Pylon.
24 *Urk.* IV, 833, 11–14.
25 C. Eyre, "The Semna Stelae: Quotation, Genre, and Functions of Literature," in S. Israelit-Groll, ed., *Studies in Egyptology Presented to Miriam Lichtheim* (Jerusalem, 1990), I, 152; Kubisch, *Lebensbilder*, 2.
26 *Urk.* I, 39, 10–12; cf. J. Stauder-Porchet, "Les autobiographies événementielles de la Ve dynastie: premier ensemble de textes continus en Égypte," in M. Bárta, F. Coppens, and J. Krejčí, eds., *Abusir and Saqqara in the Year 2010*, II (Prague, 2011), 751.
27 L. Coulon, "Véracité et rhétorique dans les autobiographies égyptiennes de la Première Période intermédiaire," *BIFAO* 97 (1997), 109–38, focused on the theme as the metadiscourse of self-presentation; cf. also Stauder-Porchet, "Les autobiographies événementielles," 750.
28 MMA 12.814, 16–18: *Aeg. Les.* 80, 1–4; R. Landgráfová, *It Is My Good Name That You Should Remember: Egyptian Biographical Texts on Middle Kingdom Stelae* (Prague, 2011), 130–34.
29 J. Osing, *Das Grab des Nefersecheru in Zawyet Sultan* (Mainz am Rhein, 1992), 43–53, pl. 35; E. Frood, *Biographical Texts from Ramessid Egypt* (Leiden-Atlanta, 2007), 144.
30 G. Martin, *The Tomb of Maya and Meryt I: The Reliefs, Inscriptions, and Commentary* (London, 2012), 20, pl. 14, lines 4–6; Frood, *Biographical Texts*, 142.
31 Stauder-Porchet, "Les autobiographies événementielles," 760–763.
32 E.g., Vischak, *Community and Identity*, 212, on appearance of cult priests with family in tombs.
33 E.g., Seidlmeyer, "People at Beni Hassan," 351–68.
34 Assmann, "Sepulkrale Selbstthematisierung"; Kubisch, *Lebensbilder*, 2; Stauder-Porchet, "Les autobiographies événementielles," 747–66.
35 Kubisch, *Lebensbilder*, 2; similarly Vischak, *Community and Identity*, 139–40.
36 BM EA 581: Landgráfová, *My Good Name*, 112–14, no. 37; his other texts are BM EA 572 = no. 38, pp. 116–19; BM EA 562 = no. 39, pp. 120–22, reign of Sesostris I.
37 So J.F. Quack, "Erzählen als Preisen: vom Astartepapyrus zu den koptischen Märtyrerakten," in H. Roeder, ed., *Das Erzählen in frühen Hochkulturen I: Der Fall Ägypten* (Munich, 2009), 305–307, making the point that plain narrative

was not the format of Egyptian myth, which survives as a part of praise and cult in ritual, and that consequently there is a small bridge from ritual aretalogy to self-presentation.

38 BM 562, x+1–2.

39 OIM 16956, D. Dunham, *Naga-ed-Dêr Stelae of the First Intermediate Period* (Boston-London, 1937), 102–103, no. 84, 4, pl. XXXII.

40 See J. Baines, *High Culture and Experience in Ancient Egypt* (Sheffield-Bristol, 2013), 237–38, on the extent to which pictures record individual experience, and the relationship of experience/reality to decorum of portrayal, and 243–44, discussing the interaction between individuation and assertion of role, upward mobility, and social solidarity.

41 B. Ockinga and Y. al-Masri, *Two Ramesside Tombs at El Mashayikh* I (Sydney, 1988), pp. 31–47, pls. 18–31; Frood, *Biographical Texts*, 107–16.

42 P. Collombert, "Une nouvelle version de l'autobiographie d'Ouni," in R. Legros, ed., *Cinquante ans d'éternité* (Cairo, 2015), 145–57.

43 Eyre, "The Practice of Literature," 122–25.

44 Osing, *Grab des Nefersecheru*, 47, pl. 35 lines 11–14; Frood, *Biographical Texts*, 145. A similar description is illustrated by scenes in the Tomb of Neferhotep (see Eyre, "The Practice of Literature," 123), or S. Binder, *The Gold of Honour in New Kingdom Egypt*, (Oxford, 2008), frontispiece for the Amarna tomb 25 of Ay.

45 M. Collier and S. Quirke, *The UCL Lahun Papyri: Religious, Literary, Legal, Mathematical and Medical* (Oxford, 2004), 16–19.

46 Eyre, "Semna Stelae," 135; S. Seidlmayer, "Zu Fundort und Aufstellungskontext der grossen Semna-Stele Sesostris' III," *SAK* 28 (2000), 233–42.

47 Eyre, "Egyptian Historical Literature." For a more limited view of the role of royal inscriptions as communication, cf. Baines, "Public Ceremonial Performance," esp. 275–76.

48 For a broader treatment of the necessity of audience reaction, related to the purpose of narrative, cf. K. Barber, *The Anthropology of Texts, Persons and Publics: Oral and Written Culture in Africa and Beyond* (Cambridge, 2007), chapter 5, and especially 139–41, contrasting modern impersonalization of public/audience and disengagement of art from social contexts and function as part of a modern commoditization of culture, with the premodern role of patronage, and linkages to specific occasion and the enhancement of prestige.

49 R. Parkinson, *The Tale of Sinuhe and other Ancient Egyptian Poems 1940–1640 BC* (Oxford, 1997), 21–26.

50 J. Allen, "L'inscription historique de Khnoumhotep à Dahchour," *BSFE* 173 (2009), 13–31.

51 A. Lloyd, "The Great Inscription of Khnumhotpe II at Beni Hasan," in A. Lloyd, ed., *Studies in Pharaonic Religion and Society in Honour of J. Gwyn Griffiths* (London, 1992), 14–36.

52 P. Anastasi I, 1, 1–2, 7: H.-W. Fischer-Elfert, *Die Satirische Streitschrift des Papyrus Anastasi I.: Übersetzung und Kommentar* (Wiesbaden, 1986), 13–30.

53 Cf. K. Jansen-Winkeln, "Lebenslehre und Biographie," *ZÄS* 131 (2004), 59–72. For specific intertextuality see G. Posener, *L'Enseignement loyaliste: sagesse égyptienne du Moyen Empire*, Geneva, 1976.

54 UC 14333, 15–16, Landgráfová, *My Good Name*, 260–63, no. 83.

55 M. Negm, *The Tomb of Samut Called Kyky: Theban Tomb 409 at Qurnah* (Warminster, 1997); Frood, *Biographical Texts*, 84–91.

56 Eyre, "The Practice of Literature," 111. For the overlap between funerary and literary laments and mortuary ritual, both generic and as performance, see R. Enmarch, "Mortuary and Literary Laments: A Comparison," in R. Enmarch and V. Lepper, eds., *Ancient Egyptian Literature: Theory and Practice* (Oxford, 2013), esp. 85–86.

57 Jansen-Winkeln, "Bemerkungen zu den Frauenbiographien der Spätzeit," 363–64, 373.

58 For a broader discussion of assemblage as literary composition, where texts are not a single organic entity, cf. Barber, *Anthropology of Texts*, 214–16.

59 A. von Lieven, "'The Soul of the Sun Permeates the Whole World': Sun Cult and Religious Astronomy in Ancient Egypt," in *Pandanus* 10–4/2 (Prague, 2010), for the tomb as archive.

60 A short section in the Ptolemaic P. Harkness—a personalized recitation for the burial ritual—seems to mix lament and formal characterizing self-presentation before moving to his reception in the other world, forgetting this world, but coming to the gods in the other world in appropriate state: M. Smith, *Catalogue of Demotic Papyri in the British Museum, III: The Mortuary Texts of Papyrus BM 10507* (London, 1987), col. II, pp. 37–38.

61 C. Eyre, "Funerals, Initiation and Rituals of Life in Pharaonic Egypt," in A. Mouton and J. Patrier, eds., *Life, Death, and Coming of Age in Antiquity: Individual Rites of Passage in the Ancient Near East and Adjacent Regions* (Leiden, 2014), 300–301.

62 On the problems of reconstructing ritual performance at funerals, see H. Willems, *The Coffin of Heqata (Cairo JdE 36418)* (Leuven, 1996), 157–77, and Willems, "The Social and Ritual Context of a Mortuary Liturgy of the Middle Kingdom (CT Spells 30–41)," in H. Willems, ed., *Social Aspects of Funerary Culture in the Egyptian Old and Middle Kingdoms* (Leuven, 2001), 253–372. On the scale and nature of performance at funerals see Eyre, "The Practice of Literature," 125–26; Baines, "Public Ceremonial Performance," 269–70.

63 F. Pumpenmeier, *Eine Gunstgabe von seiten des Königs: Ein extrasepulkrales Schabtidepot Qen-Amuns in Abydos* (Heidelberg, 1998).

64 A. von Lieven, "Zur Funktion der ägyptischen Autobiographie," *Die Welt des Orients* 40/1 (2010), 54–69.

65 M. Douglas and B. Isherwood, *The World of Goods: Towards an Anthropology of Consumption* (London-New York), 1996/1979, 42.

2

Self-Presentation in the Early Dynasties

Juan Carlos Moreno García

The early dynasties witnessed the first attempts to materialize visual and written expressions of self-presentation in the private sphere. Until then—and leaving aside 'utilitarian' documents relating to administrative day-to-day activities, like seal stamps, marks in containers and stone vessels,[1] etc.—monumental art and inscriptions were mainly restricted to the royal and divine sphere. *Serekh*s, graffiti, ceremonial palettes and mace heads, divine statuary (like the colossi of Coptos), and huge tombs (like those at Hierakonpolis and Umm al-Qaab) commemorated pharaohs and the extent of their authority.[2] Gradually, with the advent of the Early Dynastic Period, individual high officials, members of the court and king's relatives appear increasingly evoked in contemporary written sources, while their tombs, surrounding the burial place of their master, produced a new landscape of power, prestige, and status comprising the tomb of the king, the mastabas of his subordinates, and ceremonial buildings such as the enclosures discovered at Abydos. In both cases the social memory of high ranking officials seems to be concomitant with the consolidation of a true royal court, an administrative system, and a rank of titles, functions, and hierarchies. This development is also visible in the realm of iconography, whereas representations, compositions, and attitudes were, in many cases, formalized and became iconic in Egyptian art. Predynastic scenes such as those found in some palettes, in processions of ships, and in Tomb 100 at Hierakonpolis also depicted people in the company of rulers and kings. However, their conventional imagery and (quite often) enigmatic attitudes make it difficult to define their roles and the precise nature of their relation to kings, or even to assert their human (and not supernatural) condition.[3]

This situation changed with the development of writing and of formal, codified iconography. For the first time in Egyptian culture, officials were represented hierarchically, playing specific and standardized roles when they were accompanying the king. Their names and titles, combined with highly formalized poses, constitute a first step toward the expression of individuality and status, if not of self-presentation. As for tombs, their size, equipment, and location (around burials of kings or in elite necropoleis) were the main signs of the prestige, status, and closeness of their owners to the king, to the point that inscriptions and images (statues, decorated slabs) appear somewhat secondary and subordinate to massive architecture. That is why considerable debate still revolves around the identification of the owners of some huge mastabas at Saqqara and in the provinces.[4] Later on, during the Old Kingdom, particulars were better documented as their monuments, portrayals, and inscriptions became more elaborated and the use of writing expanded. Yet the expression of their individuality and their self remained confined within very narrow cultural and ideological limits, basically restricted to crucial notions like service to the king, membership of the elite, and performance of specific rituals. In fact, titles, seals, inscriptions, and scenes only conceived of officials as servants of the king, to the point that the more private aspects of their existence are virtually lacking. Under these conditions the fate of one such early official, Imhotep, is exemplary; his reputation survived for millennia and he became the object of veneration indeed, but only because of his administrative and architectural achievements during Djoser's reign.[5] Contemporary monuments actually belonging to or mentioning Imhotep are quite rare in spite of his managerial and administrative skills and the indelible memory he left in the country; quite significantly, they only consist of a brief string of titles found on the base of a statue of Djoser and in a graffito in the funerary complex of king Sekhemkhet.[6]

The scarcity of private inscriptions and images, outside the purely administrative sphere, is not the only difficulty when approaching the study of self-presentation in the First through Third Dynasties. Two additional problems are the representativeness of the preserved evidence and its socially biased nature. In many cases what has survived consists mainly in stereotypical depictions of high officials in the company of kings (as seen in rock scenes, mace heads, administrative labels, etc.) or alone, as in the slabs and reliefs of their tombs. Originally, the slabs only contained lists of offerings before the sitting figure of the dead and, in some cases, his or her name and titles completed the composition. Only in very exceptional cases, more detailed images and inscriptions provide a wealth of information about their owners, while the artistic quality of these monuments further confirmed that their owners belonged to the uppermost sectors of Egyptian society and had access to the finest craftsmanship provided by the palace workshops. However, in cases when cruder, smaller, and almost anepigraphic monuments belonged nevertheless to sons or daughters of the king, one cannot but think that exceptional artistic quality and rich epigraphy were not indispensable for expressing the importance and social position of a member of the elite.[7] Writing appears thus, once more, secondary. As for the socially biased nature of the evidence, it is worth remembering that texts and representations only concern very specific sectors of the Egyptian elite, whose closeness to the king apparently prevailed over other considerations such as individual wealth, social influence, and local power. Thus, for instance, thanks to their monuments, sculptors or palace ritualists are better attested than other sectors of the ruling class, not to speak of commoners, hardly documented at all, thus making the study of their means of self-presentation quite difficult.

Architecture, Figurative Art, and Inscriptions: Self-Presentation in the Early Dynastic Period

The recently (re)discovered rock drawing at Nag el-Hamdulab, near Aswan, depicts a royal jubilee that announces a set of scenes to become typical in Early Dynastic iconography and to continue in later times (Fig. 2.1). A ruler, followed by a fan bearer and preceded by a dog and two standard bearers, is situated above a boat with an elaborately decorated cabin. The king wears the White Crown and holds a long *heqa*-scepter. The two standard bearers have the same pose, each holding the high pole of his standard before him, while four bearded persons appear in front of the 'royal boat,' apparently holding a horizontal line that probably represents a rope. So they are most likely boat towers. Immediately behind the 'royal boat,' follows the next vessel, above which are two bearded men who continue the royal procession. The first one raises his arms above his head, holding a circular object, so it seems that the two persons are tribute bearers. Finally, another boat over the procession is followed by a brief inscription where the first sign is the hieroglyph *šms*. The whole composition could then be related to the "Following of Horus."[8] The overall composition is thus that of the king surrounded by some of his followers and involved in a ceremony, their depictions departing from those typical of servants and foreigners shown in

2.1. Rock art at Nag el-Hamdulab, near Aswan, Dynasty 0 or 1 (courtesy Maria C. Gatto)

contemporary or slightly earlier compositions such as the bearded servants in the palette Cairo JE 46418+BMA 66.175, the cloaked foreigners in this same monument and in the knife handle Abydos K 1103b2,[9] the prisoners in Narmer's knife handle,[10] and the Asiatic in a carved wood piece in King Qaa's tomb.[11] Another recent discovery is that of three reliefs dating to the reign of King Den, the fourth pharaoh of the First Dynasty, at Wadi el-Humur, in south Sinai.[12] Relief no. 2 depicts the king in the traditional attitude of beating a foreign enemy held by his hair. Before a standard appears the *ḫtmw* (treasurer) and *ṯ(t)* (vizier?) Ankhka,[13] and immediately after the king, three dignitaries are represented in two horizontal registers. In the superior one appear two officials, each one preceded by his name, while the inferior one shows a sandal bearer accompanied by his name (or perhaps more likely his title), Seper.[14] As for relief no. 3, probably belonging to a successor of Den, the king is followed by two dignitaries, one of them again designated by the name or title Seper and the other one by a hieroglyph difficult to read.[15]

The scenes from Nag el-Hamdulab and Wadi el-Humur, only separated by about two centuries, may be considered the precedent and final achievement respectively of an early imagery where officials gradually gained both in presence and individuality in Egyptian art. Intermediary steps can be found in other monuments, like Scorpion's mace head, Narmer's palette, and some labels from early kings. These objects, elaborated for royal use, contain

2.2. Line drawing of the scenes on the Narmer macehead (Free Stock Photos)

nevertheless depictions of members of the elite in a 'palatial' or at least a ceremonial environment, involving in some cases the presence of ceremonial buildings. Narmer's mace head, for instance, shows the pharaoh seated on a raised platform followed by two registers of officials: two of them also appear in the king's palette, a sandal bearer and a *ṯ(t)* (vizier?), accompanied by three men holding long sticks; in front of Narmer are four standard bearers, also quite close to those depicted in his palette, as well as a woman in a carrying-chair,[16] whose portrayal probably corresponds to a royal woman (Fig. 2.2).[17] As for his famous palette, the similar representation of some members of the king's retinue suggests that a standardized representation of the closest members of the court became somewhat canonical in their dressing and attitudes at the beginning of the First Dynasty. This is also true for some elaborated labels. In the ivory label of King Aha, for instance, four different types of people are present; the central register seems to depict a procession of high dignitaries and members of the royal family (including a woman) coming out of a palace and following the king (?), while a group of seated people, preceded by a bowing man, stay close to some offerings; as for the lower register, it depicts four men with their arms across their chests.[18]

It appears then that the advent of a unified monarchy in the Nile Valley was accompanied by the consolidation of a new, standardized imagery of the members of the elite where officials were firstly distinguished by their attitudes, position (often in registers, close to the king), and symbols of authority (sticks), and secondly by their titles and names. Judging from the standardized representations apparent in reliefs like those at Wadi el-Humur or the palette of Narmer, it seems that the figures of high dignitaries became more and more iconic and, to a certain extent, impersonal and less individualized (unlike portraits). To put it another way, the possibilities for self-presentation through 'personalized' iconographic details became paradoxically less important when Egyptian art was growing in scale and skill with the advent of a unified monarchy. Quite probably the emergence of other means of encoding status and information, including monumental architecture, writing, and large ceremonial landscapes (such as the royal funerary complexes), explain the modest role played by iconography, even statuary, in the self-presentation of officials during the Early Dynastic.

Paradoxes of Early Self-Presentation: Visible Servants versus Elusive Elites?

Means of nonroyal self-representation were apparently quite limited during the first two dynasties, a striking fact when considering that dignitaries worked now for a monarchy encompassing a large territory, with considerable resources at its disposal and with a long tradition in the representation of officials since its Nag el-Hamdulab precedents. However, monumental uses of such artistic and writing potential appear surprisingly scarce, especially in domains like statuary, epigraphy, elaborated stelae, and luxury equipment. In fact, only architecture escapes from this tendency, but its uses, as well as those of incipient carved stelae, are not without problems. Some statues interpreted as 'precanonical' represent men and women of high status (members of the royal family, in a broad sense?), but their dating points predominantly to the Third Dynasty.[19]

The rarity of statues and inscribed stelae and slabs belonging to the uppermost sectors of Egyptian society explains the considerable uncertainty about the attribution of some enormous tombs, mainly found at Saqqara as well in other places. Their dimensions suggest that they belonged to very high dignitaries, members of the royal family, even kings themselves, as in the case of those from Saqqara.[20] But for some reason, statues and monumental epigraphy were hardly employed in these monuments, making the identification of their owners rather problematic and depending essentially on the evidence provided by seals. This circumstance is the more surprising when considering that hundreds of modest tombs surrounding the burials of the First Dynasty kings at Abydos,[21] as well as about forty 'middle-class' early tombs excavated at Helwan,[22] have provided stelae and inscribed slabs with the names and, in many cases, the titles of their owners.

Thus, for instance, the attribution to Queen Neithhotep, probable wife of Narmer, of a huge mastaba excavated by De Morgan at Naqada, has been recently contested and ascribed instead to Prince Rechit (Fig. 2.3).[23] As for the vast early mastabas excavated at Saqqara, they have been alternatively assigned to First Dynasty pharaohs and to some of their more prominent officials; it has been persuasively argued that their owners were in fact not kings but members of the royal family.[24] Similar problems concern the

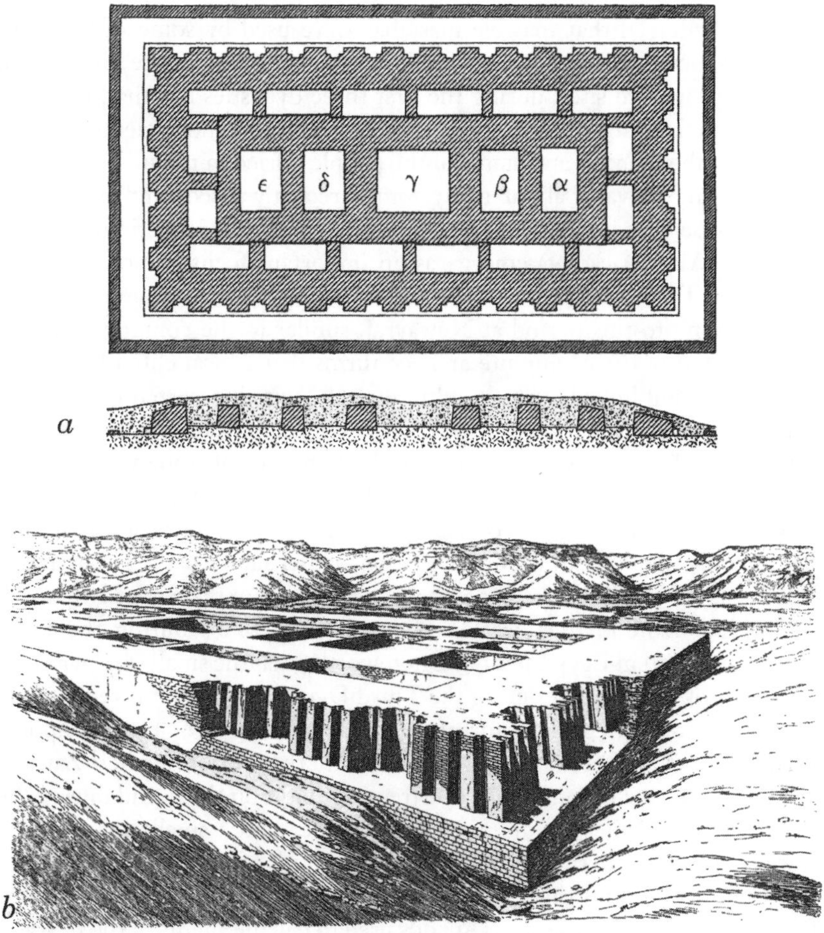

2.3. Early First Dynasty mastaba at Naqada, probably of a princess (Jacques de Morgan, *Recherches sur les origines de l'Égypte II*, 1897)

early big mastabas at Tarkhan,[25] at Abu Rawash,[26] as well as two enormous mastabas (86×45m and 64×23m respectively) discovered at Beit Khallaf, west of Girga, as well as other comparable monuments surrounding the ancient capital, Thinis, such as the mastabas of Reqaqna and of cemetery N 500–700 at Naga al-Deir.[27] Finally, big mastabas have been recently discovered at several other sites, including the one at the summit of a hill at Elkab,[28] the early (late Third–early Fourth Dynasty) mastaba found at Quesna, in the central Delta, measuring at least 17×13m,[29] and the rock tomb ascribed to the Third Dynasty found at Thot Hill near Thebes.[30] From this evidence it can be inferred that massive mastabas were used by some of the most powerful members of the king's circle, both in the Memphite area and in selected provincial sites, during the first three dynasties but that, for some reason, monumental epigraphy was absent from these monuments in order to express the identity and status of the people buried in them.

The same is valid about many tombs recently discovered in another provincial setting. The area of Bersheh and Zawiyet al-Mayetin (provinces 15–16, in Middle Egypt) emerge as an important focus of power during the Third Dynasty. The discovery of a necropolis of anepigraphic rock tombs dating to this period at Nuwayrat, similar to the contemporaneous ones attested in the Memphite area, confirms that a local elite of a certain importance and linked (at least culturally) to Memphis existed there at the beginning of the Old Kingdom.[31] It is also quite significant that the only *ḥḳꜣ* (governor) of a province mentioned in the hundreds of stone vessels found at the pyramid of Djoser ruled, precisely, the Sixteenth Nome of Upper Egypt. Finally, the discovery of many modest burials in the foothills around Bersheh, also dating to the Third Dynasty, further supports the idea that this region played an exceptional role at this early stage of the Egyptian state.[32]

Having in mind the location of many elite tombs during the Early Dynastic Period in Egypt, it is quite noteworthy that the small step pyramids built in provincial Egypt during the Third Dynasty correspond very closely to the zones where such tombs were erected: the area of Hierakonpolis/Elkab, Naqada, the area of Thinis/Abydos and the area of Bersheh/Zawiyet al-Mayetin; as for Elephantine, a fortress was built on the island during the First Dynasty, while an administrative complex and a small step pyramid were erected there in the Third Dynasty. Hundreds of seals from this dynasty mention officials and their day-to-day activities, involving cereal transfers from the state warehouses near Abydos used to pay the agents of the pharaoh at Elephantine.[33] The discovery at Elkab of a contemporary complex, dating from the Third–Fourth Dynasties and equipped with storage facilities, silos, and sites where agricultural produce was transformed, was accompanied by the recovery of many seals that reveal the activities of several high officials, also known from other seals unearthed at Beit Khallaf,[34] Abydos, Elephantine, and al-Kubanieh, who served under Khasekhemwy and Djoser and who were involved mainly in the management of plows and granaries.[35] Finally, the ink inscriptions written on several hundred vessels found in the galleries of the mortuary complex of pharaoh Djoser at Saqqara, from the Third Dynasty (partly produced during the reign of Djoser himself, but many others coming from the tombs of his ancestors), mention the officials, institutions, and regions that delivered precious products to the royal mortuary complex.[36] These texts show that some provinces had local leaders at their head, called *sšm tꜣ* (leader of the land) or *ḥḳꜣ* (governor), while others ruled over royal centers like the *ḥwt-ʿꜣt* (great *ḥwt*) and the *ḥwt*.[37]

And here precisely lies the paradox. Seals and ink inscriptions evoke a vivid world of officials and high dignitaries occupied in many different activities at the service of the kings and, as mentioned before, we can infer that the most powerful and close to the pharaoh were the owners of the huge mastabas located in key sites, like those of Merka and Hemaka (First Dynasty) and Ruaben (Second Dynasty) at Saqqara. However, these monuments remain almost mute about their owners and, in the case of the provincial mastabas, we can only deduce that the support or the alliance of prominent local families was crucial for pharaohs in order to assert their power over Egypt. In contrast, many modest tombs surrounding the burials of the first pharaohs (Abydos) or situated in 'middle-class' cemeteries (Helwan) provide the names and titles of hundreds of people connected to the king but enjoying (usually) a lesser status than the high courtiers and dignitaries of the kingdom.[38] In fact, the inscriptions from the stelae of the First Dynasty subsidiary tombs at Abydos show that their occupants were male and female courtiers, dwarfs, and even pet dogs.[39] That their condition was a modest one transpires from their more usual titles, *sẖnw ꜣẖ* and *ḥr ẖꜣsty sḳr*, the first one probably referring to a funerary priest and the second one to female prisoners or servants.[40] Their relative low status is also apparent judging from their representations, usually squatting, in some cases standing but without the symbols of status (scepters, sticks) normally associated with dignitaries. Writing was thus used to record the names and, sometimes, also the functions of these courtiers, unlike many of their upper class counterparts buried in monumental mastabas. Such a modest condition is also apparent in the inscribed slabs from Helwan. Here only forty relief slabs have been found in a cemetery comprising more than ten thousand tombs, most of which date to the Early Dynastic Period; and, while the ratio between male and female owner is rather close (20:18), the majority of individuals without titles were women, while those bearing titles were primarily men; however, among the rare women bearing titles, two of them were king's daughters and one acquaintance of the king, thus revealing a high status. Slightly later, during the Fourth Dynasty, all slabs at Helwan belonged to men. Finally, most of the titles referred to in these slabs correspond to sculptors, carpenters, ritualists, and one scribe. The only case with multiple titles corresponds to a man who held important managerial positions in government offices, dealing with storage, supplies, and logistics; he also held some religious and courtly titles.[41]

What's in a Name? Ka Dignitaries and Decorated Nonroyal Tombs

The scarcity and plainness of representational material from Early Dynastic elite tombs stands in sharp contrast not only with their large and complex mud brick mastabas, but also with the rich imagery present in previous funerary contexts, such as the painted wares of the Late Predynastic. Also the treatment of their bodies after death reveals a comparable change, from dismembering to mummification or, at least, a certain preservation in huge mastabas filled with large quantities of precious goods (wine, oil, stone vases, and objects in ivory, metal, and wood).[42] The first appearance of mastabas during the First Dynasty, as huge visual markers of status and power derived from a nascent state, went hand-in-hand with an increasing concern for the preservation of the body (not being now in contact with the sand, natural mummification became harder) and, consequently, with new perceptions of the self, including the afterlife. This perception implied that certain aspects of the deceased person should remain in the world as parts of a ritually integrated network of relations between the living and the dead.[43] One of them was the very concept of *kꜣ*, the vital essence that leaves the body after death but which should continue to be nourished thanks to the offerings presented by relatives. Thus complex networks of social relations and mutual support revolved around the dead and were entertained through rituals.[44]

A First Dynasty stone dish provides some clues about these changes. It takes the form of a *kꜣ*-sign holding with its hands the *ꜥnḫ*-sign (Fig. 2.4).[45] In fact, the very importance of the concept of *kꜣ* in its social—not only ritual—dimension certainly explains the frequency of the element *kꜣ* in many anthroponyms of First and Second Dynasty officials, like Amka, Ankhka,

2.4. First Dynasty dish of greywacke, Metropolitan Museum of Art, New York (Metropolitan Museum)

Hemaka, Henuka, Menka, Merka, Nebitka, Neska, Niyka, Saka, Sekhemka, Sekhka, Seshemka, Setka, and Wahka.[46] So names of this kind not only identified high officials; they also proclaimed their adherence to new values revolving around a novel concept of individuality and self-presentation ("my *k3*") and expressed through original, massive burials (mastabas) that marked the landscape.[47] Furthermore, the frequency of names in objects placed in royal and nonroyal tombs (recorded in ink quotations, labels, seal marks, etc.) revealed not only the extent of the duties and management capacities of their holders, but also their extensive networks of contacts within and outside the palace and in the provinces, including royals and other members of the elite. Names and titles became thus inextricably linked to the official expression of the self throughout Egyptian history.[48]

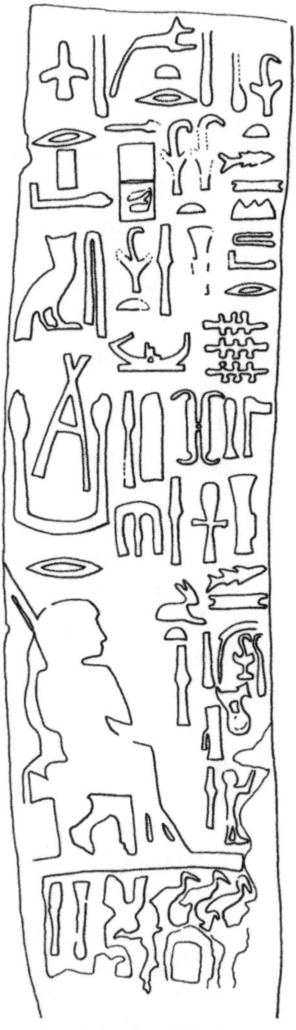

2.5. Stela of Merka (W.B. Emery, *Great Tombs of the First Dynasty* III, 1958, pl.23b, 39)

Furthermore, the memorial aspects of the self probably also explain why the newly acquired importance of titles, inscribed names, and occasional, standardized depictions of courtiers and officials appear encoded in a new kind of prestigious object placed in nonroyal tombs. They are the stelae, which also first appeared during the First Dynasty (Fig. 2.5). Later on, another type of monument was produced from the Second Dynasty on, probably under the influence of some scenes portrayed in First Dynasty cylinder seals. They were rectangular slabs placed in the wall of the burial chamber. The dead figured there sitting at an offering table and accompanied by inscriptions recording his/her name, titles and, in some cases, the goods presented.[49] Stelae and slabs appear then as inseparable from the development of the notion of *k3*, as well as from new expressions of status and individuality whose protagonists were the rising class of officials at the service of kings. The tombs of these officials more prominent or better connected to the royal court became the center of ceremonies aiming to preserve the memory of the dead and, on a more practical ground, to materialize and visualize the network of relations revolving around them, from members of their kin to friends, colleagues, and clients.[50] The deceased depicted as recipient of offerings, identified by his/her name and titles (thus marking his/her place in the hierarchy of the state and his/her closeness to the king), represented in a very limited set of poses displaying authority, and being (ideally) eternally approachable in a visible monument restricted to members of the palatial elite, codified the new values ascribed to servants of the state. An original visual culture was under elaboration and, with it, the possibilities and limits of nonroyal self-presentation. Judging from the extant evidence, the gradually expanding iconographic program in tombs, derived from these modest precedents, was to become the most elaborated embodiment of such culture during the Old Kingdom.[51]

Building Up Identities through Texts and Images

In a culture as overwhelmingly oral as that of the Early Dynastic Period, the only possibilities to gain access to its means of self-presentation are the texts and images of the protagonists themselves. Nevertheless, as previously seen, three major problems emerge. On the one hand, the scarce use of *monumental* writing is evident in contrast to its more administrative uses, such as labels, ink inscriptions, even seals. On the other hand, the highly restricted and formalized set of pictorial representations of officials and high dignitaries is evident since an early date. Finally, other means of self-representation, like the organization of nonfunerary public/ceremonial and nonroyal spaces, mural paintings, and documents (especially letters), remain largely unknown.

Seals convey key notions of authority and service to the king and, consequently, they identify officials by their names and titles. Not surprisingly, the first complex *nonroyal* depictions of officials in their tombs (stelae, slabs, also statues to a lesser extent) convey these same notions of authority and dignity through titles and a very limited set of poses considered representative of that authority: standing and accompanied by select symbols of power and status (scepter, stick, special dressing, hairstyle, and ornaments) or sitting in front of an offering table as recipients of offerings, therefore stressing their role as center of a microcosm of social networks focused in the mastaba. Thus titles, honorable poses, and specific symbols of status crystallized in early codified forms of self-presentation still to prevail for centuries, with writing playing a somewhat subordinate role. These basic elements could be expanded in tombs through a rather more elaborated iconographic program, as it happened since the Fourth Dynasty, but continuous lengthy texts still remained optional there too and were often reduced to lists of offerings and moral statements, more rarely to self-presentations and 'juridical' texts.[52] Not by chance, some of the most creative, informative, and vivid self-presentations appear far from Memphis, in the provincial world (as in the Sixth Dynasty examples of Weni of Abydos, Qar of Edfu, and Sabni and Harkhuf of Elephantine), where distance from the royal court and its normative high culture opened more possibilities for self-presentation, but always within the strict limits of the palatial codes.[53] That is why the uses of writing during the First through Third Dynasties appear so restricted and their contents so sparing in *monumental art*. However, it would be a mistake to consider these features as proof of unskillfulness, as if writing still remained an imperfect tool to record information and complex ideas during the Early Dynastic Period and the early Old Kingdom. The recent discovery of a set of papyri dating to Khufu's reign includes, for instance, a logbook where the scribe in charge of a team of workers recorded their daily activities by means of continuous phrases.[54] And some nonroyal stelae and panels, especially during the Third Dynasty, display sophisticated compositions of texts and images that point to a refined courtly culture, where writing and iconography were ably combined into harmonious and visually appealing tableaux.[55] Even if evidence of early long texts is meager, it is not completely absent, as some inscribed blocks from Heliopolis, dating from Djoser's reign, prove.[56]

The basic encoding of self-presentation was thus apparent since the First Dynasty, not by chance when mastabas, stelae, titles, and names helped express new identities related to the nascent state and its cultural values. The stela of Sabef, an official contemporary of King Qaa, is not only the earliest but also an excellent example of these innovations.[57] In his stela, Sabef appears standing, holding a stick and a scepter, while the composition is carefully divided in two almost equal parts. The first one comprises the titles of the owner while the second one conveys his depiction and name. His titles, not always easy to interpret, refer nevertheless more to courtly buildings and institutions than to practical administrative activities. Like contemporary huge mastabas, the basic meaning is that of authority and closeness to the king. Similar features appear in the stela of Merka, contemporary of Sabef (Fig. 2.5). Seated on an elegant chair, his titles identify him as a member of the highest elite (*iry pꜥt*), especially those related to the palace and the king.[58] However, it is to be noticed that occupations recorded in his seals are absent in the stela, such as those relating to the administration of some kind of fortified (or ceremonial?) enclosures.[59] Similar cases could

2.6. Wooden Panel of Hesy-Re, Egyptian Museum, Cairo (Wikicommons)

be evoked.[60] Judging from this very limited evidence, it appears then that stelae, slabs, and statues stressed rank and participation in the courtly life through a careful selection of the titles held by their owners. Incidentally, a subordinate was represented for the first time in the stela of his master; placed at the feet of Merka, he was depicted nevertheless in a much smaller scale, thus reproducing conventions present in the royal iconography.[61]

During the Third Dynasty the imagery associated with high officials became definitely codified and destined to last. Scepters and sticks conveyed the notion of authority, while the occasional presence of scribal tools further enhanced the idea of administration and service to the king. A variety of dressing (including specific priestly clothes), necklaces, hairstyles, bracelets, and other insignia strengthened the overall impression of authority, power, and membership in the elite of the kingdom and the court circles. Remarkably, the cloaks usually displayed in the statues and earlier depictions of courtiers and dignitaries disappeared, only to become restricted to the representation of foreigners and marginal populations such as herders.[62] Authority was also expressed through a limited but careful use of writing, usually reduced to lists of offerings and, above all, titles. In fact, titles stressed service to the king and missions in the palace, to the detriment of more administrative/managerial functions, thus continuing a practice well attested since the Early Dynastic. That is why many stelae and slabs dating to the Third Dynasty only evoke *wꜥb nswt* (*wab*-priest of the king) and *smr pr* (companion of the house.)[63] In the most detailed examples, like those of Hetepi, Khabausokar, Akhetaa, and Hesy-Re, this is the dominant pattern.[64] On the contrary, self-presentational information was reduced to a minimum and consisted mainly in epithets (like Khabausokar's "one who knows what is good for the heart of his lord")[65] and in official and prestige activities, such as managing property and participating at ceremonies (as in the late Third–early Fourth Dynasty inscriptions of Metjen and, perhaps, Hetepherenptah).[66] Another aspect is the careful integration of iconography and writing in the composition of scenes, which seems to combine the earlier contents of both slabs (funerary meal) and stelae (official standing and holding insignia of power). Thus the slab of Abneb, for example, combines two depictions of the owner, in one case as a dignitary, standing with a scepter and a stick, and in the other sitting at an offering table, wearing the same robe as depicted in the tombs of Khabausokar and Hetepi.[67] Finally, mastabas (more rarely hypogea, as in the area of Bersheh) retained their central role for displaying the wealth and social status of their owners.

The reliefs in the chapels of Khabausokar and Akhetaa and the wood panels in the tomb of Hesy-Re are the best examples of the consolidation of such visual expressions of self-presentation during the Third Dynasty, destined to become canonical. Thus the wood panels in the tomb of Hesy-Re depict him as a scribe, as a dignitary, and again as a scribe sitting in front of an offering table (Fig. 2.6), while Khabausokar appears both as a standing dignitary and wearing a ritual robe knotted on his shoulder

2.7. Reliefs from the Third Dynasty chapel of Khabausokar, Saqqara (M.A. Murray, *Saqqara Mastabas* I, 1905, pl. 1)

when sitting at a table (Fig. 2.7; a similar robe appears again in the tomb of Hetepi). Statues also contributed to this renewed expression of self, not only because they became more frequent in the nonroyal tombs of the Third Dynasty but, especially, because some of the most exquisite (like those of Sepa and the lady Nesa)[68] reproduced similar poses and codes present in contemporary reliefs, thus gradually departing from the style, attitudes, and characteristics dominant in the statuary of the First and Second Dynasties.[69] Also noteworthy is the importance of women either as owners of tombs, statues, and slabs or as partners of their male kinsmen in the iconography of their tombs,[70] represented at the same size, as in the case of Hathor-Neferhotepes, wife of Khabausokar.[71]

2.8. Block from the tomb of Akhetaa, late Third Dynasty (photograph by author)

These developments set the basis for still more complex compositions, leading to the characteristic decorated tomb of the Old Kingdom and its rich iconography, the first examples of which date to the end of the First Dynasty. The carved wooden panels in the tomb of Hesy-Re represent a first step, as several tableaux (literally) encompassed the current main depictions of officials: standing or sitting, and wearing the appropriate paraphernalia of power. The chapels of Khabausokar and his wife continued the same themes, but they were now directly sculpted on the walls of their tomb. However, toward the end of the dynasty, new themes appeared, but were restricted to only a few tombs owned by high dignitaries. In the case of Hetepi, the original decorative program included a panel carved in the northern wing of the entrance to the chapel of his mastaba,[72] while the unfinished southern wing might represent Hetepi standing and holding a scepter, preceded by at least two registers, one of them showing three male figures: his administrator, Nakhti, and two boys.[73] Finally, the tomb of Akhetaa constitutes a further step,[74] with his titles displayed over and in front of his standing depiction, ranged in columns separated by vertical lines, as in later monuments (Fig. 2.8). The final culmination of this long process is the decorated chapel of Metjen.[75]

Not by chance the first occurrence of decorated tombs was contemporary with the development of a new kind of royal funerary landscape in the Memphite area, centered on pyramids and the use of stone on a large scale. Carved reliefs and statuary opened further paths for the expression of ideological values, not only through the massive architectural dimensions of monuments themselves but by an increasing use of iconography.[76] The codification of artistic conventions, including the canonical representation of dignitaries in statues and reliefs, became thus one of the mainstays of self-presentation—perhaps mural painting and literary uses of writing played (even inspired) a similar role, but their traces (if any) are practically invisible.[77] Outside the Memphite area, elite funerary monuments apparently lacked this kind of decoration. Such absence reinforces the idea that it was a close product of the courtly culture, as it also transpires from the representations of officials accompanying the king in contemporary royal reliefs at Wadi Maghara, in Sinai.[78] In any case, the continuity of basic poses and themes since the Early Dynastic Period (evident in slabs, seals, and the Sinai reliefs) proves the existence of a visual tradition transmitted for centuries, whereas innovation, experiment, and withdrawal of previous dominant forms finally crystallized in potent icons of self-presentation during the Third Dynasty.

Notes

1 I. Regulski, "The Origin of Writing in Relation to the Emergence of the Egyptian State," in B. Midant-Reynes et al., eds., *Egypt at Its Origins 2: Proceedings of the International Conference "Origin of the State, Predynastic and Early Dynastic Egypt," Toulouse (France), 5th–8th September 2005* (Leuven, 2008), 985–1009.

2 B.J. Kemp, A. Boyce, and J. Harrel, "The Colossi from the Early Shrine at Coptos in Egypt," *Cambridge Archaeological Journal* 10 (2000), 211–42; D. Wengrow, *The Archaeology of Early Egypt: Social Transformations in North-East Africa, 10,000 to 2650 BC* (Cambridge, 2006), 176–217.

3 S. Hendrickx, "Iconography of the Predynastic and Early Dynastic Periods," in E. Teeter, ed., *Before the Pyramids: The Origins of Egyptian Civilization* (Chicago, 2011), 75–81; B. Midant-Reynes, ed., *Les manifestations artistiques de l'Égypte prédynastique* (Paris, 2012).

4 Wengrow, *The Archaeology of Early Egypt*, 218–58; E.F. Morris, "On the Ownership of the Saqqara Mastabas and the Allotment of Political and Ideological Power at the Dawn of the State," in Z.A. Hawass and Janet Richards, eds., *The Archaeology and Art of Ancient Egypt: Essays in Honor of David B. O'Connor*, II (Cairo, 2007), 171–90; B. Midant-Reynes, ed., *La naissance de l'architecture funéraire* (Paris, 2008).

5 D. Wildung, *Imhotep und Amenhotep: Gottwerdung im alten Ägypten* (Munich-Berlin), 1977.

6 W. Helck, *Untersuchungen zur Thinitenzeit* (Wiesbaden, 1987), 255–58; J. Kahl, N. Kloth, and U. Zimmermann, *Die Inschriften der 3. Dynastie: Eine Bestandsaufnahme* (Wiesbaden, 2003), 70–71, 132–33.

7 E. Christiana Köhler and J. Jones, *Helwan II: The Early Dynastic and Old Kingdom Funerary Relief Slabs* (Rahden, 2009).

8 S. Hendrickx, J.C. Darnell, M.C. Gatto, and M. Eyckerman, "Iconographic and Palaeographic Elements Dating a Late Dynasty 0 Rock Art Site at Nag el-Hamdulab (Aswan, Egypt)," in D. Huyge, F. van Noten, D. Swinne, eds., *The Signs of Which Times? Chronological and Palaeoenvironmental Issues in the Rock Art of Northern Africa* (Brussels, 2012), 295–326; S. Hendrickx, J.C. Darnell, and M.C. Gatto, "The Earliest Representations of Royal Power in Egypt: The Rock Drawings of Nag el-Hamdulab (Aswan)," *Antiquity* 86 (2012), 1068–83. Other contemporary or slightly later scenes, like that at Gebel Sheikh Suleiman, celebrate military campaigns against Nubia; cf. a recent study of this composition in C. Somaglino and P. Tallet, "Une campagne en Nubie sous la Ière dynastie: La scène nagadienne du Gebel Sheikh Suleiman comme prototype et modèle," *Nehet. Revue numérique d'Égyptologie* 1 (2014), 1–46. A king, several men, and boats figure in the Qustul incense burner, see Teeter, ed., *Before the Pyramids*, 162–63 [no. 10].

9 M. Hartwig, "Between Predynastic Palettes and Dynastic Relief: The Case of Cairo JE 46418 & BMA 66.175," in E.-M. Engel, V. Müller, and U. Hartung, eds., *Zeichen aus dem Sand: Streiflichter aus Ägyptens Geschichte zu Ehren von*

Günter Dreyer (Wiesbaden, 2008), 2, figs. 1–2, 4, fig. 4. Compare with the servants and the cloaked bearded foreigner in W.M.F. Petrie, *The Royal Tombs of the Earliest Dynasties*, II (London, 1901), pl. IV.

10 Wengrow, *The Archaeology of Early Egypt*, 205, fig. 9.13.

11 W.M.F. Petrie, *The Royal Tombs of the First Dynasty*, I (London, 1900), pl. XII [13], XVII [30].

12 M.R. Ibrahim and P. Tallet, "Trois bas-reliefs de l'époque thinite au Ouadi el-Humur: aux origines de l'exploitation du Sud Sinaï par les Égyptiens," *RdÉ* 59 (2008), 155–80.

13 For a different interpretation of the second title, see J. Kelder, "Narmer, Scorpion and the Representation of the Early Egyptian court," *Origini* 35 (2013), 143–56.

14 Ibrahim and Tallet, "Trois bas-reliefs," 162–69.

15 Ibrahim and Tallet, "Trois bas-reliefs," 169–73.

16 J. Spencer, ed., *Aspects of Early Egypt* (London, 1996), 31, fig. 12.

17 B. Faye, "Royal Women as Represented in Sculpture during the Old Kingdom," in C. Ziegler, ed., *L'art de l'Ancien Empire égyptien* (Paris, 1999), 113–15; V. Vasiljević, "Female Owners of Carrying-Chairs: *Sitzsänfte* and *Hocksänfte*," *SAK* 41 (2012), 395.

18 J. Vandier, *Manuel d'archéologie égyptienne*, I (Paris, 1952), 829, fig. 556.

19 M. Eaton-Krauss, "Non-Royal Pre-Canonical Statuary," in N. Grimal, ed., *Les critères de datation stilistiques à l'Ancien Empire* (Cairo, 1998), 209–25; H. Sourouzian, "Concordances et écarts entre statuaire et représentations à deux dimensions des particuliers de l'époque archaïque," in N. Grimal, ed., *Les critères de datation stilistiques à l'Ancien Empire* (Cairo, 1998), 305–52.

20 Cf. S. Hendrickx, "Les grands mastabas de la Ière dynastie à Saqqara," *Archéo-Nil* 18 (2008), 60–88; Morris, "On the Ownership of the Saqqara Mastabas," 171–90.

21 About their occupations, cf. P. Kaplony, *Die Inschriften der ägyptischen Frühzeit*, I (Wiesbaden, 1963), 364–76; G.T. Martin, *Umm el-Qaab VII: Private Stelae of the Early Dynastic Period from the Royal Cemetery at Abydos* (Wiesbaden, 2011).

22 Köhler and Jones, *Helwan II.*

23 J. de Morgan, *Recherches sur les origines de l'Égypte*, II, *Ethnographie historique et tombeau royal de Négadah* (City, Paris, 1897), 147–202; J. van Wetering, "Relocating De Morgan's Royal Tomb at Naqada and Identifying its Occupant," in J. Kabaciński, M. Chłodnicki, and M. Kobusiewicz, eds., *Northeastern Africa: New Ideas and Discoveries* (Poznan, 2012), 91–124.

24 Morris, "On the Ownership of the Saqqara Mastabas," 171–90.

25 W. Grajetzki, "The Architecture and the Signification of the Tarkhan Mastabas," *Archéo-Nil* 18 (2008), 103–12.

26 Y. Tristant, "Deux grands tombeaux du cimetière M d'Abou Rawach (Ière dynastie)," *Archéo-Nil* 18 (2008), 131–47.

27 Beit Khallaf, see J. Garstang, *Tombs of the Third Egyptian Dynasty at Reqâqnah and Bêt Khallâf* (London, 1906); Naga al-Deir, see G.A. Reisner, *Naga-ed-Dêr*

III: A Provincial Cemetery of the Pyramid Age (Oxford, 1932). Cf. also M. Baud, *Djéser et la IIIe dynastie* (Paris, 2002), 219–24.

28 L. Limme, "El-Kab, 1937–2007: Seventy Years of Belgian Archaeological Research," *BMSAES* 9 (2008), 23–24.

29 J. Rowland, "An Old Kingdom Mastaba and the Results of Continued Investigations at Quesna in 2010," *JEA* 97 (2011), 11–29.

30 G. Vörös, "Hungarian Excavations on Thot Hill at the Temple of Pharaoh Montuhotep Sankhkara in Thebes (1995–1998)," in H. Beinlich, J. Hallof, H. Hussy, and C. von Pfeil, eds., *5. Ägyptologische Tempeltagung, Würzburg, 23.–26. September 1999* (Wiesbaden, 2002), 201–11.

31 H. Willems, *Les Textes des Sarcophages et la démocratie: Éléments d'une histoire culturelle du Moyen Empire égyptien* (Paris, 2008), 16–19; M. De Meyer, S. Vereecken, B. Vanthuyne, S. Hendrickx, L.O. de Beeck, and H. Willems, "The Early Old Kingdom at Nuwayrāt in the 16th Upper Egyptian Nome," in D. Aston, B. Bader, C. Gallorini, P. Nicholson, and S. Buckingham, eds., *Under the Potter's Tree: Studies on Ancient Egypt Presented to Janine Bourriau on the Occasion of Her 70th Birthday* (Leuven-Paris-Walpole, 2011), 679–702.

32 M. De Meyer et al., "Early Old Kingdom at Nuwayrāt," 679–702; B. Vanthuyne, "The Beni Hasan el-Shuruq region in the Old Kingdom: A Preliminary Survey Report," *Praga Egyptological Studies* 21 (2018), 94–105.

33 M. Ziermann, "De l'habitat à la ville fortifiée: Éléphantine: Données choisies sur l'urbanisation et l'architecture (Ière-VIe dynastie)," *Archéo-Nil* 12 (2002), 29–46; J.-P. Pätznick, *Die Siegelabrollungen und Rollsiegel der Stadt Elephantine im 3. Jahrtausend v. Chr.* (Oxford, 2005); G. Dreyer, "Drei archaisch-hieratische Gefäßaufschriften mit Jahresnamen aus Elephantine," in J. Osing and G. Dreyer, eds., *Form und Mass: Beiträge zur Literatur, Sprache und Kunst des alten Ägypten: Festschrift für Gerhard Fecht* (Wiesbaden, 1987), 98–109, figs. 1–2; S. J. Seidlmayer, "Town and State in the Early Old Kingdom: A View from Elephantine," in J. Spencer, ed., *Aspects of Early Egypt* (London, 1996), 122–26.

34 The seals recovered from this locality reveal the existence of a well-structured central administration at this early date, whose representatives were active in southern Egypt, see I. Incordino, "I sigilli regali della III dinastia da Bet Khallaf (Abido)," *Aegyptus* 87 (2007), 45–53.

35 S. Hendrickx and M. Eyckerman, "The 1995 Excavation of an Early Old Kingdom Storage Site at Elkab," in W. Claes, H. de Meulenaere, and S. Hendrickx, eds., *Elkab and Beyond: Studies in Honour of Luc Limme* (Leuven, 2009), 1–30; I. Regulski, "Early Dynastic Seal Impressions from the Settlement Site of Elkab," in W. Claes, H. de Meulenaere, and S. Hendrickx, eds., *Elkab and Beyond: Studies in Honour of Luc Limme* (Leuven, 2009), p. 31–49.

36 P. Lacau, J.-P. Lauer, *La pyramide à degrés*, IV, *Inscriptions gravées sur les vases* (Cairo, 1959); P. Lacau, J.-P. Lauer, *La pyramide à degrés*, V, *Inscriptions à l'encre sur les vases* (Cairo, 1965). See also I. Regulski, "Second Dynasty Ink

Inscriptions from Saqqara Paralleled in the Abydos Material from the Royal Museums of Art and History (RMAH) in Brussels," in S. Hendrickx, R.F. Friedman, K.M. Ciałowicz, and M. Chłodnicki, eds., *Egypt at Its Origins: Studies in Memory of Barbara Adams* (Leuven-Paris-Dudley, 2004), 949–970.

37 J.C. Moreno García, *Ḥwt et le milieu rural égyptien du III*[e] *millénaire: Economie, administration et organisation territoriale* (Paris, 1999), 233–34.

38 Sourouzian, "Concordances et écarts," 314–17, 319–20, with references; Köhler and Jones, *Helwan II, passim*; I. Regulski, *A Paleographic Study of Early Writing in Egypt* (Leuven, Paris, Walpole, 2010), 40–42. Cf. É. Vaudou, "Les sépultures subsidiaires des grandes tombes de la Ière dynastie égyptienne," *Archéo-Nil* 18 (2008), 149–65.

39 Petrie, *The Royal Tombs of the First Dynasty*, I, pls. 30–36; Petrie, *The Royal Tombs of the Earliest Dynasties*, II, pls. 26–30; Martin, *Private Stelae of the Early Dynastic Period*, passim.

40 For these titles see, respectively, R. El-Sayed, "Quelques réflexions au sujet du titre *sẖnw ꜣḫ*," *BIFAO* 88 (1988), 63–69, and G. Godron, *Études sur l'Horus Den et quelques problèmes de l'Égypte archaïque* (Geneva, 1990), 89–96.

41 Köhler and Jones, *Helwan II*, 79–83.

42 D. Wengrow and J. Baines, "Images, Human Bodies and the Ritual Construction of Memory in Late Predynastic Egypt," in S. Hendrickx, R.F. Friedman, K.M. Ciałowicz, and M. Chłodnicki, eds., *Egypt at Its Origins: Studies in Memory of Barbara Adams* (Leuven-Paris-Dudley, 2004), 1081–1113.

43 Wengrow, *The Archaeology of Early Egypt*, 223–24.

44 They are well documented for the Old Kingdom and the First Intermediate Period. See S. Donnat and J.C. Moreno García, "Intégration du mort dans la vie sociale égyptienne à la fin du troisième millénaire av. J.-C.," in A. Mouton, J. Patrier, eds., *Life, Death and Coming of Age in Antiquity: Individual Rites of Passage in the Ancient Near East* (Leiden, 2015), 179–207.

45 H.G. Fischer, "Some Emblematic Uses of Hieroglyphs, with Particular Reference to an Archaic Ritual Vessel," *MMJ* 12 (1978), 5–19.

46 An aspect evoked by Morris, "On the Ownership of the Saqqara Mastabas," passim. Cf. also Martin, *Private Stelae of the Early Dynastic Period*, 216–18.

47 In the case of the Memphite area, the tombs of the highest elite moved according to the politics of their time. With the reign of Aha, for instance, Saqqara North was the main elite necropolis. Other cemeteries in use until then in the Memphite area (Abu Rawash, Helwan, Tarkhan) did not disappear but accommodated burials of people whose status did not merit an elite tomb at Saqqara North (I. Regulski, "Reinvestigating the Second Dynasty at Saqqara," in M. Bárta, F. Coppens, and J. Krejčí, eds., *Abusir and Saqqara in the Year 2010*, II [Prague, 2011], 697.) However, during the late Second Dynasty, the tombs of the highest elite moved about one kilometer to the south, when kings built great enclosures in the area reminiscent of those at Abydos (I. Regulski, "Investigating a New Dynasty 2 Necropolis at South Saqqara," *BMSAES* 13 [2009], 221–37, esp. 226–28).

48 Wengrow, *The Archaeology of Early Egypt*, 234–39. Cf. Also K.E. Piquette, "'It Is Written'?: Making, Remaking and Unmaking Early 'Writing' in the Lower Nile Valley," in K.E. Piquette and R.D. Whitehouse, eds., *Writing as Material Practice: Substance, Surface and Medium* (London, 2013), 213–38; and "Structuration and the Graphical in Early Dynastic Culture," in R.J. Dann and K. Exell, eds., *Egypt: Ancient Histories, Modern Archaeologies* (Amherst, NY, 2013), 51–99.

49 Wengrow, *The Archaeology of Early Egypt*, 220–23.

50 A.O. Bolshakov, *Man and His Double in Egyptian Ideology of the Old Kingdom* (Wiesbaden, 1997), 30–36; Wengrow, *The Archaeology of Early Egypt*, 218–26, 231–45; Morris, "On the Ownership of the Saqqara Mastabas," 171–90.

51 J.C. Moreno García, "La gestion sociale de la mémoire dans l'Égypte du IIIe millénaire: les tombes des particuliers, entre utilisation privée et idéologie publique," in M. Fitzenreiter and M. Herb, eds., *Dekorierte Grabanlagen im Alten Reich—Methodik und Interpretation* (London, 2006), 215–42; R. van Walsem, *Iconography of Old Kingdom Elite Tombs: Analysis and Intepretation, Theoretical and Methodological Aspects* (Leiden, 2005). As for the themes (and the ways) to be evoked in such compositions, cf. the essential remarks by J. Baines, "Restricted Knowledge, Hierarchy, and Decorum: Modern Perceptions and Ancient Institutions," *JARCE* 27 (1990), 1–23. Cf. also J. Baines and P. Lacovara, "Burial and the Dead in Ancient Egyptian Society: Respect, Formalism, Neglect," *JSA* 2 (2002), 5–36; Fitzenreiter and Herb, eds., *Dekorierte Grabanlagen im Alten Reich*, passim; S. Verma, *Cultural Expression in the Old Kingdom Elite Tomb* (Oxford, 2014). In general, M. Hartwig, ed., *A Companion to Ancient Egyptian Art* (Chichester, 2015).

52 N. Strudwick, *Texts from the Pyramid Age* (Atlanta, 2005), passim.

53 Moreno García, "La gestion sociale de la mémoire," passim.

54 P. Tallet, "Des papyrus du temps de Chéops au Ouadi el-Jarf (Golfe de Suez)," *BSFE* 188 (2014), 25–49.

55 Like the reliefs in the tomb of Khabausokar, see M.A. Murray, *Saqqara Mastabas*, I (London, 1905), pls. 1–2.

56 Kahl, Kloth, and Zimmermann, *Die Inschriften der 3. Dynastie*, 116–17.

57 Petrie, *The Royal Tombs of the First Dynasty*, I, pls. 30, 31[48], 36[48]; Helck, *Untersuchungen zur Thinitenzeit*, 194, 228–29; T.A.H. Wilkinson, *Early Dynastic Egypt* (London-New York, 1999), 133–37; Martin, *Private Stelae of the Early Dynastic Period*, 44–45, pl. 14 [48].

58 Helck, *Untersuchungen zur Thinitenzeit*, 230–33; Wilkinson, *Early Dynastic Egypt*, 148–49; G.T. Martin, "The Stela and Grave of Merka in Saqqara North," in E.-M. Engel, V. Müller, and U. Hartung, eds., *Zeichen aus dem Sand: Streiflichter aus Ägyptens Geschichte zu Ehren von Günter Dreyer* (Wiesbaden, 2008), 463–76.

59 As for the seal, cf. Kaplony, *Die Inschriften der ägyptischen Frühzeit*, III, pl. 86 [322].

60 As in the case of Setka's stela (see Petrie, *The Royal Tombs of the First Dynasty*, I, pl. 3) and seals (see Kaplony, *Die Inschriften der ägyptischen Frühzeit*, III, nos. 182–85). Cf. also Helck, *Untersuchungen zur Thinitenzeit*, 225–27.

61 Another example, dating from the late Early Dynastic, see P. Kaplony, *Die Inschriften der ägyptischen Frühzeit: Supplement* (Wiesbaden, 1964), 33 [no. 1067], pl. V.

62 Cf. note 9 supra and Sourouzian, "Concordances et écarts entre statuaire et représentations," 329, fig. 3, 337, fig. 21; Teeter, ed., *Before the Pyramids*, 59, fig. 6.7. In general, G. Vogelsang-Eastwood, *Pharaonic Egyptian Clothing* (Leiden, 1993), 159–68.

63 Kahl, Kloth, and Zimmermann, *Die Inschriften der 3. Dynastie*, 172–77, 182–83.

64 Khabausokar, see Murray, *Saqqara Mastabas I*, pls. 1–2; Helck, *Untersuchungen zur Thinitenzeit*, 261–65; Kahl, Kloth, and Zimmermann, *Die Inschriften der 3. Dynastie*, 186–91; M. Bárta, F. Coppens, and H. Vymazalová, *Tomb of Hetepi (AS 20), Tombs AS 33–35 and AS 50–53* (Prague, 2010), 398–99, pls. 32–34. Hesyre, see J.E. Quibell, *Excavations at Saqqara, 1911–1912: The Tomb of Hesy* (Cairo, 1913), pls. 29, 31; Helck, *Untersuchungen zur Thinitenzeit*, 258–60; W. Davis, "Archaism and Modernism in the Reliefs of Hesy-Ra," in J. Tait, ed., *"Never Had the Like Occurred": Egypt's Views of Its Past* (London, 2003), 31–60; Kahl, Kloth, and Zimmermann, *Die Inschriften der 3. Dynastie*, 104–11. Hetepi, see Bárta, Coppens, and Vymazalová, *Tomb of Hetepi*. For Akhetaa, see below.

65 Murray, *Saqqara Mastabas I*, pl. 1; M. Baud, "The Birth of Biography in Ancient Egypt: Text Format and Content in the 4th Dynasty," in S.J. Seidlmayer, ed., *Texte und Denkmäler des ägyptischen Alten Reiches* (Berlin, 2005), 105, with additional examples.

66 The date of Hetepherenptah is debated, ranging from the late Third to the Fifth Dynasty. See Baud, "The Birth of Biography in Ancient Egypt," 107–10; J. Stauder-Porchet, "Les autobiographies événementielles de la Ve dynastie: premier ensemble de textes continus d'Égypte," in M. Bárta, F. Coppens, and J. Krejčí, eds., *Abusir and Saqqara in the Year 2010*, II (Prague, 2011), 747–766.

67 Davis, "Archaism and Modernism," 55, fig. 3.9.

68 C. Ziegler (ed.), *L'art égyptien au temps des pyramides* (Paris, 1999), 159–61.

69 Eaton-Krauss, "Non-Royal Pre-Canonical Statuary"; Sourouzian, "Concordances et écarts."

70 Kahl, Kloth, and Zimmermann, *Die Inschriften der 3. Dynastie*, 216–17, 222–25. A trend that continued during the early Fourth Dynasty, judging from the slabs in the necropolis of Giza (P.D. Manuelian, *Slab Stelae of the Giza Necropolis* [New Haven-Philadelphia, 2003]) and from the exceptional complex of Queen Khentkaues (M. Lehner, D. Jones, L. Yeomans, H. Mahmoud, and K. Olchowska, "Re-examining the Khentkaues Town," in N. Strudwick and H. Strudwick, eds., *Old Kingdom, New Perspectives: Egyptian Art and Archaeology 2750–2150 BC* [Oxford, 2011], 143–91).

71 Murray, *Saqqara Mastabas*, I, pl. 2.

72 Bárta, Coppens, and Vymazalová, *Tomb of Hetepi*, 19–20, 391, pl. 18, 397, pl. 31.

73 Bárta, Coppens, and Vymazalová, *Tomb of Hetepi*, 19, 22, 394–95.

74 Helck, *Untersuchungen zur Thinitenzeit*, 244–55; C. Ziegler, *Catalogue des stèles, peintures et reliefs égyptiens de l'Ancien Empire et de la Première Période Intermédiaire, vers 2686–2040 avant J.-C.* (Paris, 1990), 96–100 [no. 14]; Kahl, Kloth, and Zimmermann, *Die Inschriften der 3. Dynastie*, 202–15.

75 K.B. Goedecken, *Eine Betrachtung der Inschriften des Meten* (Wiesbaden, 1976); Helck, *Untersuchungen zur Thinitenzeit*, 268–79.

76 As in the case of the monuments of Djoser at Saqqara and Heliopolis, cf. respectively F.D. Friedman, "The Underground Relief Panels of King Djoser at the Step Pyramid Complex," *JARCE* 32 (1995), 1–42, and Kahl, Kloth, and Zimmermann, *Die Inschriften der 3. Dynastie*, 114–19.

77 Painting has been only exceptionally preserved in nonroyal Early Dynastic mastabas; the very limited extant evidence consists only in nonfigurative patterns, see Wengrow, *The Archaeology of Early Egypt*, 240–41.

78 As in the scenes of kings Djoser and Sekhemkhet, see A.H. Gardiner, T.E. Peet, and J. Černý, *The Inscriptions of Sinai*, I, *Introduction and Plates* (London, 1952), pl. 1; Kahl, Kloth, and Zimmermann, *Die Inschriften der 3. Dynastie*, 120–21, 136–37.

3

Self-Presentation in the Fourth Dynasty

Hend Sherbiny

The Fourth Dynasty (2575–2450 BC) represents a major peak in ancient Egyptian history, especially for the history of the Old Kingdom or the Age of the Pyramids, Third to Eighth Dynasties (2707–2170 BC). The dynasty started with King Sneferu and ended with a possible ephemeral king. The kings of this dynasty are Sneferu, Khufu (Greek Kheops), Djedefre, Khafre (Greek Khephren), a possible ephemeral king, Menkaure (Greek Mykerinos), Shepseskaf, and another possible ephemeral king.[1]

The state and administration were very strong during this dynasty. The reign of the founder of the Fourth Dynasty, Sneferu, Lord of Maat, was a crucial episode in the history of Egyptian divine kingship. He achieved many important economic and administrative transformations, and made several funerary and artistic changes; moreover, the political ideology in his reign was dynamic. The figure of this king was intensely solarized and his sacred image was explicit.[2] Sneferu built his pyramids at Meidum, Seila, and Dahshur.[3] He was remembered by subsequent generations of Egyptians as a beneficent king, while his son and successor Khufu was recalled as a tyrant (Fig. 3.1).[4] Little is known about Khufu,[5] but the sheer size of his Great Pyramid at Giza indicates that this vast construction project was the result of a strong central administration (Fig. 3.2).[6] His son Djedefre left Giza and built his pyramid at Abu Rawash, to the north of Giza,[7] while Djedefre's brother Khafre (Fig. 3.3) returned to Giza to construct the second pyramid of Giza and the Great Sphinx.[8] Some

3.1. Statue of King Khufu, Egyptian Museum, Cairo (photograph by Nigel Fletcher-Jones)

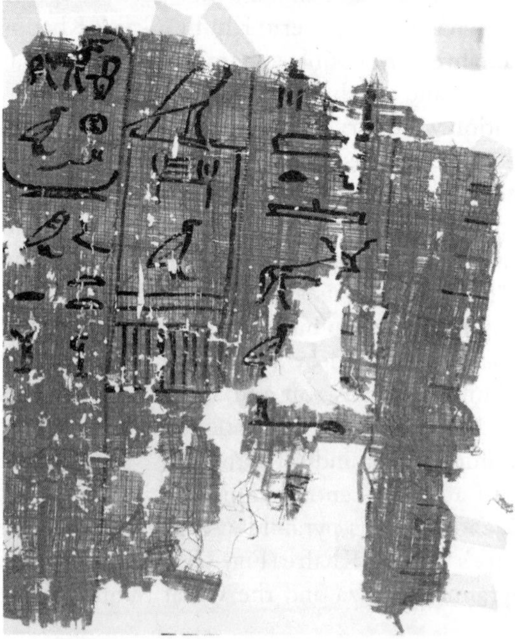

3.2. The Wadi al-Jarf papyrus from the reign of King Khufu, Egyptian Museum, Cairo (photograph by author)

3.3. Statue of King Khafre, Egyptian Museum, Cairo (photograph by author)

family instability is detectable during the later years of the Fourth Dynasty in which the two main kings were Menkaure (Fig. 3.4) and Shepseskaf. During this dynasty the architecture of the pyramids continued and reached a high level of excellence.[9] The dynasty started very strong but ended up very weak.[10]

Royal elite members administered the Fourth Dynasty and occupied most of the top offices in the state administration. This administrative move caused dramatic changes in the evolution of the state and other spheres within the society of this period. It was a turning point in the history of Old Kingdom Egypt and had a significant impact on the character of the dynasty, in general. These royal elite members holding the highest positions maintained power[11] and, in so doing, accumulated wealth and prestige. Prince Rehotep and his wife Nofret were among the true examples of these royal elite members (Fig. 3.5).

3.4. Triad of King Menkaure, Egyptian Museum, Cairo (photograph by Sandro Vannini/Laboratoriorosso)

3.5. Statues of Prince Rehotep and his wife Nofret, Egyptian Museum, Cairo (photograph by Sandro Vannini/ Laboratoriorosso)

Nonroyal Elite Self-Presentations

The Fourth Dynasty nonroyal self-presentations represent the beginnings of written self-presentations or prehistories of the genre[12] in ancient Egyptian literature. The majority of these self-presentations come from tomb contexts, especially from the Memphite Necropolis, while others are from the provinces. These self-presentations are not lengthy, and vary in both form and content. Some describe actions, careers, or events, and may be classified as either ethical or ideal biographies. Others may be characterized as intrinsic narrative titular, commented titular, appended titular, annalistic format, and commented epithets (or developed epithets).[13] The strings of titles in the Fourth Dynasty tombs are ancestors of the so-called career self-presentations, and texts dedicated to tomb protection or buildings' rewards were presumably the forerunners of the so-called ideal self-presentation.[14] The self-presentations of the nonroyal elite members of the dynasty mainly focus on highlighting their titles and epithets. The subjects of these texts present different topics and range from titles and epithets to narratives, events, and careers. These texts also focus on moral values usually expressed in later self-presentation traditions. Loyalty to the king is highly visible in these texts, especially in the titular format as epithet and comments supplementing them.[15]

Among the self-presentations of the early Fourth Dynasty is the text of Metjen, which also mentions some legal issues and property inheritances. This text presents several themes in content, displays many elements typical of self-presentation, associates text and decoration as one of the main characteristics of the Egyptian tomb program, highlights narrative and self-presentation components, and contributes to the development of self-presentation formation.[16] The relationship between the king and his high officials is well expressed in the self-presentations of the dynasty as, for example, in inscriptions of Hetepherniptah.[17] The false door or entrance jamb of the tomb of Hetepherniptah probably dates to the reign of Sneferu, based on stylistic and textual criteria.[18] The text reads:

> The king caused that a carrying-chair of *sadj*-wood (a palm-tree) be made for him, and that young recruits carry him in it following the King. This had never been done for anyone, Hetepherniptah.[19]

This text uses the word *niswt*, which is related to the state and the king as a holder of this divine position.[20] The text also states that this favor had never been bestowed upon anyone—Hetepherniptah being the first.

The self-presentation of the late Fourth Dynasty *ḫnti-š* official and singer of the palace, Ankhkhufu[21] is remarkable because it introduces the close relationship between the (unnamed) king and this high official by focusing on the nature of his post discharged at the royal palace; therefore, the king rewarded him with a false door as a royal gift. This false door bears the self-presentation of Ankhkhufu. The right and left inner jambs read, respectively, as follows:

> His majesty had this done for him as a mark of his state of *imakhu* in the sight of his majesty while he was still alive and on his feet.
> The *khenty-she* of the Great House, the singer, Ankhkhufu.
> The work was done close by the king himself in the doorway of the audience hall, and thus his majesty saw what was done daily on it there every day.
> Ankhkhufu.[22]

Ankhkhufu was a very high official in the royal house. He held the following positions: the *khenty-she* of the royal house, singer and overseer of singers of the royal house, and overseer of flautists. To show that he was a good person in the eyes of the king, Ankhkhufu described himself in this text in different ways as "beloved of his lord," "who loves his lord," "who speaks every perfect thing to his lord," "the *imakhu* in the sight of his lord," "the royal acquaintance," and "the delight of his lord daily." All these reveal the close relationship between this (unnamed) king and Ankhkhufu at the end of the Fourth Dynasty.

The self-presentation of Debehen in his tomb at Giza is one of the best known self-presentations of the period (Fig. 3.6). This text records the construction of the tomb of this nonroyal elite member as a favor from King Menkaure.[23] The phrasing of the self-presentation reads as if it were set up as a royal decree.[24] His tomb, located in the Central Field of Giza,[25] is very large, 100 cubits in length, 50 cubits in breadth, and 5 cubits in height according to his text. In his self-presentation Debehen confirms that:

> With regard to this tomb of mine,
> it was the king of Upper and Lower Egypt,
> Menkaure [may he live forever] who gave me its place,
> while he happened to be on the way to the pyramid plateau[26]
> to inspect the work being done on the pyramid of Menkaure.[27]

3.6. The tomb of Debehen, Giza (photograph by author)

Another example is the self-presentation of Merykhufu. His text states:

> The possessor of *imakh*-condition before Menkaure (says): it is because of my *imakh*-condition that my master did this for me....[28]

This text indicates that nonroyal tombs were a gift from the king, contrary to the practice in the late Old Kingdom.[29] This text also shows the interaction and close relationship of the king and his high officials at the end of the dynasty. The image of Menkaure in this text is more human than divine, in contrast to that of his grandfather, King Khufu.

The self-presentation of Ptahshepses is very interesting since it gives us a clear succession from the reign of King Menkaure, at the end of the Fourth Dynasty, to the kings of the early middle Fifth Dynasty. His self-presentation is inscribed on a false door from tomb C 1 north of the Step Pyramid at Saqqara. This door is now in London, BM EA 682, and Chicago, Oriental Institute OIM 11048. Ptahshepses was long-lived. Although the text dates to the early middle Fifth Dynasty, the text to the right of center of the door mentions kings Menkaure and Shepseskaf of the late Fourth Dynasty as follows:

> [A child born in] the time of Menkaure, he grew up among the royal children in the palace of the king, inside the royal harem.
> He was more valuable in the sight of the king than any child.
> Ptahshepses.
> [A youth who tied the headband in] the time of Shepseskaf,
> he grew up among the royal children in the palace of the king,
> inside the royal harem.
> He was more valuable in the sight of the king than any youth.[30]

This text shows that children of nonroyal elite members might be raised among the royal children at the royal house inside the royal harem. This practice was probably a royal prerogative given by King Menkaure to the family of Ptahshepses, for Menkaure had the image of a king with human qualities and was known for his close relationships with nobility, serving as a conduit between royalty and nobility during his reign.

Some self-presentations of the dynasty can be used as indicators of the succession of the kings of the dynasty, as stated in the self-presentation of Sekhemkara.[31] His self-presentation comes from his rock-cut chapel in the Central Field at Giza and mentions a long list of kings before this son of Khafre was honored as follows:

The honored one before his father, the King, before the Great God,
before the King of Upper and Lower Egypt, Khafre,
before the King of Upper and Lower Egypt, Menkaure,
before the King of Upper and Lower, Shepseskaf,
before the King of Upper and Lower Egypt, Userkaf,
and before the King of Upper and Lower Egypt, Sahure.

It is worth noting that the name of King Khufu is not mentioned in this text and it only refers to his father, the king, described as "the Great God." This is probably due to the divinity of King Khufu in the eyes of his successors and his family members. Self-presentational texts from the reign of King Khufu are few, probably due to his prohibition against making statues, for which we have only reserve heads.[32] This dearth of texts was also because King Khufu changed the cult of the king, equating himself with Re. Moreover, his sons, Kings Djedefre and Khafre, were the first kings to bear the new title *sꜣ Rꜥ* (son of Re), since their father was the god Re himself.[33] As a result, King Khufu probably did not leave much room for the nonroyal elite members to express themselves widely in text and art as was previously possible.

However, there is a block from Giza[34] which contains a text that dates to the reign of King Khufu because it contains the Two Ladies name of the king, Medjedu. The text reads:

(1) The Two Ladies, Medjedu . . .
(2) In this town of my lord (2) that I made this tomb of mine . . .[35]

Titles were also used to form the core of self-presentations. The self-presentation of Weta[36] refers to his work through his titles that indicate how he applied his craft to the pharaoh's throne. His text is inscribed on his sarcophagus in a few lines in a single string on the right side, reading:

One who made the leather-roll of the lector-priest according to his master's wish, in accordance with what was commanded, one who made anything related to the throne of the King when he came to sit in the portico-hall (*ḏꜣdw*), Weta.[37]

The text of Weta shows the nature of the position he held related to leather-making. He covered the royal throne with leather, and this throne was located in the portico-hall (*ḏꜣdw*).

Conclusions

The Fourth Dynasty nonroyal self-presentations represent an early stage in the development of Egyptian self-presentation. They are good examples for understanding the status of the nonroyal elite members of the period. Although the surviving self-presentations are few, they do, nevertheless, reflect social hierarchies,[38] political ideology, and the organization of the administration during the period. The relationship between the kings and nonroyal individuals of this dynasty is remarkable and passed through different stages (Figs. 3.4 and 3.5). This dynasty presents the different aspects of the ancient Egyptian king's image as divine, half-divine, and human.[39] Although the nonroyal elite members of this dynasty left magnificent monuments, they did not leave many self-presentational texts. This is one of the main characteristics of the nonroyal elite members' status in the period.

Fourth Dynasty self-presentations came mainly from the Memphite necropolis, especially Giza. The content of these self-presentations is basic. They are ideal biographical phrases attached to other texts, such as appeals and warnings, while some biographies commemorate individual events.[40] The self-presentations of the Fourth Dynasty are also short, mainly based on epithets and titles rather than consisting of long narratives, yet they reveal the relationship between the nonroyal individual and the king. The vast majority of these self-presentations are written in the third person.[41] This is very clear in the protagonist's titles and epithets which are "extended caption-like strings of titles whose 'biographical' potential was realized."[42]

Self-presentations from the reign of King Khufu are rare. This feature is remarkable and perhaps related to the internal policy of that king, who did not allow the sculpting of statues, even for himself. This prohibition was probably valid for the representation of nonroyal elite members in text as well. In addition, the reason for the few self-presentations from the time of King Khufu is probably that King Khufu identified himself as the sun god Re. King Khufu's wall reliefs eschew representations of him with other deities because he considered himself as the god Re. His son King Khafre worshiped him as the sun god Re in the Sphinx Temple (Fig. 3.7) in his pyramid complex; whereas his grandson King Menkaure only accepted him as a manifestation of the sun god Re, not the god Re himself.[43]

Furthermore, these nonroyal self-presentations introduce the nonroyal individual in perfect harmony with the ideals and expectations of the aristocracy of the period. These texts stress a total dependence upon the king. Although those self-presentations come from tomb contexts, mainly inscribed on tomb walls, they are condensed rather than elaborated, restricted in use of text, and do not correspond to the scenes on which they

3.7. The Great Sphinx at Giza (photograph by Sandro Vannini/Laboratoriorosso)

are inscribed. The nonroyal self-presentations of the period reflect mainly social history rather than political processes. They characterize high official individuals, summarize their professional careers, describe a few noteworthy episodes in their lives, and are linked to the social as well as the public lifestyle of the political and administrative nonroyal elites.

Notes

1 R. Bussmann, "Pyramid Age: Huni to Radjedef," *UCLA Encyclopedia of Egyptology*, 1(1), 2015, https://escholarship.org/uc/item/9wz0c837; M. Bárta, "Radjedef to the Eighth Dynasty," *UCLA Encyclopedia of Egyptology*, 1(1), 2017, https://escholarship.org/uc/item/67n4m4c4; J. Malék, "The Old Kingdom (*c.* 2686–2125 BC)," in I. Shaw, ed., *The Oxford History of Ancient Egypt* (Oxford, 2000), 89–117.

2 F.L. Borrego Gallardo, "Señor de Maat: innovaciones y cambios de la realeza divina egipcia bajo el reinado de Snefru," *ARYS: Antigüedad, Religiones y Sociedades* 12 (2014), 87–127.

3 R. Stadelmann, "Builders of the Pyramids," in J.M. Sasson, John Baines, Gary Beckman, and Karen S. Rubinson, eds., *Civilizations of the Ancient Near East*, II (New York, 1995), 724–728; R. Stadelmann, "The Pyramids of the Fourth Dynasty," in Z. Hawass, ed., *The Treasures of the Pyramids* (Cairo, 2003), 112–37.

4 As represented in Papyrus Westcar, see, for example, R.B. Parkinson, *The Tale of Sinuhe and Other Ancient Egyptian Poems, 1940–1640 BC* (Oxford, 1997), 108ff.

5 Stadelmann, "Builders of the Pyramids," 730.

6 M. Lehner and Z. Hawass, *Giza and the Pyramids: The Definitive History* (London, 2017); Stadelmann, "Builders of the Pyramids," 724–732; Stadelmann, "The Pyramids of the Fourth Dynasty," 112–37; see also P. Tallet, *Les papyrus de la mer Rouge I: Le "journal de Merer" (Papyrus Jarf A et B)* (Cairo, 2017); P. Tallet, "Les journaux de bord du règne de Chéops au ouadi el-Jarf (P. Jarf A-F): état des lieux," *BSFÉ* 198 (2017), 8–19; E.-M. Engel, "The Organisation of a Nascent State: Egypt until the Beginning of the 4th Dynasty," in J.C. Moreno García, ed., *Ancient Egyptian Administration* (Leiden, 2013), 19–40; see also M. Bietak, "Introduction to Palaces in Egypt: What They Tell Us about the Ruler, Administration and Culture," in M. Bietak and Silvia Prell, eds., *Ancient Egyptian and Ancient Near Eastern Palaces, I: Proceedings of the Conference on Palaces in Ancient Egypt, held in London 12th-14th June 2013, Organised by the Austrian Academy of Sciences, the University of Würzburg and the Egypt Exploration Society* (Vienna, 2018), 23–38.

7 M. Verner, "Contemporaneous Evidence for the Relative Chronology of Dyns. 4 and 5," in E. Hornung, R. Krauss, and D.A. Warburton, eds., *Ancient Egyptian Chronology* (Leiden-Boston, 2006), 124–43; R. Gundacker, "The Chronology of the Third and Fourth Dynasties according to Manetho's *Aegyptiaca*," in P.D. Manuelian and T. Schneider, eds., *Towards a New History for the Egyptian Old Kingdom Perspectives on the Pyramid Age* (Leiden-Boston, 2015), 76–199; Bussmann, "Pyramid Age: Huni to Radjedef"; Bárta, "Radjedef to the Eighth Dynasty."

8 R. Stadelmann, "The Great Sphinx of Giza," in Z. Hawass and L.P. Brock, eds., *Egyptology at the Dawn of the Twenty-First Century: Proceedings of the Eighth International Congress of Egyptologists*, Cairo, 2000, I (Cairo, New York, 2003), 464–69.

9 For more, see Z. Hawass, "The Programs of the Royal Funerary Complexes of the Fourth Dynasty," in D. O'Connor and David P. Silverman, eds., *Ancient Egyptian Kingship* (Leiden, 1995), 221–62; Stadelmann, "Builders of the Pyramids," 719–734; Stadelmann, "The Pyramids of the Fourth Dynasty," 112–37; J. Baines, "Kingship before Literature: The World of the King in the Old Kingdom," in R. Gundlach and C. Raedler, eds., *Selbstverständnis und Realität: Akten des Symposiums zur ägyptischen Königsideologie in Mainz 15.-17.6.1995* (Wiesbaden, 1997), 125–74.

10 See, for comparison with the Fifth Dynasty, M. Bárta, "'Abusir Paradigm' and the Beginning of the Fifth Dynasty," in I. Hein, N. Billing, and E.

Meyer-Dietrich, eds., *The Pyramids: Between Life and Death*. Proceedings of the Workshop Held at Uppsala University, Uppsala, May 31st–June 1st, 2012 (Uppsala, 2016), 51–74.

11 Bárta, "'Abusir Paradigm,'" 51–74.

12 See also J. Baines, "Forerunners of Narrative Biographies," in A. Leahy and J. Tait, eds., *Studies on Ancient Egypt in Honour of H.S. Smith* (London, 1999), 23–37.

13 M. Baud, "The Birth of Biography in Ancient Egypt: Text Format and Content in the IVth Dynasty," in S.J. Seidlmayer, ed., *Texte und Denkmäler des ägyptischen Alten Reiches* (Berlin, 2005), 119; see also A.M. Gnirs, "Die ägyptische Autobiographie," in A. Loprieno, ed., *Ancient Egyptian Literature: History and Forms* (Leiden–New York–Cologne, 1996), 203–206.

14 J. Assmann, *Stein und Zeit: Mensch und Gesellschaft im Alten Ägypten* (München, 1991), 179–80; E. Schott, "Die Biographie des Ka-em-tenenet," in J. Assmann, E. Feucht, and R. Grieshammer, eds., *Fragen an die altägyptische Literatur: Studien zum Gedenken an Eberhard Otto* (Wiesbaden, 1977), 454–55; Gnirs, "Die ägyptische Autobiographie," 200–201, 220–23; N. Klot, "Beobachtungen zu den biographischen Inschriften des Alten Reiches," *SAK* 25 (1998), 189–205; Baud, "The Birth of Biography in Ancient Egypt," 91.

15 Baud, "The Birth of Biography in Ancient Egypt," 93.

16 Baines, "Forerunners of Narrative Biographies," 29–34; Baud, "The Birth of Biography in Ancient Egypt," 92.

17 Cairo Museum JE 15048, see P.E. Newberry, "An Unpublished Monument of a 'Priest of the Double Axe,'" *ASAE* 28 (1928), 13–40; *Urk*. I, 231 (6); see also D. Farout and M. Baud, "Trois biographies d'Ancien Empire revisitées," *BIFAO* 101 (2001), 47–8; Baud, "The Birth of Biography in Ancient Egypt," 107–108.

18 N. Cherpion, *Mastabas et hypogées d'Ancien Empire: le problème de la datation* (Brussels, 1989), 108–109; M. Baud, *Famille royale et pouvoir sous l'Ancien Empire* (Cairo, 1999), 312–14; Farout and Baud, "Trois biographies d'Ancien Empire revisitées," 48; Baud, "The Birth of Biography in Ancient Egypt," 107–109.

19 Baud, "The Birth of Biography in Ancient Egypt," 109.

20 J.P. Allen, "Rē'wer's Accident," in A.B. Lloyd, ed., *Studies in Pharaonic Religion and Society in Honour of J. Gwyn Griffiths* (London, 1992), 18 (n. 36); E. Windus-Staginsky, "Der König in den Texten den Alten Reiches: Terminologie und Phraseologie," in S.J. Seidlmayer, ed., *Texte und Denkmäler des ägyptischen Alten Reiches* (Berlin, 2005), 335–49; Baud, "The Birth of Biography in Ancient Egypt," 109.

21 PM III.2, 129–30, G 4520, Giza West Field, Boston MFA 21.3081; G.A. Reisner, *A History of the Giza Necropolis*, I (Cambridge, 1942), 504–505, pl. 65, without facsimile; A. Roccati, *La littérature historique sous l'Ancien Empire égyptien* (Paris, 1982), 99–100. However, E. Brovarski, "The Washerman of the God, Senenu," in Z.A. Hawass, K.A. Daoud, and S. Abd El-Fattah, eds., *The Realm of the Pharaohs: Essays in Honor of Tohfa Handoussa*, I (Cairo, 2008), 160–61, thinks that Ankhkhufu's false door may have been executed in the reign of Userkaf.

22 Cf. N.C. Strudwick, *Texts from the Pyramid Age* (Atlanta, 2005), 263.

23 However, N. Kloth, *Die (auto-)biographischen Inschriften des ägyptischen Alten Reiches: Untersuchungen zu Phraseologie und Entwicklung* (Hamburg, 2002), 38–39, puts this text not before the middle Fifth Dynasty, suggesting that various features of the decoration and the type of the self-presentation might indicate that the scenes were executed posthumously by his son.

24 Cf. Strudwick, *Texts from the Pyramid Age*, 271.

25 PM III.2, 235–36.

26 For the translation of the word *ḥr*, as 'pyramid,' see E.J. Brovarski, "Varia," *Serapis* 3 (1975–1976), 1–8; E.J. Brovarski, "Once More on *ḥr*, 'Pyramid'?," in D. Magee, Diana, J. Bourriau, and S. Quirke, eds., *Sitting beside Lepsius: Studies in Honour of Jaromir Malek at the Griffith Institute* (Leuven, 2009), 99–114.

27 Strudwick, *Texts from the Pyramid Age*, 271.

28 Baud, "The Birth of Biography in Ancient Egypt," 107; PM III.2, 235–36, LG 90, Giza Central Field; S. Hassan, *Excavations at Gîza 4: 1932–1933* (Cairo, 1943), fig. 118, pl. 48; Roccati, *La littérature historique sous l'Ancien Empire égyptien*, 91–93.

29 For the late Old Kingdom royal involvement in the construction of nonroyal tombs, see V. Chauvet, "Royal Involvement in the Construction of Private Tombs in the Late Old Kingdom," in J.-C. Goyon and C. Cardin, eds., *Proceedings of the Ninth International Congress of Egyptologists: Grenoble, 6–12 septembre 2004*, I (Leuven, 2007), 313–21.

30 Strudwick, *Texts from the Pyramid Age*, 303–304.

31 PM III.2, 233–34, tomb LG 89; Hassan, *Excavations at Gîza 4: 1932–1933*, fig. 64, pl. 34; Roccati, *La littérature historique sous l'Ancien Empire égyptien*, 71 (no. 10, § 50); Baud, "The Birth of Biography in Ancient Egypt," 97–98.

32 B. Mendoza, "Reserve Head," in W. Wendrich, ed., *UCLA Encyclopedia of Egyptology* (Los Angeles, 2017), http://digital2.library.ucla.edu/viewItem.do?ark=21198/zz002kbwtk. For more on the recent duration of the reign of Khufu, see Tallet, *Les papyrus de la mer Rouge* I.

33 See Hawass, "The Programs of the Royal Funerary Complexes of the Fourth Dynasty," 227.

34 It was found west of the Great Pyramid at Giza and is now in the Turin museum under Turin 1853, see PM III.2, 177.

35 Strudwick, *Texts from the Pyramid Age*, 322.

36 PM III.2, 311; L. Borchardt, *Denkmäler des Alten Reiches (ausser den Statuen) im Museum von Kairo Nr. 1295–1808, Teil II: Text und Tafeln zu Nr. 1542–1808 (Manuskript abgeschlossen 1899)*, Catalogue général des antiquités égyptiennes du Musée du Caire (Cairo, 1964), CG 1295–1808, 205–206, pl. 110; Roccati, *La littérature historique sous l'Ancien Empire égyptien*, 94–95. For more on Weta, see H. Junker, *Weta und das Lederkunsthandwerk im alten Reich* (Vienna, 1957); Baud, "La date d'apparition des *ḫntiw-š*," *BIFAO* 96 (1996), 24–25.

37 Baud, "The Birth of Biography in Ancient Egypt: Text Format and Content in the IVth Dynasty," 106.

38 For more on a sociological analysis of self-presentations, see B. Hackländer-von der Way, *Biographie und Identität: Studien zur Geschichte, Entwicklung und Soziologie altägyptischer Beamtenbiographien* (Berlin, 2001).

39 For more on this, see R. Gundlach, "Zu Inhalt und Bedeutung der ägyptischen Königsideologie," in R. Gundlach and C. Raedler, eds., *Selbstverständnis und Realität: Akten des Symposiums zur ägyptischen Königsideologie in Mainz 15.-17.6.1995* (Wiesbaden, 1997), 1–8; R. Gundlach, "Die Legitimationen des ägyptischen Königs: Versuch einer Systematisierung," in R. Gundlach and C. Raedler, eds., *Selbstverständnis und Realität: Akten des Symposiums zur ägyptischen Königsideologie in Mainz 15.-17.6.1995* (Wiesbaden, 1997), 11–20.

40 Kloth, *Die (auto-)biographischen Inschriften des ägyptischen Alten Reiches: Untersuchungen zu Phraseologie und Entwicklung*, 285; Strudwick, *Texts from the Pyramid Age*, 46.

41 Baud, "The Birth of Biography in Ancient Egypt: Text Format and Content in the IVth Dynasty," 122.

42 Baines, "Forerunners of Narrative Biographies," 30.

43 Hawass, "The Programs of the Royal Funerary Complexes of the Fourth Dynasty," 252.

4

Self-Presentation in the Late Old Kingdom*

Hana Vymazalová

The King and the Elite

The second half of the Old Kingdom, including the Fifth and Sixth Dynasties, is marked by a significant change in state administration, which was closely associated with historical and political development (the change of a ruling dynasty) and had a strong impact on social transformation and perhaps also on the development of religious beliefs and important cults.[1] In addition, religious development and the adaptation or emergence of important state cults—above all of Re and Osiris—can be seen as a means of control over the country's population through the modification of belief and state ideology, in which the king continued to play the central role for his people. Some scholars consider the Fifth and Sixth Dynasties the 'standard state phase,' with fully formed and operational institutions.[2]

From the late Fourth Dynasty onwards and during the Fifth Dynasty, the highest positions in the state administration gradually came to the hands of officials of nonroyal origin.[3] This fundamental change in administration brought high social status to educated, qualified men, who owed this achievement to their family background, their loyalty to the king, and also their own capability. It was perhaps by no accident that the famous teaching of Ptahhetep was set into this time (the rule of King Djedkare),[4] providing clearly formulated advice that following the rules and being loyal to the king would bring a successful, wealthy, and happy life to any official.

This change, on the one hand, helped detach men of royal blood, who might have been the king's competitors, from executive power. On the other hand, the influence of the nonroyal elites increased over time. Naturally, both groups were to assist the king in maintaining the order of the world, the *mꜣꜥt*.[5] Whereas the former group's main (natural) intention was to keep the power in the hands of the few of royal blood, thus supporting the strongly centralized state of the Fourth Dynasty, the nonroyal officials at some point gained enough power to start giving preference to their own interests, which later resulted in the weakening of the central state.[6]

Such development can be noticed in the course of the late Old Kingdom. The first half of the Fifth Dynasty, from Userkaf to Shepseskare, shows also other apparent changes. The royal monuments of this time were built in the Saqqara–Abusir necropolis, that is, in the vicinity of the earliest step pyramid of Netjerykhet, but also of the capital Inebu-Hedj and the associated temple of Ptah. At the same time, the size of the royal pyramids decreased considerably, and the decoration program of the associated funerary and valley temples and the causeways became standardized. The symbolism that was included in the monuments and their decoration program was one way to demonstrate the king's power and role in the world.[7] In addition, Userkaf was the first king to build a sun temple, a monument associated with his own pyramid complex where the kingship was celebrated in relation to the cult of Re and Hathor.[8] Even though the Fifth Dynasty sun temples expressed in architectural form the concept that had existed in Egypt since the earliest times,[9] their form was new and enabled expansion of the administration. Functions related to the cult of Re and Hathor in royal sun temples were closely tied to the king and brought prestige and benefit to their holders.[10] Not only did priestly offices associated with the royal cults increase in number, but some other new offices started to emerge at the royal court in the early Fifth Dynasty.[11] These included, for instance, the titles of the "mouth of Nekhen of the king" or an "overseer of scribes of royal documents," which are attested perhaps from the time of Neferirkare.[12] Other titles appear much more frequently in evidence than in earlier periods, as for instance the title of the "keeper of the secrets."[13]

The reign of King Nyuserre seems to have been a turning point in the development, marking the noticeable rise of wealthy families, which accumulated power over the state administration and society.[14] This might very well be connected with the need of legitimacy on the part of Nyuserre, who ascended the throne after his brother Neferefre and the very brief reign of Shepseskare.[15] The fact that his mother Khentkaus II was promoted and her monument enlarged[16] indicates a rather influential role of the queen in his reign. Some of the high officials of his time managed to have their offspring follow their own path and take over their offices. This is apparent, for instance, in the family of Senedjemib Inti, four succeeding generations of which held the highest administrative functions associated with royal constructions during the late Old Kingdom.[17] Such was the beginning of the trend which led to the decline of the king's power and the dominance of wealthy officials and their families.

The abovementioned tendencies in the highest levels of the Egyptian administration were associated with an increasing influence and independence of powerful families, which concentrated power (numerous high administrative functions) in their hands.[18] This tendency required a continuous redefinition of the connection between the king and the elites, because, hand in hand with this development, the Old Kingdom rulers of the late Fifth Dynasty and the Sixth Dynasty attempted to remain in control.[19] It seems to be no coincidence that in the middle of the Fifth Dynasty, the nonroyal offering formulae started to include the reference to Osiris, indicating the desire of the king to control the afterlife (Fig. 4.1).[20] Marriages were among the king's political means.[21] From the early Fifth Dynasty to the early Sixth Dynasty, one may find evidence on political marriages of royal daughters, through which the king intended to ensure the loyalty of the nonroyal grooms. Marriage to a royal woman was undoubtedly an uncommon privilege for a few officials, who all belonged to the highest levels of the Egyptian society. The grooms included high-ranking individuals, mostly viziers,[22] or (usually the eldest) sons of high-ranking individuals.[23] Such was the marriage of Userkaf's eldest daughter Khamaat to Ptahshepses, a high priest of Ptah,[24] one of the most important Memphite gods. It is worth noting that the name of the princess, meaning "Maat appeared" or

4.1. The upper lintel of Neferinpu's false door with one of the earliest references to Osiris in his offering formula (Archive of the Czech Institute of Egyptology, photograph by Martin Frouz)

4.2. Relief from the mastaba of the vizier Ptahshepses, showing him with his wife Khamerernebty, a daughter of King Nyuserre (Archive of the Czech Institute of Egyptology, photograph by Martin Frouz)

"May-Maat-Appear,"[25] might have been a political message associated with the ancient Egyptian royal ideology and the role of the king.[26] The most frequent evidence on royal women married to nonroyals comes from the second half of the Fifth Dynasty,[27] and the latest attested examples date to the reign of King Teti.[28] Many of these women bore names that included the element *Nbty* (Both Ladies), which undoubtedly refers to the king[29] and indicates an intentional and thought-out pattern of the marriages (Fig. 4.2).

Changes can also be noticed in the provinces, where the provincial elites gained more independence. The officials who were responsible for the provincial administration no more lived in the residence, which was the rule previously, but from the Fifth Dynasty onwards they started to settle down in their provinces and build their tombs there.[30] In the Fifth Dynasty this tendency is apparent in the Delta and most of Middle Egypt, with the aim to improve the agricultural production.[31] This development indicates the increasing importance of ties between the members of the local elites.[32] It was a crucial moment in the development of the state because the provincial elites necessarily balanced between being fully loyal to the interests of the king and those of their province in order to secure their position within the local administration.

At the same time, we may notice an interest in provinces from the late Fifth Dynasty onwards, perhaps reflecting the undergoing social changes.[33] In reaction to the disintegrative tendencies, the king established a new office, an 'overseer of Upper Egypt,' which is attested since the reign of King Djedkare.[34] This king seems to have reformed the provincial administration, including two parallel viziers, one of whom was in provinces.[35] The kings of the Sixth Dynasty continued to reform the administrative system, especially in relation to the provinces.[36] In an attempt to regain stronger control over Upper Egypt, Pepy I, instead of marrying off royal women as did his predecessors, took himself two wives from a nonroyal family of Upper Egypt, the family of Khui from Abydos. The same family later controlled the office of the vizier of Upper Egypt under Pepy II. The development, however, resulted in more and more independent provincial administrators.[37]

The Elite and the King

The above-sketched political and social development of the Egyptian state in the Fifth and Sixth Dynasties had, naturally, an impact on the ways of the self-presentation of the Egyptian elite. As the king demonstrated his role and power through his funerary monument and its decoration program, also the nonroyal officials presented themselves to others, above all to the divine sphere, in the same way. With the development of the administration and increase of the influence of nonroyal officials, we can find a larger number of tombs of wealthy officials in the Fifth and Sixth Dynasties.[38] At the same time, however, numerous tombs of middle and lower classes of the Egyptian society can be noticed as well in this period, indicating that the share in power reflected in the well-being of the society.

The Tombs of Officials

There were many ways for officials to present themselves in their tombs. The location of a tomb reflected the owner's importance—either by proximity to a royal monument or by the position on the most prominent place on the chosen site. This trend can be, for instance, noticed in Abusir, where only the family members and very few distinguished officials, such as the vizier and the king's son-in-law Ptahshepses, were buried in the royal necropolis around the pyramids of kings.[39] The hills of the nonroyal cemetery in the southern part of Abusir contain the largest tombs of the high-ranking officials on top, while the small, simple tombs of low-ranking owners can be found at the bottom and in between the hills.[40] In the early Sixth Dynasty Teti pyramid cemetery, the royal family members and the highest-ranking tomb owners, like the viziers and the king's sons-in-law Mereruka and Kagemni, built tombs very close to the king's pyramid, whereas the tombs of the other individuals were located farther from the king. A similar situation was around the pyramid of Pepy I in south Saqqara[41] and other pyramid complexes of the late Old Kingdom.

The architecture of the tombs might have been used to demonstrate the owner's direct link to the king. Some of the highest officials in the later part of the Fifth Dynasty included in their tombs some features that referred to royal architecture. Such were, for instance, the tombs of the viziers Ptahshepses in Abusir and Ty in Saqqara.[42] Other officials gained prestige by demonstrating a close connection to a member of the royal family in their tombs. This is well apparent, for example, in the tomb complex of a king's daughter Sheretnebty in Abusir (Fig. 4.3), which contained four rock-cut tombs of four high officials, one of whom was the princess's husband. The communal courtyard of this tomb complex, which served all four tombs, was inscribed with the titles, epithets, and name of only the princess herself. This undoubtedly increased the importance of the whole wide family, which in this manner demonstrated its connection to her royal father, King Nyuserre.[43] Proximity to a tomb of another official, who had more power and was closer to the king, was another common means of expressing the same intention. Thus, officials who were related by family and/or professional ties built clusters of tombs, forming small cemeteries around one central, most-prominent tomb. In Abusir, such a cluster developed in the late Fifth Dynasty to the east of the large anonymous tomb AS 31, whose owner held titles associated with the House of Life and House of Protection,[44] and it continued even during the Sixth Dynasty, when two more tombs were attached to it from the west (Fig. 4.4).[45]

Family tombs appear in the Fifth Dynasty, usually in the form of a mastaba with many shafts for burials of a number of family members.[46] This type of tomb was often used by lower officials, but later on such tombs were built by middle or higher officials too. In the period under discussion, we can generally notice an increasing number of tombs, reflecting the growing

4.3. The courtyard of the tomb complex of Nyuserre's daughter Sheretnebty and her family, with pillars bearing exclusively her name (Archive of the Czech Institute of Egyptology, photograph by Martin Frouz)

administration of the state. Besides the well-designed and decorated mastabas and rock-cut tombs, small, simple, and undecorated tombs also occur more often in both the residential cemeteries and the provinces.

At the same time, from the middle of the Fifth Dynasty onwards, poorer individuals frequently had themselves buried within the courtyards of the more wealthy officials to whom they were associated, perhaps most often by family ties.[47] Such ties might have been intentionally maintained over a long period of time, many years after the death of the prominent figure. Therefore, for instance, over thirty individuals were buried in various parts of the abovementioned tomb complex of Princess Sheretnebty in Abusir in the period between the late Fifth Dynasty and the end of the Sixth Dynasty (and possibly even later).[48]

A similar trend can also be found in the provincial cemeteries. Above all, Abydos is worth mentioning, where large structures with relief decoration were constructed during the Sixth Dynasty. The tomb of the vizier Iuu was located at the most prominent place; very near to it was located the slightly larger tomb of Weni the Elder, and some smaller structures probably owned by their relatives were built around it.[49]

4.4. Tombs dating to the late Fifth Dynasty in Abusir South, forming a cluster around the large anonymous mastaba AS 31 (Archive of the Czech Institute of Egyptology, photograph by Vladimír Brůna)

The tombs and burials discussed above provide evidence that family ties and kinship were rather important for the tomb owners of all ranks. We might deduce that the emphasis on the relations between tomb owners and burials might reflect the tendencies toward hereditary offices in the late Old Kingdom.[50] This might be partly true especially for the high-ranking, powerful officials. The poorer echelons of Egyptian society, however, might thus simply express their dependence on the more wealthy family members in both this and the other world.

Tomb Equipment and Decoration

Besides the location and the form of the tomb, the decoration and equipment were also ways to present the importance and wealth of the owners. The equipment that was placed in the chapels, burial chambers, and burial shafts naturally reflects the status of the owners. Only the wealthy officials could afford to have a sarcophagus, canopic jars (usually filled with mud, symbolizing renewal), and miniature model vessels.[51] Moreover, the composition of the pottery vessels (bowls, jars, stands, and plates) that can be found in different parts of tombs can help us specify the status of the owners even in those tombs where no inscriptions have survived.[52]

The development of the decoration of nonroyal tombs has been studied by many scholars,[53] and the influence of royal reliefs can be well traced in evidence. A link to the king was shown indirectly, namely by imitating the forms used by the rulers in their monuments. In his tomb, the tomb owner was the central figure of the scenes, and the depictions promoted his various functions and his wealth, which enabled him to provide for his afterlife. By imitating royal scenes, the tomb owners demonstrated their link to the king himself, but any actions between the king and the tomb owner were explicit only in the inscriptions (see below), but not in the depictions—ceremonial scenes, like the king rewarding officials with gold or officials attending events in the king's presence, never occur in nonroyal tombs of the late Old Kingdom. Such scenes were carved only on the walls of the royal monuments, and it was there that the officials grew in importance based on these themes. For instance, a scene showing the king during a celebration accompanied by the royal family and elite courtiers after the return of the expedition to Punt can be found on the causeway of Sahure.[54]

The king's favor was sometimes expressed through the scenes of the personifications of funerary domains. Some officials included in their tombs royal funerary domains, which present not only the privilege given by the king but also the economic profit that the officials enjoyed from this royal property.[55]

In addition, during the Fifth Dynasty, statuary played an increasingly important role in the equipment of nonroyal tombs.[56] Some officials placed very large numbers of statues in their tomb. For instance, more than one hundred statues were discovered in the tomb of Rawer in Giza, dating to the reign of Neferirkare.[57] Some of the statuary apparently imitated forms used by kings, as for instance, the statue that was found in fragments in the serdab of the tomb of Princess Sheretnebty and her nonroyal spouse in Abusir (Fig. 4.5).[58] The three fragments of this pseudogroup statue show two male figures side by side, evidently imitating the pseudogroup statue of King Nyuserre. The fragments even show the two men in the same posture as the king's statue, both striding with arms along their bodies, dressed in pleated kilts. Only one head has been preserved, showing nice features and a short curly wig (instead of the royal headdress). Another similar statue

4.5. Fragments of a pseudo-group statue found in the serdab of Sheretnebty's tomb, imitating the statue of King Nyuserre (Archive of the Czech Institute of Egyptology, photograph by Martin Frouz)

was discovered in the neighboring tomb of Nefershepes, but this time with one figure striding and the other figure standing with an arm bent across his chest.[59]

Besides the tomb owner himself, some of the figures shown in his tomb might have been presented with their names. This includes not only the members of his family, but identifications were sometimes added to the figures of the offering bearers, craftsmen, and other figures. In this manner, poorer members of the family and of the owner's household received their share of eternity, fully depending on their master. In other tombs, however, no names are given in such scenes, and we might find numerous cases of names scratched additionally in reliefs by those who desired to present themselves for eternity and insisted to do so even against the plan of the tomb owner.

Tomb Inscriptions

Tomb inscriptions are perhaps the richest, or the most assorted, source relating to the self-presentation of officials. Various types of inscriptions were carved in tombs, among which above all the titular strings and the self-presentational inscriptions provide us with relevant information.

The titles of the tomb owner usually consisted of various types of offices, combining honorary, administrative, judicial, and priestly duties. The lists of titles carved in a tomb often included lower- and higher-ranking variants of the same office, reflecting the stages in the tomb owner's career. It is worth mentioning that while the hieroglyphic inscriptions in tombs emphasized the highest offices and titles, the hieratic inscriptions on the tomb's masonry often included only one, perhaps the most common or most typical of the titles. In Neferinpu's tomb in Abusir, for instance, we can hence find his numerous middle- and high-ranking titles, including "overseer of all works ordered to him," "property custodian of the king," "speaker of Nekhen of the king," "priest of Maat and Horus," "priest of kings Neferirkare and Nyuserre," "*wab*-priest of the pyramid complex of Nyuserre," and other titles, carved on his fine limestone false door. The hieratic inscriptions on the masonry of Neferinpu's tomb, however, include mainly his middle-ranking title of the "elder of the (judicial) court of the king" and only once the title of the "*wab*-priest."[60] The hieroglyphic inscriptions served the eternity and were intended to include all that the tomb owner considered important for his presentation for eternity, while the hieratic texts were related only to the construction of the tomb. The hieratic inscriptions, however, provide evidence that the highest-ranking titles attested for the owners did not necessarily have to be the most important ones during their lives.[61]

Attachment to the king is, however, more clearly expressed in the biographical inscription where the importance of an official was fabricated into a story with a narrative frame. In the Fifth and Sixth Dynasties, it is possible to distinguish several different types of biographical inscriptions, which developed from the early examples of the Fourth Dynasty. Some of the inscriptions refer mainly to the principles and qualities of the tomb owners. Various phrases of this kind had developed by the end of the Fifth Dynasty into the so-called ideal-biographies.[62] These inscriptions promote the tomb owners' fairness in relation to their family, other people, the tomb owner's office duties and their general respect for the principle of *mꜣꜥt*.[63] For instance Mehu wrote:

> I came forth from my town, I went down into the afterlife . . . I carried out *maat* which is what the god loves; I propitiated the god in respect of all that which he loves; I made invocation offerings to the *ankhs*; I was respectful of my father and kind to my mother. I buried him who had no son; I ferried him over who had no boat; I rescued the wretched man from the (more) powerful one; I gave the share of the father to his son.[64]

To promote themselves, some officials tried to show a more personal link to the ruler in their biographical inscriptions by mentioning the king's satisfaction with their work and the king's gifts for them.[65] Donations from the king, like for instance Debehni's inscription on the donation of his whole tomb by King Menkaure,[66] occur in the tombs in Giza and Saqqara during the Fifth Dynasty and later even in the provinces. Many of the inscriptions concern the equipment, mostly sarcophagi or false doors, which the king donated to a lucky official, or to his sons who equipped his tomb.[67] The false door of Nyankhsekhmet bears a rare detailed description of how the official asked for and received this false door from King Sahure, who personally looked after its decoration: "His majesty had two false doors of Tura stone brought for him . . . . The great controller of craftsmen and a workshop of craftsmen were then set to work on them in the presence of the king himself . . . . His majesty arranged for pigments to be placed on them and they were decorated in blue."[68]

Other officials mention rewards that they received from the king during their lives as a manifestation of the king's satisfaction with their work and loyalty. For instance, Akhethetep in his inscription recorded that the king donated to him precious jewelry and oxen after being satisfied with the manners of his son "as a reward for having educated him to the satisfaction of the king."[69]

Some tomb inscriptions, however, mention a more personal relationship with the king and refer to a very special, unusual deed that the king performed on the owner's behalf. In one of the early biographical inscriptions, the vizier Washptah describes a great privilege allowed by King Neferirkare during an inspection to the pyramid construction site where Washptah collapsed (or was injured)[70] and the king said to him: "Do not kiss the ground. Kiss my foot!" Later on in the palace, the king called his chief doctors and lector priests to treat Washptah, he prayed for him, all the royal children and companions feared for him, and afterwards he gave him many gifts for his tomb.[71]

Another exceptional event was recorded in the tomb of Rawer, who hit (or was hit by) a scepter of the king but was not punished for it: "His majesty said: 'It is the desire of my majesty that he be very well, and that no blow be struck against him.'" Moreover, Rawer was given permission by the king to carve this event in his tomb.[72] This, too, happened in the reign of Neferirkare, and it is difficult to say whether the events reflect the increasing power of the highest officials or just the exceptionally kind character of the king.

Those biographical inscriptions that describe the career of the officials also highlight their special bond to the king(s).[73] The early Fifth Dynasty inscription of Ptahshepses from Saqqara demonstrates that he received education together with the king's children in his palace and lists his credits that led the king to reward him:

> He grew up among the royal children in the palace of the king . . . . His majesty gave him his eldest royal daughter, Khamaat, as his wife, for his majesty wished that she be with him more than with any other man . . . . When his majesty favored him because of the things (which he had done), his majesty allowed him to kiss his foot.[74]

Some other high officials raised their importance by including in the inscriptions carved in their tombs the king's entire letters or decisions in which the kings express their appreciation to the officials. An early example of this kind might be the inscription that was carved on the facade of the tomb of Iaib in Deir el-Bersha.[75] It is a hieroglyphic copy of an assignment decree, in which King Neferefre assigned some high-ranking offices to Iaib.[76]

The other attested royal letters, which date to a later part of the Fifth Dynasty, are more elaborate and were usually incorporated into the biographical inscriptions of the tomb owners. The tomb of the vizier Rashepses[77] contains the king's letter,[78] which is a reply to a report sent to the king by the tomb owner: "Seeing this letter of yours is what my majesty desired above all else, for you indeed know how to say what my majesty loves . . . . O, Rashepses, I say to you millions of times: (You are) one whom his lord loves, one whom his lord favors, one who is close to his lord."[79] Inscriptions in the tomb of Senedjemib Inti in Giza[80] are more extensive and describe the favors that the king did for his vizier, rewarding him for his duty with jewelry and cosmetic treatment by the king's personal hairdresser but also with documents written by the king: "Isesi made for me a decree which his majesty wrote with his own hand in order to favor me for everything which I had done nobly, perfectly and excellently in relation to his majesty's wish concerning it."[81] In these letters, the king assures his vizier of his satisfaction with Senedjemib's work, and of his fondness of him: "O Senedjemib the elder, I do love you and it is known that I love you."[82] In both of these cases, it was King Djedkare who sent these letters to Rashepses and Senedjemib Inti and apparently allowed them to use these writings for the presentation of their own importance. Interestingly, yet another letter concerns the favors done by Djedkare for his officials, but indirectly. It is the Sixth Dynasty inscription with another letter by the king from the tomb of Harkhuf, which includes the remark: "When you draw to the residence, and this pygmy in your charge is alive, prosperous and healthy, my majesty shall do great things for you, more than what was done for the seal-bearer of the god Werdjedba in the time of Izezi."[83] The same official is referred to also in the Sixth Dynasty inscription of Iny, probably from Saqqara:[84] "I was more valuable in the sight of his majesty than the sealbearer of the god Werdjedba in the time of Isesi."[85] Werdjedba thus appears to have been especially favored by the king and was used by the later officials for comparison of their own importance.

Since the late Fifth Dynasty, we can find inscriptions that mention how the tomb owner fulfilled his duties to the king.[86] Some of them do it in a more general manner, like Hesi, who claims that:

> His majesty permitted that (this) be done for me as his majesty knew my name from when I took (the office of) scribe from his hands . . . . I carried out the role of a scribe in the presence of his majesty actually at the forefront of the scribes, and I carried out the role of an official in the presence of his majesty actually at the forefront of the officials.[87]

Other officials mention even specific duties, which they were so proud of themselves to have fulfilled, like Kaiemtjenenet, who refers to his technical skills. His inscription describes that he proposed a way to move a sphinx onto its pedestal in the pyramid temple of King Djedkare: "Then his majesty said 'Look at what is the matter with this sphinx.' [I gave the answer] so that it was as when the shadows run away at daybreak . . . . [I took over the work] likewise, constructing it of bricks."[88] It is at this time that we can notice the tomb owner placing himself in the focus of the inscription.[89]

This type of biographical inscription, where the tomb owner comes to the front, continued to appear in the Sixth Dynasty in both the residence and in the provincial cemeteries. As the cited inscriptions show, the tomb owners changed from the third to the first person singular and highlighted their honors and privileges guaranteed by the offices and thanks to their achievements.[90] One of the best-known biographical inscriptions is that of

Weni the Elder,[91] who lived in the time of Teti, Pepy I, and Merenre. He presents himself as the most trusted of the king's men: "When there was a legal case in secret in the royal harem against the royal wife, the 'great of affection', his majesty had me proceed to hear it on my own. No vizier or official was present apart from myself because I was excellent, I was rooted in his heart, and his heart was full of me."[92] Besides the achievements in the residence and promotion in offices which Weni describes in his inscriptions, he also lists his own capabilities in military expeditions: "His majesty sent me to lead this force five times, with these same troops, to drive away the Sand-dwellers each time they rebelled . . . . Only after I had apprehended them all, slaughtering every insurgent among them, did I return."[93] His military success brought to Weni more professional promotion. He also adds information concerning several expeditions to quarries, where he was sent to bring stone for the equipment of the king's pyramid complex, and he boasts over his capability to conclude the mission successfully and quickly:

> His majesty sent me to Hatnub . . . and I organized that this offering table was brought down (after) seventeen days of quarrying at Hatnub. I had it travel north in a barge. I made for it (this) barge . . . assembled in seventeen days in the third month of the Shemu season. Despite there being no water on the sandbanks, I moored successfully at the pyramid of Merenre.[94]

In the late Sixth Dynasty, we can find more-numerous biographical inscriptions referring to military activities outside of Egypt in the tombs of officials who were responsible for the southern border of the country, for instance in the tombs of Pepynakht, Harkhuf, and Sabni at Elephantine.[95] These officials present in their inscriptions their experience with the foreign lands and their military dominance. In addition, the abovementioned inscription of Iny records his expeditions to the east, which seem to have been of a trading character:

> I was sent to Byblos under the majesty of Merenre, my lord . . . . I brought back lapis lazuli, lead/tin, silver, *sefetj*-oil and every good product his ka desired.[96]

The above-presented examples show that there was an apparent shift in the form and also the content of the biographical inscriptions between the Fifth and Sixth Dynasties, which undoubtedly reflects the increasing independence of the officials. While in the Fifth Dynasty the biographies emphasize the king as the one who gives favor and gifts to the official in return for the fulfillment of his duties, in the Sixth Dynasty the tomb owner became the central focus and the main agent of the inscriptions, presenting himself as an active historical figure.[97] In the Sixth Dynasty, moreover, some new motifs occur in the biographical inscriptions, including a special emphasis on the themes of the province and especially its economic welfare.[98] It can be noticed since the reign of Pepy I in the inscriptions of provincial officials like Kar of Edfu: [99]

> I was taken to Pepy (I) to be given an education among the children of the chiefs . . . . Then the majesty of Merenre had me go south to the second nome of Upper Egypt . . . . I measured out the grain of Upper Egypt from my funerary estate for a hungry man whom I found in this nome . . . . I buried every man of this nome who had no son with linen from the property of my estate.[100]

These inscriptions followed the pattern of the earlier biographies, but they also started to contain features that later became typical of the inscriptions of the local rulers in the First Intermediate Period[101] and that clearly demonstrate that the officials in provinces considered the local politics to be more important for themselves than the king's interests.

Notes

* This study was written within the Programme for the Development of Fields of Study at Charles University, no. Q11: "Complexity and Resilience: Ancient Egyptian Civilisation in Multidisciplinary and Multicultural Perspective".

1 For the changes that occurred during this period, see above all, K. Baer, *Rank and Title in the Old Kingdom: The Structure of the Egyptian Administration in the Fifth and Sixth Dynasties* (Chicago, 1960); W. Helck, *Wirtschaftsgeschichte des Alten Ägypten im 3. und 2. Jahrtausend vor Chr.* (Leiden, 1975); J.C. Moreno García, *Études sur l'administration, le pouvoir et l'idéologie en Égypte, de l'Ancien au Moyen Empire* (Liège, 1999); N. Kanawati, *Conspiracies in the Egyptian Palace: Unis to Pepy I* (London, New York, 2003); J.C. Moreno García, "Building the Pharaonic State: Territory, Elite and Power in Ancient Egypt in the Third Millennium BCE," in J.A. Hill, P. Jones, and A. Morales, eds., *Experiencing Power, Generating Authority: Cosmos, Politics, and the Ideology of Kingship in Ancient Egypt and Mesopotamia* (Philadelphia, 2013), 185–217; and other works cited below.

2 M. Bárta, "Egyptian Kingship during the Old Kingdom," in J.A. Hill, P. Jones, and A. Morales, eds., *Experiencing Power, Generating Authority: Cosmos, Politics, and the Ideology of Kingship in Ancient Egypt and Mesopotamia* (Philadelphia, 2013), 261.

3 W. Helck, *Untersuchungen zu den Beamtentiteln des ägyptischen alten Reiches* (Glückstadt, 1954), 58; Baer, *Rank and Title in the Old Kingdom*, 300; Helck, *Wirtschaftsgeschichte des Alten Ägypten*, 18–22; Bárta, "Egyptian Kingship during the Old Kingdom," 270; M. Bárta, "Kings, Viziers, and Courtiers: Executive Power in the Third Millennium B.C.," in J.C. Moreno García, ed., *Ancient Egyptian Administration* (Leiden, Boston), 2013, 85–151.

4 The teaching itself was perhaps composed in the early Middle Kingdom, see for instance, E. Eichler, "Zur Datierung und Interpretation der Lehre des Ptahhotep," *ZÄS* 128 (2001), 97–107; P. Vernus, "Le discours politique de l'Enseignement de Ptahhetep," in J. Assmann and E. Blumenthal, eds., *Literatur und Politik im pharaonischen und ptolemäischen Ägypten: Vorträge der Tagung zum Gedenken an Georges Posener 5.–10 September 1996 in Leipzig* (Cairo, 1999); R.B. Parkinson, *Poetry and Culture in Middle Kingdom Egypt: A Dark Side to Perfection* (London, New York, 2001), 314–15; all provide the reader with further bibliography on this subject. For translations of the teaching of Ptahhetep, see for instance, M. Lichtheim, *Ancient Egyptian Literature I: The Old and Middle Kingdoms* (Berkeley, Los Angeles, London, 1975), 61–80.

5 Bárta, "Kings, Viziers, and Courtiers," 156. For the concept of *mꜣꜥt*, see above all, J. Assmann, *Maꜥat: Gerechtigkeit und Unsterblichkeit im alten Ägypten* (Munich, 1990).

6 Bárta, "Kings, Viziers, and Courtiers," 156.

7 Bárta, "Egyptian Kingship during the Old Kingdom," 264.

8 For the sun temples, see above all, H. Ricke, *Die Sonnenheiligtum des Königs Userkaf* (Cairo, 1965); S. Voss, "Untersuchungen zu den Sonnenheiligtümer der 5. Dynastie: Bedeutung und Funktion eines singulären Tempeltyps im Alten Reich" (PhD Diss., Univ. Hamburg, 2010). Recently, also, M. Verner, *Sons of the Sun: Rise and Decline of the Fifth Dynasty* (Prague, 2014). Newly also M. Nuzzolo, *The Fifth Dynasty Sun Temples: Kingship, Architecture and Religion in Third Millennium BC Egypt* (Prague, 2018).

9 See, for instance, J. Janák, H. Vymazalová, and F. Coppens, "The Fifth Dynasty 'Sun Temples' in Broader Contexts," in M. Bárta, F. Coppens, and J. Krejčí, eds., *Abusir and Saqqara in the Year 2010*, I (Prague, 2011), 430–42.

10 M. Nuzzolo, "The V Dynasty Sun Temples Personnel: An Overview of Titles and Cult Practice through the Epigraphic Evidence," *SAK* 39 (2010), 289–312.

11 For the expansion of the administration, Baer, *Rank and Title*, 296–302; Helck, *Untersuchungen zu den Beamtentiteln*, 29–44, 106–19; Bárta, "Kings, Viziers, and Courtiers," 169–70.

12 V.G. Callender, "À propos the title of *r Nḫn n zꜣb*," in M. Bárta and J. Krejčí, eds., *Abusir and Saqqara in the Year 2000* (Prague, 2001), 361–80, with a summary of the previous discussion and further bibliography. N. Strudwick, *The Administration of Egypt in the Old Kingdom: The Highest Titles and Their Holders* (London, 1985), 202–203; P. Andrassy, "Zur Struktur der Verwaltung des Alten Reiches," *ZÄS* 118 (1991), 1–10.

13 Bárta, "Egyptian Kingship during the Old Kingdom," 271; Bárta, "Kings, Viziers, and Courtiers," 170. In detail in K.T. Rydström, "*ḥry sšt3* 'In Charge of Secrets': The 3000-Year Evolution of a Title," *DE* 28 (1994), 53–94.

14 M. Bárta and V. Dulíková, "Divine and Terrestrial: The Rhetoric of Power in Ancient Egypt (the Case of Nyuserra)," in F. Coppens, J. Janák, and H. Vymazalová, eds., 7. *Symposium zur ägyptischen Königsideologie: Royal Versus Divine Authority* (Wiesbaden, 2015), 31–47.

15 For instance, M. Verner, "Archaeological Remarks on the 4th and 5th Dynasty Chronology," in *ArOr* 69/3 (2001), 401–404; Verner, *Sons of the Sun*, 61–75.

16 M. Verner, *Abusir III: The Pyramid Complex of Khentkaus* (Prague, 1996).

17 Bárta, "Kings, Viziers, and Courtiers," 168–69.

18 Bárta, "Egyptian Kingship during the Old Kingdom," 272.

19 Bárta, "Egyptian Kingship during the Old Kingdom," 272; Moreno García, "The Territorial Administration of the Kingdom in the 3rd Millennium," 121–24.

20 Bárta, "Egyptian Kingship during the Old Kingdom," 268; Bárta and Dulíková, "Divine and Terrestrial," 46–47.

21 Bárta, "Kings, Viziers, and Courtiers," 170; Bárta and Dulíková, "Divine and Terrestrial," 47.

22 The viziers included Sekhemankhptah, Ptahshepses (Abusir), and Senedjemib Mehi, while other high officials Ptahshepses (Saqqara), Kakhenet, and Khufuhaf II. For an overview of the princesses and their nonroyal spouses, see, for instance, Bárta and Dulíková, "Divine and Terrestrial," 36.

23 Including Seshemnefer III, the son of a vizier, and Sankhuptah and Iymery II, the sons of high-ranking officials. See Bárta and Dulíková, "Divine and Terrestrial," 36–39.

24 M. Baud, *Famille royal et pouvoir sous l'Ancien Empire égyptien* (Cairo, 1999), 452–53.

25 For this name, see K. Scheele-Schweitzer, *Die Personennamen des Alten Reiches: Altägyptische Onomastik unter lexikographischen und sozio-kulturellen Aspekten* (Wiesbaden, 2014), 586 [2676].

26 Assmann, *Maʿat*, 244–45.

27 Bárta and Dulíková, "Divine and Terrestrial," 37–41.

28 For instance Teti's daughters Watetekhor and Nubkhetnebty married his viziers Mereruka and Kagemni.

29 For these names, see V.G. Callender, "Curious Names of Some Old Kingdom Royal Women," *JEA* 97 (2011), 127–42; H. Vymazalová and V. Dulíková, "Sheretnebty, a King's Daughter from Abusir South," *ArOr* 80 (2012), 341–42. For the element *Nbtj* as a reference to the king, see Callender, "Curious Names," 135.

30 J.C. Moreno García, "The Territorial Administration of the Kingdom in the 3rd Millennium," in J.C. Moreno García, ed., *Ancient Egyptian Administration* (Leiden, Boston, 2013), 107–51; Moreno García, "Building the Pharaonic State: Territory, Elite and Power in Ancient Egypt in the Third Millennium BCE," 203–208. A few cases have been attested since the early Fifth Dynasty,

see Bárta, "Kings, Viziers, and Courtiers," 170–72; E. Pardey, *Untersuchungen zur ägyptischen Provinzialverwaltung bis zum Ende des Alten Reiches*, (Hildesheim, 1976), 41–108.

31 Moreno García, "The Territorial Administration of the Kingdom in the 3rd Millennium," 119–20.

32 Bárta, "Egyptian Kingship during the Old Kingdom," 269.

33 R. Bussmann, *Die Provinztempel Ägyptens von der 0. bis zur 11. Dynastie: Archäologie und Geschichte einer gesellschaftlichen Institution zwischen Residenz und Provinz* (Leiden, Boston, 2010), 468; Bárta and Dulíková, "Divine and Terrestrial," 45.

34 Pardey, *Untersuchungen zur ägyptischen Provinzialverwaltung*, 152.

35 Bárta, "Kings, Viziers, and Courtiers," 171–72; Helck, *Untersuchungen zu den Beamtentiteln*, 136 ff.; Strudwick, *Administration*, 321–28; E. Martin Pardey, "Die Verwaltung im Alten Reich: Grenzen und Möglichkeiten von Untersuchungen zu diesem Thema," *BiOr* 46 (1989), 546–47.

36 Bárta, "Egyptian Kingship during the Old Kingdom," 272–74; Moreno García, "The Territorial Administration of the Kingdom in the 3rd Millennium," 124–38.

37 Bárta, "Kings, Viziers, and Courtiers," 171–73.

38 Bárta, "Egyptian Kingship during the Old Kingdom," 268.

39 See for instance M. Verner, *Abusir: Realm of Osiris* (Cairo, New York, 2002); M. Verner and V.G. Callender, *Abusir VI: Djedkare's Family Cemetery*, Prague, 2002, J. Krejčí, *Abusir XI: The Architecture of the Mastaba of Ptahshepses* (Prague, 2009); J. Krejčí, *Abusir XVIII: The Royal Necropolis in Abusir*, Prague, 2010.

40 See, for instance, M. Bárta, F. Coppens, and H. Vymazalová *et al.*, *Abusir XIX: The Tomb of Hetepi (AS 20), Tombs AS 33–35 and AS 50–53* (Prague, 2010), 1–2, 183.

41 See, especially, the archaeological reports of A. Labrousse and P. Collombert. For the recent works, see, for instance, P. Collombert, "Découvertes récentes de la mission archéologique française à Saqqâra (campagnes 2007–2011)," *CRAIBL* 2011, 921–938; Ph. Collombert, "Découvertes récentes dans la nécropole de Pépy Ier à Saqqâra," *Pharaon* 21 (2015), 10–18, with further bibliography.

42 M. Bárta, *Journey to the West: The World of the Old Kingdom Tombs in Ancient Egypt* (Prague, 2011), 175–78; Bárta, "Egyptian Kingship during the Old Kingdom," 268.

43 H. Vymazalová and V. Dulíková, "New Evidence on Princess Sheretnebty from Abusir South," *ArOr* 82/1 (2014), 2.

44 For preliminary information on this tomb, see M. Bárta, "A New Old Kingdom Rock-cut Tomb from Abusir and Its Abusir-South Context," in N. Strudwick and H. Strudwick, eds., *Old Kingdom, New Perspectives: Egyptian Art and Archaeology 2750–2150 BC* (Oxford, 2011), 9–21, esp. 19. Similar titles were attested also in the tomb of Shepseskafankh located east of the tomb AS 31, see M. Bárta, "Tomb of the Chief Physician Shepseskafankh," *PES* 15 (2015): 15–27.

45 The tombs of the vizier Qar and the tomb of his son Inti, see M. Bárta *et al.*, *Abusir XIII: Tomb Complex of the Vizier Qar, His Sons Qar Junior and Senedjemib, and Iykai: Abusir South 2* (Prague, 2009); M. Bárta and B. Vachala, *Abusir XXI: The Tomb of Inti*, Prague (forthcoming).

46 Bárta, *Journey to the West*, 185; Bárta, "Egyptian Kingship during the Old Kingdom," 269.

47 Bárta, "Egyptian Kingship during the Old Kingdom," 269.

48 H. Vymazalová, "Exploration of the Burial Apartments in the Tomb-Complex AS 68: A Preliminary Report of the 2013 Fall Season," *PES* 15 (2015), 57; H. Vymazalová and K.A. Kytarová, "The Development of Tomb AS 68c in Abusir South: Burial Place of the King's Daughter Sheretnebty and Her family," in M. Bárta, F. Coppens, and J. Krejčí, eds., *Abusir and Saqqara in the Year 2015* (Prague, 2017), 436.

49 J. Richards, "The Archeology of Excavations and the Role of Context," in Z.A. Hawass and J. Richards, eds., *The Archaeology and Art of Ancient Egypt: Essays in Honor of David B. O'Connor*, II (Cairo, 2007), 327–33.

50 Bárta, "Egyptian Kingship during the Old Kingdom," 269.

51 For studies of the sarcophagi and stone model vessels, see for instance the recent V. Nováková, "Old Kingdom Sarcophagi: The Abusir Corpus", in I. Incordino, S. Mainieri, E. D'Itria, M.D. Pubblico, F.M. Rega and A. Salsano, eds., *Current research in Egyptology 2017: proceedings of the eighteenth annual symposium, University of Naples "L'Orientale" 3-6 May 2017* (Oxford, 2018), 139–60; L. Jirásková, "Model Stone Vessels of the Old Kingdom: Their Typology and Chronology," in M. Bárta, F. Coppens and J. Krejčí eds., *Abusir and Saqqara in the Year 2015* (Prague, 2017), 145–56.

52 The socio-economic aspect of the pottery finds from the Abusir necropolis has been studied by Katarína Arias within her Ph.D. diss., "Social Dynamics in the Material Culture: Pottery of the Late Old Kingdom from the Complex of Princess Sheretnebty at Abusir South," (Charles Univ., Prague, 2017).

53 Especially Y. Harpur, *Decoration in Egyptian Tombs of the Old Kingdom: Studies in Orientation and Scene Content* (London, New York 1987).

54 T. El Awady, *Abusir XVI: Sahure—The Pyramid Causeway: History and Decoration Program in the Old Kingdom* (Prague, 2009), 166–84, pl. 6.

55 For instance, M.I. Khaled, "The Donation of Royal Funerary Domains in the Old Kingdom," in R. Landgráfová and J. Mynářová, eds., *Rich and Great: Studies in Honour of Anthony J. Spalinger on the Occasion of his 70th Feast of Thoth* (Prague, 2016), 169–85; see also H. Vymazalová, *The Administration and Economy of the Pyramid Complexes and Royal Funerary Cults in the Old Kingdom* (habilitation thesis, Prague: Charles University of Prague, 2015), 205–18.

56 Bárta, *Journey to the West*, 178.

57 Bárta, *Journey to the West*, 178.

58 Vymazalová and Dulíková, "New Evidence on Princess Sheretnebty from Abusir South," 4–5; M. Bárta and H. Vymazalová, "Created for Eternity: Statues and Serdabs in the Late Fifth Dynasty Tombs at Abusir South," in K.O.

Kuraskiewicz, E. Kopp, and D. Takács, eds., *'The Perfection that Endures . . .': Studies in Old Kingdom Art and Archaeology* (Warsaw, 2018), 61–76.

59 Bárta and Vymazalová, "Created for Eternity," 64, pl. VI, fig. 2.

60 M. Bárta *et al.*, *Abusir XXIII: The Tomb of the Sun Priest Neferinpu (AS 37)* (Prague, 2014), 8–9, for the hieratic inscriptions, H. Vymazalová in the same volume, 71–80.

61 H. Vymazalová, "Hieratic inscriptions in the Old Kingdom tombs at Abusir," in S.A. Gulden, K. van der Moezel, and U. Verhoeven, eds., *Ägyptologische "Binsen"-Weisheiten III. Formen und Funktionen von Zeichenliste und Paläographie. Akten der internationalen und interdisziplinären Tagung in der Akademie der Wissenschaften und der Literatur, Mainz im April 2016* (Mainz, 2018), 185–216.

62 N. Kloth, *Die (auto-)biographischen Inschriften des ägyptischen Alten Reiches: Untersuchung zu Phraseologie und Entwicklung* (Hamburg, 2002), 229–39; N. Kloth, "Zur Überlieferung (auto-)biographischer Inschriften im Alten Reich," *SAK* 32 (2004), 245–54. The recently published N. Kloth, *Quellentexte zur ägyptischen Sozialgeschichte I: Autobiographien des Alten Reichs und der Ersten Zwischenzeit*, (Münster, 2018) was not available to the author during the writing of this contribution.

63 Kloth, *Die (auto-)biographischen Inschriften*, 236.

64 Transl. Strudwick, *Texts from the Pyramid Age*, 295.

65 Kloth, *Die (auto-)biographischen Inschriften*, 239–48.

66 For discussion of Debehni's tomb and its dating, see for instance P. Jánosi, *Giza in der 4. Dynastie* (Vienna, 2005), 386–93.

67 Kloth, *Die (auto-)biographischen Inschriften*, 241–43.

68 Transl. Strudwick, *Texts from the Pyramid Age*, 303.

69 Transl. Strudwick, *Texts from the Pyramid Age*, 261.

70 Kloth, *Die (auto-)biographischen Inschriften*, 240; For the reason of Washptah's collapse, see, above all, N.S. Picardo, "(Ad)dressing Washptah: Illness or Injury in the Vizier's Death, as Related in His Tomb Biography," in Z. Hawass and J.H. Wegner, eds., *Millions of Jubilees: Studies in Honor of David P. Silverman*, II (Cairo, 2010), 93–104; for the translation of the abovementioned passages, see 94–95.

71 Transl. Strudwick, *Texts from the Pyramid Age*, 318–20.

72 Kloth, *Die (auto-)biographischen Inschriften*, 240. J.P. Allen, "Rewer's Accident," in A.B. Lloyd, ed., *Studies in Pharaonic Religion and Society in Honour of J. Gwyn Griffiths* (London, 1992), 14–20.

73 Kloth, *Die (auto-)biographischen Inschriften*, 243–44.

74 Transl. Strudwick, *Texts from the Pyramid Age*, 304–305. P.F. Dorman, "The Biographical Inscription of Ptahshepses from Saqqara: A Newly Identified Fragment," *JEA* 88 (2002), 95–110.

75 M. De Meyer, "Old Kingdom Rock Tombs at Dayr al-Barsha: Archaeological and Textual Evidence of their Use and Reuse in Zones 4 and 7," (PhD. diss., Katholieke Univ., Leuven, 2008), 28–36; M. De Meyer, "The Fifth Dynasty royal decree of Ia-ib at Dayr al-Barsha," *RdE* 62 (2011), 57–72.

76 De Meyer, "Old Kingdom Rock Tombs," 29–32; De Meyer, "The Fifth Dynasty royal decree."

77 Only a few scenes and texts from the tomb of Rashepses, including this letter, have been published until today. The tomb has been explored and documented by the Egyptian mission headed by H. El Tayeb.

78 E. Eichler, "Untersuchungen zu den Königsbriefen des Alten Reiches," *SAK* 18 (1991), 149–52.

79 Transl. Strudwick, *Texts from the Pyramid Age*, 181.

80 E. Brovarski, *The Senedjemib Complex*, I, *The Mastabas of Senedjemib Inti (G 2370), and Senedjemib Mehi (G 2378)* (Boston, 2001), 92–101.

81 Transl. Strudwick, *Texts from the Pyramid Age*, 312.

82 Transl. Strudwick, *Texts from the Pyramid Age*, 313.

83 Transl. Strudwick, *Texts from the Pyramid Age*, 333.

84 M. Marcolin and A.D. Espinel, "The Sixth Dynasty Biographic Inscription of Iny: More Pieces to the Puzzle," in M. Bárta, F. Coppens, and J. Krejčí, eds., *Abusir and Saqqara in the Year 2010*, II (Prague, 2011), 570–615.

85 Marcolin and Espinel, "The Sixth Dynasty Biographic Inscription of Iny," 574, 581.

86 Kloth, *Die (auto-)biographischen Inschriften*, 243–46.

87 Transl. Strudwick, *Texts from the Pyramid Age*, 276–77.

88 Transl. Strudwick, *Texts from the Pyramid Age*, 284.

89 Kloth, *Die (auto-)biographischen Inschriften*, 254.

90 Kloth, *Die (auto-)biographischen Inschriften*, 243–44.

91 For Weni's epithet, see H.G. Fischer, *Egyptian Studies*, I: *Varia* (New York, 1976), 81–86. For newly uncovered inscriptions of Weni, see Ph. Collombers, "Une nouvelle version de l'autobiographie d'Ouni," in R. Legros, ed., *Cinquante ans d'éternité: jubilé de la Mission archéologique française de Saqqâra. Mission archéologique de Saqqarah V* (Cairo, 2015), 145–57.

92 Transl. Strudwick, *Texts from the Pyramid Age*, 353.

93 Transl. Strudwick, *Texts from the Pyramid Age*, 355.

94 Transl. Strudwick, *Texts from the Pyramid Age*, 356.

95 Kloth, *Die (auto-)biographischen Inschriften*, 244–46.

96 Marcolin and Espinel, "The Sixth Dynasty Biographic Inscription of Iny," 582.

97 Kloth, *Die (auto-)biographischen Inschriften*, 247.

98 Kloth, *Die (auto-)biographischen Inschriften*, 254.

99 J.C. Moreno García, *L'autobiographie des Ḳ3r*; transl. Strudwick, *Texts from the Pyramid Age*, 344.

100 Transl. Strudwick, *Texts from the Pyramid Age*, 343–44.

101 Kloth, *Die (auto-)biographischen Inschriften*, 255.

5

Self-Presentation in the Eleventh Dynasty

Renata Landgráfová

The Eleventh Egyptian Dynasty saw the return of the king after the First Intermediate Period, which was characterized by a disintegration of the centralized state into smaller (city-based) units led by troop commanders and local governors. The southern kingdom was centered around Thebes and involved in prolonged periodical military conflicts with the Heracleopolitan rulers of the Ninth/Tenth Dynasty, who succeeded the Memphite Eighth Dynasty in the north. The origins of the Theban family that rose to power as the Eleventh Dynasty is rather difficult to reconstruct with precision. All that is known for certain is that the lineage of the Theban kings stemmed from a nonroyal ancestor named Antef, who was in later inscriptions called *iny-ity.f ꜥꜣ* (Antef the Great). Altogether eight inscriptions[1] are currently ascribed to this ancestral figure, who seems to have served as a nomarch of the fourth (Theban) nome of Upper Egypt and may have attained the title *ḥry-tp ꜥꜣ ni šmꜥw* (great chief of the South).[2] The first Eleventh Dynasty king who appears in the Karnak king list is Mentuhotep I, whose name *tpy-ꜥw* (The Ancestor), alongside his complete absence from contemporary sources, suggests that he may have been added to the lineage later,[3] for the purposes of legitimization. The first of the Thebans to have been king was thus Antef I (*shrw-tꜣwy*), but the first self-presentations dated to this dynasty come from the reign of his successor, Antef II (*wꜣḥ-ꜥnḫ*) The pre-unification self-presentations thus date to the reigns of three kings,

Antef II, Antef III, and the first part of the reign of Mentuhotep II. Some of the testimonies of the officials contain important historical information on the fighting[4] and negotiations[5] that led to the gradual extension of the Theban realm and finally to the rise of Mentuhotep II as king of re-unified Egypt. It comes as no wonder that both fighting and negotiating skills play a major role in the self-presentations of these men, alongside loyalty and access to their kings, which return to the fore after the feudal[6] time of the earlier First Intermediate Period. Some other topics were born in the times when nome governors had no king to rely on and answer to. They stress the independence, self-reliance[7] and provider/guardian (or good shepherd)[8] role of the (auto)biographers. At the same time, the renewed presence of the king and especially the time after the unification of Egypt by Mentuhotep II, which was marked by a consolidation of royal power and attempts at integration of the former Heracleopolitan realm into the Theban structures, caused the rise in importance of court culture and court roles, and the officials found it more important to present themselves as true and trusted servants of their kings.

The image of the ideal official of the first half of the Eleventh Dynasty is thus a complex one: a powerful self-made man whom the king (or even a royal lady)[9] selected from among others for his excellent qualities (usually at an exceptionally young age),[10] who gained an exclusive close access to the ruler and continued to excel in whatever task was entrusted to him, towering over his peers yet continuing to care for his city or district, especially in the role of a provider in need. Any potential doubts and mistrust are addressed with veracity statements and a sort of negative confession in the form of a short list of transgressions that he had not done (despite having had ample opportunity).[11]

Media of Self-Presentation

Unlike in the Old Kingdom, when an official's self-presentation typically was carried on one or more walls of his tomb,[12] the Eleventh Dynasty self-presentations appear mostly on commemorative stelae set up in tomb chapels. As the stela (which became an important medium for self-presentation in the course of the First Intermediate Period) offers a much more limited space than the whole tomb, the texts were condensed and only the essential parts were left—even if, at times, two[13] or even three[14] stelae with self-presentational information are associated with a single tomb.[15] The stela had, however, also offered advantages—such as a transferability to other contexts, for example, the commemorative *mʿḥʿt*-chapels at Abydos,[16] or, usually in the form of graffiti or rock-cut stelae, to expedition sites such as Wadi

Hammamat or the alabaster quarries at Hatnub, where the self-presentations take the form of (more or less) extensively commented achievement reports. Tomb walls, too, continue to be used as carriers of self-presentations,[17] but the number of known Eleventh Dynasty tombs with self-presentations inscribed on walls is currently rather limited.

The preferred media—the stone and rock-cut stelae—and their placement clearly show that the self-presentations were meant to be accessed and read (or heard)[18] by the widest possible audiences. The necropoleis were lively spots of the ancient Egyptian cultural landscape, and stelae with self-presentations were placed in the accessible chapels (or even in the facades), where visitors would regularly come to present offerings—and probably also to just stroll around, as visitor graffiti (of a later date) inform us.[19] The texts at expedition sites tend to appear in clusters and are located at well-visible places, accessible and readable for any future expedition leader, to whom they promise a safe journey home and a successful life for the favor of reading the text without damaging it, thus preserving it for future generations to see. Finally, Abydos was the site of a periodic major gathering of people during the annual festivities of Osiris, and to set up a stela there meant securing for oneself an additional audience that would otherwise surely remain out of reach. The practice of visiting the chapels and reading the texts is well documented in the Middle Kingdom, both in the Appeals to the Living and in the practice of copying (from) earlier texts.[20]

Motivation for Self-Presentation

The motivation for the setting up of commemorative stelae and inscribing large areas of one's tomb with texts containing elaborate self-presentations of the owners is often explicitly expressed in the texts themselves: "I did all of this so that my name might be good upon earth, and so that the memory of me might be good in the necropolis" (Berlin 13272, 11),[21] or (the words of the same man, Antef son of Myt, on hiring priests and ensuring proper inflow of offerings), "so that my name would be good and the memory of me would last today, . . . so that my name would live forever" (BM EA 1164, 14). It is clear from these and similar texts that the main motivation for self-presentation of these officials was to create or promote their name—that is, their good reputation[22]—among their contemporaries and, even more importantly, in the minds of future generations. Being remembered as a man of *maat*, as one whose actions were righteous and charitable, guaranteed not only a potential influx of offerings or at least numerous recitations of the offering formula,[23] but also a form of social immortality,[24] which appears to have been the main motivation not only for the composing and setting up of self-laudatory texts, but also for righteous conduct of the Egyptians of this time. (Contemporary wisdom texts emphasize conduct that lead to generating a good name for oneself though controlled and self-restricted behavior.)[25] The awareness of the link between (good) reputation and a testimony of one's life in written form has even been stated explicitly by the chamberlain of three successive Eleventh Dynasty kings, Henwen, who proudly states in his self-presentation that "[his] son, [his] heir . . . shall let the memory of [him] live, for he is a scribe" (Cairo E. 36346, 10).

Means and Methods of Self-Presentation

The aim of the self-presentation of Egyptian officials, fashioning for oneself a good reputation, remained unchanged throughout most of Egyptian history (exceptions can perhaps be found in some Ramesside texts[26] and a few Greco-Roman[27] ones), the means and methods of achieving this, and, thus, the character traits and actions most valued in an Egyptian official, changed through time. How then did an Eleventh Dynasty official ensure "that [his] name would live forever" (BM EA 1164, 14)?

To be a good man meant first and foremost to follow the principles of *maat*, the universal order of things given to Egypt by the gods. The opposite of *maat* was chaos, *isfet*—and thus, to be a *maaty*, a "righteous" one, one had to know and occupy one's proper role in the Egyptian society, to adhere to the principles of order.[28] The officials, thus, present themselves as "one who knows his position" (Cairo CG 20543, 3), "one who knows his rank in the palace" (MMA 57.95, 8), or, "one who knows his rank among officials" (BM EA 159, 10).

An important aspect of the social self of a high official was his relationship to authority and the way he was perceived by this authority. Often, officials aim at creating for themselves a kind of secondary reputation through the close connection to a reputable authority. In the Eleventh Dynasty self-presentations, four distinct sources of authority can be identified: first and foremost comes the king, who is mentioned most frequently, but the officials also refer to their district, their (city-) god, as well as to their immediate superiors, such as the queen (Cairo CG 20543; Cairo CG 20001), a priestess of Hathor,[29] and the overseer of the Treasury Bebi.[30] The latter text is as much a self-presentation as an exhortation of the superior and can be understood only through the concept of "secondary reputation" as introduced in this paragraph.

As far as the authority of the king is concerned, officials throughout the Eleventh Dynasty describe themselves as loyal and beloved followers, who had more personal access to the king than others. They are "beloved, praised" and "foremost of place in the house of [their] lord" (Moscow, Pushkin Museum I.i.a 1137a, b, 4–5). Loyalty to the king is a much-praised and frequently mentioned trait—the officials are "loyal in the house of [their] lord" (Cairo 3/6/25/2, 3–4), and they "follow the king to all his good places" (Moscow, Pushkin Museum I.i.a 1137a, b, 2). In the second half of the Eleventh Dynasty, the relationship of the official to the king is perhaps best characterized by the recurring phrase "his true and trusted servant" (MMA 5795, 1; Cairo 3/6/25/2, 2–3; Louvre C 14, 2). It is interesting to note that, while in the first part of the Eleventh Dynasty, the officials who mention being "beloved of [their] city" (Cairo JE 41437, 9; Cairo CG 20500, 5–6) or nonroyal superior(s) (Cairo E 36346, 2–3) are about equally frequent as those concentrating solely on the king, after the re-unification of the country, it is almost exclusively the king who is mentioned in these contexts. Perhaps the most interesting of the pre-unification examples is that of the seal bearer Ity, who states that he "followed a great lord as . . . a small lord, and there never came a (bad) thing in it" (Cairo 20001, 8–9).

The rather frequent occurrence of the theme of loyalty—which culminates in the interesting self-presentation of Hetepi (Cairo CG 20506) from the late Eleventh Dynasty, who presents himself as the loyal dog at the feet (actually, in the tent and in the bed) of his mistress—is a direct consequence of the patronage-based social organization of the earlier First Intermediate Period, when loyalty of the subjects was no longer granted, but had to be earned, and being a truly loyal follower of one's lord was, if not exceptional, then at least a commendable trait. Despite the renewed presence of the king in the Eleventh Dynasty, the topic of loyalty continued to be used and expanded upon, and it remained in use well into the Middle Kingdom.

Closely related to being trusted by the king is the concept of having unique and special access to him. An overseer of the work camp[31] who served under Mentuhotep II states that he was a "king's favorite in the palace in keeping the commoners away from him" (MMA 5795, 6). The chamberlain Heny describes himself as a "servant of trust in the secret hall of solitude" (Moscow, Pushkin Museum I.i.a 1137a, b, 6), and a certain Khety was "one who entered to his lord without (the need of) being announced" (London UC 14430, x+4).

The authority of the city god appears much less frequently in the texts, and the format is usually a simple phrase stating that the official was "praised by his god" (Cairo JE 41437, 9). The city itself is used metonymically to refer to the city's inhabitants, as in the statement on the fragment Cairo 20503 "[I nourished] my city in the year of hunger so that my name would be good" (line 3). This use of the word "city" takes us, however, from relationship to authority to relationship in the other direction, to the lower-ranking and the common people in general. As the above-quoted sentence indicates, the (auto)biographers present themselves above all as caretakers and benefactors of the common folk, in keeping with one of the main principles of *maat*, vertical solidarity.[32] Especially the role of provider in need[33] is most prominent in the first half of the Eleventh Dynasty, when officials call themselves "great provider of the home in the year of hunger" (Brussels E 4985, 3–4), and say that they "measured out barley for the nourishment of this entire city . . . in the miserable years of famine" (Cairo CG 20500, 2–5), or "nourished Gebelein in hard years" (Cairo CG 20001, 3–4). In the second half of the dynasty, the topic of providing nourishment to the needy disappears and it is only expressed by the stock phrase "I gave bread to the hungry" (MMA 5795, 3; Cairo CG 20506, 4; Turin Suppl. 1447, 6).

Besides the frequent and long-lived motif of nourishment of the needy, the (auto)biographers' role of a good guardian is reflected in statements such as "I was a protector of his subjects" (Cairo CG 20503, 4),[34] or, referring to the petitioner made famous by the Instructions of Ptahhotep,[35] "I received the one who made petition to me" (London UC 14430, x+10) and "friendly to the one who comes so that he might say what is in his heart" (Cairo 20543, 5). As caretakers and guardians, the (auto)biographers also stress that they were impartial: "I helped the one I did not know like the one I knew, so that my name would be good in the mouth of those who are on earth" (Cairo 20543, 15–16).[36]

A theme that is loosely connected to the provider-and-caretaker role described above and can be found only in texts from the First Intermediate Period to the Early Middle Kingdom is the (rightful) acquisition of property.[37] The (auto)biographers describe having acquired various items of (movable) property, thus extending the possessions they inherited from their parents. The property that is acquired through the effort of the (auto) biographer often comes from the patron (or, later, king): "I equipped myself with my own things which the Majesty of my lord gave to me because he loved me" (BM EA 614, 12).

The complex network of relationships in which the (auto)biographers were involved included also other similarly ranked officials. Especially in the second half of the Eleventh Dynasty, the (auto)biographers stress their exceptional abilities and position that brought them to stand out from among their peers. The overseer of the work camp, Antef, states that he was "one to whom the great ones come bowing" and "a leader of officials, whom the great ones greet" (MMA 5795, 6–7). The overseer Abkau was "one noble and unique at the fore of officials" (Louvre C15, x+5) and the priest Antef, son of Myt, "one about whose condition the great ones . . . ask, touching the ground with their foreheads for him" (Ny Carlsberg 1241, 6).

The parts of the self-presentations that speak about the (auto)biographer's social ties to other officials and to his inferiors reflect his unique qualities (for which he was chosen by the highest authority mentioned in the text, usually the king) and his readiness to use his good fortune to help the less fortunate ones, thus, maintaining the stability of the Egyptian social order. Phrases such as "one with whom no man stayed angry overnight" (BM EA 159, 11–12), or "I have done what the great ones love and what the small ones praise so that my life might endure on earth and [in] the necropolis" (Brussels E 4985, 4–6), and "I did what the great ones love and what the small ones praise" (Cairo CG 20503, 1) show the high value that Egyptians placed on general consensus.[38]

Being known as a man of *maat*, one who knows his position within the Egyptian society and acts according to it, was a goal shared by all (auto)biographers of this time. Most of them added to this the secondary reputation through access and close relationship with a personage of reputable authority, usually the king. The third constituent part of an official's reputation, his career, (or, in the case of ancient Egypt, its bright moments), is where his individual achievements, talents, and character traits were brought to the fore. Here a mere listing of epithets gives way to a (semi-)narrative account, and the official lays claim to achievements unique in his time, or even in recorded history, to having "[surpassed] the sum of that which was made" (Louvre C15, x+2).[39]

The beginning of the official's career is one of the rare moments when the self-presentation appears to give us a glimpse of the life of his inner self—namely, his childhood and youth. A careful analysis of these instances shows, however, that mentions of childhood and/or youth only appear to emphasize the official's unique abilities and special status with the king.[40] One example may suffice to illustrate this point. The steward Rediukhnum sums up his childhood as follows: "I grew up under the feet of Her Majesty since (my) earliest youth, because she knew that my actions were excellent and that I followed the path of officials" (Cairo CG 20543, 10–11). The point that Rediukhnum thematizes here has little to do with his childhood: the queen selected him due to his inherent qualities and excellent performance. This statement appears to connect the earlier First Intermediate Period self-made-man accounts with the return of the king's authority into official (auto)biographies. In the Twelfth Dynasty, this is reflected in the frequently occurring ambivalent phrase "It was my own heart that advanced my position . . . It was, however, the king . . . who placed me in the midst of his officials" (Leiden V4, 6–7). Throughout the Middle Kingdom, however, (auto)biographers continue to thematize the importance of their own character and effort in their success in statements such as the following: "It was his character that produced love of him (and) that advanced his place in the royal palace" (Cairo E. 36436, 9), or, to return to Rediukhnum again, "It was my heart that promoted my place, it was my character that caused my top (position) to last" (Cairo CG 20543, 17).

Before we take a closer look at the parts of the self-presentations that are dedicated to the text owners' careers, it should be noted that none of these texts actually contain anything like a career description. Firstly, the texts only select the pinnacles of their owners' official, military, priestly, or artistic achievement—the aim of the entire self-presentation is to create and forever preserve a good reputation of their owners, and, thus, only the positive and outstanding moments are selected for self-presentation. Secondly, as there was no real specialization in Middle Kingdom Egypt,[41] the officials also chose that aspect of their professional life that they considered constitutive for their identity. All of them were first and foremost officials of the state administration, but some identified more as priests, others as warriors, and yet others as artists. The accounts are highly variable, but all aim at portraying the text owners as reputable members of the Egyptian society. The (semi-)narrative accounts are not numerous, but they add significantly to our knowledge of possible sources of good reputation in ancient Egypt.

An interesting testimony comes from the chief treasurer, Tjetji:

> The treasury was in my hand and under my seal, consisting of the choicest of all good things which were being brought to the Majesty of my lord from Upper and Lower Egypt, as every thing pleasing the heart, as a tribute of this entire land for the fear of him throughout this land, (and) which were being brought to the Majesty of my lord from the rulers and chieftains of the desert for the fear of him throughout the foreign countries. (BM EA 614, 5–6)

In his text, Tjetji shows great pride in his function of chief treasurer, and his career description, thus, shifts the focus from Tjetji's activities to the character of the treasury that was in his charge. In other words, Tjetji is attempting to derive his reputation from the responsibility over the highly prestigious collection of royal tribute and its management. This complements the secondary reputation through proximity to the king, which forms the main part of the rest of Tjetji's text.

Rediukhnum, from whose text we have already quoted extensively, reports on his role as a manager of an estate in Dendera:

> I reorganized it, improving its administration to be better than before. I restored what I had found broken, I set up that which I had found fallen. I took (back) that which I had found stolen. . . . I managed the estate well, I enlarged all its portals. (Cairo CG 20543, 12–15)

Like that of Tjetji, Rediukhnum's text is mostly concerned with secondary reputation through proximity to his mistress, whose praise even takes up lines 7 to 10 of his self-presentation. In this short narrative part, Rediukhnum emphasizes his own achievement in the management of the estate that was entrusted to him in exceedingly deteriorated state.

The overseer of foreign mercenaries Djari describes an incident in which he served as a messenger for his king. He mentions his own role in the fights[42] against the Heracleopolitan forces in passing, and concentrates on the royal missive:

> Horus Wahankh . . . sent to me, after I had fought with the house of Khety to the west of Thinis: He made his assignments come. The ruler caused me to sail downstream to acquire food of weak[43] barley for this entire land, southward to Elephantine and northward to the Aphroditopole nome, because I knew my word(s) and my speaking was good. I was one weighty among the officials, one with an avid heart at the moment of striking, saying: 'Approach me, Khety, who made storm-clouds over the district, one strong of rule! I made (my) boundary at the valley of Hezi!' (Cairo JE 41437, 2–6)

Djari's Brussels stela (E 4985) presents him mainly as a provider in need, which is repeated here, but alongside two other moments that build Djari's excellent reputation: firstly, he is the one selected by the king to pass his all-important message to the Heracleopolitan opponents, a fact that emphasizes that the Theban ruled held Djari in great esteem; secondly, Djari himself shows courage and determination in delivering the threat/challenge to the enemy forces.[44]

The hunter Antef, son of Ka, limits his career description to a mere listing of (highly prestigious) people and institutions that employed him: "I was a hunter for my lord, Horus Wahankh, son of Re Antef the Great, for my lord Horus Nakht-neb-tep-nefer son of Re Antef, (and) for my lord, Horus Sankh-ib-tawy, son of Re Mentuhotep. I was a hunter for the West, for the

East, and for the temples. I was a hunter for the administration of provisions. I was a hunter for the Qenbet-council" (BM EA 1203, 2–5). Among others' self-presentations, Antef's functions appear to be quite modest, and it is, thus, not surprising that he chose to derive his reputation mainly through the personages and institutions in whose employ he was. The hunter Antef is, thus, a prime example of secondary reputation in the Eleventh Dynasty.

The priest Antef, son of Myt, set up three stelae, two of which contain a nearly identical text dedicated to his sacred knowledge:

> Governor in the estate of Monthu, noble of the first primeval time, who knows the offerings of the temples, experienced in the time of carrying (offerings) to them, who detests their abomination for them, who knows what their heart receives, each god according to his need, who knows his offering bread of primeval times, who knows the demons of the highland and the lowland as well as all their affairs, one for whom is opened the content of the spell-book, who knows the Morning house, one apt in its doors. (Berlin 13272, 2–6)

Antef's three stelae touch upon many of the topics that were used for reputation building at this time (restoring deteriorated properties, the provider/guardian role, and acquisition of property), but in this part he adds his access to sacred knowledge derived from his role as a priest.

Irtisen describes his artistic abilities:

> I know the secret of hieroglyphs, (and) the performance of offering-lists. Every magical spell, I employed it, there being nothing therein that escaped me—for I was an artisan excellent in his art, who advanced to the top by means of what he had learned. I know the rules of proportion (?): the determination of the correct method of carving and incising as it goes out and in until the body comes to its (proper) place. I know the going of a male statue, the coming of a female statue, and the standing of a bound (?)bird, the defiance(?) of a single captive, while one eye looks to the other, and the terror of the face of the captive who is frightened, the raising of the arm of the one who spears a hippopotamus, the gait of a runner. I know how to make inlays and the things that go in them, not allowing fire to burn them, and without them being washed away by water either. (Louvre C 14, 6–12)

His text is in many ways parallel to that of the priest Antef. Just like him, Irtisen describes his exclusive knowledge which no one else could access in order to create a long-lasting reputation for himself. Unlike Antef, though, Irtisen appears to rely exclusively on this knowledge and adds none of the other possible sources of reputation found in contemporary texts.

These (semi-)narrative accounts usually describe unusual, unique achievements in military and pseudomilitary expeditions, performance in an exceptional office,[45] or access to sacred, exclusive knowledge. The Eleventh Dynasty officials whose narrative testimonies have come down to us are few, but their achievements and abilities clearly stand out from the accounts of their contemporaries. It is interesting to note one phenomenon in this connection, namely the veracity statements that have appeared at the end of the Old Kingdom and were most numerous in First Intermediate Period texts, asserting the truthfulness of the accounts in which they appear and dismissing all others as "lies" and "offices of the necropolis."[46] They are rather rare in the Eleventh Dynasty, but reappear again in the Twelfth, where they are closely tied to narrative accounts of military and pseudomilitary character.[47] Perhaps these veracity statements are a direct consequence of these rare Eleventh Dynasty narrative accounts that stood out so clearly from the rest of similar texts that they needed a special means of legitimization beyond the mere *pacte autobiographique*.[48]

Those officials that could not rightfully claim to have achieved the levels of mastery of Irtisen or to have possessed the knowledge of Antef, son of Myt, usually concentrate the description of their abilities especially on rhetorical prowess and cleverness. In the early Eleventh Dynasty, the statements contain more concrete information on the employment of the (auto)biographer's rhetorical prowess: "I am one open of mouth, beneficient of counsel and strong of utterance on the day of assembly, one who gives a statement, [self-controlled on the day of] council" (Strassbourg 345, 6–8), or "one control[led of speech in] the council of the offic[ials], one sel[f-controlled on the day] of trou[b]le" (Cairo CG 20502, x+1). After the reunification of the country, the motif appears mostly in phrases that become part of the stock phrases used throughout the rest of the Middle Kingdom in the "encomiastic"[49] style: "one knowledgeable, wise and [clever?]" (MMA 5795, 2), "wise and clever" (Cairo 3/6/25/2, frg. x+3),[50] "one knowledgeable, who has no equal" (Louvre C 15, x+5), and "who knew things, one wise, acute of mind" (BM EA 1164, 1).

Conclusions

In the Eleventh Dynasty, the main goal of self-presentation was to create for oneself a good reputation which was the source of social immortality. There were three sources of reputation: the primary source, that is, the inherent qualities and achievements of the text owner; the secondary source, that is, the proximity to and favored status by a highly prestigious individual (usually, but at this time not exclusively, the king); and the negative source, the self-restraint, that is, the despicable deeds that the text owner may have had an opportunity to do, but refrained from. While narrative segments are rare, the use of stock phrases that flourished fully in the later Middle Kingdom is only just beginning in the second half of the Eleventh Dynasty.

Notes

1 L. Gestermann, *Kontinuität und Wandel in der Politik des frühen Mittleren Reiches in Ägypten* (Wiesbaden, 1987), 24; L. Postel, *Protocole des souverains égyptiens et dogme monarchique au début du Moyen Empire* (Turnhout, 2004), 7–26.

2 Stela Cairo 11/5/18/7, found in Dendera; see W. Schenkel, *Memphis—Herakleopolis—Theben: Die epigraphischen Zeugnisse der 7.–11. Dynastie* (Wiesbaden, 1965), 65–66. This seems to have been the motivation of the Thebans for having selected this one of their ancestors as the one to whom they would explictly trace their origins.

3 Gestermann, *Kontinuität und Wandel*, 26; for a recent appraisal, see Postel, *Protocole*, 27–53.

4 Stela of Djari, Cairo JE 41437; R. Landgráfová, *It Is My Good Name that You Should Remember: Biographical Texts on Middle Kingdom Stelae* (Prague, 2011), 8–9. See also the translation of the narrative segment below.

5 Antef, stela Strassburg 345; see H.G. Fischer, *Egyptian Studies III: Varia Nova* (New York, 1996), 83–90. Antef states that he sailed "with a mission" of the "great chief of Upper Egypt, Antef, to the place where the rulers of Upper and Lower Egypt were headed," and that he made the assembled rulers happy with his speech (i.e., that he succeeded in presenting his lord's message well). This early text appears to bear witness to early negotiations between various local rulers that eventually led to the rise of the Theban realm.

6 I.e., patronage-based, see D. Franke, "Erste und Zweite Zwischenzeit: ein Vergleich," *ZÄS* 117, (1990), 120–21.

7 M. Lichtheim, *Ancient Egyptian Autobiographies Chiefly of the Middle Kingdom: A Study and an Anthology* (Freiburg, 1988), 21.

8 D. Franke, "Fürsorge und Patronat in der Ersten Zwischenzeit und im Mittleren Reich," *SAK* 34 (2006), 159–85; D. Franke, "The Good Shepherd Antef: Stela BM EA 1628," *JEA* 93 (2007), 149–74.

9 Stela of Rediukhnum, CG 20543; see Landgráfová, *It Is My* Good *Name that You Should Remember*, 74–79.

10 R. Landgráfová, "In the Realm of Reputation: Private Life in Middle Kingdom Auto/Biographies," in W. Grajetzki and G. Miniaci, *The World of Middle Kingdom Egypt*, I (London, 2015), 177–86.

11 These phrases occur predominantly in the first half of the Eleventh Dynasty, and include statements such as: "I was not drunken, I was not forgetful, I was not feeble in my performance" (Cairo CG 20543, 16); I never did that which anyone hated (Cairo CG 20499, 7); "I did not let any strife arise against me. I did not seize a thing of a man" (BM EA 1203, 12–13); "I was not rebellious, I did not damage the land, (for which) people are hated" (Cairo E 36346, 2); "I did not accept things of the evil man" (London UC 14430, x+9 – x+10); and "I did not seize a man's daughter, I did not seize his field" (Cairo CG 20001, 4–5).

12 N. Kloth, *Die (auto-)biographischen Inschriften des ägyptischen Alten Reiches: Untersuchungen zur Phraseologie und Entwicklung* (Hamburg, 2002), 3–44.

13 Djari, stelae Cairo JE 41437 and Brussels E.4985.

14 Antef, son of Myt, stelae Berlin 13272, BM EA 1164 and Ny Carlsberg Glyptothek 1241.

15 See also Lichtheim, *Ancient Egyptian Autobiographies*, 39.

16 W.K. Simpson, *The Terrace of the Great God at Abydos: The Offering Chapels of Dynasties 12 and 13* (New Haven, 1974), 1–29.

17 E.g., Deir al-Bersha; H. Willems, *Dayr al-Barsha*, I. *The Rock Tombs of Djehutinakht (No. 17K74/1), Khnumnakht (No. 17K74/2), and Iha (No. 17K74/) With an Essay on the History and Nature of Nomarchal Rule in the Early Middle Kingdom* (Leuven, 2007), 42–58, 64–73.

18 Given the low levels of literacy in ancient Egypt in general (current estimates are around 1–2 percent of the population, see J. Baines, "Literacy and Ancient Egyptian Society," in J. Baines, ed., *Visual and Written Culture in Ancient Egypt* [Oxford, 2007], 49–50), it should not surprise us that the (auto)biographers expected their texts to be read aloud to assembled audiences by the literate passersby. This is mentioned explicitly by the steward Montuwoser of the Twelfth Dynasty, whose appeal to the living is addressed to "all people who shall hear this stela" and "any scribe who shall read" it (MMA 12.184, 16–17).

19 H. Navrátilová, *Visitors' Graffiti of Dynasties 18 and 19 in Abusir and Northern Saqqara: With a Survey of the Graffiti at Giza, Southern Sakkara, Dahshur and Maidum* (Oxford, 2015); see also J.A. Peden, *The Graffiti of Pharaonic Egypt: Scope and Roles of Informal Writings* (Leiden-Boston-Cologne, 2001).

20 R.J. Leprohon, "The Cairo Stela of Sehetepibre (CG 20538): Borrowings and Innovation," in D.P. Silverman and J. Wegner, eds., *Archaism and Innovation: Recent Perspectives on Middle Kingdom Egypt* (Philadelphia, 2009), 277–92.

21 For the sake of space, self-presentational stelae are quoted by inventory number and line. The entire texts can be found in Landgráfová, *It Is My Good Name that You Should Remember*.

22 For the connection between name and reputation, and the way from one to the other, see J. Wells and S. Strickland, "Biological Ends and Human Social Information Transmission," in J. Wells, S. Strickland, and K. Laland, *Social*

Information Transmission and Human Biology, (Boca Raton, FL–London–New York, 2006), 111.

23 As the treasurer, Meru puts it in his appeal to the living: "If there is nothing in your hand, say it with your mouth" (Turin 1447, 14); for similar statements see P. Vernus, "La formule 'Le Souffle de la Bouche' au Moyen Empire," *RdE* 28 (1976), 139–45.

24 For construing one's reputation as a means of transcending death, see Wells and Strickland, "Biological Ends," 111–13.

25 F. Junge, *Die Lehre Ptahhoteps und die Tugenden der ägyptischen Welt*, (Freiburg, Göttingen, 2003), 140–47; M. Lichtheim, "Didactic Literature," in A. Loprieno, ed., *Ancient Egyptian Literature: History and Forms*, (Leiden, New York, Cologne, 1996), 243–62.

26 See the texts translated in E. Frood, *Biographical Texts from Ramessid Egypt* (Atlanta, 2007).

27 Especially those that speak about death, e.g., Taimhotep, see M. Panov, "Die Stele der Taimhotep," *LingAeg* 18, (2010), 169–91.

28 This is best reflected in contemporary wisdom texts, see Junge, *Ptahhotep*, 150–59; Lichtheim, *Didactic Literature*, 244–47, as well as in the lamentations, which portray the world devoid of order and in a state of ruin and desolation (for a contextualized appraisal of these texts see R.B. Parkinson, *Poetry and Culture in Middle Kingdom Egypt: A Dark Side to Perfection*, [London, New York, 2002], 193–234). Such descriptions of disaster lend even more prominence to good character traits.

29 Stela of Nynebshemau; see J.J. Clère, "Une stèle de la 1ère période intermédiaire comportant un hieroglyphe nouveau," in *Miscellanea Gregoriana. Raccolta di Scritti publicati nel i centenario dalla fondazione del museo egizio* 1838–1939 (Rome, 1941), 455–66.

30 In the stela of Maati, whose self-presentational part reads: "I was one beloved of his overseer, the royal chamberlain and treasurer, Bebi. He, moreover, is the one who causes air to be breathed in all houses" (MMA 14.2.7, 3–5).

31 *imy-r3 ḫnrt*; for the title, see, W. Grajetzki, *Die höchsten Beamten der ägyptischen Zentralverwaltung zur Zeit des Mittleren Reiches: Prosopographie, Titel und Titelreihen* (Berlin, 2000), 158–62; S. Quirke, "State and Labour in the Middle Kingdom: A Reconsideration of the Term *ḫnr.t*," *RdE* 39 (1988), 83–105.

32 J. Assmann, *Ma'at: Gerechtigkeit und Unsterblichkeit im alten Ägypten* (Munich, 1990), 92–121.

33 The role of guardian and provider in need appears prominently in the First Intermediate Period, after the disintegration of the central authority and as a reaction to it. The local land owners were facing new problems and new responsibilities, with the well-being of their spheres of influence being now exclusively in their hands. The fact that they present themselves as providers, caretakers, and guardians of those who depended on them thus largely corresponds to reality. For an in-depth analysis of this situation, see Franke, "Fürsorge und Patronat."

34 The role of protector is most strongly reflected in the self-presentations on the rock inscriptions at Hatnub, the precise date of which is still a matter of debate. See R. Anthes, *Die Felseninschriften von Hatnub: nach den Aufnahmen Georg Möllers* (Leipzig, 1928); E. Brovarski, "The Hare and Oryx Nomes in the First Intermediate Period and Early Middle Kingdom," in A. Woods, A. McFarlane, and S. Binder, eds., *Egyptian Culture and Society: Studies in Honour of Naguib Kanawati*, I (Cairo, 2010), 31–85; L. Gestermann, "Die Datierung der Nomarchen von Hermopolis aus dem frühen Mittleren Reich: eine Phantomdebatte?," *ZÄS* 135 (2008), 1–15; E. Brovarski, "A Phantom Debate?" in E. Bechtold, A. Gulyás, and A. Hasznos, eds., *From Illahun to Djeme: Papers Presented in Honour of Ulrich Luft* (Oxford, 2011), 25–30.

35 The 17th maxim; Junge, *Ptahhotep*, 195.

36 At times, this motif is taken to an almost absurd extreme, such as in the claim of Shensetji to have given to "the one I loved as to the one I hated." See Franke, "Fürsorge und Patronat," 161.

37 Franke, "Fürsorge und Patronat," 162–65.

38 This preference of consensus seems to have been important even in court proceedings, which is reflected in the (stock) phrase "I judged the two brothers to (mutual) satisfaction" (Kloth, *Die (auto-)biographischen Inschriften*, 80).

39 On surpassing the deeds of one's predecessors, see P. Vernus, *Essai sur la conscience de l'histoire dans l'Égypte pharaonique* (Paris, 1995).

40 Landgráfová, *In the Realm of Reputation*, 179–81.

41 D. Franke, "Erste und Zweite Zwischenzeit: ein Vergleich," *ZÄS* 117 (1990), 124.

42 Expedition reports are the most frequent narrative self-presentations from the Eleventh Dynasty. They have been recorded either on tomb stelae, like that of Djari or of the overseer of the workplace Khety, who dedicated one of his two Theban stelae to his mining expedition (Cairo JE 45058, 2–9). Other accounts are found in the destinations of expeditions, such as the Wadi Hammamat inscription of Henu (M114, see Schenkel, *Memphis—Herakleopolis—Theben*, 253–58), the stela of Djemi from Gebelein (see Schenkel, *Memphis—Herakleopolis—Theben*, 116–17), or the aforementioned texts in Hatnub.

43 R. Müller-Wollermann, "Die sogenannte ober- und unterägyptische Gerste," *VA* 3 (1987), 39–42.

44 J.C. Darnell, "The Message of King Wahankh Antef II to Khety, Ruler of Heracleopolis," *ZÄS* 124 (1997), 101–108.

45 Tjetji seems to have been one the first holders of the title *ỉmy-r3 ḫtmt* (S. Desplancques, *L'institution du Trésor en Égypte des origines à la fin du Moyen Empire* [Paris, 2006], 158–61), and repeats it several times on his stela.

46 L. Coulon, "Véracité et rhétorique dans les autobiographies égyptiennes de la Première Période Intermédiaire," *BIFAO* 97 (1997), 109–38.

47 R. Landgráfová, "No Imagined Worlds, No Imagined Achievements: Veracity Statements in Twelfth Dynasty Auto/biographies," in W. Grajetzki and G. Miniaci, *Company of Images: Modelling the Ancient Egyptian Imaginary World of the Middle Bronze Age (2000–1500 BC)* (London, forthcoming).

48 A.M. Gnirs, "Die ägyptische Autobiographie," in A. Loprieno, ed., *Ancient Egyptian Literature: History and Forms*, (Leiden, New York, Cologne, 1996), 191–241.

49 Gnirs, "Die ägyptische Autobiographie," 205.

50 G. Daressy, "Fragments de stèles de la XIe dynastie," *ASAE* 8 (1907), 243–44.

6

Self-Presentation in the Twelfth Dynasty*

Ronald Leprohon

The written[1] material on self-presentation[2] from the Twelfth Dynasty comprises largely short non-narrative phrases—the so-called epithets—that officials used to describe themselves, their qualities, circumstances, and behavior toward their fellow men.[3] The locations of these phrases would indicate that they were meant to be read—or heard—by future passersby.[4] The latter could be visitors in the funerary chapels of the great necropoleis of Elephantine, Assiut, Meir, Deir el-Bersheh, or Beni Hasan.[5] The other major sites with this material were Abydos[6] as well as mining and quarrying areas (Fig. 6.1).[7] The proliferation of such texts in the Middle Kingdom allowed for a higher number of individuals heralding their personal virtues. From local magnates in their magnificent tombs to middle-ranking officials sent on royal missions or recounting their success at the court, this increase was a contrast from the Old Kingdom, when the majority of texts came from high court officials.

The location of the texts would presumably have influenced their composition. The ample space in the funerary chapels allowed the tomb owners to be more effusive, as lengthy narratives complemented their visual self-presentations. Obvious examples are the nomarch Amenemhat of Beni Hasan, who recounted his military exploits in Nubia at the side of King Senwosret I and the crown prince Ameni, the future Amenemhat II (*Urk.* VII, 14–16), and Khumhotep II, also of Beni Hasan, who proudly narrated his family's rise to power under the Twelfth Dynasty rulers (*Urk.* VII, 26–27).

On a single stela, however, the limited space forced individuals to carefully choose the way they were to be presented, usually in a single scene. Thus, they used status indicators such as dress, wigs, implements, furniture, and so forth, along with the relative placement of the figures within the tableau, to show their importance.[8] The space for the written narrative itself was restricted and hence was often reduced to a few sentences accompanied by epithets that expanded the account. An example is the stela of the assistant seal bearer Sa-Hathor (BM 569), who recounted his various good works on behalf of Amenemhat II interspersed with self-laudatory phrases. Alternatively, the stela of the overseer of the inner

6.1. Graffito no. 43 from the Wadi Hammamat, reign of Amenemhat III (photograph by author)

palace (*imy-r ꜥḫnwty*),[9] Intef son of Senet (BM 572), mostly consists of epithets specific to his work, in between which are a few narrative sentences that add information about his longevity and his children's success in the royal palace.

A number of individuals left longer narratives that chronicled their achievements. A notable example is the soldier Khuwisobek (Manchester 3306), who described his exploits in Asia and Nubia and his consequent reward at the palace, as well as his rise in the military ranks.[10] Another significant monument is the stela of the chief treasurer Iykhernofret (Berlin 1204), who recounted his early education at the palace, quoted a letter from Senwosret III charging him with a mission at Abydos, and told of his participation in the festival of Osiris there. Although succinct, his account remains the fullest description of the festival in Egyptian sources.[11]

Self-presentation statements were often proclaimed to be true.[12] In his great tomb, the nomarch Amenemhat stated that he had "spoken with true words" (*ḏd.f m mdt mꜣꜥt*; *Urk.* VII, 18:3). Such claims were perhaps even more pertinent in funerary chapels, since the events recounted there were probably familiar to the local community. At Abydos, the steward Intef also claimed to "speak the truth" (*ḏd mꜣꜥt*; Louvre C 167), while in the Sinai, the seal bearer Sobekhotep ended his self-presentation with an oath: "As the king lives for me, truthfully have I spoken" (*ꜥnḫ n.i nsw ḏd.n.i m mꜣꜥt*; Sinai 405). The placement of the last two texts is relevant. It is easy to dismiss such declarations as hyperbolic, but the fact that they are found close to temples—dedicated to Osiris and Hathor, respectively—must be taken into consideration. If the audiences for such texts were human as well as divine,[13] the gods, as arbiters of human destiny,[14] had to be taken seriously. As such it would have been improper to overstate one's qualities and good deeds.[15] An example of this reverence is the early Nineteenth Dynasty chief sculptor Userhat, who began his list of good qualities with an invocation to the divine world: "Oh gods who are in the Thinite nome, (the very) lords of life on earth, who hate lies (*grg*) and wrongdoing (*isft*) and live upon Maat, I am a righteous one (*mꜣꜥ*)" (KRI I, 361:5–6).

The Composition of Self-Presentational Texts

Oral Component

That the narrators claimed to have "spoken" truthfully is significant. Many self-presentational texts begin their narrative sections or list of epithets with the phrase *ḏd.f* (he says), possibly betraying an oral genesis for such compositions.[16] This feature of the Twelfth Dynasty texts followed a long tradition seen in self-presentations from the Old Kingdom onward, and one that would continue into the New Kingdom.[17] The importance of the spoken word should perhaps not be surprising in a society where literacy was so low that the oral testimony of witnesses could actually confirm or overrule the value of written documents.[18] This is emphasized by the nomarch Amenemhat, who proclaimed that he was "one who could make writing speak" (*di mdw drf*; II Bm 96).[19]

The highly formulaic composition of self-laudatory epithets found in ancient Egypt—including repetition, episodic organization of material, juxtaposition of contrasting notions, a tendency toward exaggeration, and the intermingling of longer narratives and short declarations mentioned earlier—is, in fact, characteristic of the stock phrases strategically employed by traditional storytellers.[20]

Groupings of Epithets

The use of words that convey complementary notions is a device commonly found in epithets.[21] For example, a man would claim to be "important in his office" (*wr m i3t.f*; I R) as well as "great in his rank" (*ˁ3 m sˁḥ.f*; I H), while another boasted that he was "important for the king of Upper Egypt" (*wr n nsw*; I R 9, 14, 24) and "great for the king of Lower Egypt" (*ˁ3 n bity*; I H 14, 30, 32). An official could also "say" then "repeat," as in "one who said what was good" (*ḏd nfrt*; II Hc) and "repeated what was appreciated" (*wḥm mrrt*; II V). One notable juxtaposition is found in groupings where the nouns "mind" (*ib*), "heart" (*ḥ3ty*), and "tongue" (*ns*) occur. An overseer of priests of Min described himself as "one who suppressed (his) desires" (*hrp-ib*; II Br 1) and was, thus, "free from lightness of tongue" (*šw m isw n ns*; VI J); he followed this pair of epithets with a declaration that he was "sound of mind" (*wḏ3-ib*; I V 2), repeating the word *ib*. An overseer of masons claimed to be "excellent of speech" (*ikr st-ns*; I G 45) and "precise of heart" (*mty-ḥ3ty*; I Ac 14), and finished that set of phrases by repeating the word *ib* in declaring to be "content" (*hrw-ib*; I Ak 18). The same association of words is found in the Instructions of Ptahhotep, where an official's "perfect opportunity" (*sp.f nfr*; 527)[22] was "due to the action of his mind and his tongue" (*m-ˁ n ib.f ns.f*; 528), and is well known from the Memphite Theology, where Ptah's heart (*ḥ3ty*) and tongue (*ns*) allowed him to create the gods.[23]

Other groupings consist of pairs of epithets that convey a progression of ideas within a similar topic. One man asserted he was "guarded of speech" (*ḏns mhwt*; I Bh 1), which made him "efficient of words" (*mnḫ ḏd*; I Aa 45). Another declared that he was "knowledgeable, (indeed) one who had taught himself knowledge" (*rḫ sb3 sw rḫ*; CII Bl 3, 6 and II Dr 5, 10) yet kept on "consulting so as to cause that he be consulted" (*nḏnḏ rdi nḏ.tw.f*; II Dj 2, 4).

In other sequences, individuals announced they were "firm-footed" (*mn-rd*; I Z 7) or "firm of sandals" (*mn-ṯbw*; I Z 12, 13), which allowed them to "adhere to the road of the one who could advance him" (*mḏd mtn n/w3t nt smnḫ sw*; II Bc 15, 20–21).

A remarkable sequence of phrases was formulated by—or for—the previously mentioned overseer of priests, whose graffito (Hammamat 199) contains three pairs of epithets. The first line of each pair contains an adjective preceding the noun *ib* followed by a second line that details the beneficial consequences of the original statement by stating that the individual was "free from" (*šw m*) a negative attribute. He first claimed to be "strong-minded regarding what was said to him" (*nḏr-ib ḥr ḏdt n.f*; II Bk 1), which allowed him to be "free from an occasion of forgetfulness" (*šw m sp n mht*; VI J 16). Next he professed to be "clear-headed regarding what happened in his charge" (*sḫm-ib r sḫprt m-ʿ.f*; I Au 1) and "(thus), free from an occasion of remissness" (*šw m sp n b3gy*; VI J 17). These statements are concluded with the pair of phrases mentioned earlier, "one who suppresses his desires" (*hrp-ib*; II Br 1), which enabled him to be "free from lightness of tongue" (*šw m isw n ns*; VI J). Similar examples[24] include being "patient" (*w3ḥ-ib*; I N 10–25), which kept someone from being overly "passionate" (*šw m prt-ib*; VI J 38), "free of improprieties" (*šw m rrit*; VI J 23),[25] or of "anxiety" (*šw m nhrhr*; VI J 12).[26] Being "generous" (*wsḫ-ib*; I T 6) helped an individual be "free of greed" (*šw m ḥns-ib*; VI J 33), while being "content" (*hrw-ib*; I Ak 8, 15) led to his being "free from passion" (*šw m prt-ib*; VI J 10).[27] Remembering that the ancient Egyptians recognized the *ib*-mind as the origin of proper conduct, these collections of epithets are striking.[28]

A collection of epithets where both contrast and progression are found was employed by an overseer of the inner palace (Louvre C 170). He began the series with the pairing of "one who is firm of sandals" (*mn-ṯbw*; I Z 9–22), but who could also be "quiet of steps" (*hrw nmtwt*; I Ak 19–32).[29] He then declared himself to be "wise and splendid" (*s3i sbḳ*; I As 4), wisdom that allowed him to be "one who knew his proper standing" (*rḫ st rdwy.f(y)*; II Bl 21)[30] and also to "adhere to the road of the one who could advance him" (*mḏd w3t nt smnḫ sw*; II Bc 19). The phrases first used the nouns "sandals," "steps," and "feet," then concluded with the phrase "adhering to a road," certainly a noteworthy progression.

Self-presentations Describing Positions

The narratives in the funerary chapels of the nomarchs described in glowing terms their service to the crown and the good works they performed in their domains. After recounting various missions for the king, the great overlord of the Oryx nome Amenemhat mentioned that all the taxes (*b3kw*) for the palace were in his charge, taxes he duly delivered on a yearly basis, boasting that there were never any arrears (*ḥrt-ʿ*) against him in any royal office (*ḫ3*). This was accomplished because the entire nome was said to have worked steadily (*m nmtwt w3ḥwt*) for him, a nice juxtaposition of his diligence toward the palace compared to his own people's efforts on his behalf. Following this are a series of denials of any wrongdoings against a "citizen's daughter" (*s3t nḏs*), "widow" (*ḫ3rt*), "farmer" (*iḥwty*), "herdsman" (*mniw*), or an "overseer of five" (*imy-r diw*)—a variety of people with whom he may have come into contact on his estate.[31] His subsequent claim that there were never any "unfortunate" (*m3r*) or even "hungry people" (*ḥḳr*) in his time then cleverly serve as preliminary remarks to what follows, which is an account of the famine that swept through his area and his efforts to overcome the problem (Urk. VII, 15–16).

Such narratives of an official's work-related responsibilities are, unfortunately, rare in the ancient Egyptian records, especially on stelae and graffiti, where space was restricted. A few individuals did, however, give some indication of what their position entailed. Within the catalogue of his many good qualities (stela MMA 12.184, Fig. 6.2), the steward Mentuwoser, who worked in the royal palace, stated, "I provided clothing to the Treasury, with (its) accounting being directly in my charge in the palace" (*ḫrp.n.i. ḥbsw r pr-ḥḏ iw ip m-ʿ.i m pr-nsw*),[32] which gives a glimpse of some of his duties. At times an official would also hint at some of his responsibilities. The vizier Mentuhotep suggested that he had to be "secretive concerning the affairs of the palace" (*ḥ3p ḥr sšm ʿḥ*; II Bs 1) and be "one whose mouth was sealed concerning what he had heard" (*ḫtm r3.f ḥr sḏmt.f*; II Cl 1).

Similarly, two other officials revealed some of their obligations within a series of self-laudatory epithets. As the man in charge of a section of the inner palace, Intef son of Senet stated that he was "one who ushered in the great ones of Upper Egypt" (*sṯ3 wrw t3-šmʿw*; II Fj 1) and "placed (them) on their bellies in the office of the member of the elite and vizier" (*rdi m-b3ḥ ḥr ḫwt.sn m ḫ3 n iry-pʿt ṯ3ty*; II Bm 4).[33] There, he also "presented (cases) for judgment at the time a matter was heard" (*rdi m tp n m3ʿ-ḫrw ḫft sḏm ḫt*; II Bm 4), which sometimes entailed "punishing the one who was remiss in his duty (*ʿ3 skn kni ḥr wnwt.f*; I H 63 and II Bu 1) and "giving explanations to[34] the quarrelsome man" (*sḥḏ n šntw*). He also stated that officials "stood or sat according to[35] my good will" (*ʿḥʿ.tw ḥms.tw ḫr nfrt.i*), which presumably meant he was in charge of protocol in that particular component of the palace. Further details emerge with his mention of "knowing the procedure of the rules[36] of (proper) behavior" (*rḫ nmtt hpw nw irt*; II Ae 7, II Bl 45), which

6.2. Stela of the Steward Mentuwoser, reign of Senwosret I, Metropolitan Museum of Art, New York, no. 12.184 (photograph by author)

may have also necessitated "teaching how to judge between two men" (*sbꜣ m wḏꜥ s snw*; II Ae 7).

A herald of the entrance approach (*wḥmw ꜥrrt*)[37] claimed to have "said what was good" (*ḏd nfrt*; II Hc 71) "(and then) repeated what was desired" (*wḥm mrrt*; II V 24). Although these are not original phrases, the repetition of the verb *wḥm* (to repeat) within his title and an epithet is noteworthy. After mentioning that his efficiency occasioned the king to give him a task, he added that he "paid attention to business procedures" (*dd ḥr sšmw*; II Bm 6) and could be "loud of voice in a quiet place" (*ḳ3i-ḫrw m st sgr*; I Az 4), surely a mark of his importance. He then concluded this portion of his self-presentation by claiming that he was "one to whom were reported the affairs of the Two Lands (*smi(w) n.f ḫrt t3wy*; II Dy 13) and "who (subsequently) repeated (them) in a perfect way to the Lord of the Two Lands" (*wḥm nfrt n nb t3wy*; II V 25). These are attributes one might have expected from a *wḥmw*-herald.

Themes

Service to the King

With the advent of a new family led by Sehetepibre Amenemhat (I), a number of individuals recounted their role in the sometimes turbulent transition of power.[38] The nomarch Khnumhotep I went on a military expedition with the new king, at which time the latter is said to have "expelled him from the Two Banks" (*dr.n.f sw m idbwy*; Urk. VII, 12), with the pronoun *sw* referring to an unnamed, and possibly Egyptian, enemy, while the hunter Kay mentions pursuing a refugee in the "Western Oasis," presumably Dakhleh (Berlin 22820).[39] Additionally, General Nysumontu's account of his military exploits (Louvre C 1) suggests an ongoing civil war into the reign of Senwosret I.[40]

The officials at Amenemhat I's court may also have felt a certain urgency to declare their allegiance to the new family. Thus, the lector priest Ihy,[41] who held a number of cultic positions at the palace, claimed to be "foremost of position at the *sema*-throne of Horus" (*ḫnty-st r sm3 ḥr*; III S 8) and "in his lord's mind every day" (*imy ib nb.f rꜥ nb*; III A). Farther from the palace, the great overlord of the Hare nome Nehri (Hatnub 25) pronounced himself "friendly to the Residence and subject to the plan that had been said to him" (*hrw n ḫnw ḫr sḫr ḏd n.f*; I Ak5) as well as "a precise one for the king" (*mtr n nsw*; I Ac 1).[42] While not all of these phrases were new, the unambiguous references to the new king and his palace are noteworthy.

Indeed, full devotion to the king—close proximity to whom was recognized as the key to success[43]—was a theme that pervaded the self-presentation epithets throughout the period.[44] An official claimed to be a "true servant" (*b3k m3ꜥ*; IV Q), "who was in his lord's mind" (*imy ib n nb.f*; III A) and who in fact "regularly acted according to what was in his (lord's) mind" (*irr mi ntt m ib.f*; II F 190). He was "pleasant to his lord's house" (*bnr n pr nb.f*; I W4) and "did what was beneficial to the Palace" (*ir 3ḫt n pr-nsw*; II F 118). He also ensured that he was "vigilant of his duties" (*rs-ḫrwt.f;* I Aj 14), "steadfast in his office" (*ḳni m i3t.f*; I Bb 17), "precise of heart regarding what had been commanded to him" (*mtr-ḥ3ty ḥr wḏt n.f*; I Ac 9), and, generally, "precise in his lord's house" (*mtr m pr nb.f*; I Ac 5). This diligence led him to be "effective of speech within his lord's mind" (*3ḫ-ḏd ḥry-ib n nb.f*; I C 4), which allowed him to be "efficient of counsels" (*mnḫ nḏwt-r3*; I Aa 50), with advice that his lord knew to be "excellent" (*rḫ.n nb.f iḳr sḫr.f*; II Bl 71) and which was, perhaps, even offered "at his lord's side" (*mnḫ r-gs nb.f*; I Aa 39). He also "knew his proper place in the Palace" (*rḫ st rd(wy).f(y) m pr-nsw*; II Bl 17–20, 23–24) and was "disciplined regarding a royal mission" (*s3ḳ-ib ḥr wpt-nsw*; II Cy 6). He always made sure he "adhered to the road of the one who advanced him" (*mḏd w3t nt smnḫ sw*; II Bc 24) and never considered "neglecting the governance of the ceremonial palace or the instructions of the *Setep-sa*-(royal service) committee" (*tm thi tp-rd n ʿḥ tpt-r3 n stp-s3*; VI L 8).[45]

Such qualities resulted in an official being "unique in his lord's mind" (*wʿ m ib n nb.f*; I P 21) as one "whose excellence his lord/the Lord of the Two Lands had observed" (*ptr.n nb.f/nb t3wy iḳr.f*; II Aq 2–3) and "whose lord had caused him to be appreciated" (*rdi.n nb.f mr.tw.f*; II Bm 104). Indeed, he was "one whom the king exalted after he saw the officials of the *Setep-sa*-committee" (*ḳ3i nsw m3.f srw nw stp-s3*; Sinai 115) and "one who was (actually) known in his lord's house (*nty rḫw m pr n nb.f*; II Bl 70). A further, and more personal, result would be to become "one whose name his lord knew" (*rḫ.n nb.f rn.f*; II Bl 80) and possibly even be "hailed by name" (*nḏ-ḥr rn*; IV Aw 4) by the king. And the ultimate goal was then to be one whom the king "promoted before multitudes" (*ṯn.n nb.f ḫnt ḥḥw*; II Gk 7) or before "his peers" (*sṯn.n.f ḫnty mityw.f*; II Fk 4). Officials also claimed to have been "one whose plenty[46] the Lord of the Two Lands furnished, and the love of whom advanced his position" (*rdi.n nb t3wy f3w.f sḫnt.n mrwt.f st.f*; II Ev 19) or "his office" (*sḫnt nb.f i3t.f*; II Ev 6).[47] Such praise meant access to the inner circles, where one could boast of being "wide of stride" (*wsḫ-nmtwt*; I T 3) and "truly unhindered" (*wsṯn m3ʿ*; II Y 1).

Efficiency at Work

Competence was not limited to serving at the palace. An official could boast of his skills by declaring to have "performed a job according to its (proper) purpose" (*ir i3t mi iry.s*; II F 3) or, generally, "successfully" (*ir ḫt n tp-nfr*; II F 84–86). His "ideas" or "advice" (*sḫr*) were always "important" (*ʿ3*; I H 66), "excellent" (*iḳr*; I G 52–56), or "efficient" (*mnḫ*; I Aa). He was a veritable "possessor of (good) advice" (*nb sḫrw*; IV Ac 41) and proud enough to have come up with his ideas himself (*ḳm3 sḫr.f*; II Fz 1)[48] that he could claim to be "one about whom it is regularly said, 'His advice was useful'" (*ḏdd r.f mnḫ sḫr.f*; Sinai 101A, 143, 405).

Personal Qualities

Individuals also wished to be remembered for personal qualities. They presented themselves as "amiable" (*ỉmꜣ*; I E) and "great of kindness" (*ꜥꜣ-ỉmꜣt*; I H 36), a kindness they consistently "possessed" (*nb ỉmꜣt*; II Ac 2, 5, 7). They were "friendly to commoners" (*ḫnms n nḏsw*; IV Ak), in fact "kindly disposed to everyone" (*ꜣms-ib n rmṯ nb*; I B 2), all of whom they "welcomed" (*ỉr ỉỉ.w(y) n bw nb*; II F 119). They also claimed to "know kindness when the right time (lit., 'his opportunity') came" (*rḫ sfn n ỉw n sp.f*; II Bl 51) and could even "silence weeping with the perfect remark" (*sgr rmỉw m ḫnw nfr*; II Fe 2).

Their kindness led to acts of generosity, which was defined as being "long of hand" (*ꜣw-ḏrt*; I A), "broad-hearted" (*wsḫ-ib*; I T 6), and "free from indifference" (*šw m ḥbs-ḥr*; VI J 33). They "regularly gave things to the one <in> poverty" (*dd ḫt n nty <m> snw*; II Bm 11), "always looked after the afflicted" (*mꜣꜣ r ỉnd*; II Au 3), "fed commoners" (*sꜥnḫ rḫyt*; II Dg 13), "nourished the young" (*šd nḫn*; II Fy 4), and were veritable "fathers to orphans" (*it n nmḥ*; IV H). They also made sure to "rescue the one who was nothing" (*nḥm iwty sw*; II Bh 13) and "protect the unfortunate" (*nḫ mꜣr*; II Bi).

General assistance to people was summed up as doing "what everyone always appreciated" (*ỉr mrr bw-nb*; II F 137). Specific instances could be when someone "calmed fear" (*swḏꜣ snḏ*; II Dq 1) or "unraveled what had been knotted" (*wḥꜥ ṯsst*; II W5), that is, solved people's problems. An official made sure he was "patient in order to hear words" (*wꜣḥ-ib r sḏm mdwt*; I N 17), to which he "truly listened" (*sḏmw r wn-mꜣꜥ*; II Fo 7). He would never be "partial to the owner of bribes" (*tm nmꜥ n nb ḏbꜣw*; VI L 4)[49] since he only "evaluated a man according to his speech" (*siꜣ s r tpt-rꜣ.f*; II Cz 2). The result of this was that he "always caused two fellows to leave satisfied with what had come from his mouth" (*dd pr snw ḥtp(.w) m prw n rꜣ.f*; II Bm 95).

Self-Presentations and Instructional Literature

The relationship between self-presentation texts and instructional literature has been much discussed.[50] Although they were separate genres and intended for different audiences, the similarities between the vocabulary used in epithets and Ptahhotep's maxims are striking.[51]

The king began his instructions to Ptahhotep by recommending that the vizier "first and foremost teach him[52] to speak" (*sbꜣ rk sw r mdt ḫr ḥꜣt*; 37). Such advice had certainly been taken to heart by Middle Kingdom officials, who claimed to be "good at listening and excellent at speaking" (*nfr-sḏm ỉḳr-ḏd*; I G 61–62). Indeed, a man would "know the outcome of his words" (*rḫ prw n mdw.f*; II Bl 31, 53), and he would be "respected for the excellence of his utterances" (*mḫy ḥr ỉḳr mdw.f*; II Ay 1). At the court he would be "precise of words on the day of serving, and could speak a phrase at its (proper) time" (*ʿḳ3-mdw hrw msbb ḏd ṯs r h3w.f*; I L 3, II Bm 44). Ptahhotep went on to describe his instructions as "teaching the ignorant to be knowledgeable according to the principles[53] of perfect speech" (*sb3 ẖmw r rḫ r tp-ḥsb n mdt nfrt*; 47–48), which would be "beneficial to the one who will listen" (*m 3ḫt n sḏm.ty.fy*; 49). This passage finds a parallel in Intef son of Senet's description of himself as "one who is knowledgeable for the one who doesn't know and who teaches a man what will be beneficial to him" (*rḫ n nty n rḫ.f sb3 s 3ḫ.t(y).s(y) n.f*; II Bl 2 and II Dr 4).[54]

In their inscriptions men described themselves as being "self-contained," which they expressed by claiming to be *s3ḳ-ib* (II Cy), a phrase that echoes Ptahhotep's dictum to "gather every heart toward excellence" (*s3ḳ ib nb r bw iḳr*; 364), or having "self-control" (*d3r-ib*; II Go), also found in Ptahhotep (*rmn.n d3r ib.k ʿḥʿw.f*; 67). Officials wished to be remembered as "trustworthy" (*kf3-ib*; I Bc), a presumably common phrase since Ptahhotep used it a number of times.[55] They also claimed to be "patient" (*w3ḥ-ib*; I N), as Ptahhotep reiterated when he urged his charges to "be patient when you speak" (*w3ḥ ib.k tr n mdwy.k*; 624). Another desired personal quality was to be "one who is without greed" (*iwty ʿwn-ib.f*; VI C 15), a transgression mentioned a number of times by Ptahhotep,[56] or "without falsehood" (*šw m grg*; VI J 45), a phrase found verbatim in Ptahhotep (532).

In social or professional contexts, a man knew to "bend down to great ones" (*ẖ3m n wrw*; II Ce 5) or "bend his back" (*ẖms s3.f*; II Cm 1), that is, bow, which Ptahhotep taught his son by enjoining him to "bend your arms and bow" (*ẖ3m ʿwy.k(y) ẖms s3.k*; 62) and "bow down to your superior" (*ẖms s3.k ḥry-tp.k*; 441). In a culture where information may have been delivered orally, it is interesting to see an epithet used to profess precise communication. The phrase "the one who reports his affairs without forgetting" (*smi sšm.f nn ʿm-ib*; II Dy 10) is mirrored by Ptahhotep's advice to "report your business without forgetfulness" (*smi sšm.k nn ʿm-ib*; 249).[57]

Interestingly, a number of laudatory epithets contradict some of Ptahhotep's directives. Although Ptahhotep declared that "no one is born wise" (*nn msy s3.w*; 41), one individual asserted that he "had been born as one who is (already) wise and who can act" (*ms.n.tw.i m s33.f ir.f*; I Ar 4), while others bragged about having "come out of the womb (already) wise" (*pr m ẖt s3.w*; II Ak 25) or "knowledgeable" (*pr m ẖt iw.f m rḫ*; II Ak 24). Similarly, while Ptahhotep warned that "no one can know what will happen when planning for tomorrow" (*n rḫ.n.tw ḫprt si3.f dw3w*; 343), one individual boasted that he was "one who knew tomorrow before it had come" (*rḫ dw3w n iwt.f*; II Bl 41).

Conclusions

Amiable and helpful, well spoken and knowledgeable, diligent in his work, and dedicated to the crown to the point of obsequiousness, the Middle Kingdom official was proud of his accomplishments and of belonging to the upper registers of society. His self-presentation walked a fine line between braggadocio and humility, as he wished his contemporaries and future generations to remember him well. His entreaty to posterity could have been spoken by the magic snake in the story of the Shipwrecked Sailor: "Cause my reputation to be good in your city. Look here, it is my (only) request from you" (*imi rn.i nfr(.w) m niwt.k mk ḫrt.i pw im.k*).[58]

Notes

* I wish to thank the anonymous referees, whose suggestions made this chapter better (and significantly shorter).

1 This chapter deals mostly with the written documents. For the pictorial record, see the recent studies in M. Hartwig, ed., *A Companion to Ancient Egyptian Art* (Oxford, 2014). For an iconographic study on one specific tomb from the period, see J. Kamrin, *The Cosmos of Khnumhotep II at Beni Hasan* (London, 1999).

2 For the term *self-presentation* rather than *(auto)biography*, see L. Morenz, "Tomb Inscriptions: The Case of the 'I' Versus Autobiography in Ancient Egypt," *Human Affairs: A Postdisciplinary Journal for Humanities & Social Sciences* 13 (2003), 179–96.

3 The *locus classicus* for the epithets dating from the Old to the late Middle Kingdoms remains J. Janssen, *De traditioneele Egyptische Autobiografie vóór het Nieuwe Rijk*, 2 vols. (Leiden, 1946). The Middle Kingdom examples have been studied by D. Doxey, *Egyptian Non-Royal Epithets in the Middle Kingdom: A Social and Historical Analysis* (Leiden, 1998). See also B. van de Walle, "Biographie," in W. Helck and E. Otto, eds., *Lexikon der Ägyptologie*, I (Wiesbaden, 1974), 815–822; M. Lichtheim, *Ancient Egyptian Autobiographies Chiefly of the Middle Kingdom: A Study and an Anthology* (Göttingen, 1988); O. Perdu, "Ancient Egyptian Autobiographies," in J.M. Sasson, ed., *Civilizations of the Ancient Near East* (New York, 1995), 2243–54; P. Vernus, *Essai sur la conscience de l'histoire dans l'Égypte pharaonique* (Paris, 1995); A. Gnirs, "Die ägyptische Autobiographie," in A. Loprieno, ed., *Ancient Egyptian Literature: History and Forms* (Leiden, 1996), 191–241; S.-A. Naguib, "Mémoire de soi: Autobiographie et identité en ancienne Égypte," in E. Wardini, ed., *Built on Solid Rock: Studies in Honour of Professor Ebbe Egede Knudsen on the Occasion of His 65th birthday, April 11th 1997* (Oslo, 1997), 216–25; A. Gnirs, "Biographies," in D. Redford, ed., *The Oxford Encyclopedia of Ancient Egypt*, I (New York, 2001), 184–89.

4 Cf. the Abydos stela of the steward of counting barley, Ankhren (Queen's College (Oxford) 1113; P. Smither and A. Dakin, "Stelae in the Queen's College, Oxford," *JEA* 25 [1939], 163–65, no. 4), where the Appeal to the Living begins with the phrase, "Oh you who (still) live on earth, every scribe, every lector priest, and every *wab*-priest who will read aloud (*šd*) this stela (of mine)." On the question of the audience for such texts in the Middle Kingdom, see Doxey, *Non-Royal Epithets*, 6–7. That stelae were, indeed, read can be surmised from the fact that some were copied by later visitors. For a Middle Kingdom copy of sections of the earlier stela of the vizier Mentuhotep (CG 20539), see R.J. Leprohon, "The Stela of Sehetepibre (CG 20538): Borrowings and Innovation," in D. Silverman, W.K. Simpson, J. Wegner, eds., *Archaism and Innovation: Studies in the Culture of Middle Kingdom Egypt* (New Haven, 2009), 277–92. For a New Kingdom copy of the same stela, see B. Russo, "La stele di Kares (CGC 34003): semplice copia o voluta ripresa della grande stele di Mentuhotep (CGC 20539)?" in P. Minà, ed., *Imagines nell'Egitto antico: per i novant'anni di Sergio Donadoni. Atti del IX Convegno Internazionale Colloqui di Egittologia e Papirologia in onore del Prof. Sergio Donadoni* (Palermo, 2004), 235–41.

5 For Elephantine, see *Urk.* VII, 1–9. For other sites, see F.Ll. Griffith, *The Inscriptions of Siût and Dêr Rîfeh* (London, 1889); A.M. Blackman, M.R. Apted, eds., *The Rock Tombs of Meir*, 6 vols. (London, 1914–53); P.E. Newberry, *El Bersheh*, 2 vols. (London, 1893–94). The latter site is currently being investigated by the Egyptology Department at Leuven University; for a bibliography, see the project's website, http://www.dayralbarsha.com. For Beni Hasan, see P.E. Newberry, *Beni Hasan*, 4 vols. (London, 1893–97) and A. Shedid, *Die Felsgräber von Beni Hassan in Mittelägypten* (Mainz, 1994).

6 These comprise the majority of the texts. They were mostly inscribed on stelae left at the site, in the hope of spiritually participating in the festival of Osiris. The major collections of these stelae are in Berlin, Cairo, Leiden, London, and Paris, and published, respectively, in: G. Roeder, ed., *Aegyptische Inschriften aus den Königlichen Museen zu Berlin* (Leipzig, 1913); H. Lange and H. Schäfer, *Grab- und Denksteine des Mittleren Reiches im Museum von Kairo*, 4 vols. (Cairo 1902, 1908, 1925); P. Boeser, ed., *Beschreibung der ägyptischen Sammlung des niederländischen Reichsmuseums der Altertümer in Leiden*, 2 vols. (The Hague, 1905–1909); E.A.W. Budge, ed., *Hieroglyphic Texts from Egyptian Stelae etc. in the British Museum*, especially vols. 2–4, (London, 1912–13); A. Gayet, *Stèles de la douzième dynastie* (Paris, 1889). Excellent photographs of a good number of the stelae can be found in W.K. Simpson, *The Terrace of the Great God at Abydos: The Offering Chapels of Dynasties 12 and 13* (New Haven, 1974).

7 The major sites are Hatnub, Wadi Hammamat, Wadi el-Hudi, and the Sinai. These are published, respectively, in: R. Anthes, *Die Felseninschriften von Hatnub* (Leipzig, 1928); J. Couyat and P. Montet, *Les Inscriptions hiéroglyphiques et hiératiques du Ouâdi Hammâmât* (Cairo, 1912); G. Goyon, *Nouvelles inscriptions rupestres du Ouadi Hammamat* (Paris, 1957); A. Sadek, *The Amethyst Mining Inscriptions of Wadi El-Hudi*, 2 vols. (Warminster, 1980, 1985); A.H. Gardiner and J. Černý, *The Inscriptions of Sinai* (London, 1955). The texts found in the Eastern Desert near the Gulf of Suez, published by M. Abd el-Raziq, G. Castel, P. Tallet, and V. Ghina, eds., *Les Inscriptions d'Ayn Soukhna* (Cairo, 2002), mostly consist of titles and short narratives describing the official's mission.

8 W. Grajetzki, *Two Treasurers of the Late Middle Kingdom* (Oxford, 2001), 77; Leprohon, "Ideology and Propaganda," in Hartwig, *A Companion to Ancient Egyptian Art*, 316–17.

9 On the *ʿẖnwty*, see G. Pagliari, "Function and Significance of Ancient Egyptian Royal Palaces from the Middle Kingdom to the Saite Period: A Lexicographical Study and its Possible Connection with the Archaeological Evidence" (University of Birmingham PhD Diss., Birmingham, Rome, 2012), 266–67.

10 J. Garstang, *El Arábah* (London, 1900), pl. 5; T. Peet, *The Stela of Sebek-khu* (Manchester, 1914); J. Baines, "The Stela of Khusobek: Private and Royal Military Narrative and Values," in J. Osing and G. Dreyer, eds., *Form und Mass: Beiträge zur Literatur, Sprache und Kunst des alten Ägypten* (Wiesbaden, 1987), 43–61. Other examples include stelae BM 574, Leiden V4, Louvre C 3, etc.; such narratives have been designated "historical autobiographies" by Gnirs, "Die ägyptische Autobiographie," 204; and Gnirs, "Biographies," 185.

11 M.-C. Lavier, "Les mystères d'Osiris à Abydos d'après les stèles du Moyen Empire et du Nouvel Empire," in S. Schoske, ed., *Akten des vierten Internationalen Ägyptologen Kongresses München 1985*, III (Hamburg, 1989), 289–95.

12 Gnirs, "Biographies," 185; C. Eyre, "*The Semna Stelae: Quotation, Genre, and Functions of Literature," in* S. Israelit-Groll, ed., *Studies in Egyptology Presented to Miriam Lichtheim* (Jerusalem, 1990), 152–53; Perdu, "Autobiographies," 2244; L. Coulon, "Véracité et rhétorique dans les autobiographies égyptiennes de la Première Période Intermédiaire," *BIFAO* 97 (1997), 109–38.

13 Lichtheim, *Ancient Egyptian Autobiographies*, 2.

14 J. Griffiths, "Intimations in Egyptian Non-royal Biography of a Belief in Divine Impact on Human Affairs," in J. Baines, T.G.H. James, A. Leahy, and A.F. Shore, eds., *Pyramid Studies and Other Essays Presented to I.E.S. Edwards* (London, 1988), 92–102.

15 Fully realizing that someone like Weni the Elder had clearly exaggerated what he portrayed as humble beginnings in his self-presentation, as the rediscovery of his Abydos mastaba has shown; see J. Richards, "Text and Context in Late Old Kingdom Egypt: The Archaeology and Historiography of Weni the Elder," *JARCE* 39 (2002), 75–102.

16 Van de Walle, "Biographie," 816, 820; Eyre, "*The Semna Stelae*," 147, 152–53; Perdu, "Autobiographies," 2243; Gnirs, "Die ägyptische Autobiographie," 196; R.J. Leprohon, "Remarks on Private Epithets Found in the Middle Kingdom Wadi Hammamat Graffiti," *JSSEA* 28 (2001), 127–28; R.B. Parkinson, *Poetry and Culture in Middle Kingdom Egypt: A Dark Side to Perfection* (London, 2002), 50–51, 55–57, 142–43, etc. In the context of Chinese storytelling, this has been described as "the oral communication of 'telling' and 'listening'"; see V. Børdahl, *The Oral Tradition of Yangzhou Storytelling* (Richmond, 1996), 241.

17 H.G. Fischer, "Occurrences of *in*, Agential and Dative," *GM* 107 (1989), 71, and fig. 1. A few examples from various periods include *Urk.* I, 9:13, 18:9, 49:17; Berlin 24032; Cairo CG 20500; J. Clère and J. Vandier, *Textes de la Première Période Intermédiaire et de la XIe dynastie*, Brussels, 1948, nos. 14, 15, 17; BM 101, 202; Cairo CG 20026, 20040; Leiden V4, V6; Louvre C 3, C 11; Hatnub 24, 49; Sinai 53, 86; Wadi el-Hudi 14, 143; Wadi Hammamat 43, 87; *Urk.* IV, 1:16, 2:8, 30:7; and *KRI* I, 290:5, 299:13, etc.

18 See Pap. Berlin 9010 (= N. Strudwick, *Texts from the Pyramid Age* [Atlanta, 2005], 186–87, no. 103), where the court would only accept the authenticity of a legal document if witnesses could testify orally to its veracity; see A. Théodoridès, "The Concept of Law in Ancient Egypt," in J. Harris, ed., *The Legacy of Egypt*, 2nd ed. (Oxford, 1971), 299. On literacy, see J. Baines, "Literacy and Ancient Egyptian Society," *Man* 18 (1983), 572–99; J. Baines and C. Eyre, "Four Notes on Literacy," *GM* 61 (1983), 65–96; Parkinson, *Poetry and Culture*, 15, 66–67.

19 Unless otherwise noted, the numbers in the brackets following epithets will refer to Janssen's catalogue in *De traditioneele Egyptische Autobiografie*.

20 W. Ong, *Orality and Literacy: The Technologizing of the Word* (London, 1982), 38–42; A. Lord, "Perspectives on Recent Work on the Oral Traditional Formula," *Oral Tradition* 1 (1986), 480–82; A. Lord, "Characteristics of Orality," *Oral Tradition* 2 (1987), 57; Eyre, "*The Semna Stelae*," 162; C. Bryan, *A Preface to Mark: Notes on the Gospel in Its Literary and Cultural Settings* (Oxford, 1993), 73, 126–51; Gnirs, "Biographies," 185; B. Incigneri, *The Gospel to the Romans: The Setting and Rhetoric of Mark's Gospel* (Leiden, 2003), 44; C. Thomas and C. Conant, *The Trojan War* (Norman, Oklahoma, 2007), 63. On parataxis, see E. Havelock, *Preface to Plato* (Cambridge, 1963), 180; Børdahl, *The Oral Tradition*, 241; M. Moeser, *The Anecdote in Mark: The Classical World and the Rabbis* (London, 2002), 189–90.

21 Doxey, *Non-Royal Epithets*, 167.

22 The numbers following the quotes from Ptahhotep's Instructions are those found in Z. Žába, *Les Maximes de Ptaḥḥotep* (Prague, 1956).

23 Shabako Stone col. 53, K. Sethe, *Dramatische Texte zu altägyptischen Mysterienspielen Das "Denkmal memphitischer Theologie": Der Schabakostein des Britischen Museums* (Leipzig, 1928), 50–56.

24 Doxey, *Non-Royal Epithets*, 69–70.

25 For *rrit*, see R. Hannig, *Ägyptisches Wörterbuch* II: *Mittleres Reich und Zweite Zwischenzeit* (Mainz, 2006), 1503.

26 For *nhrhr*, see Hannig, *Ägyptisches Wörterbuch* II, 1309.

27 The reverse could also be case; although the phrase *hrw-ib* precedes here, being "free from passion" may have led to being "content." I owe this observation to a reviewer.

28 M. Lichtheim, "Autobiography as Self-Exploration," in Anonymous, ed., *Sesto Congresso internazionale di egittologia: Atti* I (Turin, 1992), 409–14. On the *ḥ3ty* as part of the body and the *ib* as the "interior," see R. Nyord, "Taking Phenomenology to Heart: Some Heuristic Remarks on Studying Ancient Egyptian Embodied Experience," in R. Nyord and A. Kjølby, eds., *"Being in Ancient Egypt": Thoughts on Agency, Materiality and Cognition: Proceedings of the Seminar Held in Copenhagen, September 29–30, 2006* (Oxford, 2009), 63–74.

29 The same pairing is seen in the stela of Amunwoser (*JEA* 51 [1965], 63–68); Manchester 3306; Sinai 33, 35, 71, and 118; and Wadi el-Hudi 16 and 21.

30 Lit., "the place of his feet."

31 Noticeably, such specific groups of people are mostly absent in epithets found on stelae or graffiti, perhaps because high- or middle-level court officials would not have dealt with them on a regular basis. For a useful summary of various classes of people in this period, see W. Grajetzki, *The Middle Kingdom of Ancient Egypt* (London, 2006), 142–61.

32 K. Sethe, *Ägyptische Lesestücke zum Gebrauch in akademischen Unterricht* (Leipzig, 1924), 79:9–10.

33 On this passage, see G. van den Boorn, *The Duties of the Vizier: Civil Administration in the Early New Kingdom* (London, 1988), 35, n. 149.

34 Lit., "enlightening."

35 Lit., "under."

36 On the noun *hp* meaning "a rule to be observed" rather than simply "law," see M. Bontty, "Concerning *hp*," *JSSEA* 27 (1997), 1–8; B. Menu, "La règle fiscale comme source du droit," *Recherches sur l'histoire juridique, économique et sociale de l'ancienne Égypte*, II (Cairo, 1998), 21–25; P. Vernus, "The Royal Command (*wḏ-nsw*): A Basic Deed of Executive Power," in J.C. Moreno García, ed., *Ancient Egyptian Administration* (Leiden, 2013), 272.

37 For the ʿrrt, see Pagliari, "Function and Significance of Ancient Egyptian Royal Palaces," 260–62.

38 R.J. Leprohon, "The Programmatic Use of the Royal Titulary in the Twelfth Dynasty," *JARCE* 33 (1996), 167; J.P. Allen, "The High Officials of the Early Middle Kingdom," in N. Strudwick and J. Taylor, eds., *The Theban Necropolis: Past, Present and Future* (London, 2003), 14–29; L. Postel, *Protocole des souverains égyptiens et dogme monarchique au début du Moyen Empire* (Turnhout, 2004), 266–67; H. Willems, "The First Intermediate Period and the Middle Kingdom," in A. Lloyd, ed., *A Companion to Ancient Egypt* (Oxford, 2010), 90–91.

39 R. Anthes, "Eine Polizeistreife des Mittleren Reiches an die westliche Oase," *ZÄS* 65 (1930), 108–14; for the dating of the stela to the reign of Amenemhat I, see R. Freed, "A Private Stela from Naga ed-Der and Relief Style of the Reign of Amenemhet I," in W.K. Simpson and W. Davis, eds., *Studies in Ancient Egypt, the Aegean, and the Sudan* (Boston, 1981), 76.

40 C. Obsomer, *Sésostris Ier: Étude chronologique et historique du règne* (Brussels, 1995), 54–81; for archaeological evidence of the war, see C. Barbotin, "II: Guerre civile et guerre étrangère d'après la stèle de Nysoumontou (Louvre C1)," *RdE* 56 (2005), 193–94.

41 C. Firth and B. Gunn, *Excavations at Saqqara: Teti Pyramid Cemeteries*, II (Cairo, 1926), 280–88, pl. 83.

42 For the dating of the Hatnub graffiti, see H. Willems, "The Nomarchs of the Hare Nome and Early Middle Kingdom History," *JEOL* 28 (1984), 80–102; L. Gestermann, "Die Datierung der Nomarchen von Hermopolis aus dem frühen Mittleren Reich—ein Phantomdebatte?" *ZÄS* 135 (2008), 1–15.

43 Such allegiance became codified in the so-called Loyalist Instructions, for which see G. Posener, *L'Enseignement loyaliste: Sagesse égyptienne du Moyen Empire* (Geneva, 1976); see also A. Gnirs, "The Language of Corruption: On Rich and Poor in The Eloquent Peasant," in A. Gnirs, ed., *Reading the Eloquent Peasant: Proceedings of the International Conference on The Tale of the Eloquent Peasant at the University of California, Los Angeles, March 27–30, 1997* (Göttingen, 2000), 149.

44 Such epithets formed part of what has been designated "encomiastic autobiographies"; see Gnirs, "Die ägyptische Autobiographie," 205; Gnirs, "Biographies," 186–87.

45 On *stp-s3*, see O. Goelet, "The Term *stp-s3* in the Old Kingdom and Its Later Development," *JARCE* 23 (1986), 85–98; G. Shaw, "The Meaning of the Phrase *m ḥm n stp-s3*," *JEA* 96 (2010), 175–90. For *ʿḥ* and *stp-s3*, see Pagliari, "Function and Significance of Ancient Egyptian Royal Palaces," 233–44 and 246–48, respectively.

46 On *f3w*, see E. Blumenthal, *Untersuchungen zum ägyptischen Königtum des Mittleren Reiches*, I: *Die Phraseologie* (Berlin, 1970), 373.

47 For a comprehensive study on phrases used to describe promotions, see M. Trapani, *La Dévolution des fonctions en Égypte pharaonique: Étude critique de la documentation disponible* (London, 2015).

48 Lit., "one who created his (own) ideas."

49 For a discussion of this expression in its social context, see the cogent remarks by Gnirs, "The Language of Corruption," 134–35.

50 H. Brunner, "Zitate aus Lebenslehren," in E. Hornung and O. Keel, eds., *Studien zu altägyptischen Lebenslehren* (Freiburg, 1979), 105–77; J. Assmann, "Schrift, Tod und Identität: Das Grab als Vorschule der Literatur im alten Ägypten," in A. Assmann, Ch. Hardmeier, eds., *Schrift und Gedächtnis: Beiträge zur Archäologie der Literarischen Kommunikation* (Munich, 1983), 64–93; Eyre, "The Semna Stelae"; R. Parkinson, *Voices from Ancient Egypt* (Norman, 1991), 17, 24; Gnirs, "Die ägyptische Autobiographie," 207–09; M. Lichtheim, "Didactic Literature," in A. Loprieno, ed., *Ancient Egyptian Literature* (Leiden, 1996), 244–47; Doxey, *Non-Royal Epithets*, 5–7; Parkinson, *Poetry and Culture*, 111–12; F. Junge, *Die Lehre Ptahhoteps und die Tugenden der ägyptischen Welt* (Göttingen, 2003); K. Jansen-Winkeln, "Lebenslehre und Biographie," *ZÄS* 131 (2004), 59–72; and N. Lazaridis, "Ethics," in E. Frood and W. Wendrich, eds., *UCLA Encyclopedia of Egyptology* (Los Angeles, 2008), http://escholarship.org/uc/item/4q20j8mw.

51 On the transmission of texts, see, e.g., J. Kahl, *Siut-Theben: zur Wertschätzung von Traditionen im alten Ägypten* (Leiden, 1999), 28–52; and Eyre, "The Semna Stelae," 155–58.

52 His son.

53 On *tp-ḥsb* as precise rules of protocol, see L. Coulon, "La rhétorique et ses fictions: Pouvoirs et duplicité du discours à travers la littérature égyptienne du Moyen et du Nouvel Empire," *BIFAO* 99 (1999), 103–32.

54 Ptahhotep reiterated this maxim when he also urged his son to "teach a great man what will be beneficial to him" (*sb3 wr r 3ḫt n.f*; Ptahhotep 399). Ong, *Orality and Literacy*, 40–41, makes the point that oral societies needed to repeat information time and again for the knowledge to properly sink in; for this reason, learned people were highly valued.

55 Ptahhotep Maxims 233, 234, and 433.

56 Ptahhotep 91, 300, 315, 316, and 318.

57 Additional Middle Kingdom phrases that warned against "forgetfulness" (*mht*, VI C 16, VI J 16 and 36) can be paralleled by Ptahhotep's admonition to not be "forgetful concerning what has been said to you, and beware of the occasion of forgetfulness" (*m ꜥm ib.k ḥr ḏdt n.k s3w.ti ḥr sp n mht-ib*;

153–54). However, this particular passage is from an Eighteenth Dynasty manuscript of Ptahhotep (L2 [Pap. BM 10509]), so may perhaps be a New Kingdom addition. For the dating of Pap. BM 10509, see Eyre, "*The Semna Stelae,*" *156, n.* 77; Junge, *Die Lehre Ptahhoteps,* 10–14.

58 A. Blackman, *Middle Egyptian Stories* (Brusssels, 1932), 46:14–15.

7

Self-Presentation in the Second Intermediate Period*

R. Gareth Roberts

By the Second Intermediate Period, Egyptian self-presentation had reached the stage where the well-to-do apparently felt comfortable with expressing many facets of their lives on commemorative monuments. S. Kubisch, whose *Lebensbilder der 2. Zwischenzeit* provided the examples used for this chapter, observed that those who dwelt during this period elaborated on the personal bonds they had to the king, the gods, and the community; boasted of the fine characteristics they possessed, such as strength in combat or natural eloquence; and often claimed that these had manifested during childhood. Kubisch sees these themes as being pragmatic, if perhaps exaggerated, reflections of lived experience.[1] Implicit in this assessment, along with many commentaries on self-presentation material, is the notion that such information was autobiographical, and that it contained what the deceased wanted to personally communicate to the community, gods, and posterity: the 'self' in the term *self-presentation*. M. Lichtheim was very clear about this, calling Egyptologists "apologetic" for regarding such texts as anything but autobiography.[2]

I am not convinced. While it has long been recognized that Egyptians with the resources to do so would seek to prepare for their inevitable demise, there must have been circumstances where this was not possible. Unexpected death from illness or misadventure, for example, might have struck before preparations were complete, as evidenced most famously by the tomb of Tutankhamun.[3] Children who had risen high might seek to create postmortem funerary monuments for their more humble parents or grandparents. If the norm in the Second Intermediate Period was for the elite to express thematically appropriate aspects of their lives on funerary monuments, then there must have been times when this was done for them. What was expressed in such cases cannot have been autobiographical.

This does not mean that presentation was not personal. Portraying the deceased as being alive and active, and evoking elements of their 'self,' implies personal commitment and investment, even if it was done while following societal conventions. If that is so, then studies of self-presentation ought to draw from methodologies that incorporate the lived experience of real people. What follows is an examination of Second Intermediate Period self-presentation data from the perspective of what is both intrinsically personal and, I argue, common to all self-presentation material: human memory.

Self-Identity and Memory

Self-presentation, even apparent self-presentation, requires recognition of the self and of self-identity. The philosophical consensus appears to be that identities are in some way constructed via a reciprocal relationship between individuals and the societies in which they live: society affects the individual, and the individual affects their society (some more than others). Memory plays a part in this process because individuals and societies persist through time, changing so that the identities a person recognizes in him- or herself in a given present might be very different from those they recognize of themselves in the past.

Psychologists distinguish between a number of interrelated memory states,[4] the most pertinent for identity being the 'working memory.' This term refers to the conscious process of manipulating information in the ongoing present, and is where sensory perceptions are interpreted. The working memory interacts with other memory states, including short-term memory, which processes (and then possibly discards) information relevant to a current task, and long-term memories that are recalled either deliberately or via sensory cues. If reading this chapter brings something to mind, then that recollection will be collated in the working memory and assessed against what is currently being read. There is a reciprocal relationship between the working memory and other memory states, particularly long-term ones, because what is encountered in the present continually manipulates, modifies, or reaffirms the understanding of the past.

The cumulative effect of this interplay is an ongoing personal narrative: a working self.[5] Working selves change over time because social contexts change, and memories recalled from the distant past might appear to be of someone (or of a society) very different to that of the present. If a person remembers a naïve teenage self, or, if the past generally seems better than today, then this is partly because memories of the past are being assessed against perceptions of the present in the working memory, and informing the working self. If this is true of modern humans, it must also have been true of ancient Egyptians.

The relationship between long-term memories and the working self is crucial to self-presentation because presentation data—such as stelae, tombs, or statues—are constructed by individuals or groups of individuals who access long-term 'declarative' memories (facts or knowledge) in a personal present. We include what we know in what we create. Such knowledge need not be autobiographical: the long-term memory state called 'semantic' memory relates to knowledge or beliefs held without personal experience of them, such as the early life of a parent, or an interpretation of the ancient past.

Long-term memories that relate to what has personally been experienced are known as 'episodic' memories, and include a subset of autobiographical memories that are associated with personal identity. Three categories of episodic memory are normally recognized: 'lifetime periods' that cover extended durations, such as jobs and relationships; 'general events' or episodes within such periods that so closely resemble one another that it is not easy to distinguish between them (the 'daily grind'); and 'event-specific' memories of actual single events. Recall is rarely perfect, however, because of imperfect transference between short- and long-term memory states, because of neural or synaptic degradation due to age or infirmity, or because there are things that we, as humans, would rather not remember, or would wish to remember differently. Memory is sometimes a motivated choice.

Modes of Self-Presentation

If the person commissioning a self-presentation datum was the one commemorated on it and had direct input in its creation, then that person would have accessed their episodic autobiographical memories for the purpose. The datum would then contain expressions of memories *by* a person.

If the person who commissioned a piece was a relative, say a child or grandchild, then the memories presented there are less likely to have been autobiographical, even if expressed in the first person. They might still seem to be episodic memories expressed by a person, and, thus, be presented as autobiography, but would instead be closer to what modern writers might term biography. Any events thus portrayed would be semantic memories pertaining to what was known, or believed, *of* a person.

A third category exists because it is unlikely that any individual would have dictated all aspects of a commission, let alone created it. Specialized workshops appear to have been common,[6] and the people employed there would have had experience of what ought to appear in a given funerary text or monument, having built up a repertoire of suitable options. The final form of a piece is likely to have been tailored to specific requirements but, because the workers may not have known the client at all, much of what survives might instead include memories of a *sort* of person. Elements that were deemed appropriate for a priest, for example, might be different from those deemed appropriate for a soldier. The fact that researchers can identify themes or 'icons' of self-presentation attests to this.[7]

These distinctions should not be regarded as mutually exclusive, because the act of commissioning and creating a funerary monument must have been a collaborative exercise. Moreover, in many—perhaps most—cases it is not easy to differentiate memories *by* a person from memories *of* a person: Egyptian mortuary data perpetuates the deceased as being alive. Yet sometimes a case can be made.

Memories *by* a Person

Actual autobiographical memories *by* a person are likely to be on pieces that demonstrate event-specific knowledge, but which lack evidence that another person commissioned them. These do not necessarily reveal historical 'truth,' because imperfect or motivated recall can distort the events of the past, and reconstructing 'what happened' is a tenuous exercise at best.

For example, a stela from Buhen (Seventeenth Dynasty; Helck no. 121) bears a degraded text commemorating a certain *Iʿḥ-ms* (Ahmose),[8] including:

> *ink ʿḥ3wti ḳn n ḥḳ3 nḫt* [. . . *K3?*]*-ms ʿnḫ ḏt ini.n.i tp rmṯw 46 iw.i ḥr šms ḥḳ3 di ʿnḫ*
>
> I am a brave warrior of the strong ruler [. . . Ka]mose, given life. I carried off the heads of forty-six people when I followed the ruler, given life.

The statements that follow, so far as they are preserved, tend to be more general, such as *nḫ.i niwtyw.i* (I protected my townspeople). No other individuals are named in the surviving text, so it is possible, though not certain, that Ahmose commissioned his own funerary stela. The text generally corresponds to the Second Intermediate Period 'strong warrior' theme, which manifests as an autobiographical (lifetime period, theme of work as a warrior) remembered self. It also contains the very specific claim that Ahmose took forty-six heads, which reads as viable (though perhaps exaggerated) and suggests direct input. This may, therefore, be a genuine autobiographical (general event or event-specific) expression of self-presentation: an event or series of events that Ahmose wished to be remembered for. Less specific claims, such as protecting townspeople, are appropriate for the strong warrior theme, but might have been chosen or suggested by whoever composed the final text.

A second example is contained in the Edfu stela presenting *sꜣ nswt ṯsw Ḫnsw-m-wꜣst* (the king's son and commander Khonsuemwaset; Sixteenth Dynasty; Cairo JE 38917),[9] which includes a very specific recollection:

> *rdi.n.f n.i sbḫt r ḥꜥt.i m ḫt mk (?) ḥḏ* [. . .] *2 m nbw*
> He (the king) gave me a pectoral for my chest, of wood covered with silver and two [. . .] of gold.

The only other person named on the stela is King Dedumose, so Khonsuemwaset may have commissioned and had some direct input into the content of his own stela. If so, then this detail appears to be an autobiographical (event-specific) memory. More general statements are listed, including royal satisfaction *ḥis.f wi m iꜣwt* [*rdi.n.f w*]*i im.s* (inasmuch as he favored me in the office in which he placed me), and that Khonsuemwaset was one who *irr iꜣwt m nḫn.f* (exercised the office since childhood). These might be autobiographical or contextually appropriate lifetime period (theme of relationships with the king, theme of 'work' during childhood) elements from a repertoire of suitable Second Intermediate Period statements.

A third example might be the Hierakonpolis stela dedicated to *sḥḏ ḥmw-nṯr tpy n Ḥr Nḫn imy-rꜣ tꜣwt Ḥr-m-ḫꜥw.f* (the chief inspector of the priests of Horus of Hierakonpolis and overseer of lands Heremkhawef; Fig. 7.1; Thirteenth or Sixteenth Dynasty; New York, MMA Nr. 35.7.55),[10] whose stela relates that he was tasked by *Ḥr-nḏ-ḥr-it.f* (either the deity later known as Harendotes or a superior of that name) with retrieving the cult statues of Horus of Hierakonpolis and Isis from the royal residence:

> *rdi.n.f wi m ḥry imw ist isṯ grt rḫ.n.f wi m sr mnḫ n ḥwt-nṯr.f rs-tp ḥr swḏ n.f ꜥḥꜥ.n.i ḫd.kwi* ⟨*m*⟩ *mꜣꜥw nfr šd.n.i Ḥr Nḫn ḥr ꜥwy*⟨*.i*⟩ *ḥnꜥ mwt.f nṯrt . . . ḫft-ḥr nsw ḏs.f*
> He made me captain of a vessel and its crew, because he knew me as a trustworthy official of his temple, alert to what was assigned to him. And so I went downstream with a fair breeze. I brought away Horus of Hierakonpolis with my own hands, along with his mother the goddess . . . into the presence of the king himself.

a) Hierakonpolis 1 (New York, MMA 35.7.55)

7.1. Stela dedicated to Heremkhawef, Metropolitan Museum of Art, New York, 35.7.55

This is reported speech presented as an event-specific autobiographical memory. It is followed by general statements, including of being a decent person, giving bread to the hungry and clothes to the naked, and caring for a sister, which are more likely to be stock inclusions. There is little on the stela to suggest that it was a postmortem commission. Heremkhawef is depicted and named, without being called *mꜣꜥ-ḫrw* (true of voice or justified), in the lower left, next to visual representations of the standard voice offerings. Below this, and separated by a line, are several names, including of his sons, Djehuty and Sebeknakht, and his daughter, Hermaakherew, but they are relatively inconspicuous. It is, therefore, possible that the stela might have been commissioned by Heremkhawef while he was still alive, and that the episode was included to present an autobiographical memory of a significant event in his life.

Memories *of* a Person

If there are indications of a postmortem commission, if descendants have a meaningful presence on a piece, or if there are subtexts, then there is a chance that the 'self' being presented is not truly autobiographical, but instead is a memorial to a person, and, thus, contains memories *of* that person.

An example is the stela set up in Buhen for *Sr-kꜣ* (Serka; Thirteenth or Sixteenth Dynasty; Khartoum no. 18),[11] which was created at a time when Buhen was not part of the Egyptian ambit but still held a sufficiently large Egyptian population for their funerary traditions to be preserved and followed. The piece was not commissioned by Serka but by his grandson:

> *in sꜣ sꜣt.f sꜥnḫ rn.f sr pw Ꞽꜥḥ-wsr ḏd.f ink bꜣk ḳn n ḥḳꜣ n Kšì iw iꜥ⟨.ì⟩ rdwy(w) ⟨.ì⟩ ḥr mw nw Kšwì ḥr šmsw pꜣ ḥḳꜣ Nḏḥ iw.ì ìì.kw ꜥḏ⟨.kw⟩ wḏꜣ.kw ⟨n⟩ ẖrw⟨.ì⟩*
> It is the son of his daughter who causes his name to live: this official Iahuser. He says: I am a brave servant of the ruler of Kush. I washed my feet in the waters of Kush while following the ruler of Nedjeh. I arrived with my family safe and intact.

There is a strong possibility that this commission was postmortem, or at least so late in Serka's life that neither he nor his children were directly responsible for its contents. This does not necessarily mean that the events alluded to on the stela are untrue, but rather that they are more likely to be semantic memories (theme of relationships, with the king) that Iahuser recalled of his grandfather at the time when the stela was commissioned, and which correspond to the strong warrior theme of the Second Intermediate Period. However, the subjects of *in PN sꜥnḫ rn.f* formulae have an active voice in this period,[12] so the *ḏd.f* reported speech that immediately follows Iahuser's name appears to relate in part to his own working self. Claiming that Serka was a loyal follower of the ruler of Kush might be as much a statement of loyalty by Iahuser as a remembrance of his grandfather.

Another example appears on a stela from Edfu presenting *ḥ3ti-ʿ imy-r ḥmw-nṯr Ḥrw-ḥr-ḫwt.f* (the mayor and overseer of priests Heruherkhewetef; Thirteenth or Seventeenth Dynasty; Cairo JE 31612).[13] Some of the reported speech is generic (and ancient: *di.n.i t n nty ḥḳr ḥbsy n nty ḫ3w* [I gave bread to those who were hungry, clothes to those who were naked]), but a line stands out:

> *di.n⟨.i⟩ prt n t3 ⟨r⟩ ḏr.f šdn⟨.i⟩ niwt.i m ḥḳr n iri ky irt.i*
> I gave grain to the whole country, and I freed my town from hunger. Never did another do what I have done.

Kubisch sees this as autobiographical, albeit with Heruherkhewetef presenting himself "in an exaggerated way," [14] which assumes his direct input. But Heruherkhewetef and his wife Iritpat are shown seated as the revered dead, with their children prominent before them. The presence of their children in such a notable fashion suggests that a postmortem commission is, at least, possible, so the detail about feeding the whole country might be a semantic memory (general event or event-specific) of their father's alleged deeds, and appropriate for the Second Intermediate Period theme of community. If so, then this apparent self-presentation by Heruherkhewetef might be as much a statement of his children's working selves through their association with a notable forebear.

A further example might be seen in a funerary stela from Elephantine (Berlin 19500) that was set up for *3ṯw n Styw ỉnny* (attendant of Nubians, Inny) and his wife *Ddt-ʿnḳt* (Dedetanqet), who are both presented in the offering formula as being *m3ʿ-ḫrw* (true of voice) and, therefore, as deceased.[15] The reported speech reads:

> *ink grw šw m grg wʿ mnḫ mrr.w niwtyw.f iri.n⟨.i⟩ ʿš3w n wpwt m ḫnt r Kš n iw sp.i n ḫpr sk.i n spr⟨w⟩ ḥr⟨.i⟩ n wḥmw n sḏr⟨.i⟩ šnʿ.kwi*
> I was silent and free from falsehood, uniquely effective, being beloved of his townspeople. I undertook numerous missions while sailing upstream into Kush. No fault of mine ever came out, for I was never accused. No petitions were upon me, and there were no reports of my inactivity or being detained.

The remaining legible reported speech is generic and contains no information that stands out as a potential autobiographical memory from Inny's life. Five other people, Inny's descendants, are depicted and named on this stela: his daughters, Iby, Dedetanqet (apparently named for her mother), Satetjeny, Inetwaw, and Bebew. The general statements, use of *mȝʿ-ḫrw*, and significant inclusion of five daughters on the stela suggest that the piece may have been a postmortem creation, and the detail about sailing to Kush probably constitutes a (rather vague) semantic memory of a deceased father. If so, and if the statements of blamelessness were not merely formulaic, then his daughters apparently wished to stress his innocence and the stela might have had relevance to the family's circumstances at the time it was created, the details of which are long since lost.

Memories of a *Sort* of Person

Repeated patterns, such as statements about feeding the hungry and clothing the naked, or depictions of the deceased before an offering table, are common in funerary texts and monuments. These are present on the stela set up for Heremkhawef (Fig. 7.1), for example. The decision to include such elements may or may not have rested with whoever commissioned a given piece, but they would have been familiar to the workers who actually created it.

At least ten stela workshops were identified by R. Freed from the early Twelfth Dynasty,[16] and the 'signature' of individual studios can be seen at least into the Roman period.[17] If Deir el-Medina was representative of the organization, if not the scale, of a typical Egyptian workshop, then personnel would have included a senior scribe, probably with assistants, an overseer to supervise technical details, and a crew of workers and apprentices including those with specialized functions, such as draftsmen, sculptors, and colorists.[18] Any of these people might have influenced the final product, because whoever commissioned a piece need not have issued detailed instructions. An ostracon from the New Kingdom, perhaps from the reign of Ramesses III,[19] seems to preserve self-presentation instructions in which the beneficiary, the scribe Pentaweret, was to be depicted venerating Monthu:[20]

> *twt n Mnṯw snḏm(.w) ḥr bḥd twt n sẖ Pn-tȝ-wrt ḥr sn-tȝ m-bȝḥ.f ḥr dwȝ.f m sẖ ḳdw.t*
>
> An image of Monthu sitting on a throne, and an image of the scribe, Pentaweret, kissing the ground before him in his reverence. To be drafted by a scribe.

Pentaweret (or his family; it may have been a postmortem commission) issued a general description of what was required, but the details were to be left to the artisans at the workshop.

Further examples of workshops following patterns, from shortly after the Second Intermediate Period, can be seen in tomb decorations from the reigns of Thutmose IV or Amenhotep III. M. Hartwig has identified 'styles' among these decorations, which she suggests were specialisms of particular studios: her 'temple' style predominates in the tombs of those whose titles associate them with temples or the estate of the king; her 'court' style corresponds to tombs in which titles are of those engaged in palace, civil, or military roles.[21] Within these styles Hartwig identifies 'icons' that might be used for a given tomb. For example, the 'offering table' icon, of the deceased (and often his wife) seated before such an item, appears more often in tombs of those whose titles suggest duties in religious institutions, and is connected with the temple style. The 'royal kiosk' icon, of the deceased shown interacting with the king, seems to be associated with those whose titles suggest more civil roles, and appears within Hartwig's court style.[22] There is some crossover (an individual might have held a variety of positions during life) but the trend is that the offering table icon is typically used for those with roles in temple administration, and the royal kiosk icon is for those with roles in civil or military administration.

The decision to include one icon over another might have been made with the input of the client, but that decision is likely to have been influenced by the workers in a studio. Experts are expected to offer their expertise. As a consequence, a text or a relief need not entirely reflect the memories of whoever commissioned it, but might derive most directly from the experience (and thus the memories) of an expert who would know what ought to be included on a funerary monument for a *sort* of person. Priests would be expected to have certain duties and privileges and their monuments ought to reflect these; soldiers would have different duties and privileges, so their monuments would contain different elements.

This was alluded to by Kubisch in her article "Biographies of the Thirteenth to Seventeenth Dynasties," though she discussed it from a different perspective. Her assessment seems to have been for active, personal input by the one being commemorated, stating for example that "all priests [in Second Intermediate Period monuments] lay the same emphasis in presenting their professional activities."[23] That may have been the case for some, but given the probability of postmortem commissions, it cannot have been the case for all, and repeated patterns might lend credence to the idea that a third party was involved in the decision-making process.

One repeated pattern that Kubisch observed is the number of texts indicating that a priest, or other temple worker, had the right to access parts of the temple that were otherwise off-limits.[24] These include a seated statue from Elephantine (probably Seventeenth Dynasty; Louvre AF 9916) upon which is a line stating that *sẖ ḥwt-nṯr H̱nm-ḥtp* (scribe of the temple, Khnumhotep) was one:[25]

> *ˁḳ r pt m33 ntt im.s sip [n]tt im.s*
> who enters heaven [presumably the sanctuary], sees what is in it, and inspects what is in it.

Another example is from the Edfu stela commemorating *ẖry-ḥbt tpy n Ḥr Bḥdty ˁḳ Iby* (chief lector-priest of Horus of Edfu and one who enters, Iby; Seventeenth Dynasty; Cairo JE 46200),[26] where a line relates that he was:

> *ḥry-tp n st-wrt ẖtm ẖt.f ḥr m33t.f*
> chief of the sanctuary, sealed is his belly [discreet] about what he sees.

Both of these examples convey the notion that priests and those with administrative roles in the temple had access to its innermost areas. They are consistent with Second Intermediate Period themes of expressing personal relationships with the gods and community, and of personal qualities (in these cases discretion). They might even have been true, because those who have reached a significant position in a hierarchy might reasonably be expected to have commensurate duties and privileges. Whether a statement to that end on a funerary statue or stela represents an autobiographical memory is another matter, because these are not event-specific expressions of the sort that might relate memories *by* a person, but rather are of lifetime periods (theme of work) or general events. They appear more to be the day-to-day elements that would be expected of a *sort* of person, and are more relevant to a social self—one that society would expect to see—than a personal self-identity. Accordingly, statements that the deceased had the right to access restricted areas in a temple might indicate the input of the workshops where they were created, as being appropriate for those who had reached a certain position within the temple hierarchy. As such, they might be precursors to Hartwig's temple style.

A precursor to Hartwig's court style, which was applied to those who had military careers, might be seen among Kubish's examples of the strong warrior theme who are called *ḳn* (brave).[27] These tend to be on stelae from Thirteenth or Seventeenth Dynasty Buhen (including two discussed above:

Khartoum no. 18, Helck no. 121),[28] or in the case of one (Cairo JE 52456) on a Seventeenth Dynasty stela from Edfu commemorating a man from the south,[29] whose reported speech begins:

> *ink ꜥḥꜣwty ḳn ꜥḳ Ḏbꜣ sfḫ.i ḥmt⟨.i⟩ ẖrdw⟨.i⟩ rḫt⟨.i⟩ m rsy Kšỉ m 13 hrw*
> I am a brave warrior entering Edfu. I removed my wife, children, and household from the south of Kush in thirteen days.

None of these stelae shows a depiction of the deceased, so they are not directly comparable to Hartwig's notion of icons, but the repeated phrase *ink ꜥḥꜣwty ḳn* or its variations—*ink bꜣk ḳn* (I am a brave servant; Khartoum no. 18) and *ink ṯsw ḳn* (I am a brave commander; Philadelphia 10984)[30]—suggests a pattern. Any pattern is unlikely to have derived from whoever commissioned the pieces. At least one, commemorating Ahmose (Helck no. 121), has elements that suggest general and/or event-specific memories that may be autobiographical, while another, for Serka (Khartoum no. 18), was set up by his grandson. The obvious alternative source would be the staff of the workshops where the stelae were created, who are likely to have had the expertise to know that warriors from the south should be remembered as being "brave."

Conclusions

There is enough in this brief survey to call into question Lichtheim's assertion that self-presentation material is autobiography, should that be necessary, or even that the person whose self was ostensibly being presented needed to be part of the self-presentation process. The finished product might contain a socially appropriate memory of someone's life experience, stand as a personal statement projected into posterity (perhaps via an ancestor), exemplify typical practice from a lifetime of remembered experience, or be some meaningfully constituted expression of each. Whatever else it may be, a presented self is a remembered self, and probably an edited remembered self.

There is an implication in this. Literate members of the Egyptian elite are likely to have encountered presentation material regularly, but the workers who created their texts and stelae would have encountered it daily. These workers may even have seen the form and content of such material develop over the years, and over generations, as styles evolved and master instructed apprentice. Indeed, what we, now, see on self-presentation material might have evolved through them.

The staff of ancient Egyptian workshops, including those of the Second

Intermediate Period, had the knowledge (autobiographical, declarative memories) to suggest self-presentation material for their clients, and the experience (episodic, lifetime period, and general event memories) to make them. Each client is likely to have had specific requirements, but the workers would have incorporated these into accepted styles and patterns. Each slight difference on each individual commission would have resulted in small but incremental changes to what the workers remembered as being appropriate. As each commission passed into memory and became a basis for later ones, those styles and patterns must have evolved: a working self, which is manifested in what an individual creates, evolves because what is encountered in the present continually manipulates, modifies, or reaffirms the understanding of the past. Elites—even kings—who based their self-presentation material on the what they encountered during their lives, and on what their artisans recommended, would only have been one part of this evolution, albeit an influential part. Thus, any assumption that Egyptian elites were wholly or even primarily responsible for the form and content of their self-presentation material, and for how it changed over time, may be flawed.

Notes

* I wish to express my grateful thanks to E. Frood, C. Khoo, and K. Streit for reading, commenting on, and making helpful suggestions about drafts of this chapter, even when they did not always agree with its contents.

1 S. Kubisch, *Lebensbilder der 2. Zwischenzeit: Biographische Inschriften der 13.–17. Dynastie* (Berlin, New York, 2008), 135.

2 M. Lichtheim, *Ancient Egyptian Autobiographies Chiefly of the Middle Kingdom: A Study and an Anthology* (Freiburg, Göttingen, 1988), 2.

3 Many royal burials in the Valley of the Kings appear to be incomplete; see, for example, the survey in N. Reeves and R.H. Wilkinson, *The Complete Valley of the Kings: Tombs and Treasures of Egypt's Greatest Pharaohs* (London, 1996).

4 These brief notes are a précis of fuller discussions in A. Baddeley, M.W. Eysenck, and M.C. Anderson, *Memory* (London, New York, 2015), which includes definitions of the terms used here.

5 M.A. Conway, "Memory and the Self," *Journal of Memory and Language* 53.4 (2005), 597.

6 Such as the Middle Kingdom examples studied in R.E. Freed, "Stela Workshops of Early Dynasty 12," in P.D. Manuelian, ed., *Studies in Honor of William Kelly Simpson*, I (Boston, 1996), 297–36.

7 For example M.K. Hartwig, *Tomb Painting and Identity in Ancient Thebes, 1419–1372* BCE (Turnhout, 2004).

8 Kubisch, *Lebensbilder der 2. Zwischenzeit*, 175–77.

9 Kubisch, *Lebensbilder der 2. Zwischenzeit*, 195–200.

10 Kubisch, *Lebensbilder der 2. Zwischenzeit*, 310–14.

11 Kubisch, *Lebensbilder der 2. Zwischenzeit*, 166–68.
12 M.G. Nelson-Hurst, "'. . .Who Causes His Name to Live': The Vivification Formula through the Second Intermediate Period," in Z. Hawass and J.H. Wegner, eds., *Millions of Jubilees: Studies in Honor of David P. Silverman*, II (Cairo, 2010), 17–19.
13 Kubisch, *Lebensbilder der 2. Zwischenzeit*, 203–206.
14 S. Kubisch, "Biographies of the Thirteenth to Seventeenth Dynasties," in M. Marée, ed., *The Second Intermediate Period (Thirteenth–Seventeenth Dynasties): Current Research, Future Prospects* (Leuven, 2010), 319.
15 Kubisch, *Lebensbilder der 2. Zwischenzeit*, 251–54; I. Müller, "Eine Stele des Mittleren Reiches von Elephantine," *Forschungen und Berichte* 24 (1984), 30–33.
16 Freed, "Stela Workshops of Early Dynasty 12."
17 S. Gupta-Agarwal, "Cultural Transmission and Consumer Demand: A Case Study Using Ceramics from Karanis, Egypt," in N. Poulou-Papadimitriou, E. Nodarou, and V. Kilikoglou, eds., *LRCW 4: Late Roman Coarse Wares, Cooking Wares and Amphorae in the Mediterranean: Archaeology and Archaeometry. The Mediterranean: A Market without Frontiers*, I (Oxford, 2014), 125–31.
18 J. Černý, *A Community of Workmen at Thebes in the Ramesside Period* (Cairo, 1973).
19 J. Moje, "O.DeM 246: Ein Auftragsbeleg aus einer altägyptischen Werkstatt," *BIFAO* 106 (2006), 190.
20 Moje, "O.DeM 246," 184.
21 Hartwig, *Tomb Painting and Identity in Ancient Thebes*, 36.
22 Hartwig, *Tomb Painting and Identity in Ancient Thebes*, 201–203, tables 1–2.
23 Kubisch, "Biographies of the Thirteenth to Seventeenth Dynasties," 313.
24 The following examples were used by Kubisch, "Biographies of the Thirteenth to Seventeenth Dynasties," 314.
25 Kubisch, *Lebensbilder der 2. Zwischenzeit*, 264–68.
26 Kubisch, *Lebensbilder der 2. Zwischenzeit*, 234–38.
27 Examples taken from Kubisch, "Biographies of the Thirteenth to Seventeenth Dynasties," 323–25.
28 Kubisch, *Lebensbilder der 2. Zwischenzeit*, 166–68, 168–71.
29 Kubisch, *Lebensbilder der 2. Zwischenzeit*, 227–30.
30 For Philadelphia 10984, see Kubisch, *Lebensbilder der 2. Zwischenzeit*, 175–77.

8

Self-Presentation in the Eighteenth Dynasty*

Hana Navratilova

The Eighteenth Dynasty offers remarkably rich archaeological and written sources[1] for a study of the Egyptian personal and cultural identity, its conceptualization, and its representation.[2] There were signs[3] of social identities and interactions shown in material culture,[4] as well as conceptualizations of both, embedded in written culture. Especially the concepts of an idealized personality and social communication were expressed in written culture, which consequently set important channels available for a self-representation,[5] or for broader phenomena of 'impression management,' which included processes of formation and presentation of private and public selves.[6]

Identities of an Eighteenth Dynasty Egyptian were defined mainly within his/her family affiliation, hierarchy, occupation, and devotion,[7] and registered or represented accordingly in administrative, devotional, and funerary context. In particular the written representation of identity and, also, individuality, shown in the tomb and similar contexts, comes to the forefront,[8] as we may reasonably claim that this was a personalized presentation, although chosen from a culturally sanctioned, appropriate systemic repertoire.[9] However, there were other venues of self-representation that either complemented the commemorative message-board of a tomb, stela, or statue in the funerary context, or entirely differed from it, playing out the self-representation performance, for example, on the field of correspondence.[10] In context of other cultural texts—that is, texts that also may be included in the Egyptian literature—the instructions and other literary texts offered a model to be followed in order to achieve the desirable format of a successfully culturally adapted, socialized—in short, 'encultured'—individual. At the risk of presenting an unfocused chapter, this contribution presents a large text corpus that stretched over several centuries and addressed the process of self-fashioning that had underwritten different performances of self-representation. Interplay with nontextual representation is referred to wherever possible.[11]

Men and Women of the Eighteenth Dynasty: (Self-)Fashioning and (Self-)Representation

"Fashioning of human identity as a manipulable, artful process" with a resulting "distinctive personality, a characteristic address to the world, a consistent mode of perceiving and behaving"[12] was not limited to early modern Europe, even though it is well illustrated in its culture and social relations. For the Egyptian Eighteenth Dynasty, the self-representation in texts was an aspect of the complex process of self-fashioning. The self-representation encompassed more than texts (witness the extensive development of forms of art), yet the elite textual representations have had the discriminating advantage of giving a seemingly privileged insight into the formation of the social self and into a conceptualization of its representations—from comportment and courtesy to personal commemorative monuments.

This is especially true for the Egyptian administration, military, and court, in short the executive elite of the New Kingdom, whose memory was embodied in the funerary and temple monuments. A salient example is the fact that texts of the period characterize mainly the concept of a public career, such as a civil servant, or more particularly a dignitary in the royal service, that is, a career reserved mostly for men.[13] Egyptian women, however, were not deleted from history, but were represented differently, suggesting a self-fashioning along multiple lines of social position and gender.[14]

Women play a part in the visual record in tombs, statues, and stelae.[15] The textual representation of women appears in tombs, statues, stelae, and on objects of daily life,[16] as it does for men, and may therefore be treated together with theirs, with the exception that women did not possess the self-presentational record. However, women appear in the family tombs together with men, and it is in the immediate vicinity of the tomb owner's self-presentational stelae that we often find the depictions of him with his spouse or other female relatives.[17] Daughters offer to their parents,[18] spouses accompany each other.[19] Women are never absent from the larger picture of an ideal society, be it in agricultural scenes or in monumental records of families that ran the country. How do they self-represent, or are they only presented? It would be easy to assume that the monumental (and in particular the written) record was controlled by men, and that women are only presented and never self-represented. Yet we do not know the details of the actual decision-making processes within a household, let alone in commissioning personal monuments. Concerning the former, a *nebet per* was the actual head of the household,[20] a woman's household could have been taxed, and so on. Concerning the latter, a female monumental record shared with men is large, if not fully equal to men in quantity and in contents, but an independent female record is smaller.[21] Eventually, it may well be that our understanding of the tomb as a vehicle of the tomb owner's self-presentation underestimates the character of the tomb as a shared family memorial.[22]

It may be then cautiously suggested that there were self-representations of women, but our access to them is rather complicated, due to an absence of self-presentations that would be presenting their *cursus honorum*. In fact, there are female names, epithets, and other laudatory statements, and despite no self-presentational material fully comparable to that of men, there is an undoubted identity and prominence. Social positions achieved by skills, reliability, and loyalty were not limited to men. Women with an exclusive access to the king, such as royal nurses, wielded considerable influence that reflected on their family connections, and so on,[23] and not least on their exceptional monuments.[24]

Consequently, to present the Eighteenth Dynasty exclusively as the age of an identity formation of the male executive administrator, or a warrior, or a courtier, would be a shortcut going in direction of the bias of selecting the accessible (or the better quantifiable) source without admitting its opposite number. Asking where the ladies have gone will lead, however, into a field of study exceeding the written culture record of self-presentation. There is much in the culture, and, consequently, representations of Eighteenth Dynasty women, that is lost to us because the textual record is lacking.

A later New Kingdom instruction of Any mentions that men are asked about their job and women about their husband.[25] This reads like an anathema to modern feminism, but only if read at face value and through the lens of a modern industrial age, where the executive power in society is alienated from any domestic connection. It may well be suspected that the Egyptian societal concept was not against women as independent and valuable human beings (note that concepts of independence and value are also flexible), but that they were included together with their husbands as participating in different roles in the process of keeping Egypt on its toes. A dignitary was backed in his efforts by his efficient and intelligently run household. That being said, views held by men on women and vice versa were likely to be multifaceted and may remain at present largely inaccessible to us.[26]

Therefore, this chapter on the Eighteenth Dynasty ought to open with a commonplace, but perhaps no less true, statement that, as in any other period of Egyptian history, the Egyptian society was composed of men and women who were subjects to the king—a pivot of the Egyptian society—but who also wielded authority in various ranks and took part in the formation of the society and its culture on different levels. In order to do so successfully, both men and women fashioned a sufficient facade of self-presentation helping them to carry out their roles, even though they chose different media to indicate and record it.

Texts and Their Materiality, Script, and Language

Texts with a self-presentative purpose have correspondingly a distinct materiality that is part of their message. Similarly, the script and language play a role, and the Eighteenth Dynasty is a germane platform for their analysis, as language change took place throughout its duration.

A typical textual trace of an elite Eighteenth Dynasty self-fashioning lies in the area of a dignitary's self-presentation, be it located on stelae or in a series of tomb texts or statue inscriptions. Monumental edifices and objects were of crucial importance given their representative role within an important space (necropolis, temple area), durability, and often also the quantity and quality of texts that they could bear.

The tomb, usually a rock-cut chapel- or temple-like structure, was a privileged space of cultural communication, with a fittingly emphasized aspect of commemoration. In the Eighteenth Dynasty, it contained a combination of written and visual[27] representations[28] of the tomb owner, his family, his office, his social recognition, and also his king and communications with the king.[29]

A New Kingdom nonroyal tomb was, also, a place of literary tradition, as its texts constituted a link in transmission of religious literature, which was often reworked creatively on the tomb walls in different combinations of spells from Coffin Texts,[30] Pyramid Texts,[31] and, also, the Book of the Dead,[32] or in variants of the solar hymns.[33] The choice of texts and their arrangement, as well as the choice of a tomb type and location (for example, close to an important landmark[34] or a processional road or in contact with a royal building as in the case of Senenmut or Maiherperi[35]) was in itself an act of (self-)presentation.[36] It was an active process that used selected texts and their location as part of the communicative role of the tomb in a realm of memory, devotion, and literature.[37]

The tomb was also accompanied by stelae that bore further textual representations, by funerary cones, and eventually by funerary equipment also marked with texts (on which see below). The false door in a tomb functioned chiefly as a passage to the netherworld, the statue of the tomb owner as a recipient of offerings, but it was the stelae with self-presentational texts that bore his individuality and personal identity.[38] Toward the end of the Eighteenth Dynasty, the stelae became less a means of communication of the self-presentation of the tomb owner and more a means of cult presentation and communication with the deity,[39] but for most of the time the tomb stelae were one of the most important conveyors of identity in the tomb.[40]

All elements of tomb decoration were combined to produce the definitive imprint, which the tomb owner intended to leave for posterity. The above textual elements also showed clearly that the tomb was meant to be a space of communication with different audiences.[41] The divine audience and a successful transition to the Afterlife were of crucial importance; however, the tomb was decisively the vehicle of an earthly commemoration. Alongside prayers to the gods there was the Appeal to the Living and elements of self-presentational information, with varying degrees of detail. Apart from particular elements (individual titles, details of a formulaic 'job description,' a particular career path),[42] we may also identify desirable skills, behavior, and personality traits that brought success to the official in question.

Understanding the complex message of a tomb required literacy at least in part of the audiences. The Appeal to the Living specifies that scribes (apt at their work, that is, probably able to read hieroglyphs) were to read out the texts to spread the impact of the communication to those who were either largely illiterate or in any case not able to read hieroglyphic inscriptions.[43] Eventually, the tomb space was party to a specific textual communication in the form of visitors' graffiti, a newly emphasized and developing element in written culture of Eighteenth Dynasty (see also further below).

In the instance of cenotaph stelae and texts (such as those located in Abydos), the physical closeness to important sacred spaces[44] was combined with the written message intended for mixed audiences of the temporal and spiritual worlds. The shrines, stelae, or texts that commemorated an important personage were also found in places connected with significant activity undertaken by or rather under orders of that particular person—witness the dignitaries' shrines at Gebel el-Silsila, chiefly in the reigns of Hatshepsut and Thutmose III (Hapuseneb, Minnakht, Nehesi, Senenmut,

User),[45] or rock texts at Aswan (Senenmut[46] or Bak,[47] sculptor of Amenhotep IV) or texts at Sinai (Nakht, Senenmut, Sennefer,[48] etc.), all locations being connected with quarrying and mining as well as with specific divine presence (exemplified by Hathor at Sinai). There may be an ambiguous dividing line between rock stelae, rock inscriptions, and eventually graffiti, but they certainly share an aim of self-presentation of an important personage in a space already endowed with specific meaning.[49]

Both local notables and dignitaries with ties to the Residence were commemorated at places of importance. A prototypical example is provided by the monuments of Senenmut, who left memorials of his activity in the service of his sovereigns at all three of the above said locations. Nubian viceroys[50] located their texts and copies of royal documents accordingly on Nubian soil.[51]

An innovative New Kingdom status symbol were statues in an important temple (and marked with appropriate self-presentational information and Appeals to the Living) that offered a new stage for the self-presentational performance,[52] located within a preeminent sacred commemorative space of a major divine temple. Such statues were also either donated[53] or otherwise legalized by the king. The privileges of being granted temple statues and offerings by the king were referred to in tomb texts, as did Kenamun (TT 93)[54] and on the statues themselves (Senenmut, CG 42114,[55] and Amenhotep son of Hapu, BM EA 103).[56] Senenmut, rather exceptionally, asked that his statues were to be "in the following of the images of your majesty."[57] Royal connections and closeness to divinity and often, also, direct relations to the temple and its personnel and rites were all encapsulated in a private temple statue,[58] "made to ensure the eternal well-being of the individual represented by preserving his name, his physical manifestation, and ability to receive offerings, and being remembered amongst and interact with the living."[59]

The stage for textual presentations of the nonroyal Egyptians, however, was wider than the above examples—the materiality of texts that bore or reflected period self-presentations includes objects of daily life as well as context of secondary and seemingly impromptu texts such as graffiti or rock inscriptions.

Objects of daily life that bore titles and other texts have been often, but not exclusively, located in a funerary setting.[60] Hence inscribed palettes of scribes and painters, cubit rods of overseers of works, a whip handle of a skipper bearing his name, or furniture marked with names and funerary formulae[61] were perhaps not necessarily always so marked when in active use, but some of them might well have been and evidence is inconclusive.[62] At least one example of a scribal palette was inscribed after the death of its user by a professional colleague.[63] In any case, the ownership as well as other social messages were marked in writing on objects of daily use, and it is interesting that the practice concerned also utensils of writing themselves.[64]

Thus far, the textual traces were identified on man-made surfaces, where they were located mostly as part of the primary purpose of the object. However, Egyptians of the Eighteenth Dynasty also transformed natural spaces into cultural landscapes by means of writing. Rock inscriptions and graffiti turned land into landscape,[65] that is, into a meaningful cultural space. Texts, often in company of figural rock art or figural graffiti, created markers along roads[66] or turned rock shelters and cavities into rock shrines.[67] They also invigorated or transformed older edifices. The graffiti production is not a new phenomenon, but it is emphasized in the New Kingdom with a newly widespread graffiti genre, visitors' graffiti.

The visitors' graffiti were a peculiar branch of the cultural practice that re-appropriated and adapted spaces by a new layer of human presence and activity.[68] The graffiti were left in buildings both a generation and hundreds of years older and reflected cultural strategies, such as a response to a commemorative effort from the past, combined with perpetuating personal memory and devotion of the visitor. Accordingly, they contained a medley of devotional and commemorative elements, including offering formulae for the benefit of the visited (tomb owner) and the visitor. The visitors' graffiti that adorn both nonroyal and royal funerary monuments were left by nonroyal persons of varied social status, including court dignitaries (for example, the herald Amunedjeh).[69]

The location of texts concerned with leaving a representative sign was, thus, spread from spaces that were already of high status to areas where the text itself contributed to a remaking of the space into a stage for performance of cultural practices including self-presentation of individuals.[70] The media and surfaces[71] of the above-listed examples vary widely and, perhaps, apart from select graffiti and some hieratic notes on the scribal palettes, were probably not executed by the self-representing person himself, but ordered to be effected on his behalf.

The script and language of most of the above texts are hieroglyphs and formal Middle Egyptian, demonstrating a monumental commemorative context and a classical language. However, some of the texts on objects of daily use as well as—and most notably—the graffiti and rock inscriptions were written in hieratic. Also elements of the impending new language phase—the Late Egyptian—crept in. In one graffito, contemporary to other more formal texts in Middle Egyptian, Late Egyptian features appear in an untypical text berating other graffiti writers for their incompetence.[72]

The Literary and Nonliterary Image of Enculturation

Literary (cultural) texts copied and select nonliterary texts composed in the Eighteenth Dynasty give another insight into the elite mentality of the period. The literary texts offer perhaps a set of normative views. The surviving papyri are mostly instructions or teachings: Instructions of Khety, Teaching of a Man for His Son, Teaching of Amenemhat, Teaching for Merykara, Ptahhotep, The Loyalist Teaching but, also, The Story of Sinuhe[73] that show norms of loyalty, self-control, and Egyptianness. Finds of ostraca, even though less frequent than the Ramesside avalanche, also show that the didactic text of Kemit, as well as instructions and other literary texts portraying the loyal elite, were copied and used.[74] Interestingly, direct intertextual relations between normative texts and individual commemoration are limited.[75] The overlap may be better described as consisting of values of loyalty, courtesy, and efficiency.

The nonliterary texts, specifically letters, offer another view on the personages of the Eighteenth Dynasty, on occasion on personages known from the self-presentative repertoire of tomb and statue texts. In Egyptian epistolography, superiors, inferiors, as well as equals communicate. Letters mostly use polite well-wishing formulae and enquiries concerning the addressee's health.[76] The tone is often practical, determined, and on occasion also rigorous. The Mayor of Thebes, Sennefer, berated his employee, Baki, severely, whereas Mentuhotep, superior to scribe Ahmose, Peniaty's man, was practical but kind.[77] Amenhotep II writing to his viceroy, Usersatet, was both practical, probably unofficial, and yet demanding—and all these aspects possibly made his letter especially prized for Usersatet.[78] A situational setting, now irretrievable, no doubt played a role. A letter apparently demanded a different level of self-presentation for a different audience and as such cannot be directly compared to an official self-presentation. However, it was still at least a semipublic face of the official.

Being an Eighteenth Dynasty Egyptian

The Eighteenth Dynasty self-presentational texts were, like Egyptian texts from other periods, "generally sparing in the kind of biographical detail that modern historians find useful for reconstructing the careers of influential personages."[79] The lack of self-presentational information as understood within modern conventions is not detracting from the value of the texts as examples of ancient rhetorical repertoire and commemorative practices,[80] and indeed of historical information.[81] The texts have a definite historicity, which concerns behavioral and intellectual concepts, as well as ideas and practices of governance plus the everyday presentation of the self.[82]

Tomb, stelae, and statue texts mostly address the existential aspect of transition from this world to the netherworld, as well as the linear-temporal aspect of a three-way communication covering the ancestors, the present, and posterity with a consistent message of personal commemoration.

Both aspects are well demonstrated, for example, by the 'great funerary text,' a comprehensive set of inscriptions appearing in the tombs of dignitaries, with examples dated to the time span of Thutmose III to Amenhotep III.[83] The text covers a *ḥtp di nsw* offering formula opening, followed by a statement by the deceased attesting to his qualities demonstrated in his earthly existence, including unreserved trustworthiness, discretion, prudence, and discernment, alongside courtly manners. A shorthand description of an ideal civil servant would be a master of ethics-cum-etiquette.

The qualities were both inborn and trained—hence the consistent 'instructions' character of many Egyptian texts (including the king instructing, for example, his vizier).[84] These merits also qualified the deceased for good service in life, the respect of posterity on earth, and a good afterlife, all of which he claims in his Appeal to the Living.[85]

The temporal aspect may also concern self-presentational details related to different reigns. A typical example of service to multiple sovereigns is demonstrated in texts of Ahmose son of Abana,[86] Ineny,[87] an unnamed viceroy of Nubia,[88] etc. A transition of office from one family member to the next (and equally worthy) generation is shown, for example, in the text of the vizier Useramun.[89] The elite is thus relating to the past,[90] either as a positive model (for example, taking over from previous generations[91]) or in a competitive way (by outdoing the ancestors by one's originality).[92]

What is in the focus of the self-presentation of the Egyptian elite of the Eighteenth Dynasty? The individuality is always shown in a social context,[93] showing values shared by the (literate) executive elite of the Egyptian state and consequently centered on the access to the king and a successful discharge of duties of an executive administrator in varied governmental and similar roles. A sense of *maat* as the abstract principle is not always invoked theoretically, but demonstrated practically in good governance and care.[94] The substance[95] of the service may differ (fighting for and alongside the king, accompanying him, registering his campaigns, or organizing his court, his edifices, or his finances—great attention is paid to the actual details of the function, especially in texts dated to the period from Ahmose I to Amenhotep II) but the key elements of reliability, communication skills within and without the office—in short a dutiful, dedicated, and accountable service—remain the same.

A successful service required fulfilment of king's wishes, but not always in the royal presence (the herald Amunedjeh made a point of referring to his king's Syrian campaign, while he himself was in Memphis,[96] and other self-presentational texts suggest that the protagonist only appeared alongside his sovereign at a certain point of his campaign).[97] However, the reward and recognition were very much tied to the sovereign's presence.

Some of the personality traits considered advantageous or desirable, as well as skills used, had a more general interest that might have exceeded the social sphere of high positions of responsibility. The righteousness of superiors was to cause positive attitudes in their servants (sculptor Djehuty claimed that people worked happily for him)[98] and dependability of an inferior was to be rewarded also in the case of persons of originally lower status, for example, former prisoners of war (for example, Sibastet, barber of the king, adopts one such person as member of his family).[99]

Amarna

The inevitably exceptional element at the end of Eighteenth Dynasty is the Amarna Period. Some elements that came to a head after Amarna and in the early Ramesside Period, and that concern self-presentation, foremostly the personal piety, had longer roots. Deities appear in a more important role in the tomb representations in the second half of the Eighteenth Dynasty,[100] and the intense focus on the king and the court service and functions is already in the forefront in the reign of Amenhotep III, if not earlier. However, the Amarna intermezzo shows a decisive specificity. The Amarna tomb communications focus almost exclusively on the king and the interaction of the tomb owner with his sovereign. The emphasis is less on the 'I' of the tomb owner and his achievements but on 'He' the king, and what the king did for his (trusted) official, whose trustworthiness resides in doing what "issued from his (= the king's) mouth."[101] The Atenist hymn replaces other devotional texts, as the communication with other deities altogether disappears, as does the emphasis on the biographical element in the tomb,[102] except said court scenes.

If a plain definition were sought, then Amarna is perhaps actually somewhat uniform after previous changeable and diverse (both descriptively and conceptually) identities that only shared a set of beliefs and attitudes. An active loyalty that sought a fulfilment of the sovereign's wishes and of *maat* was replaced by a dominating adherence to an exclusive doctrine mediated by the king.[103]

Conclusions: Impression Management and Memory

What was the personality behind the elite Egyptian of the Eighteenth Dynasty? It was not preordained in a fixed pattern, although there are shared forms and shared principles, but there is also some flexibility in terms of how the social roles were carried out. The self-presentation as shown in written culture in this period emphasized a successful enculturation, socialization, and functioning within a community, with similar principles to the preceding periods,[104] but went to greater detail concerning both an occupational identity and personality traits that had to be enumerated, characterized in detail, and immortalized.[105] The literate Egyptian was eventually asserting his own self, especially in order to perpetuate a renowned remembrance—the ultimate battlefield of social competition seems to be the field of memory. A self-presentative act was balancing the need for competitive impression management against expectations of collective memory.

Throughout the Eighteenth Dynasty, careers developed and changed, literacy was emphasized by some but not all,[106] social mobility existed alongside inherited offices. The self was, also, fashioned in deference, or at least in relationship to the authorities (or to the concept of authority).[107] The dignitary or the literato was always a distinctive personality, consistent in his perceiving and behaving—his utter reliability and good character should have distinguished him, whether he was in a role of a dependent or in a role of superior. He was also obliged to be conciliatory and righteous, if strict, with his subordinates.

Both authorities and character of relationship to them changed throughout the Eighteenth Dynasty, chiefly in the post-Amarna Period. It may be excessive to suggest that the Eighteenth Dynasty brought such a swerve as that suggested by Greenblatt for the European Renaissance as "a heightened awareness of the existence of alternative modes of social, theological, and psychological organization" accompanied dialectically by a "new dedication to the imposition of control upon those modes and ultimately to the destruction of alternatives."[108] And yet, the pre-Amarna expansion of Egyptian identities and the Amarna imposition on them and their following transformation echo an indication of such developments.

Notes

* The research was conducted within the Programme for the Development of Fields of Study of Charles University in Prague, no. 14: Archaeology of Non-European Areas, Sub-Programme Research of Ancient Egyptian Civilisation, Cultural and Political Adaptation of the North African Civilizations in Ancient History (5000 BC–AD 1000). The author gratefully acknowledges helpful comments and critique of the anonymous reviewers, and would also like to thank H. Bassir, the editor of this book, as well as colleagues and friends, especially N. Allon, C. di Biase-Dyson, and R. Landgráfová.

1 Texts may be found chiefly in *Urk.* IV., although the selection is not comprehensive; further documents of individual dignitaries were outlined in W. Helck, *Zur Verwaltung des Mittleren und Neuen Reichs* (Leiden, 1958); also in H. Guksch, *Königsdienst: Zur Selbstdarstellung der Beamten in der 18. Dynastie* (Heidelberg, 1994); for the late Eighteenth Dynasty and the specific military roles, also, A. M. Gnirs, *Militär und Gesellschaft: Ein Beitrag zur Sozialgeschichte des Neuen Reiches* (Heidelberg, 1996).

2 Cf., also, W. Wendrich, "Identity and Personhood," in W. Wendrich, ed., *Egyptian Archaeology* (Chichester, 2010), 200–19. Compare, also, the application of New Kingdom material culture studies in I. Shaw, "Identity and Occupation: How Did Individuals Define Themselves and Their Work in the Egyptian New Kingdom?" in J. Bourriau and J. Phillips, eds., *Invention and Innovation: The Social Context of Technological Change 2: Egypt, the Aegean and the Near East, 1650–1150 BC. Proceedings of a Conference Held at the McDonald Institute for Archaeological Research, Cambridge, 4–6 September 2002* (Oxford, 2004), 12–24. Some observations, also, M. Horbury, *Personal Identity and Social Power in New Kingdom and Coptic Egypt* (Oxford, 2009).

3 Cf. Wendrich, "Identity and Personhood," 209–10.

4 Compare, also, recent broader approaches, e.g., a division of domestic space as a social marker: K. Spence, "Settlement Structure and Social Interaction at el-Amarna," in M. Bietak, E. Czerny, and I. Forstner-Müller, eds., *Cities and Urbanism in Ancient Egypt: Papers from a Workshop in November 2006 at the Austrian Academy of Sciences* (Vienna, 2010), 289–98; and an attempt at identifying possible variations on the concept of prestige (including, but not limited to material social markers), albeit in a specific privileged community, G. Neunert, *Mein Grab, mein Esel, mein Platz in der Gesellschaft: Prestige im alten Ägypten am Beispiel Deir el-Medine* (Berlin, 2010).

5 As suggested by Wendrich, "Identity and Personhood," 213.

6 For the term borrowed from psychology, see a review in M.R. Leary and R.M. Kowalski, "Impression Management: A Literature Review and Two-Component Model," Psychological Bulletin 107.1 (1990), 34–47. For details of the concept, see E. Goffman, *The Presentation of Self in Everyday Life* (New York, 1959).

7 See, e.g., D. Valbelle, "La notion d'identité dans l'Égypte pharaonique," in Anonymous, ed., *Sesto Congresso internazionale di egittologia: atti* 2 (Turin, 1993), 551–56.

8 Valbelle, "La notion d'identité," 555; J. Assmann, *Sonnenhymnen in thebanischen Gräbern* (Mainz, 1983), XVI.

9 Assmann, *Sonnenhymnen*, XIVff. with further references.

10 Identities and aspects of social behavior in correspondence were addressed by D. Sweeney, *Correspondence and Dialogue: Pragmatic Factors in Late Ramesside Letter Writing* (Wiesbaden, 2001), and an attempt at a survey was presented also by Horbury, *Personal Identity and Social Power*, 21ff. Both publications, however, are chiefly concerned with the Ramesside Period.

11 See, further, e.g., M. Hartwig, *Tomb Painting and Identity in Ancient Thebes, 1419–1372 BCE* (Turnhout, 2004).
12 S. Greenblatt, *Renaissance Self-Fashioning* (Chicago, 1980), 2.
13 See, also A. Gnirs, "Die ägyptische Autobiographie," in A. Loprieno, ed., *Ancient Egyptian Literature: History and Forms* (Leiden, 1996), 191–241.
14 Cf. methodological and theoretical issues connected with the aspect of gender in Egypt—C. Eyre, "Source Mining in Egyptian Texts: The Reconstruction of Social and Religious Behaviour in Pharaonic Egypt," in A. Verbovsek, B. Backes, and C. Jones, eds., *Methodik und Didaktik in der Ägyptologie: Herausforderungen eines kulturwissenschaftlichen Paradigmenwechsels in den Altertumswissenschaften* (Mainz, 2011), 599–615; D. Sweeney, "Sex and Gender," in E. Frood and W. Wendrich, eds., *UCLA Encyclopedia of Egyptology* (Los Angeles, 2011), http://digital2.library.ucla.edu/viewItem.do?ark=21198/zz0027fc04. A contribution with different viewpoints, also, G. Robins, "Gender and Sexuality," in M.K. Hartwig, ed., *A Companion to Ancient Egyptian Art* (Chichester, 2015), 120–40.
15 Family statues, see, also, F. Kampp, *Die Thebanische Nekropole*, I (Mainz, 1996), 49.
16 Alongside visual representations, see, Hartwig, *Tomb Painting and Identity in Ancient Thebes*, 93–95.
17 Also, A. Hermann, *Die Stelen der Thebanischen Felsgräber der 18. Dynastie* (Glückstadt, 1940), 67ff.
18 S. Whale, *The Family in the Eighteenth Dynasty of Egypt: A Study of the Representation of the Family in Private Tombs* (Sydney, 1991), 257.
19 Compare, also, Whale, *The Family in the Eighteenth Dynasty of Egypt*, and B. Engelmann-von Carnap, *Die Struktur des Thebanischen Beamtenfriedhofs in der ersten Hälfte der 18. Dynastie: Analyse von Position, Grundrißgestaltung und Bildprogramm der Gräber* (Berlin, 1999), 408ff.
20 Treating most female non-administrative titles as honorary or ranking may perhaps be too dismissive, although it may largely be attributed to insufficient knowledge of tasks or job descriptions of the ladies.
21 In some categories, such as rock inscriptions and similar monuments, the differences can amount to significant numbers—the corpus of Aswan monuments mapped by S.J. Seidlmayer and his team and analyzed by A. Herzberg contained 96 men and 5 women. A. Herzberg, "Felsinschriften und -bilder als Medium der Selbstrepräsentation lokaler Amtsträger des Neuen Reiches: Ein Befund aus der Aswâner Region," in G. Neunert, A. Verbovsek, and K. Gabler, eds., *Bild: Ästhetik - Medium – Kommunikation: Beiträge des dritten Münchner Arbeitskreises Junge Ägyptologie* (Wiesbaden, 2013), 137–54, esp. 141–42. The situation is different in the Ramesside period and in specific communities such as Deir al-Medina, but the subject matter is not fully comparable. For the Ramesside women of Deir al-Medina, see J. Toivari-Viitala, *Women at Deir el-Medina: A Study of the Status and Roles of the Female Inhabitants in the Workmen's Community during the Ramesside Period* (Leiden, 2001), with comprehensive references.

22 See P.F. Dorman, "Family Burial and Commemoration in the Theban Necropolis," in N. Strudwick and J.H. Taylor, *The Theban Necropolis: Past, Present and Future* (London, 2003), 41.

23 C.H. Roehrig, "The Eighteenth Dynasty Titles Royal Nurse (*mnʿt nswt*), Royal Tutor (*mnʿ nswt*) and Foster Brother/Sister of the Lord of the Two Lands (*sn/snt mnʿ n nb t3wy*)" (PhD Diss., Univ. of California, Berkeley, 1990), esp. 318f.

24 Compare the statue of Sitre, royal nurse of Hatshepsut, see C.H. Roehrig, "The Statue of the Royal Nurse Sitre with her Nursling Maatkare Hatshepsut," in M. Eldamaty and M. Trad, eds., *Egyptian Museum Collections around the World*, II (Cairo, 2002), 1003–10; also, H.E. Winlock, "The Museum's Excavations at Thebes: 1. Excavations at the Temple of Hatshepsut," *BMMA* 27 (1932), 5, 10.

25 J.F. Quack, *Die Lehren des Ani: Ein neuägyptischer Weisheitstext in seinem kulturellen Umfeld* (Freiburg, 1994), 105, 171.

26 Compare the gender debate: Sweeney, "Sex and Gender," T. Wilfong, "Gender in Ancient Egypt," in W. Wendrich, ed., *Egyptian Archaeology* (Chichester, 2010), 164–79, T. Wilfong, "Gender and Sexuality," in T. Wilkinson, ed., *The Egyptian World* (London, 2007), 205–17.

27 Among many examples see an exemplification of a combination of visual and written message in J. Assmann, "Bild und Schrift: Interdependenz and komplementäre Multimedialität," in J. Assmann. *Stein und Zeit* (Munich, 2003), 3rd edition, 81–85 (demonstrated on material from the tomb of Paheri), followed by R.J. Leprohon, "A Wall for all Seasons: The Funerary Chapel of Pahery at El Kab," *KMT* 24.3 (2013), 49–58. See, also, the classic outline, based, however, in part on pre-New Kingdom material, by H.G. Fischer, *L'écriture et l'art de l'Égypte ancienne: quatre leçons sur la paléographie et l'épigraphie pharaoniques* (Paris, 1986).

28 Outline of themes in L. Manniche, *Lost Tombs: A Study of Certain Eighteenth Dynasty Monuments in the Theban Necropolis* (London, 2010); changes in tomb plan and larger schemes in Kampp, *Thebanische Nekropole*, I, passim. Analysis of themes in Hartwig, *Tomb Painting and Identity.*

29 Detailed list in A. Radwan, *Die Darstellungen des regierenden Königs und seiner Familienangehörigen in den Privatgräbern der 18. Dynastie* (Berlin, 1969).

30 L. Gestermann, "Die Überlieferung der Sargtexte nach dem Mittleren Reich," in C.J. Eyre, ed., *Proceedings of the Seventh International Congress of Egyptologists, Cambridge, 3–9 September 1995* (Leuven, 1998), 437–46. See also B. Lüscher, *Die Vorlagen-Ostraka aus dem Grab des Nachtmin (TT 87)* (Basel, 2013).

31 Liturgies, defined so by J. Assmann, an unpublished lecture as quoted by P.F. Dorman, *Monuments of Senenmut* (London, 1988), 82–83.

32 Book of the Dead was used selectively during Eighteenth Dynasty, see M. Saleh, *Das Totenbuch in den Thebanischen Beamtengräbern des Neuen Reiches* (Mainz, 1984), 95. The dominant resource remained the Coffin Texts, but passages from the Pyramid Texts are also well attested.

33 A later example shown by C. Traunecker, "The 'Funeral Palace' of Padiamenope: Tomb, Place of Pilgrimage, and Library: Current Research," in E. Pischikova, J. Budka, and K. Griffin, eds., *Thebes in the First Millennium BC* (Newcastle upon Tyne, 2014), 205–34. We lack such explicit material for the New Kingdom, yet the role of tombs as repositories of cultural texts and other representations seems highly likely—see A. Den Doncker, "Theban Tomb Graffiti during the New Kingdom: Research on the Reception of Ancient Egyptian Images by Ancient Egyptians," in A.K. Kothay, ed., *Art and Society: Ancient and Modern Contexts of Egyptian Art: Proceedings of the International Conference Held at the Museum of Fine Arts, Budapest, 13–15 May 2010* (Budapest, 2012), 23–34, in context of older royal edifices; also Hana Navratilova, "Thutmoside graffiti and Thutmoside traditions: a view from Memphis," in Todd Gillen, ed., *(Re)productive traditions in ancient Egypt: proceedings of the conference held at the University of Liège, 6th–8th February 2013* (Liège: Presses universitaires de Liège, 2017), 537–61.

34 Compare changing popularity of various parts of the Theban necropolis throughout the Middle and New Kingdom, Dorman, *Monuments of Senenmut*, 85.

35 C.H. Roehrig, "The Tomb of Maiherperi in the Valley of the Kings," in C.H. Roehrig, R. Dreyfus, and C.A. Keller, eds., *Hatshepsut: From Queen to Pharaoh* (New York, 2005), 70–72, with further references.

36 Assmann, *Sonnenhymnen*, XI.

37 J. Assmann, "Schrift, Tod und Identität: Das Grab als Vorschule der Literatur im alten Ägypten," in A. Assmann, J. Assmann, and C. Hardmeier, eds., *Schrift und Gedächtnis: Beiträge zur Archäologie der literarischen Kommunikation* (Munich, 1983), 64–93.

38 Assmann, *Sonnenhymnen*, XV- XVII.

39 Summed up in Kampp, *Thebanische Nekropole*, I, 54–55, with further references.

40 Assmann, *Sonnenhymnen*, XVI, Hermann, *Stelen*. Also Kampp, *Thebanische Nekropole*, I, 75f., stelae located in the courtyard.

41 Cf. outline of tomb communication functions in Kampp, *Thebanische Nekropole*, I, 117–19.

42 Categories of self-presentation outlined in Gnirs, "Ägyptische Autobiographie".

43 The distinction probably realized by the tomb owner in the calls addressing priesthood and scribes knowledgeable in god's words (e.g., *Urk*. IV, 509, TT 127, Senemiah), or, at least, "capable scribes".

44 On communication spaces see summarily S.J. Seidlmayer, "Frohe—und andere—Botschaften: Kult und Kommunikation im alten Ägypten," in U. Peter and S.J. Seidlmayer, eds., *Mediengesellschaft Antike? Information und Kommunikation vom Alten Ägypten bis Byzanz; altertumswissenschaftliche Vortragsreihe an der Berlin-Brandenburgischen Akademie der Wissenschaften* (Berlin, 2006), 93–111.

45 For an outline see *PM* V, 213–16.
46 *PM* V, 248.
47 *PM* V, 249.
48 *Urk.* IV, 532ff. *PM* VII, 351.
49 Compare further Herzberg, "Felsinschriften und -bilder." On a related topic of interacting with deities in a sacred space using different written media in diverse registers: Elizabeth Frood, "Le vite del tempio: devozione, pietà e il divino," in P. Giovetti and D. Picchi, eds., *Egitto: Splendore millenario: la collezione di Leiden a Bologna* (Milan: Skira, 2015), 316–23; and E. Frood, "Temple lives: devotion, piety, and the divine," in P. Giovetti and D. Picchi, eds., *Egypt: Millenary Splendour: The Leiden Collection in Bologna* (Milano: Skira, 2016), 316–23.
50 Shorter texts and graffiti of Nubian viceroys near Aswan, see, also *PM* V, 252–53.
51 Beginning with the road from Aswan, Island of Biga (*PM* V, 255–65).
52 Cf. outline in Gnirs, "Ägyptische Autobiographie," 199.
53 The privilege was accorded both to men and to women in devoted royal service, cf. Roehrig, "The Statue of the Royal Nurse Sitre with her Nursling Maatkare Hatshepsut."
54 A collection of tomb and statue texts of Kenamun *Urk.* IV, no. 421. The reference to offerings *Urk.* IV, 1398ff.
55 Dorman, *Monuments of Senenmut*, 125, C. Meyer, *Senenmut: Eine prosopographische Untersuchung* (Hamburg, 1982), 169–70.
56 *Urk.* IV. 1829.9, *PM* II, 2, 88, and H. Sourouzian, "La statue d'Amenhotep fils de Hapou, âgé, un chef-d'oeuvre de la XVIIIè dynastie," in *MDAIK* 47 (1991), 341–55.
57 CG 42114, l. 12, translation Dorman, *Monuments*, 125.
58 A. Kjølby, "Decision-Making Processes: A Cognitive Study of Private Statues in New Kingdom Temples," in J.-C. Goyon and C. Cardin, eds., *Proceedings of the Ninth International Congress of Egyptologists: Grenoble, 6–12 septembre 2004*, I (Leuven, 2007), 991–1000. Also A. Kjølby, "Material Agency, Attribution and Experience of Agency in Ancient Egypt: The Case of New Kingdom Private Temple Statues," in R. Nyord and A. Kjølby, eds., *"Being in Ancient Egypt": Thoughts on Agency, Materiality and Cognition; Proceedings of the Seminar Held in Copenhagen, September 29–30, 2006* (Oxford, 2009), 31–46.
59 Kjølby, "Material agency, attribution and experience," 35.
60 Cf. Wendrich, "Identity and Personhood," 210.
61 See an outline of the furniture study in H.G. Fischer, "Möbel," *LÄ* IV, 180–89, also Fischer, *L' écriture et l'art*, 169–249. Texts clearly shown e.g., on furniture of Kha (Deir al-Medina), Sennefer (Deir al-Medina), but also Yuya and Thuya (Valley of the Kings) to mention only select nonroyal contexts.
62 The whip handle of captain Nebiri was almost certainly in active use and it would perhaps be somewhat forced to assume that the captain's favorite disciplining tool would have been marked with his name only after his death. See P.F. Dorman, "Whip Handle of Nebiri," in C.H. Roehrig, R. Dreyfus, and C.A. Keller, eds., *Hatshepsut: From Queen to Pharaoh* (New York, 2005), 56.

63 Offering and similar texts located on the palettes, e.g., S.R.K. Glanville, "Scribes' Palettes in the British Museum part 1," *JEA* (1932), 18, 53–61, text inscribed probably posthumously by a colleague, p. 57.

64 The importance of which is also demonstrated by their presence in tomb decoration, burial equipment, and even in the hand of the tomb owner; compare also N. Allon, "Writing, Violence and the Military: Visualizing Literacies at the Time of Horemhab (1550–1295 BCE)," (PhD diss., Yale Univ., 2014); B. Bryan, "Evidence for Female Literacy from Theban Tombs of the New Kingdom," *BES* 6 (1984), 17-32.

65 The concept of landscape as a cultural category was exemplified by S. Schama, *Landscape and Memory* (London, 1995), and may be adapted for the ancient material.

66 J.C. Darnell, *Theban Desert Road Survey II: The Rock Shrine of Pahu, Gebel Akhenaton, and Other Rock Inscriptions from the Western Hinterland of Qamula* (New Haven, CT, 2014).

67 See also further A. Garnett, "'Landscape Is Time Materialising': A Study of Embodied Experience and Memory in Egypt's Eastern Desert," in A.M. Chadwick and C.D. Gibson, eds., *Memory, Myth and Long-term Landscape Inhabitation* (Oxford, 2013), 226–39; also, H. Köpp, "Desert Travel and Transport in Ancient Egypt: An Overview Based on Epigraphic, Pictorial and Archaeological Evidence," in F. Förster and H. Riemer, eds., *Desert Road Archaeology in Ancient Egypt and Beyond* (Cologne, 2013), 107–32.

68 For a survey of graffiti interpretation, see most recently: C. Ragazzoli, Ö. Harmanşah, C. Salvador, and E. Frood, eds., *Scribbling through History: Graffiti, Places and People from Antiquity to Modernity* (London, 2018).

69 For visitors' and similar graffiti see M. Marciniak, *Deir El Bahari*, I: Les inscriptions hiératiques du temple de Thoutmosis III (Varsovie, 1974); and A.J. Peden, *The Graffiti of Pharaonic Egypt: Scope and Roles of Informal Writings (c. 3100–332 B.C.)* (Leiden, 2001); also H. Navratilova, *Visitors' Graffiti of Dynasties 18 and 19 in Abusir and Northern Saqqara. With Survey of Visitors' Graffiti in Giza, Southern Saqqara, Dahshur and Maidum* (Liverpool, 2015), 60–62, with further references.

70 Compare further E. Frood, "Egyptian temple graffiti and the gods: appropriation and ritualization in Karnak and Luxor," in D. Ragavan, ed., *Heaven on Earth: Temples, Ritual, and Cosmic Symbolism in the Ancient World* (Chicago, 2013), 285–318.

71 Compare K.E. Piquette and R.D. Whitehouse, "Introduction: Developing an Approach to Writing as Material Practice," in K.E. Piquette and R.D. Whitehouse, eds., *Writing as Material Practice: Substance, Surface and Medium* (London, 2013), 1–13.

72 A graffito by a scribe Amenemhat, located in the Step Pyramid complex, in Navratilova, *Visitors' Graffiti of Dynasties 18 and 19*, 156–58.

73 Manuscripts of Eighteenth Dynasty listed in S. Quirke, "Archive," in A. Loprieno, ed., *Ancient Egyptian Literature: History and Forms* (Leiden, 1996), 388, 392.

74 Ostraca identified, e.g., in Western Thebes, Quirke, "Archive," 392, see, further, R.B. Parkinson, *Reading Ancient Egyptian Poetry Among Other Histories* (Chichester, 2009), 178–81, texts of Sinuhe and Instruction of Amenemhat I read by the Theban elite and subelite. For a discussion on their dating see G. Moers, K. Widmaier, A. Giewekemeyer, A. Lümers, and R. Ernst, eds., *Dating Egyptian Literary Texts, Lingua Aegyptia, Studia Monographica* 11 (Hamburg, 2013).

75 K. Jansen-Winkeln, "Lebenslehre und Biographie," *ZÄS* 131 (2004), 59–72.

76 Translations in E. Wente, *Letters from Ancient Egypt* (Atlanta, 1990), 90–92, with further references.

77 Especially P. BM 10102.

78 Stela Boston MFA 25.632, *editio princeps* W. Helck, "Eine Stele des Vizekönigs Wsr-st.t," *JNES* 14.1 (1955), 22–31; see, also, P.D. Manuelian, *Studies in the Reign of Amenophis II* (Hildesheim, 1987), 157–58; see, also, C. Vandersleyen, *L'Egypte et la vallée du Nil 2 – de la fin de l'Ancien Empire à la fin du Nouvel Empire* (Paris, 1995), 330–31.

79 Dorman, *Monuments of Senenmut*, 110. However, compare observations by H. Bassir, *Image and Voice in Saite Egypt: Self-presentation of Neshor Named Psamtikmenkhib and Payeftauemawyneith*, Wilkinson Egyptology Series 2 (Tucson, AZ, 2014).

80 L.D. Morenz, "Tomb Inscriptions: The Case of the I versus Autobiography in Ancient Egypt," *Human Affairs* 13 (2003), 179–96.

81 See, for instance, C. di Biase-Dyson, "Amenemheb's Excellent Adventure in Syria," in G. Neunert, H. Simon, A. Verbovsek, and K. Gabler, eds., *Text, Wissen, Wirkung, Wahrnehmung: Beiträge des vierten Münchner Arbeitskreises Junge Ägyptologie (MAJA 4)*, 29.11. bis 1.12.2013. Göttinger Orientforschungen, 4. Reihe: Ägypten 59. Wiesbaden: Harrassowitz, 2015), 121–50.

82 See also Goffman, *The Everyday Presentation of Self.*

83 Menkheper, Nakhtmin (TT 87), Ptahmose (stela Lyon 88), Pehsuker (TT 88), and others, Cf. summary in B. Cumming, *Egyptian Historical Records of the Later 18th Dynasty*, III (Warminster, 1984), 197–206, with further references.

84 A comprehensive edition by G.F. van den Boorn, *The Duties of the Vizier: Civil Administration in the Early New Kingdom* (London, New York, 1988).

85 C. Salvador, "From the Realm of the Dead to the House of the God: The New Kingdom Appeals to the Living in Context at Thebes," in A. Kelly, R. Fellinger, S. Musselwhite, P.L. Conçalves, and W. Paul van Pelt, eds., *Current Research in Egyptology 2013: Proceedings of the Fourteenth Annual Symposium, University of Cambridge, United Kingdom, March 19–22, 2013* (Oxford, 2014), 153–67, containing references to preceding studies.

86 *Urk.* IV 1ff.

87 TT 181, *Urk.* IV, 53ff.

88 *Urk.* IV, 40ff.

89 Connections of the vizieral family, see Dorman, "Family Burial and Commemoration."

90 See, also, J. Baines, "Ancient Egypt," in A. Feldherr and G. Hardy, eds., *The Oxford History of Historical Writing*, I: *Beginnings to AD 600* (Oxford, 2011), 53–75; C. Eyre, *The Use of Documents in Pharaonic Egypt* (Oxford, 2013), 286–98.

91 Amenhotep son of Nakhtmin, palette BM 12786, or TT 131, Useramun, installation of a new vizier. Cross-referencing of family members: TT 83, Ahmose Ametju, father to Useramun (also TT 61) and Rekhmire (TT 100), viziers, *Urk.* IV, 490ff. On Useramun, also, E. Dziobek, "Theban Tombs as a Source for Historical and Biographical Evaluation: The Case of User-Amun," in J. Assmann, E. Dziobek, H. Guksch, and F. Kampp, eds., *Thebanische Beamtennekropolen: Neue Perspektiven archäologischer Forschung. Internationales Symposion, Heidelberg, 9.–13.6.1993* (Heidelberg, 1995), 129–40.

92 Senenmut, JE 47278 or Berlin 2296, Meyer, *Senenmut: Untersuchungen*, 161–63; Dorman, *Monuments*, 188, 192–93.

93 E.g., an interplay of the royal propaganda and corresponding elite social identity was analyzed by Guksch, *Königsdienst* and D.B. Redford, *Wars in Syria and Palestine of Thutmose III* (Leiden, 2003), 165ff.

94 Compare, also, J. Assmann, *Ma'at: Gerechtigkeit und Unsterblichkeit im Alten Ägypten* (Munich, 1990), 213–24.

95 See also Ramesside examples of group roles and identities discussed by E. Frood, "Role-play and group biography in Ramessid stelae from the Serapeum," in R. Landgráfová and J. Mynářová, eds., *Rich and Great: Studies in Honour of Anthony J. Spalinger on the Occasion of his 70th Feast of Thot* (Prague, 2016), 69–87.

96 See references to the Amunedjeh graffito above.

97 See di Biase-Dyson, "Amenemheb's Excellent Adventure."

98 *Urk.* IV, 130ff.

99 *Urk.* IV, 1396; compare, also, observations by M. Horbury on a self-fashioned, accultured identity that was open to the foreigners in Egypt (summing up several previous surveys) Horbury, *Personal Identity and Social Power.*

100 Kampp, *Thebanische Nekropole*, I, 76, 116–19.

101 Compare W.J. Murnane, *Texts from the Amarna Period in Egypt* (Atlanta, 1995), 107–204.

102 J. Assmann, "The Ramesside Tomb and the Construction of Sacred Space," in N. Strudwick and J.H. Taylor, eds., *The Theban Necropolis: Past, Present and Future* (London, 2003), 46–52, esp. 51.

103 Gnirs, "Ägyptische Autobiographie" 230–31, and on the the Amarna change in particular 232–33; Guksch, *Königsdienst*, 29–39, 62–65, 73–77.

104 See J. Assmann, "Persönlichkeitsbegriff und –bewusstsein," *LÄ* IV, 966–968.

105 Gnirs, "Ägyptische Autobiographie," 228–33. Compare, also, S.-A. Naguib, "Mémoire de soi: autobiographie et identité en ancienne Égypte," in E. Wardini, ed., *Built on Solid Rock: Studies in Honour of Professor Ebbe Egede Knudsen on the Occasion of His 65th Birthday, April 11th 1997* (Oslo, 1997), 216–25.

106 Allon, "Writing, Violence and the Military."

107 Greenblatt, *Self-Fashioning*, 9.

108 Greenblatt, *Self-Fashioning*, 2.

9

Self-Presentation in the Ramesside Period*

Colleen Manassa Darnell

O people who are discerning in their hearts, who exist,
who are upon earth,
and who will come after me,
for millions and millions (of years), after hoary old age,
whose hearts are skilled in recognizing worth,
I will cause you to know my character when (I) was upon earth,
in every office which I performed since my birth.[1]

The ancient Egyptians possessed no term for such concepts as 'art,' 'history,' or 'religion,' so it is unsurprising that the concept of 'self-presentation' lacks a corresponding word in the Egyptian lexicon. Nevertheless, just as the ancient Egyptians were consummate artists, wrote their own historical texts and historical fiction, and expressed in innumerable icons and texts the tenets of the longest visually and textually traceable religion, so they also practiced self-presentation, albeit with greater frequency during certain periods of their history. If one examines the concept of the 'self' for the ancient Egyptians, the underlying complexity and richness of material suggests an explanation for the lack of so specific and limiting a term as *self-presentation*. In the tomb of Amenemhat (Theban Tomb 82, reign of Thutmose III), two unique offering scenes list the components of the tomb owner's personhood:[2] *kꜣ*-spirit, fate (*šꜣy*), lifetime (*ʿḥʿ*), *ꜣḫ*-spirit, body (*ẖ3t*), shadow (*šwt*), and all of his manifestations (*ḫprw.f nb*).[3] A full exploration of the definition of each of these components of personhood is beyond the scope of the present work, but their contours provide a framework for understanding what the Egyptians conceived of as the self. The self had both a personal and social identity, much like the *b3*-soul embodied individual personality traits, while the *k3*-soul represented family or social traits.[4] Personal efficacy, represented by the *3ḫ*-soul, may be compared to more modern notions of agency.[5] It is the unity of these diverse elements—individual and corporate identities combining with personal acumen and achievements—that makes the Egyptian self, which then may find representation through text and image in tombs and temples.

Returning to Amenemhat's list of personal attributes, both offering scenes in his tomb state that offerings are presented not just to his *k3*, *b3*, and *3ḫ*, but to another element of Amenemhat's self: *ʿb3.f* (his stela),[6] which is clearly not part of his body, but certainly provides a means of self-expression. The stela was a means of self-presentation, a place where tomb visitors could read someone's titles and epithets as they interacted with his or her monument—the stela can be the nexus between this world and the next, the focus of reciprocity between the actions of the living and the corresponding benefactions of the deceased.[7] The inclusion of Amenemhat's stela among his personal attributes to which one could offer indicates that Egyptian notions of the self and self-presentation were, thus, inextricably intertwined. Although self-presentational material appears already—albeit in a skeletal and titular form—in the inscriptions of the late Third/early Fourth Dynasty official Metjen, and sees some particularly idiosyncratic manifestations during the Middle Kingdom,[8] the New Kingdom (and in particular the Ramesside Period) is rich in monuments of self-presentation.

Self-presentation in ancient Egypt incorporates not only the genre of (auto)biography, but also the artistic and architectural context of any textual material[9] as well as anepigraphic representations of self.[10] During the Ramesside Period, self-presentation continues the career-oriented biographies of the Eighteenth Dynasty, but can transform these event-based texts into psychological evaluations of those events. In some cases, we appear to witness a transformation of a self-presentational text into a memoir: "[n]ot as ambitious as traditional autobiography in the goal of telling the whole life, memoirs tend to centre on significant moments of a life and use the devices of prose fiction to narrate those moments."[11] Ramesside self-presentation within (auto)biographical texts emphasizes how an individual's career and life-choices impact his relationship to the divine—within tombs and statues dedicated to temples, and increasingly upon the walls of the temples themselves as the Twentieth Dynasty progresses, Ramesside self-presentation transforms an individual's life into an act of devotion.[12]

Self-Presentation of the Deceased: Funerary Contexts

Ramesside tombs, in their architecture and decoration, display multiple developments from earlier Eighteenth Dynasty sepulchers.[13] Temple architecture, including pylons and columned halls, was adopted for large tomb complexes of the late Eighteenth Dynasty at Saqqara, most famously in the tomb of Horemhab;[14] in the Ramesside Period, such tombs continued to be built at Saqqara (for example, the tomb of Tia and Tia), and on the west bank of Thebes, rock-cut tombs could be augmented with large colonnaded courtyards and pylons, albeit poorly preserved now.[15]

In the exceptional case of the tomb of Imiseba (TT 65), a reused Eighteenth Dynasty tomb was transformed—through its additional, Twentieth Dynasty painted decoration—into "a royal memorial temple context for the purpose of integrating his [Imiseba's] own mortuary cult within it."[16] Two scenes of Ramesses IX offering to the barques of the Theban triad and the barque of Amun, icons of the temple, not traditionally part of the funerary sphere, signal that the columned, transverse hall in the tomb is functioning as the hypostyle hall of a temple; such an identification is enhanced by the prototype for the scene of Ramesses IX offering to the barque of Amun: Seti I burning incense before the barque of Amun in the Hypostyle Hall of Karnak Temple.[17] Imiseba, whose titles included "chief of the temple archives of the estate of Amun," is thus presenting himself both as an initiate with access to the iconography of interior temple walls and as a keeper of that temple's archives, which would have included the templates for the temple's own decoration.[18] Although not (auto)biographical in the sense of focusing on stages and events in the tomb owner's career, the tomb-as-temple of Imiseba emphasizes his knowledge and priestly status.

Decoration within more typical Ramesside tombs enhanced the 'sacralization' of the funerary space—most often, two continuous registers of scenes depict the interaction of the deceased with the gods (above) and funerary rituals (below);[19] thus, the few Ramesside self-presentational texts that appear within such cultically charged spaces focus on the individual's interactions with deities, such as the multifaceted 'autobiography' of Samut-Kyky (TT 409), which begins as a third-person "Tale of Samut" and ends with a hymn extolling the protective powers of Mut.[20] The self-presentation of Djehutyemheb (TT 194) contains an equally remarkable 'conversation' between the tomb owner and his patron goddess, Hathor, who refers to herself with the nickname "Hely."[21]

Changing textual descriptions of death in the Ramesside Period can be expressed in lamentations that essentially deny the efficacy of funerary rituals—death becomes a dark and lonely existence.[22] The insistence of (auto) biographical texts, such as that of Samut-Kyky, on the physical aspects of the afterlife might be rooted in such transformations of funerary belief.[23] A similar motivation may lie behind the transition in tomb decoration during the Ramesside Period, which de-emphasizes the 'professional' scenes of the Eighteenth Dynasty in favor of ritual activities and interactions with the divine in the Nineteenth and Twentieth Dynasties. The presentation of self as an individual deserving of eternal salvation becomes ever more significant during the Ramesside Period. Thus, the tomb as locus of self-presentation in this period must be considered in the context of later visitors to the decorated chambers.

On the west bank of ancient Thebes, the necropoleis were integrated into the larger cultic landscape of temples of millions of years (mortuary temples), and in exceptional cases, New Kingdom tombs could themselves become stopping points for festival processions, such as the Beautiful Festival of the Valley.[24] In such cases, the tomb as locus for self-presentation extended beyond one's own descendants to a wider swath of pious individuals; even if a tomb was not directly associated with a processional route, it could be a focus for later visitors, a pilgrimage destination that provided a physical space and surfaces for a conversation through time—a dialogue between the tomb owner's original act of self-presentation and future scribal acts of self-presentation in graffiti.[25]

As a transitional situation between Ramesside graffiti in Egyptian tombs and the practice of votive surcharging in temple contexts, one may note the interesting corpus of graffiti located within Memphite contexts, situated on surfaces of royal monuments of the necropolis. The graffiti—mostly *dipinti*[26]—are visitor's inscriptions[27] that name both the visitor and the owner of the monument being admired. A similar phenomenon appears within the Theban necropolis, with certain earlier tombs becoming the focus of scribal visits and the use of graffiti to present their veneration for the past, as well as boast of their literacy: [28]

> [I]t is highly significant that the practice of visitors' inscription, which was limited in time to the 18th and 19th dynasties, is almost exactly contemporaneous with the elaboration of a scribal identity and ideals in a range of texts that can be called "scribal literature", including the *Late Egyptian Miscellanies* and related compositions. The social identity of the graffitists, in other words the identity that they choose to emphasize

when visiting a tomb and leaving a visitors' inscription is the one of *sš*-scribe, "the one who can write."

In a First Intermediate Period tomb in the necropolis of Asyut (N13.1), more than two dozen New Kingdom graffiti incorporate literary texts of the classical, Middle Egyptian tradition, a perfect illustration of visitors showcasing their scribal knowledge in a chronologically appropriate setting.[29] The self-presentation of visitors' inscriptions is that of a literate individual who is knowledgeable about the history and literature of the past,[30] possessing an aesthetic appreciation for already ancient monuments, and desiring that this small evidence of his identity is recorded for all eternity.[31]

Self-Presentation and the Divine: Temple Contexts

Ramesside temples—from the elaborate and monumental complex at Karnak to the simple rock-shrine at Timna—provided abundant opportunities for self-presentation. Even seemingly ephemeral actions, such as prayer or participation within a festival, could be recorded within a temple context[32] or even in a private shrine within a desert landscape.[33] Votive surcharging, more commonly called graffiti,[34] within temple contexts provides expressions of personal devotion to a divinity. Even the simple outlines of a sandal could function as a form of self-expression and memorialization,[35] and the leaving of one's name or footprints on a temple roof enabled a lower-ranking priest to accrue the same divine benefits as the higher-ranking officials who could afford to place private statues within the temple.[36] While inscriptional votive material attests to male self-presentation within the temple sphere, votive *objects*, often humble, may provide a corresponding activity for female worshipers in specific contexts.[37]

Private statuary placed within temple contexts represented a form of distributed personhood: "the statues should be seen not simply as images of the individuals represented, but as (detached) parts of their distributed person, i.e., personhood distributed or extended in the milieu, beyond the body-boundary."[38] Inscriptions on the statuary dedicated to temples could include a resume of official positions, a description of beneficent actions in such offices,[39] or a narrative of participation in ritual events.[40] The statues can be of truly monumental proportions, such as the pillar statue of the high priest of Osiris Wennefer (Louvre A. 66), and the appeals to the living that are often incorporated into the hieroglyphic inscriptions (as well as the standard *ḥtp di nsw* formulae) demand both an audience and reciprocal actions; for example, a block statue of the high priest of Amun Romaʿ-Roy from Karnak requests verbal and physical offerings:[41]

ḏd.f i ḥmw-nṯr itw-nṯr wꜥbw ꜥ3yw nw pr-Ỉmn
ḏ3mww ꜥš3yw ntyw r ḫpr
imi [ꜥnḫw n ḫnty.i ḳbḥw] n k3.i
sḫ3 rn.i m ḫrt-hrw
ir ḥtp di nsw n ḫnty.i
mi w3ḥ.i ib.i r irt 3ḫwt n Ỉmn

He says: "O priests, divine fathers, *wab*-priests, great ones of the domain of Amun,
and numerous generations who will come to be!
Give [garlands to my statue, libations] to my *k3*.
Remember my name in the course of the day.
Perform the offering ritual to my statue
in as much as I set my heart to performing benefactions for Amun"

The statue not only assists in the remembrance of Roma'-Roy's name, but is the specific locus of the offering ritual, creating a paragon of the concept of distributed personhood. In an exceptional case, the high priest of Amun Bakhenkhons, a stela describes his restoration of divine statues that was complemented by adding a statue of his own, *n mrwt di.tw mn.f mi ḳd.sn r nḥḥ ḥnꜥ ḏt m pr Ỉmn* 'in order that it (his statue) might be made enduring like them (the divine statues) forever and ever in the domain of Amun.'[42]

In addition to the texts written on the statues, elements of iconography may also signal important elements of identity. Possibly the most extreme examples of iconography in the service of self-presentation are the cuboid statues in the begging pose, their hands cupped to their mouths, which can be combined with an unusual representation of baldness.[43] The texts on these statues refer to men as a "bald one" associated with a manifestation of the goddess of the eye of the sun, most commonly Hathor, but also Isis, Mehyt, and Mut.[44] The role of these statues as mediators for their divine mistresses does not necessarily correspond to the career of the individual presented on his statue.[45] The statues' iconography and their texts—as in so many other cases of ancient Egyptian monuments—provide complementary perspectives,[46] allowing a single monument to present multiple aspects of a personality, combining their official career achievements with their moral character into a cohesive unity.

Another development of the Ramesside Period is the use of temple walls—especially the Temple of Karnak—to display inscriptions and reliefs of the high priests of Amun. While royal investiture texts could be prominent aspects of tomb decoration of Eighteenth Dynasty viziers[47] and a high official such as Senenmut could place an image of himself within the doorways of temples, including Deir el-Bahri and the temple of Mut at Karnak,[48] large-scale personal monuments on temple walls is a Nineteenth Dynasty innovation[49] that becomes increasingly bold towards the end of the Twentieth Dynasty. The self-presentational texts of the high priest of Amun Roma'-Roy carved on the Eighth Pylon at Karnak use an exterior wall that would have otherwise remained undecorated to vaunt his improvement of the temple (especially the *wabet*), thus, requesting offerings and verbal memorialization for his good deeds.[50] At the conclusion of the Twentieth Dynasty, the high priest of Amun Amunhotep commissioned texts and scenes around a doorway on the eastern wall of the open court between the seventh and eighth pylons of the north–south axis of Karnak Temple.[51] A hieroglyphic text inside the temple and the door jambs is complemented by two large reward scenes on the exterior wall, which flank an even more-monumental dual depiction of Amunhotep. A smaller inscription, almost certainly commissioned by Amunhotep (although his name is not preserved) on a Thutmoside shrine nearby offers another form of self-presentation within a temple context: one in which the high priest juxtaposes his successful career with a time of tribulations—a 'transgression'—that was ended through the intervention of Amun and the pharaoh.[52]

The existence of royal acquiescence to such private monuments in a context otherwise suited to pharaonic display (for example, military texts and reliefs) and interaction with divinities is unknowable with surviving evidence. However, the necessity of high priestly control over the Thebaid, far removed from the Ramesside capital at Pi-Ramesses, may indicate royal sponsorship of such personal display, rather than private abrogation of royal prerogatives on the part of the high priests.[53] The high priest Amunhotep's decision to feature his reward with the gold of honor in his monumental scenes in the Temple of Karnak may provide evidence for the former proposition, since the gold of honor is "the symbol of trust between the king and his official," and neither the representation of Ramesses IX as a statue nor the scale of the statue in Amunhotep's reliefs is out of proportion with earlier scenes.[54] A careful consideration of the multiple factors at work in the self-presentation of Ramesside high priests may thus provide clues to the more dramatic developments under Herihor,[55] who included the high priest title within his own royal cartouches and whose military power allowed the creation of a "state within a state"[56] in Upper Egypt.

The temple of Timna mentioned above is one of many cult areas incorporated into Egyptian settlements and fortresses in the far-flung Ramesside empire. Self-presentation by high officials and military commanders within these marginal areas display some interesting parallels with the high priestly co-opting of sacred spaces during the Nineteenth and Twentieth Dynasties. Nebre, the commander of the fortress of Zawiyet Umm el-Rakham during the reign of Ramesses II, dedicated a large (half–life-size) statue of himself holding a standard of Sakhmet as well as additional monuments: a naos with Sakhmet and Ptah and at least two stelae;[57] Snape has suggested that the intentional damage done to the name of Nebre on his monuments suggests that the military commander is an Egyptian Kurtz who overstepped his bounds and "may well, rather unwisely, have regarded this area as his own personal fiefdom."[58] While such a scenario fits well with modern conceptions of decorum and authority, it is important to emphasize that seemingly royal self-presentation per se may not have led to the *damnatio memoriae* of Nebre.[59] One can equally imagine a scenario in which a loyal Nebre was rewarded with specific monumental privileges and the ability to finance them, a situation overturned at a later date because of Nebre's official malfeasance or replacement by another commander, not because of his self-presentation.[60]

Self-Presentation in the Landscape: Rock Inscriptions

While the distribution of rock inscriptions within a landscape is inherently dependent upon the availability of stone suitable for carving, the ancient Egyptians did not simply seek out suitable flat surfaces, but intentionally chose specific locations for their epigraphic activities. Foremost among the rock artist's considerations was often the accessibility of a site, and the frequency with which it would be seen by later visitors; for this reason, rock inscriptions in an otherwise 'unmarked' landscape tend to cluster along ancient tracks.[61] Even when suitable stone is located a few meters from the road, a rougher surface will be utilized if it would be more easily seen by future travelers; this basic principle of rock art distribution coincides with the 'memory' function of inscriptions, equivalent to tomb chapels intended for visitation, particularly during annual festivals (for example, the Beautiful Festival of the Valley in Thebes). A second principle, in regions replete with suitable stone, such as the area of Aswan and the First Cataract, is that rock inscriptions will cluster in areas of religious significance, portions of the desert or islands sacred to a particular deity, or located near processional routes.[62] In other, less frequent, cases, an ancient rock artist could choose a location remote from existing tracks in order to create a sacred space, a personal shrine, within an otherwise unsocialized landscape.[63] Small votive offerings and shrines could serve as a modest form of distributed personhood within a sacred landscape devoid of large architectural features; *tꜣ dhnt*, the peak that rises above the west bank of Thebes and forms a dramatic backdrop to the Valley of the Kings, was sacred to Meretseger, and during the Ramesside Period, the tracks along her slopes could be the loci of votive cairns and shrines.[64]

As early as the Naqada II Period, rock art could be used to create self-presentation in a desert landscape—from images carved by hunters of themselves and their desert game to elaborate tableaux of royal ritual power, late Predynastic rock inscriptions demand a human audience to 'complete' the inscriptions.[65] Textual expressions dominate similar self-presentation in Old Kingdom quarrying expedition inscriptions, which commemorate personal achievements as well as emphasize family relationships, paralleling the presence of family members in tomb contexts.[66] By the time of the Ramesside Period, rock inscriptions in the Eastern and Western Deserts (the latter concentrated in the Thebaid) display similar functions. The major Nineteenth and Twentieth Dynasty inscriptions in Eastern Desert landscapes concentrate in quarrying regions (Wadi Hammamat, Gebel el-Silsila, and Wadi Allaqi) and record the names and titles of officials working within those areas. While no rock inscriptions are attested for the Nineteenth or Twentieth Dynasties in the turquoise mines in Sinai, stelae continue to be dedicated at Serabit el-Khadim during the Ramesside Period; since rock inscriptions can be called *wḏ* 'stela' as early as the First Intermediate Period,[67] the presence of Ramesside stelae, but lack of rock inscriptions, should not be interpreted as a meaningful difference in overall commemorative activity at the site. The greatest concentration of Ramesside rock inscriptions appears in the gebel of western Thebes, particularly in the Valley of the Kings, Valley of the Queens, and adjacent wadis that were easily accessible to the workmen of Deir el-Medina.[68] While most of the inscriptions were made by the workmen themselves, some inscriptions record visits by high officials who were on site to inspect the progress of royal tomb construction; in these cases, even a small hieratic inscription was a form of self-presentation, confirming duties properly discharged.

The inscription of the "second priest of Amun, Roma'"[69] atop the caravansary at Gebel Roma' (on the Farshut Road crossing the Qena Bend of the Nile) provides a potentially fascinating confirmation of the self-presentation of a priest in a temple inscription. If the Roma' of the rock inscription at Gebel Roma' is indeed Roma'-Roy, eventual high priest of Amun who left a self-presentational text on the Eighth Pylon of Karnak Temple,[70] which seems likely, then the rock inscription provides additional evidence for Roma'-Roy's statements about his craftsmanship and administrative abilities.[71]

Conclusions

The foregoing discussion has concentrated on three loci for self-presentation: tombs, temples, and rock inscription sites; in each case, self-presentation can take the form of an original dedication, such as a self-presentational text within one's own tomb, or of a surcharging of a pre-existing monument—another individual's tomb, a temple, or a rock-art location. Interestingly, one of the spaces that *appears* to be the least susceptible to self-presentation is within an active household, which may be as much due to the lack of evidence (outside of the community of Deir el-Medina) as to meaningful patterns of ancient Egyptian behavior. The lintels of New Kingdom elite houses could include the name and titles of the building's owner, paralleling self-presentational statements and expressions of loyalty to the king otherwise found in tomb contexts.[72] Within domestic contexts, the ancestor busts that embody the *3ḫ iḳr* (effective spirits) were (for the most part) intentionally devoid of individual features (for example, name or even gender), and, thus, represent the worship of deceased family members in a manner divorced from an ancestor's self-presentation.[73]

Notes

* I would like to dedicate this article to E. Frood, whose work on the Ramesside Period has been fundamental to understanding the self-presentation of so many ancient Egyptian individuals.

1 Excerpt from the self-presentational inscription of the high priest of Amun Bakenkhons—transl. E. Frood, *Biographical Texts from Ramessid Egypt* (Atlanta, 2007), 40–41.

2 N. Davies and A. Gardiner, *The Tomb of Amenemhet (No. 82)* (London, 1915), pls. XIX–XX, XXII–XXIII; the list also appears in *Urk.* IV 1060–61.

3 For the complete list, see also J. Gee, "A New Look at the Conception of the Human Being," in R. Nyord and A. Kjølby, eds., *'Being in Ancient Egypt': Thoughts on Agency, Materiality and Cognition, Proceedings of the Seminar Held in Copenhagen, September 29–30, 2006* (Oxford, 2009), 2. See, also, the overview of C. Riggs, "Body," in E. Frood and W. Wendrich, eds., *UCLA Encyclopedia of Egytpology*, https://escholarship.org/uc/item/8f21r7sj

4 J. Assmann, *Death and Salvation in Ancient Egypt* (Ithaca, 2005), 97: "The *ka*, however, was the vehicle of the vindication that restored the individual's status as a social person, which had been destroyed by death. In other words, the *ba* belonged to the physical sphere of the deceased, restoring his movement and his ability to take on form, while the *ka* belonged to his social sphere and restored his status, honor, and dignity." See also A. Loprieno, "Drei Leben nach dem Tod, Wieviele Seelen hatten die alten Ägypter?" in H. Guksch,

E. Hofmann, and M. Bommas, eds., *Grab und Totenkult im alten Ägypten* (Munich, 2003), 203–207.

5 L. Meskell, *Object Worlds in Ancient Egypt, Material Biographies Past and Present* (Oxford, 2004), 69–85. For ancestor busts, see also note 73 below.

6 Davies and Gardiner, *Tomb of Amenemhet*, pl. XIX; *Urk.* IV 1060.11 (locating the offering stone specifically within the necropolis) and 1061.4; the stela appears in the following sequence: "for his *k3*, for his stela, [... for] his [*b3*], for his *3ḫ*, for his corpse, for his shade, and for all of his manifestations."

7 H.M. Hays, "Between Identity and Agency in Ancient Egyptian Ritual," in Nyord and Kjølby, eds., *Being in Ancient Egypt* (Oxford, 2009) 21–24. A particularly powerful expression of the unity of self and offering place appears in the mastaba of Idu, where Idu emerges (visible from the waist up) below his false door, ready to accept his offerings (W.K. Simpson, *The Mastabas of Qar and Idu, G 7101 and 7102* (Boston, 1976), pl. XXIX).

8 Note particularly the significant self-presentation of the artist Irtysen in his stela (Louvre C12)—W. Barta, *Das Selbstzeugnis eines altägyptischen Künstlers [Stele Louvre C 14]* (Berlin, 1970); H.-W. Fischer-Elfert, "Das verschwiegene Wissen des Irtisen (Stele Louvre C14)," in J. Assman and M. Bommas, eds., *Ägyptische Mysterien?* (Munich, 2002), 27–35.

9 Compare J. Baines, "Egyptian Elite Self-Presentation in the Context of Ptolemaic Rule," in W.V. Harris and G. Ruffini, eds., *Ancient Alexandria between Egypt and Greece* (Leiden, 2004), 34–35: "I term these practices 'self-presentation,' rather than the more traditional 'biography' or 'autobiography,' both because they encompassed visual media at least as much as textual ones and because the visual and the textual existed in a social context that must have included ceremonies and performances in which a person's self was presented. The audience for those presentations included peers and—in the terms of the declared purpose of the artifacts—deities, the next world, and posterity."

10 For the relationship between the terms autobiography, biography, and self-presentation, see H. Bassir, *Image & Voice in Saite Egypt: Self-Presentations of Neshor Named Psamtikmenkhib and Payeftjauemawyneith* (Tucson, AZ, 2014), 5–11.

11 H. Buss, "Memoirs," in M. Jolly, ed., *Encyclopedia of Life Writing: Autobiographical and Biographical Forms*, http://search.credoreference.com/content/entry/routlifewrite/memoirs/0 (July 31, 2015).

12 Frood, *Biographical Texts from Ramessid Egypt*, 20–23; note, also, the overview of the issue of 'decorum' in self-presentation (particularly piety) in J. Baines and E. Frood, "Piety, Change and Display in the New Kingdom," in M. Collier and S. Snape, eds., *Ramesside Studies in Honour of K.A. Kitchen* (Bolton, 2011), 1–17.

13 E. Hofmann, *Bilder im Wandel: Die Kunst der ramessidischen Privatgräber* (Mainz, 2004); F. Kampp, *Die thebanische Nekropole: Zum Wandel des*

Grabgedankens von der XVIII. bis zur XX. Dynastie (Mainz am Rhein, 1996).

14 G. Martin, *The Hidden Tombs of Memphis: New Discoveries from the Time of Tutankhamun and Ramesses the Great* (London, 1991).

15 Temple-like features, as with tomb size itself, should not necessarily be correlated with the status of the tomb owner; for example, 'prestige' and status at Deir al-Medina appears to be related to more elaborate and larger tombs during the Nineteenth Dynasty, but this relationship does not obtain for the Twentieth Dynasty (G. Neunert, *Mein Grab, Mein Esel, Mein Platz in der Gesellschaft: Prestige im alten Ägypten am beispiel Deir el-Medine* [Berlin, 2010], 213).

16 T.A. Bács, "The Last New Kingdom Tomb at Thebes: The End of a Great Tradition?" *BMSAES* 16 (2011), 12; see, also T.A. Bács, "Art as Material for Later Art: The Case of Theban Tomb 65," in W.V. Davies, ed., *Colour and Painting in Ancient Egypt* (London, 2001), 94–100. Textual material within the tomb is also remarkable; the tomb texts remain unpublished—for a translation of an important hymn to Osiris as the Mendesian ram, see J.C. Darnell, *The Enigmatic Netherworld Books of the Solar-Osirian Unity: Cryptographic Compositions in the Tombs of Tutankhamun, Ramesses VI and Ramesses IX* (Fribourg, 2004), 398–401 (and pl. 38A for a copy of the text); the four-headed solar ram in the TT 65 hymn relates to the depiction of the Mendesian ram in the first hall of the royal tombs of Ramesses IX, X, and XI in the Valley of the Kings (Darnell, *The Enigmatic Netherworld Books of the Solar-Osirian Unity*, 400–401, n. 132).

17 The inclusion of the prenomen of Seti I (rather than Ramesses IX) in TT 65 argues strongly for the identification of the specific earlier template (Bács, "Art as Material for Later Art: The Case of Theban Tomb 65," 97).

18 J. Kahl, *Siut-Theben: Zur Wertschätzung von Traditionen im alten Ägypten* (Leiden, 1999), 278–79. In the tomb of Djehuty (TT 11, time of Hatshepsut/Thutmose III), cryptographic texts provide another means of signaling scribal skill and restricted knowledge—in addition to guarding the arcana of the solar cycle, the cryptographic texts "served both as Djehuty's 'business card' for the most educated visitors, and as a lure for trained scribes ready to face up to, or play in, an intellectual challenge" (A.D. Espinel, "Play and Display in Egyptian High Culture: The Cryptographic Texts of Djehuty (TT 11) and their Sociocultural Contexts," in J. Galán, B.M. Bryan, and P.F. Dorman, eds., *Creativity and Innovation in the Reign of Hatshepsut: Papers from the Theban Workshop 2010* (Chicago, 2014), 297–335 (quote from p. 326).

19 Literature abounds on this topic; for a recent analysis, see A. El-Shahawy, *Recherche sur la décoration des tombes thébaines du Nouvel Empire: Originalités iconographiques et innovations* (London, 2010), 281–82; J. Assmann, "The

Ramesside Tomb and the Construction of Sacred Space," in N. Strudwick and J.H. Taylor, eds., *The Theban Necropolis, Past, Present and Future* (London, 2003), 46–52 (with earlier literature cited therein).

20 Frood, *Biographical Texts*, 20–23 (and her translation of Samut-Kyky on pp. 84–91); the textual analysis of P. Vernus, "Littérature et autobiographie: Les inscriptions de *s3-mwt* surnommé Kyky," *RdE* 30 (1978), 115–46 remains useful. The tomb owner's name "Samut" may be an additional facet of his self-presentation, a name likely adopted after his dedication to the goddess, rather than a name bestowed upon him by his actual mother (U. Rummel, "'Ramsesnacht-dauert': Die Beziehung zwischen Namespatron und Namensträger am Beispiel einer Besucherinscrift aus Dra' Abu el-Naga," in N. Kloth, K. Martin, and E. Pardey, eds., *Es werde niedergelegt als Schriftstück, Festschrift für Hartwig Altenmüller zum 65. Geburtstag* [Hamburg, 2003], 370–71).

21 Frood, *Biographical Texts*, 91–94; for the nickname Hely and other 'familiar' names of deities, see J.C. Darnell, *Theban Desert Road Survey II: The Rock Shrine of Pahu, Gebel Akhenaton, and Other Rock Inscriptions of the Western Hinterland of Qamûla* (New Haven, CT, 2014), 23.

22 J. Assmann, *Death and Salvation in Ancient Egypt*, trans. D. Lorton (Ithaca, 2005), 113–27 (addressing the phenomenon of death as separation from a diachronic perspective).

23 A.M. Gnirs, "Der Tod des Selbst, Die Wandlung der Jenseitsvorstellungen in der Ramessidenzeit," in Guksch, et al., eds., *Grab und Totenkult*, 185.

24 Compare tomb complex K93.11/K93.12 at Dra Abu al-Naga—U. Rummel, "Der Tempel im Grab, Die Doppelgrabanlage der Hohepriester des Amun Ramsesnacht und Amenophis (K93.11/K93.12) in Drā' Abū el-Nagā/Theben-West," in I. Gerlach and D. Raue, eds., *Sanktuar und Ritual: Heilige Plätze im archäologischen Befund* (Rahden, 2013), 221–33 (especially the analysis on pp. 230–32).

25 Definitions of graffiti include J.C. Darnell, "Graffiti and Rock Inscriptions," in J. Allen and I. Shaw, eds., *Oxford Handbook of Egyptology* (Oxford, forthcoming); A.J. Peden, *Graffiti of Pharaonic Egypt: The Scope and Role of Informal Writing (c. 3100–332 BC)* (Leiden, 2001), (with the review of J.C. Darnell, *JAOS* 122 [2002], 4885–86); H. Navrátilová, "Graffiti Spaces," in L. Bareš, F. Coppens, and K. Smoláriková, eds., *Egypt in Transition: Social and Religious Development of Egypt in the First Millennium BCE* (Prague, 2010), 307–13. E. Cruz-Uribe, *Hibis Temple Project 3: The Graffiti From the Temple Precinct* (San Antonio, 2008), 199–225; his definition no. 15 is false: "[graffiti] is normally not written within an area of a sacred place (such as a temple) that is still functioning as an active community, holy place"—for a refutation,

see *inter alia* E. Frood, "Horkhebi's Decree and the Development of Priestly Inscriptional Practices in Karnak," in L. Bareš, F. Coppens, and K. Smoláriková, eds., *Egypt in Transition: Social and Religious Development of Egypt in the First Millennium BCE* (Prague, 2010), 123.

26 C. Ragazzoli, "The Social Creation of a Scribal Place: The Visitors' Inscriptions in the Tomb of Antefiqer (TT 60), with Newly Recorded Graffiti," *SAK* 42 (2013), 270.

27 H. Navrátilová, *Visitor's Graffiti of Dynasties XVIII and XIX in Abusir and North Saqqara*, 2nd rev. ed. (Prague, 2015); Navrátilová, "Graffiti Spaces," 321–26.

28 Ragazzoli, "The Social Creation of a Scribal Place," 281.

29 U. Verhoeven, "The New Kingdom Graffiti in Tomb N13.1: An Overview," in *Seven Seasons at Asyut: First Results of the Egyptian-German Cooperation in Archaeological Fieldwork* (Wiesbaden, 2012), 47–58; U. Verhoeven, "Literatur im Grab: Der Sonderfall Assiut," in G. Moers, K. Widmaier, A. Giewekemeyer, A. Lümers, and R. Ernst, eds., *Dating Egyptian Literary Texts* (Hamburg, 2013), I, 139–58.

30 H. Navrátilová, "Intertextuality in Ancient Egyptian Visitor's Graffiti," in F. Hagen, J. Johnston, and W. Monkhouse, eds., *Narratives of Egypt and the Ancient Near East: Literary and Linguistic Approaches* (Leuven, 2011), 259–63; C. Ragazzoli, "Weak Hands and Soft Mouths, Elements of Scribal Identity in the New Kingdom," *ZÄS* 137 (2010), 165–66. A small corpus of literary texts from the Ramesside Period that may be classified as historical fiction show a similar knowledge of history linked the aesthetic appreciation and enjoyment of the stories; see C. Manassa, *Imagining the Past: Historical Fiction in New Kingdom Egypt* (Oxford, 2013).

31 D. Frank, "Graffiti," in D. Redford, ed., *The Oxford Encyclopedia of Ancient Egypt*, II, (New York, 2001), 38–41, particularly p. 38: "Ancient Egyptian elite culture was the first to leave graffiti for eternity, to perpetuate individual achievements and names, and to communicate with future generations."

32 E. Frood, "Egyptian Temple Graffiti and the Gods: Appropriation and Ritualization in Karnak and Luxor," in D. Ragavan, ed., *Heaven on Earth: Temples, Ritual, and the Cosmic Symbolism in the Ancient World* (Chicago, 2013), 285–318; H. Jacquet-Gordon, *Temple of Khonsu*, III. *The Graffiti on the Khonsu Temple Roof at Karnak: A Manifestation of Personal Piety* (Chicago, 2003). For more official votive surcharging of temple surfaces, see P. Brand, "Veils, Votives, and Marginalia: The Use of Sacred Space at Karnak and Luxor," in P. Dorman and B. Bryan, eds., *Sacred Space and Sacred Function in Ancient Thebes* (Chicago, 2007), 51–83.

33 Darnell, *Theban Desert Road Survey II*; for more on rock inscriptions, see below.

34 See note 25 above for definitions of 'graffiti' in Egyptian contexts.

35 J.C. Darnell, *Theban Desert Road Survey in the Egyptian Western Desert I* (Chicago, 2002), 121; Darnell, *Theban Desert Road Survey II*, 15.

36 Jacquet-Gordon, *Temple of Khonsu*, III, 5, writes of the authors of the graffiti on the roof of Khonsu Temple: "These were generally humble people who probably did not have the means or possibly even the right to place statues of themselves in the sacred precinct, but they did have access to the interior of the temple and to its roof, to which some of their functions may have introduced them. It would seem then that these people seized the opportunity of leaving their names on the roof slabs in lieu of statues, and added their footprints as a kind of substitute for themselves so that they would remain forever, at least as long as the temple lasted, in the presence of their god and under his protection." Compare, also, the remarks of Frood, "Horkhebi's Decree and the Development of Priestly Inscriptional Practices in Karnak," 116–22; R. Fazzini, "Aspects of the Mut Temple's Contra-Temple at South Karnak, Part II," in S.H. D'Auria, *Offerings to the Discerning Eye: An Egyptological Medley in Honor of Jack A. Josephson* (Leiden, 2010), 93–94.

37 For votive offerings at temples of Hathor showing women in the role of principal donor, see G. Pinch, *Votive Offerings to Hathor* (Oxford, 1993), 342–43. For graffiti possibly left by chantresses at Deir al-Bahri, see Navrátilová, "Graffiti Spaces," 318.

38 A. Kjølby, "Material Agency, Attribution and Experience of Agency in Ancient Egypt, The case of New Kingdom Private Temple Statues," in Nyord and Kjølby, eds., *'Being in Ancient Egypt'*, 35; for the concept of "distributed personhood," she cites the studies of A. Gell, *Art and Agency: An Anthropological Theory* (Oxford, 1998).

39 The two statues of the high priest of Amun, Bakhenkhons, provide complementary texts with these two themes; Frood, *Biographical Texts*, 39–46.

40 Compare the description of the Osiris mysteries of Abydos on the statue of the high priest of Osiris, Wennefer; Frood, *Biographical Texts*, 97–99. The memorial chapel of the artist, Userhat, most likely from Abydos, shows all three of these self-presentational elements in door jambs and a stela (Frood, *Biographical Texts*, 117–29), rather than statuary, indicating that similar forms of self-presentation could extend across media in the Ramesside Period.

41 K. Kitchen, *Ramesside Inscriptions: Historical and Biographical*, IV (Oxford, 1982), 209, lls. 11–14.

42 M. Boraik, "Stela of Bakenkhonsu, High Priest of Amun-Re," *Memnonia* 18 (2007), 122, fig. 1, lns. 14–15. As Boraik notes, the restoration of divine monuments found destroyed, a situation rectified by Bakhenkhons rather than the king, is an example of the royal novel genre adapted to a nonroyal context.

43 J.J. Clère, *Les chauves d'Hathor* (Leuven, 1995).

44 Clère, *Les chauves d'Hathor*, 5–6.

45 For example, Amenemone's statue (Luxor Museum no. 227) juxtaposes a self-presentational text that describes his military career and overseeing of royal monuments (on the right side), with his role as "bald one of the goddess" who effectively hears petitions to her due to his moral rectitude (Clère, *Les chauves d'Hathor*, 87–94; Frood, *Biographical Texts*, 189–91).

46 "Complementary" appears to capture the intent of Egyptian monuments better than the proposed "disjunction" by B.M. Bryan, "The Disjunction of Text and Image in Egyptian Art," in P.D. Manuelian, ed., *Studies in Honor of William Kelly Simpson* (Boston, 1996), 161–68.

47 G.P.F. van den Boorn, *The duties of the Vizier: Civil Administration in the Early New Kingdom* (London, 1988); for mid-Eighteenth dynasty viziers and their duties, see B. Bryan, "Administration in the Reign of Thutmose III," in E.H. Cline and D. O'Connor, eds., *Thutmose III: A New Biography* (Ann Arbor, 2006), 70–77.

48 P.F. Dorman, "The Royal Steward, Senenmut, the Career of Senenmut," in C. Roehrig, ed., *Hatshepsut: From Queen to Pharaoh* (New York, 2005), 108–9 and n. 12.

49 The Viceroy of Nubia Setau commissioned reliefs of himself in the small temple of Thoth at Elkab during the reign of Ramesses II (basic description in Frood, *Biographical Texts*, 204–206; original publication: P. Derchain, *Elkab I: Les monuments religieux à l'entrée de l'Ouady Hellal* [Brussels, 1971]).

50 Frood, *Biographical Texts*, 54–59.

51 Frood, *Biographical Texts*, 61–81. The reward scenes are translated in S. Binder, *The Gold of Honour in New Kingdom Egypt* (Oxford, 2008), 135–40.

52 Frood, *Biographical Texts*, 77–81, following the interpretation proposed already by E. Wente, "The Suppression of the High Priest Amenhotep," *JNES* 25 (1966), 74–83. The lexicography of *thi* as a series of violent 'transgressions' rather than 'suppression' has been analyzed by K. Ridealgh, "A Tale of Semantics and Suppressions: Reinterpreting Papyrus Mayer A and the So-called 'War of the High Priest' during the Reign of Ramesses XI," *SAK* 43 (2014), 359–73; archaeological material that can be brought to bear on the topic is discussed as part of the historical debate in U. Rummel, "War, Death and Burial of the High Priest Amenhotep: The Archaeological Record at Dra' Abu el-Naga," *SAK* 43 (2014), 375–97.

53 As D. Polz, "The Ramsesnakht Dynasty and the Fall of the New Kingdom: A New Monument in Thebes," *SAK* 25 (1998), 289–90 notes, the power of the Ramsesnakht 'dynasty' (of which Amunhotep was a member as one of Ramsesnakht's sons) was not done to contravene royal power: the activities of

this private family "were definitely carried out *on behalf of* and not *against* the interests of the court" (p. 290).

54 Binder, *Gold of Honour*, 250–51; the text of the Amunhotep reward scenes, which mention an annual presentation of the *šbyw* collar, may provide a slight caveat as Binder notes: "If indeed the *šbyw* evolved from being the unpredictable token of trust and merit, to being part of an agreement between the king and an official, then a significant shift has taken place."

55 Discussions of Herihor's 'kingship' and his chronological placement (especially in relation to Piankh) abound; a summary of the most reasonable series of events—Herihor followed by Piankh—appears in J. Palmer, "The High Priests of Amun at the End of the Twentieth Dynasty," *Birmingham Egyptology Journal* 2 (2014), 1–22, modifying, but not rejecting the important study of K. Jansen-Winkeln, "Das Ende des Neuen Reiches," *ZÄS* 119 (1992), 22–37. Studies that try to place Piankh after, or even during, the tenure of Herihor are problematic, such as P. James and R. Morkot, "Herihor's Kingship and the High Priest of Amun Piankh," *JEgH* 3.2 (2010), 231–60.

56 Polz, "The Ramsesnakht Dynasty," 293.

57 S. Snape, "Neb-Re and the Heart of Darkness: The Latest Discoveries from Zawiyet Umm el-Rakham (Egypt)," *Antiquity* 75 (2001), 19–20; a forthcoming publication of the monuments of Nebre, as *Zawiyet Umm el-Rakham II* is listed in S. Snape and P. Wilson, *Zawiyet Umm el-Rakham I: The Temple and the Chapels* (Bolton, 2007), 127.

58 Snape, "Neb-Re and the Heart of Darkness," 19.

59 For *damnatio memoriae* more generally, see R.H. Wilkinson, "*Damnatio Memoriae* in the Valley of the Kings," in R.H. Wilkinson and K.R. Weeks, eds., *The Oxford Handbook of the Valley of the Kings* (Oxford, 2016), 335–46.

60 A similar argument is presented in K. Exell, *Soldiers, Sailors and Sandalmakers: A Social Reading of Ramesside Period Votive Stelae* (London, 2009), 136–37.

61 For the concept of "socialization" of the desert landscape, see J.C. Darnell, "The Narrow Doors of the Desert: Ancient Egyptian Roads in the Theban Western Desert," in B. David and M. Wilson, eds., *Inscribed Landscapes, Marking and Making Place* (Honolulu, HI, 2002), 114; J.C. Darnell, "Iconographic Attraction, Iconographic Syntax, and Tableaux of Royal Ritual Power in the Pre- and Proto-Dynastic Rock Inscriptions of the Theban Western Desert," *Archéo-Nil* 19 (2009), 85; for the impact of this concept in the study of desert roads, see H. Riemer and F. Förster, "Ancient Desert Roads: Towards Establishing a New Field of Archaeological Research," in F. Förster and H. Riemer, eds., *Desert Road Archaeology in Ancient Egypt and Beyond* (Cologne, 2013), 42.

62 A. Herzberg, "Felsinschriften und -bilder als Medium der Selbstrepräsentation lokaler Amsträger des Neuen Reiches, Ein Befund aus der Aswâner Region,"

in G. Neunert, A. Verbovsek, and K. Gabler, eds., *Bild: Ästhetik – Medium – Kommunikation, Beiträge des dritten Münchner Arbeitskreises Junge Aegyptologie (MAJA 3)* (Wiesbaden, 2014), 137–54.

63 The best example of this practice is the rock shrine of the priest Pahu west of Naqada (dating to the reign of Amunhotep II/Thutmose IV)—Darnell, *Theban Desert Road Survey II*.

64 Darnell, *Theban Desert Road Survey II*, 76, citing J. Yoyotte, "À propos de quelques idées reçues: Méresger, la Butte et les cobras," in G. Andreu, *Deir el-Médineh et la Vallée des Rois* (Paris, 2003), 281–307.

65 J.C. Darnell, "Homo Pictus and Painted Men: Depictions and Intimations of Humans in the Rock Art of the Theban Western Desert," in *"Whatever Happened to the People?" Humans and Anthropomorphs in the Rock Art of Northern Africa* (Brussels, 2018), 397–418.

66 D. Sweeney, "Self-Representation in Old Kingdom Quarrying Inscriptions at Wadi Hammamat," *JEA* 100 (2014), 275–91. Middle Kingdom rock inscriptions and free-standing monuments in quarry landscapes can also emphasize relationships to both contemporaries as well as the king; among the many possible references, see R. Leprohon, "Remarks on Private Epithets Found in the Middle Kingdom Wadi Hammamat Graffiti," *JSSEA* 28 (2001), 124–46; J.C. Darnell and C. Manassa, "A Trustworthy Seal-Bearer on a Mission: The Monuments of Sabastet from the Khephren Diorite Quarries," in R. Parkinson and H.-W. Fischer-Elfert, eds., *Studies in Honor of Detlef Franke* (Wiesbaden, 2013), 55–92.

67 J.C. Darnell, "The Rock Inscriptions of Tjehemau at Abisko," *ZÄS* 130 (2003), 35.

68 An overview of rock inscriptions in western Thebes during the Nineteenth and Twentieth Dynasties appears in Peden, *The Graffiti of Pharaonic Egypt*, 146–237.

69 Darnell, *Theban Desert Road Survey I*, 159 (Wadi el-Hol Rock Inscription 44).

70 Frood, *Biographical Texts*, 54–59.

71 Darnell, *Theban Desert Road Survey I*, 160.

72 J. Budka, *Der König an der Haustür: Die Rolle des ägyptischen Herrschers an dekorierten Türgewänden von Beamten im Neuen Reich* (Vienna, 2001).

73 Recent studies include N. Harrington, *Living with the Dead: Ancestor Worship and Mortuary Ritual in Ancient Egypt* (Oxford, 2013); J.L. Keith, *Anthropoid Busts of Deir el Medineh and Other Sites and Collections: Analyses, Catalogue, Appendices* (Cairo, 2011). Older studies remain useful: R.J. Demarée, *The ꜣḫ iḳr n Rꜥ Stelae: On Ancestor Worship in Ancient Egypt* (Leiden, 1983); F. Friedman, "On the Meaning of Some Anthropoid Busts from Deir el-Medina," *JEA* 71 (1985), 82–97 (note particularly her observation on p. 96 of the likely textual reference to offerings made to ancestor busts in P. Sallier IV, the "Calendar of Luck and Unlucky Days": "make invocation offerings to the *akh*-spirits in your house").

10

Self-Presentation in the Third Intermediate Period*

Roberto B. Gozzoli

The collapse of the Egyptian New Kingdom was a watershed in Egyptian dynastic history. While Ramesses II and his conquests were memories by the end of the Twentieth Dynasty, the passing of the last Ramesside was the end of an epoch. During the Twenty-first and Twenty-fourth Dynasties—the Libyan Period—the political capital moved to Tanis, a fact already partially accomplished by the end of the Twentieth Dynasty, as described in the Report of Wenamun.[1] Wenamun also highlights the increasing importance of the high priests of Amun at Thebes and their usurpation of royal prerogatives. The duality between Tanis, earlier, and Bubastis, later as political capitals, and Thebes, as religious capital, was a situation fated to last until the end of the Libyan Period.[2]

The nonroyal self-presentations of the Twenty-first Dynasty are scarce, a sort of Dark Age for such a genre.[3] The archaeological disappearance of many Delta sites might be an explanation for such absence.[4] It is more than an impression, however, that the political uncertainty of the Twenty-first Dynasty also reduced the number of nonroyal self-presentations.

Theban Self-Presentations in Uncertain Political Times

As a collateral dynasty grew up in Thebes and the independence of the Theban region was a fait accompli, the self-presentations of the period reflect such parochialism. Statues with the cartouche of Osorkon II on one shoulder and the name of the high priest Harsiese on the other shoulder are found. While Harsiese's control over Thebes was temporally limited, Osorkon II's cartouche and Harsiese's name demonstrate that Theban officials easily accepted a local 'ruler.'[5]

Confirmation of the division of Egypt between Tanis and Thebes comes from texts that are outside the boundaries of nonroyal self-presentations: the Priestly Annals from Karnak, spanning chronologically from King Psusennes I, Twenty-first Dynasty, to the Nubian king Kashta, early Twenty-fifth Dynasty, are usually simple and repetitive—sometimes simply a succession of dates and induction.[6] A further example is Priestly Annals no. 7. The text is dated to year 39 of Sheshonq III, but Prince Osorkon (B) is immediately mentioned after the royal titulary.[7] It is an acknowledgment of a joint control over Egypt by the king at Tanis, with the high priest of Amun having control over Thebes.[8]

Theban Self-Legitimacy and Royal Connections

The Karnak cachette is the major source of nonroyal self-presentations during the Libyan Period. As they come from temple settings, such province limits the set of expressions present in these texts.[9] Many of those statues are also family connected, such as is the case of *Ḏd-Ḫnsw-iw.f-ꜥnḫ* (A), in whose honor his son *Nḫt.f-Mwt* erected a statue in Luxor Temple; he is also celebrated by other statues ordered by his children and other relatives within the Temple of Amun at Karnak.[10] From the historical point of view, many of the families flourishing during the Libyan Period itself were later supplanted by other families during the subsequent Nubian Period.[11]

A few self-presentations of the Libyan Period simply consist of the name of the donor followed by an invocation to the god Amun.[12] An example of the genre is the statue (CG 559) of *Ḏd-Ḫnsw-iw.f-ꜥnḫ* (A) in Luxor Temple, which has a pattern of such a genre:

1. Priestly titles (+ name in final position + father's and mother's names and titles) (lls. 1–3)[13]
2. Invocation to future visitors, celebrate my name for my wisdom (lls. 3–4)
3. Refusal of the riches (lls. 4–5)
4. Parents honored by their son's behavior (lls. 5–6)
5. Honored by the pharaoh and his successors (lls. 6–7)
6. Loyalty to the king (l. 8)
7. Following the king's precepts (lls. 8–13)
8. Hope to see family members in his position (l.13)

9. Liberal provision of food (back pillar, 1–4)
10. Avoiding quarrels

Ḏd-Ḫnsw-iw.f-ˁnḫ (A) was established in his position by Osorkon I, who was his uncle-in-law; therefore, he should have demonstrated loyalty and respect toward the various pharaohs he found himself serving. Instead, he points out that the honors come from him respecting the rules. In fact, all the elements described here seem to belong to a desire for political justice missing from the previous Ramesside Period.[14]

In this respect, *Ḏd-Ḫnsw-iw.f-ˁnḫ* (A)'s self-presentation is quite different from its Ramesside examples. His career is marked by his good deeds, which are recognized by the pharaohs, but his career develops independently from royal favor—at least he would like to give such an impression. Bakekhonsu, for instance, gives a *cursus honorum*, in which the stages of the career advancement are chronologically placed and dependent on the god's favor:

I spent 4 years as an excellent youngster.
I spent 11 years as a youth, as a trainee stable-master
for king Men-maat-Re (Sety I).
I was a wab-priest of Amun for 4 years.
I was a God's Father of Amun for 12 years.
I was Third Priest of Amun for 15 years.
I was Second Priest of Amun for 12 years.

He favored me; he perceived me because of my character.
He appointed me High Priest of Amun for 27 years.[15]

Furthermore, *S3-mwt* called Kiky celebrates Mut for his rise from humble conditions, thereby simply highlighting deference to the goddess, without any reference to royal favor.[16] *Ḏd-Ḫnsw-iw.f-ˁnḫ* (A) celebrates current and past achievements as a way to strengthen his family's grip over Thebes. *Ḏd-Ḫnsw-iw.f-ˁnḫ*—or better, his son speaking through him—celebrates, not the pharaoh per se, but the sequence of pharaohs during whose reigns *Ḏd-Ḫnsw-iw.f-ˁnḫ* (A) was able to demonstrate his ability to perform duties asked. Having demonstrated his worthiness, he feels the right to settle his progeny in the position. Among this list, *Ḏd-Ḫnsw-iw.f-ˁnḫ* (A)'s offspring were fated to succeed him in important positions, and *Ḏd-Ḫnsw-iw.f-ˁnḫ* (A) was, certainly, successful in such enterprise.[17]

From a historical point of view, Ramesside self-presentations and everything else were connected with the king, who was the one to decide whether or not an official continued in his position. To have control over the city of Amun, kings of the Libyan Period sought the connections of Theban families that were showing independence from the royal court. Later in the dynasty, Osorkon II prayed to Amun to prevent his children from killing each other in the course of their struggles for power.[18]

Ḏd-Ḫnsw-iw.f-ʿnḫ also makes another statement: the god is judging his behavior and this message closes the text on the front of the statue. The parochialism of *Ḏd-Ḫnsw-iw.f-ʿnḫ* (A) appears in other self-presentations as well, in which their local dimension is dictated by invocations such as: "I searched for the good of my town during my period in charge."[19] More similar to Ramesside examples, Harsiese (C) celebrates the preferred position within the palace, thanks to the royal favor and his obedience to royal orders.[20] Such introduction uses the long prayer of Harsiese (C)'s son, *Ḏd-Ḫnsw-iw.f-ʿnḫ* (C), in favor of his father, therefore, celebrating high positions.

Ḥrw, dated to the reign of Pedubastis I, is, indeed, more focused on expressing the links with the pharaoh.[21] The long inscription on the back of the statue in fact focuses much more on the benefaction received from the pharaoh and the purity of *Ḥrw*'s actions. The same concept of purity pervades the inscription on the socle as well. As *Ḥrw* accomplishes Pharaoh's will, he also declares himself friend of Maat.[22] As inspired by Maat, he restores order in his land, and puts the *wꜥb*-priest in the place of his father, therefore, earning the respect of the higher ranks.

Still connected to royal perspectives, yet more related to a memento mori, the self-presentation of *Nb-nṯrw* is a reflection about the official position and his duties.[23] *Nb-nṯrw*, in fact, acknowledges that his life has been spent knowing that one day he should leave this world. As he dies—and his family suffers for it—*Nb-nṯrw* is able to issue a warning to the reader to avoid excesses and unworthy desires.[24]

Family Connections

The Libyan Period self-presentations usually mention the son of the family founder as the statue donor. The prologue itself is usually limited to "Given through the king's favor" in addition to name and titles of the statue's owner, as well as his parents.[25]

The father as receiver of the statue talks at first, but other members of the family talk as well. Daughters and sons repeat the good things received by the god, and pray to the deity for their well-being. A pattern is visible: the donor, usually a son of the deceased, celebrates his father and raises a hymn toward the god Amun, with a wish of a long and good life to the donor.[26] Among many other self-presentations, CG 42208, from the reign of Osorkon II, is striking for its structure and resemblance to a contemporary royal statue. In fact, CG 42208 points out the fact that the family inheritance was distributed equally among the various children so they would not quarrel with each other.[27] The kneeling statue of Osorkon II offers the reversed version of the prayer, as he invokes the god's help in order to stop the royal children quarrelling.[28]

One of the most frequent patterns of Libyan self-presentations is the list of ancestors each official mentions in his monument. Ancient Egyptian self-presentations of earlier periods were usually limited to the names of the statue donor's father and mother, for instance. In the Libyan Period, the reference to at least three or four generations before the statue owner is quite the norm. But statues CG 42221 and 42224 together allow the creation of a family tree that is fifteen generations long for the Neseramun family.[29]

The father is honored in order to legitimize the father-to-son succession. The reference reads, *st.i pw ꜣḫ n kꜣ.i imy-ib ḥr nb snn.i* ("My successor is the one who is useful for my *kꜣ* and beloved for making my statue.")[30] The inscription then concludes by stating that the son has set up the statue for his father in order that the latter would not to be forgotten.[31] As the father makes such a remark, the statement is the cornerstone of the entire group of Libyan genealogies: keeping the same positions generation after generation. A similar statement appears in Prince Osorkon's Chronicle (l. 37): "The children of the magnates of the interior of this land who were knowledgeable [to] cause [that they occupy the] positions of their fathers."[32]

Statues are one of the media on which genealogies are carved, but they are not the only ones. A graffito on the roof of the Khonsu temple at Karnak, from year 7 of Takeloth III, gives the genealogy of the God's Father *ꜥnḫ.f-n-Ḫnsw* on the day of his induction.[33] Listing all his paternal and maternal ancestors, *ꜥnḫ.f-n-Ḫnsw* went back to the beginning of the Twenty-first Dynasty to his most remote ancestor, the first prophet of Amun, Menkheperre. The Libyan genealogy of *Pꜣ-sn-Ḥr* was inscribed on a stele from the Serapeum.[34] *Pꜣ-sn-Ḥr* went back to the Libyan Buyuwawa, four generations earlier than Pharaoh Sheshonq I.[35]

Even Priestly Annals no. 6, possibly from the reign of Osorkon II, uses the contemporary long geneaologies:

> (1) [Regnal year . . . of] the Majesty of the King of Upper and Lower Egypt, Lord of the Two Lands, *Wsr-Mꜣꜥt-Rꜥ Stp-n Imn*, son of Re, lord of diadems, [. . . the day of induction of . . .] (2) [. . . of A]mun-Re, King of the Gods, deputy of the estate of Mut the great, lady of Asher[u], Hor, the justified, son of the God's Father of Amun-Re, King of [the Gods . . .] (3) [. . . Amun]-Re, Ankhefenmut, the justified, born by the

sistrum-player of Amun-Re, Tabaketenmut, the justified, [daughter of . . .] (4) [. . .] of the estate of [A]mun, chief temple scribe of the estate of Amun, Hor, the justified, [son of . . .] of [Amun-Re,] King of the God[s], and chief of [. . .][36]

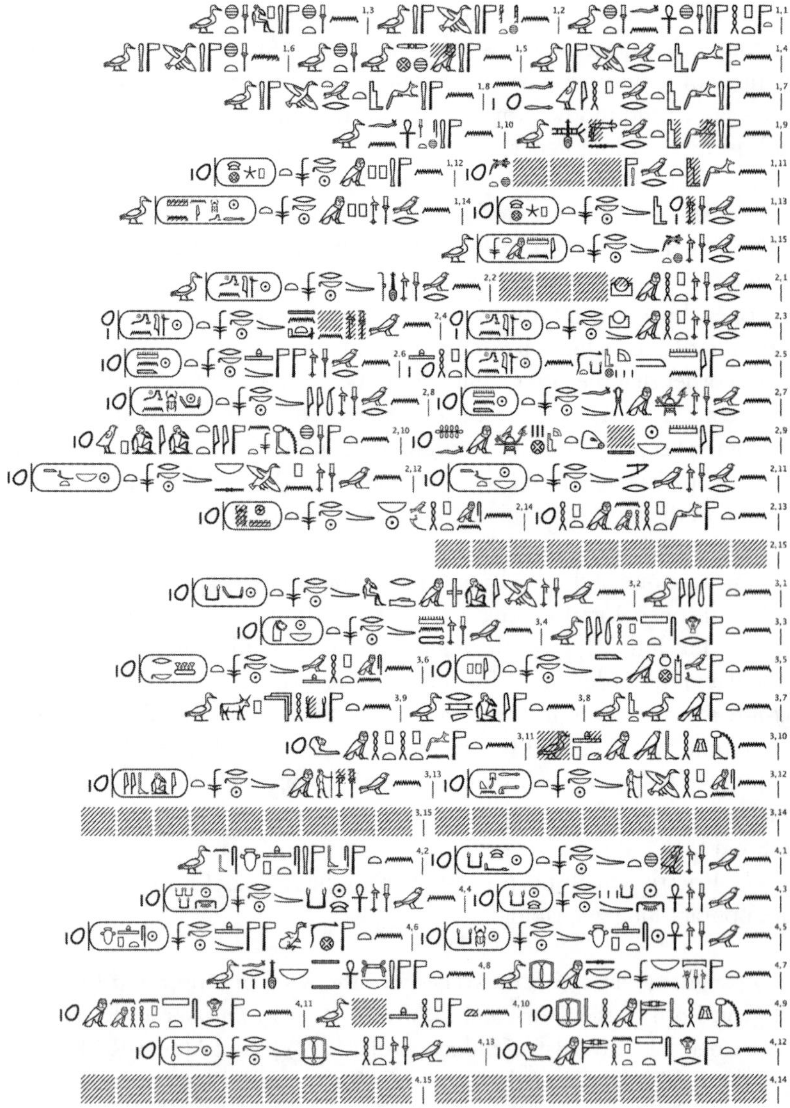

10.1. The Berlin genealogy main text (computer-generated version after K. Jansen-Winkeln, Inschriften der Spätzeit, II: Die 22.-24. Dynastie, 2007)

Any account of the genealogical lists of the Libyan Period would not be complete without the so-called Berlin genealogy (Fig. 10.1).[37]

Starting with the God's Father of Amun *ˁnḫ.f-n-Sḫmt*, the genealogy goes back to the reign of Pharaoh Montuhotep I. While there are many gaps in such a list, the intention of justifying the rights to titles and relative benefits through ancestors having already held a similar position is obvious. In a similar attempt, the statue of *B3s3* goes back to the beginnings of the Nineteenth Dynasty, as *Nbwn.f* mentioned in the genealogy was high priest of Amun at Karnak from year 1 of Ramesses II.[38]

The usual scholarly statement is that the long Libyan-Period genealogies are due to the particularity of the Libyan conceptions of kinship, for which family connections were very important.[39] This does not, however, take into consideration that long genealogies appear both for long-established Egyptian as well as newly arrived Libyan families. An Egyptian adaptation to the new Libyan pattern of family identification might be a possibility. Long nonroyal genealogies are known at least since the Ramesside Period, pointing to their 'pure' Egyptian origin.[40] Moreover, Libyans did not have any written tradition before coming to Egypt, while the creation of genealogical lists implies their written existence.[41] Before coming to Egypt, Libyan genealogies might have been passed from one generation to another through oral traditions. Orality cannot be disregarded, but the balance seems to tilt toward pure Egyptian traditions.

As the old families of Egyptian origin claimed their rights going back to ancient times, *homines novi* like the Libyan *P3-sn-Ḥr* employed the same strategy. His genealogy was not as long as the Egyptians of old, but it was employed nonetheless.

The reasons for such appearance should be considered within the political context of the period: genealogies stated the importance of being Egyptian as a term of distinction over Libyan newcomers. In addition, as the ruling families changed from indigenous to Libyan pharaohs, the only way local officials and priests could justify their rights in front of the new pharaohs was by going back to the antiquity of their position.[42]

The Discovery of Archaism

During the Libyan Period, statues dated to the Middle and New Kingdoms were usurped and new inscriptions were carved on them, completely obliterating those of the original owners.[43] The exception was the statue of *Ḏd-Ḏḥwty-iw.f-ˁnḫ*, where the name of the original owner was preserved, while a new inscription replaced the original.[44] Leaving the name both respects the original owner and highlights the importance of antiquity as an important element of self-presentation.

The reuse of older statues did not happen for the lack of material, as new statues were carved at the same time by the same donors. It should be considered instead as part of the same archaism that started during the Libyan Period and continued at a much larger scale during the Twenty-fifth and Twenty-sixth Dynasties.[45] Artistic models coming from the past were part and parcel of the pharaonic culture. Archaeological interest, such as that demonstrated by Prince Khaemwaset during the Ramesside Period, is one possible example.[46] Religion also contributed to keep older models, as demonstrated by Osorkon II's reliefs from Bubastis, with their return to Old and New Kingdom models. The other element of employing the past could be legitimization, as the New Kingdom royal names were adjusted and re-employed by the Libyan pharaohs.[47] As they repeated the same actions of distant ancestors, the ruling pharaohs were legitimized.[48] Libyan nonroyal self-presentations should be considered to be following the same patterns of the royal self-presentation, with antiquity as a way to state priorities and legitimacy.

Notes

* For more on the period, see K. Jansen-Winkeln, *Ägyptische Biographien der 22. und 23. Dynastie* (Wiesbaden, 1985); K. Jansen-Winkeln, *Inschriften der Spätzeit*, II–III, (Wiesbaden, 2007); H. Brandl, *Untersuchungen zur steinernen Privatplastik der Dritten Zwischenzeit: Typologie, Ikonographie, Stilistik* (Berlin, 2008); R.K. Ritner, *The Libyan Anarchy: Inscriptions from Egypt's Third Intermediate Period* (Atlanta, 2009). Previous literature is only cited when needed, while studies published after both of Jansen-Winkeln's monographs are quoted in full. The high priests' inscriptions within the temple of Karnak are not considered here, as they are not an expression of nonroyal self-presentations, but they appropriate iconography and textual topics belonging to the royal sphere. For instance, the Chronicle of Prince Osorkon, cf. R.A. Caminos, *The Chronicle of Prince Osorkon* (Rome, 1958), which employs many royal elements within its text, cf. R.B. Gozzoli, *The Writing of History in Ancient Egypt during the First Millennium BC (ca. 1070–180 BC): Trends and Perspectives* (London, 2006), 41–49.

1 The period between the Twenty-first Dynasty and the Twenty-fourth Dynasty has usually been called the Third Intermediate Period; here, following the Birmingham School, it is called the Libyan Period, cf. A. Leahy, "The Libyan Period in Egypt: An Essay in Interpretation," *Libyan Studies* 16 (1985), 51–65; A Leahy, "Abydos in the Libyan Period (with Appendix: The Twenty-Third Dynasty)," in A. Leahy, ed., *Libya and Egypt c1300–750 BC* (London, 1990), 155–200; D.A. Aston, "Takeloth II: A King of the 'Theban' Twenty-Third Dynasty," *JEA* 75 (1989), 139–53; D.A. Aston, "Takeloth II, a King of the Herakleopolitan/Theban Twenty-Third Dynasty Revisited: The Chronology of Dynasties 22 and 23," in G.P.F. Broekman,

R.J. Demarée, and O.E. Kaper, eds., *The Libyan Period in Egypt: Historical and Cultural Studies into the 21st-24th Dynasties. Proceedings of a Conference at Leiden University, 25–27 October 2007* (Leiden, Leuven, 2009) 1–28; D.A. Aston and J.H. Taylor, "The Family of Takeloth III and the 'Theban' Twenty-Third Dynasty," in A. Leahy, ed., *Libya and Egypt c1300–750 BC* (London, 1990), 131–54. For the report of Wenamun, see A.H. Gardiner, *Late-Egyptian Stories* (Brussels, 1932), 61–76; B.U. Schipper, *Die Erzählung des Wenamun: Ein Literaturwerk im Spannungsfeld von Politik, Geschichte und Religion* (Freiburg, 2005); M. Lichtheim, *Ancient Egyptian Literature*, III (Berkeley, Los Angeles,London, 1980), 224–29, for a translation.

2 As noted by J. Assmann, *The Mind of Egypt* (New York, 2002), 289, the creation of the *wḥm mswt* era by Herihor means the attribution of royal prerogatives to a nonroyal figure, as years were counted at the beginnings of a new pharaoh's reign.

3 As remarked by Jansen-Winkeln, *Ägyptische Biographien*, 1: "Die zeitliche Isolierung dieser Texte ist weitgehend ohne künstliche Einschnitte möglich. Die Grenze nach oben ergibt sich problemlos: Aus der 21. Dynastie sind keine längeren biographischen Inschriften überliefert." For the passage between the Twenty-first and Twenty-second Dynasties, see A. Dodson, "The Transition between the 21st and 22nd Dynasties Revisited," in G.P.F. Broekman, R.J. Demarée, and O.E. Kaper, eds., *The Libyan Period in Egypt: Historical and Cultural Studies into the 21st-24th Dynasties. Proceedings of a Conference at Leiden University, 25–27 October 2007* (Leiden, Leuven, 2009), 103–12.

4 A. Leahy, "A Battered Statue of Shedsunefertem, High Priest of Memphis (BM EA 25)," *JEA* 92 (2006), 181, notes the scarcity of self-presentations for the Twenty-first Dynasty, as only a couple of statues could be attributed to the entire dynasty.

5 See CG 42208 and 42225, Jansen-Winkeln, *Inschriften Spätzeit*, II, 141–44 (18.78), 135–39 (18.75); Brandl, *Untersuchungen*, 56 (Doc. O–3.2), 149 (Doc. O–5.2.25). The single name of Harsiese as king also appears in CG 42254, Jansen-Winkeln, *Inschriften Spätzeit*, II, 156–59 (19.7), and JE 37348; Jansen-Winkeln, *Inschriften Spätzeit*, II, 159 (19.8). Osorkon II took back the control of the entire country by year 17, cf. F. Payraudeau, "Ioufâa, un gouverneur de Thèbes sous la XXIIe dynastie," *BIFAO* 105 (2005), 207; F. Payraudeau, *Administration, société et pouvoir à Thèbes sous la XXIIIe dynastie bubastite* (Cairo, 2014), 53–54, 151–52. Payraudeau, "Ioufâa," 202, is able to date the division of the country in two independent entities to the last years of Osorkon I.

6 Text no. 4 mentions Sheshonq (I) at the beginning of the text as simply "Chief of Ma," and later he has become pharaoh; see Jansen-Winkeln, *Inschriften Spätzeit*, II, 36 (12.49); Ritner, *Libyan Anarchy*, 51. From a historical point of view, any Theban doubts about Sheshonq I's ability to rule as pharaoh were solved by year 6: the Nile Record no. 1 dates to year 6 of

Sheshonq I, see J. Beckerath, "The Nile Level Records at Karnak and Their Importance for the History of the Libyan Period (Dynasties XXII and XXIII)," *JARCE* 5 (1966), 49. For the problems of accepting Nile Record no. 3, dated to an unnamed king, as belonging to Sheshonq I, see G.P.F. Broekman, "The Nile Level Records of the Twenty-Second and Twenty-Third Dynasties in Karnak: A Reconsideration of Their Chronological Order," *JEA* 88 (2002), 164.

7 Jansen-Winkeln, *Inschriften Spätzeit*, II, 203–204 (22.38); Ritner, *Libyan Anarchy*, 52–54. See, also, J.H. Taylor, "Coffins as Evidence for a 'North-South Divide' in the 22nd–23rd Dynasties," in G.P.F. Broekman, R.J. Demarée, and O.E. Kaper, eds., *The Libyan Period in Egypt: Historical and Cultural Studies into the 21st–24th Dynasties. Proceedings of a Conference at Leiden University, 25–27 October 2007* (Leiden-Leuven, 2009), 375–415 for the North-South division as revealed by tomb coffins.

8 Most of the discussion about Prince Osorkon is mostly based on his Chronicle, carved on the Bubastite Gate at Karnak. The hieroglyphic text has been published by Survey Epigraphic, *Reliefs and Inscriptions at Karnak*, III (Chicago, 1954), pls. 16–22. The classic commentary is Caminos, *Prince Osorkon*, and a more recent translation appears in Ritner, *Libyan Anarchy*, 348–77. As noted by Ritner, *Libyan Anarchy*, 65 n. 21, Shoshenq III's power was possibly limited to the Delta, and Prince Osorkon had control over the Southern territory.

9 For the discovery of the cachette and the preliminary publication, see G. Legrain, "Reinsegnements sur le dernières découvertes faites a Karnak," *RT* 27 (1905), 61–82. Most of the statues, with photos and bibliography are now present in the Karnak Cachette Database by IFAO: http://www.ifao.egnet.net/bases/cachette.

10 See CG 559, CG 42206–42207, for which Jansen-Winkeln, *Inschriften Spätzeit*, II, 95–98 (17.17) 144–47 (18.79–80), Brandl, *Untersuchungen*, 113–14 (Doc. O–5.2.7), 228–231 (Docs. U–2.2–3).

11 Jansen-Winkeln, *Ägyptische Biographien*, I, as well as F. Payraudeau, "Fin de partie pour une famille de grand commis de l'État (Statuette Caire JE 37025)," *CdE* 84 (2009), 121 and n. 19, discuss the family of *Nb-nṯrw*, who disappeared by the end of the Libyan Period.

12 See CG 42214 belonging to *Ḥr-m-3ḫbit*, Jansen-Winkeln, *Inschriften Spätzeit*, II, 239–240 (25.45), Brandl, *Untersuchungen*, 58–59 (Doc. O–3.3) as well as CG 42218, belonging to *P3-di-mwt*. The statue was originally dated to the Libyan Period by Jansen-Winkeln, *Ägyptische Biographien*, I, 112–116, but such a date has been disputed, and it has now been attributed to the Twenty-fifth Dynasty; cf. Jansen-Winkeln, *Inschriften Spätzeit*, III, 509–510 (52.288); Brandl, *Untersuchungen*, 135–136 (Doc. O–5.2.18); Payraudeau, *Administration*, 150 and n. 135.

13 The initial titulary simply list all the titles the official had during his entire lifetime; cf. Payraudeau, *Administration*, 170.

14 See Payraudeau, "Ioufâa," 200, who states, referring to the statue of *Iwfˁ3* (JE 37374), Jansen-Winkeln, *Inschriften Spätzeit*, II, 156–159 (19.7): "Cette première statue de Ioufâa s'inscrit dans la plus pure tradition des statues de temples de la Troisième Période intermédiaire. Elle comporte les éléments nécessaires au maintien de la mémoire du défunt auprès du dieu, grâce aux prières et appels aux vivants portés sur ses parois. Ces textes reflètent aussi l'affirmation d'un idéal social qui traverse presque toutes les biographies de l'élite thébaine à l'époque libyenne: la nécessité d'une administration efficace et surtout incorruptible, à l'encontre de la réalité peu reluisante révélée par les procès de la fin du Nouvel Empire."

15 Block statue of Bakekhonsu, from the reign of Ramesses II (Munich statue), *KRI* III 297.4–299.6, transl. E. Frood, *Biographical Texts from Ramessid Egypt* (Atlanta, 2007), 41.

16 The inscription of Samut comes from his tomb TT 409, and the most recent studies are *KRI* III 336.1–341.12; P. Vernus, "Littérature et autobiographie: Les inscriptions de *S3-mwt* surnommé *Kyky*," *RdE* 30 (1978), 115–46; M. Negm, *The Tomb of Simut called Kyky: Theban Tomb 409 at Qurnah* (Warminster, 1997); Frood, *Biographical Texts*, 84–91.

17 CG 42206, CG 42207, CG 42208, 42211, 42221, 42231 are other examples celebrating *Ḏd-Ḫnsw-iw.f-ˁnḫ* (A) and his family; see Jansen-Winkeln, *Inschriften Spätzeit*, II, 141–47, 243–45, 247–50, 320–23 (18.78–80, 25.51, 25.53); Brandl, *Untersuchungen*, 125–26 (Doc. O–5.2.13), 141–42 (Doc. O–5.2.21, 157–58 (Doc. O–5.2.29); see, also, Payraudeau, *Administration*, 140–44, for the family genealogy.

18 See Jansen-Winkeln, *Inschriften Spätzeit*, 108–109 (18.3); Payraudeau, *Administration*, 323–24.

19 See Cairo CG 42207 (inscription on the back, cols. 3–4) and CG 42225, Jansen-Winkeln, *Inschriften Spätzeit*, II, 135–39 (18.75).

20 Statue CG 42210, Jansen-Winkeln, *Inschriften Spätzeit*, II, 234–36 (25.36); Brandl, *Untersuchungen*, 123–24 (Doc. O–5.2.12).

21 CG 42226, Jansen-Winkeln, *Inschriften Spätzeit*, II, 213–216 (23.18); Brandl, *Untersuchungen*, 151–52 (Doc. O–5.2.26). The main text simply contains a list of good deeds done by the official, without any invocation toward the reader. For a short version of *Ḥrw*'s self-presentation, see CG 42227, Jansen-Winkeln, *Inschriften Spätzeit*, II, 216–17 (23.19); Brandl, *Untersuchungen*, 153–54 (Doc. O–5.2.27).

22 For the concept of Maat, see J. Assmann, *Ma'at: Gerechtigkeit und Unsterblichkeit im alten Ägypten* (Munich, 1995); E. Teeter, *The Presentation of Maat* (Chicago, 1997).

23 CG 42225, from the reign of Osorkon II.

24 See CG 42228, Jansen-Winkeln, *Inschriften Spätzeit*, II, 139–41 (18.76); Brandl, *Untersuchungen*, 50–51 (Doc. O–2.4) for the Mistress of the House, *Šb-n-Spdt*.

25 Variations are also admitted: a double donation to Amun on one side and the combined Theban Ennead on the other as present in CG 42207, instead of the usual final invocation to Amun.

26 See the block JE 43359 from Mendes, Jansen-Winkeln, *Inschriften Spätzeit*, II, 387–88 (44.9–10), on which the Chief of Ma, *Ns-bꜣ-ḏdt*, celebrates the fact that he inherited the position from his father: "I was your servant, to whom your *kꜣ* talks, the son of your servant beforehand."

27 CG 42208, stela inscription, 12–13: *nn ḏd kw sꜣw(.i) sꜣwt(.i) imi n.i mitt n di.k ꜣr.w s(y) m ḫꜥw nb nty m pr.i m-sꜣ hrw-ꜥḥꜥ* "As none of my sons and daughters should say: 'Give me the same.' Do not let them oust her from all the possessions, what is in my estate after my death."

28 For Philadelphia E 16199 and Cairo JE 37489 statue, see Jansen-Winkeln, *Inschriften Spätzeit*, II, 108–109 (18.3); Ritner, *Libyan Anarchy*, 283–288.

29 For the family reconstruction and detailed analysis of the specific family, see K.A. Kitchen, *The Third Intermediate Period in Egypt (1100–650 BC)* (Warminster, 1995), 211–30; and, now, Payraudeau, *Administration*, 133–36, for the other families.

30 Statue of Bakekhonsu (CG 42213), l. 1, Jansen-Winkeln, *Inschriften Spätzeit*, II, 134–35 (18.74); Brandl, *Untersuchungen*, 129–30 (Doc. O–5.2.15).

31 This is also the theme of CG 42206, where it is noted: *bn wsf.s it.s mwt.s*, "She has not forgotten her father and her mother."

32 Transl. Ritner, *Libyan Anarchy*, 356.

33 Jansen-Winkeln, *Inschriften Spätzeit*, II, 326–28 (30.11); Ritner, *Libyan Anarchy*, 11–16.

34 Serapeum stele IM 2846, originally published by M. Malinine, G. Posener, and J. Vercoutter, *Catalogue des stèles du Sérapéum de Memphis* (Paris, 1968), 30–31 and pl. 10 (31), and, now, Jansen-Winkeln, *Inschriften Spätzeit*, II, 271–72 (28.12); Ritner, *Libyan Anarchy*, 17–21. For the genealogical tree, see Payraudeau, *Administration*, fig. 3.

35 Nespekashuty's family had important positions within the Egyptian army during the Twenty-first Dynasty; they lost their status after Osorkon II and Sheshonq III; cf. F. Payraudeau, "Une famille de generaux de domaine d'Amon sous les 21eme et 22eme dynasties (statue Caire JE 36742)," in M.M. Eldamaty and M. Trad, *Egyptian Museum Collections around the World: Studies for the Centennial of the Egyptian Museum, Cairo*, II (Cairo, 2002), 925.

36 For the text, see Jansen-Winkeln, *Inschriften Spätzeit*, II, 437 (45.91); for the translation, see, Ritner, *Libyan Anarchy*, 52.

37 Relief Berlin 23673. The basic reference is still L. Borchardt, *Die Mittel zur zeitlichen Festlegung von Punkten der ägyptischen Geschichte und ihre Anwendung* (Cairo, 1935), 96–112. See, now, Jansen-Winkeln, *Inschriften Spätzeit*, II, 278–280 (28.24); Jansen-Winkeln, "The Relevance of Genealogical Information for Egyptian Chronology," *Ägypten und Levante* 16 (2007), 260 and fig. 2; Ritner, *Libyan Anarchy*, 21–25.

38 Chicago OIM 10729, for which see Jansen-Winkeln, *Inschriften Spätzeit*, II, 407–409 (44.57); Ritner, *Libyan Anarchy*, 25–31.

39 This explanation is given by R.K. Ritner, "Fragmentation and Re-integration in the Third Intermediate Period," in G.P.F. Broekman, R.J. Demarée, and O.E. Kaper, eds., *The Libyan Period in Egypt: Historical and Cultural Studies into the 21st–24th Dynasties. Proceedings of a Conference at Leiden University, 25–27 October 2007* (Leiden–Leuven, 2009), 336, for instance.

40 K.A. Kitchen, *Ramesside Inscriptions*, I (Oxford, 1968), 329–30; cf. Payraudeau, *Administration*, 109 and n. 21. See, also, D.B. Redford, *Pharaonic King-Lists: Annals and Day-Books* (Mississauga, Ont., 1986), 197 for the Ramesside Period interests for the past as a way of legitimization.

41 See Payraudeau, *Administration*, 109, for the statement.

42 A few centuries later, Herodotus (Book II, 143) reports in his book on Egypt the answer to Hecataeus of Myletus stating that there was a god among his family members twelve generations before his time. They showed him 345 generations of priests, and none of them had a deity among them. While the intents of Herodotus's passage are certainly different from those given by the Libyan genealogies, the message is quite clear in both, legitimacy through genealogical lists was an important criterion of legitimacy in Egyptian society. For the archive which Peteisis used in his peroration in front of the Satrap in Papyrus Rylands IX; cf. G. Vittmann, *Der demotische Papyrus Rylands 9*, Wiesbaden, 1998. That implies the ability of having written records on which information can be employed.

43 For Baltimore, Walters Art Gallery 22.203, see Jansen-Winkeln, *Inschriften Spätzeit*, I, 431 (45.75). For statue JE 37382, see F. Payraudeau, "Les prémices du mouvement archaïsant à Thèbeds et la statue du Caire JE 37382 du quatrième prophète Djedkhonsouieoufânkh," *BIFAO* 107 (2007), 141–156. For statue JE 37880, see F. Payraudeau, "Généalogie et mémoire familiale à la Troisième Période intermédiaire," *RdE* 64 (2013), 72–73. The same Djedkhonsuiewfankh carved his inscriptions on a usurped statue (CG 42206). The self-presentation of Shedsunfertem, from early Dynasty 22, was carved on a statue of prince, Khaemwaset, son of Ramesses II. The statue was published by A. Leahy, "A Battered Statue."

44 The statue is now Cairo CG 42207; see Jansen-Winkeln, *Inschriften Spätzeit*, II, 144–47 (18.79–80); S. Aufrère, "Les anciens Égyptiens et leur notion de l'antiquité," *Méditerranées* 17 (1998), 28 n. 76.

45 Many studies have been written about archaism in ancient Egypt. Only mentioning the most significant, see I. Nagy, "Remarques sur le souci d'archaïsme en Egypte a l'epoque saïte," *Acta Antiqua Academiae Scientiarum Hungaricae* 21 (1973), 53–64; H. Brunner, "Zum Verständnis der archaisierendern tendenzen in der ägyptischen Spätzeit," *Saeculum* 21 (1970), 151–61; S. Neureiter, "Eine neue Interpretation des Archaismus," *SAK* 21 (1994), 219–254. For Kawa and its reliefs, see R. Morkot and W.J. Tait, "Archaism and Innovation in Art from the New Kingdom to the Twenty-Sixth Dynasty," in W.J. Tait, ed., *'Never Had the Like Occurred': Egypt's View of Its Past* (London, 2003), 80–82. Morkot seems to ignore, however, that archaism developed independently from the

royal court, and the cases reproduced for Kawa and the Jubilee reliefs by Osorkon II at Bubastis could be considered more as examples of reference to models established by the tradition. The jubilee ceremonies continued elements going back to the archaic times. The same trampling scenes by Kawa were part of a crystallized tradition of celebrating the pharaoh himself. For the late archaistic examples, see Gozzoli, *Writing of History*, 104–106.

46 For Khaemwaset, see F. Gomaà, *Chaemwese. Sohn Ramses' II. und Hohenpriester von Memphis* (Wiesbaden, 1973); Aufrère, "Les anciens Égyptiens," 16, 18–22. See, also, H. Navrátilová, *The Visitors' Graffiti of Dynasties XVIII and XIX in Abusir and Northern Saqqara* (Prague, 2007).

47 See M.-A. Bonhême, *Les noms royaux dans l'Égypte de la Troisième Période Intermédiaire* (Cairo, 1987), 241–42, 263–64 for the series of names going back to New Kingdom ones. For the repeated presence of the name Menkheperre in scarabs; cf. B. Jaeger, *Essai de classification et datation des scarabées Menkhéperrê* (Fribourg-Göttingen, 1982). For Demotic literature, such as Setne II, cf. F.L. Griffith, *Stories of the High Priests of Memphis* (Oxford, 1900), 41–66; Gozzoli, *Writing of History*, 261–64. Aufrère, "Les anciens Égyptiens," 34–35, discusses the strong connection between new rulers and desire of legitimacy.

48 For this, see, Aufrère, "Les anciens Égyptiens," 28.

11

Self-Presentation in the Twenty-fifth Dynasty

Jeremy Pope

In its most general outline, the Kushite era appears a seamless transition between the Third Intermediate and Late Periods. Pi(ankh)y's kinsmen were neither the first nor the last dynasty across this span to bring foreign ancestry to the throne of Horus. Like the Libyan pharaohs who preceded them and the Near Eastern and Mediterranean invaders who would follow, the Kushite royals were also joined by immigrants from their homeland who obtained positions of military, ecclesiastical, and civil authority in Egypt.[1] Moreover, the period of Kushite rule continued and intensified a much longer florescence of artistic and literary archaism: characteristics of Old and Middle Kingdom statuary, phraseology, and hieroglyphic orthography were increasingly revived on both royal and nonroyal monuments. In similar fashion, the Kushite Period sustained the growth of personal piety and especially of Egyptian biography; in no part of the Near East was this genre more central to cultic life.[2] The Twenty-fifth Dynasty exemplified the steady development of foreign rule, immigration, archaism, personal piety, and nonroyal self-presentation in Egypt across the first millennium BC.

Yet the Kushite era is no mere dynastic periodization artificially dividing the *longue durée* of Egyptian social history. Inspection of the self-presentational corpus and its associated images uncovers some peculiarities in the expression of nonroyal attitudes toward the king and compatriots that subtly distinguish the Twenty-fifth Dynasty from preceding and succeeding epochs. The chapter that follows considers these attitudes in their Egyptian context before turning to the question of self-presentation in the Nubian half of the Double Kingdom.

Kushite Kingship and the Nonroyal Self in Egypt

A brief but insightful commentary upon the Twenty-fifth Dynasty by Price has recently drawn attention to the absence of royal names "from most non-royal self-presentations during the Late Period proper (25th Dynasty and later)," a departure from the more frequent appearance of royal names upon "private monuments of the 22nd–24th Dynasty."[3] Thanks to the subsequent publication of Jansen-Winkeln's invaluable two-volume set of Saite inscriptions, it is now possible to refine this observation: close scrutiny of the evidence cataloged by the *Inschriften der Spätzeit* series reveals that the absence of royal names upon nonroyal self-presentations was, in fact, far more characteristic of the Kushite Twenty-fifth Dynasty than of the Saite Twenty-sixth.[4] When one looks beyond the functionaries of the God's Wife of Amun, the contrast becomes particularly stark: whereas the Saite kings were mentioned upon dozens of nonroyal statues commissioned by numerous individuals, cartouches for the names of Kushite kings appeared only upon the statues of Montuemhat, Pesdimen, and Ity (Fig. 11.1).[5] Nonroyal papyri, burial linens, and funerary cones, as well as donation and Apis stelae, more frequently mention the Kushite pharaohs by name, but arguably with less explicit connection to any self-presentational subject—namely, as regnal date and imprimatur.[6] The available corpus for the Twenty-fifth Dynasty is not so small that royal absence upon nonroyal statuary may be dismissed as a simple accident of survival, so it warrants some attempt at explanation.[7] The omission of Kushite royal names from so many Egyptian nonroyal statues may be variously attributed to intentional disregard for an immigrant regime, to social distance from the royal house, or to a change in the stylistic conventions of self-presentation with limited significance for political history.

Several points would seem at first to suggest an intentional disregard for the Kushite regime across the nonroyal corpus. Firstly, it is notable that Kushite royal names are altogether missing from nonroyal statuary in Lower Egypt, precisely where Kushite political control was most tenuous; in this regard, the landscape of the Twenty-fifth Dynasty may be likened to the divided rule of the Twenty-first, a period whose kings were similarly absent from most nonroyal monuments.[8] Secondly, the authority of the Kushite kings was sometimes understated even within those nonroyal inscriptions where their names appear: Pi(ankh)y and Shabako were both named upon

11.1. Statue of Ity, BM EA 24429 (© The Trustees of the British Museum)

the aforementioned statue of Ity (Fig. 11.1), but Rößler-Köhler has perceived in the laconic royal epithets of that text a "'leise' Kritik an Schabako" that she would tentatively attribute to "der königlichen Personalpolitik (Einsetzung von Äthiopen in entscheidende klerikale und weltliche Ämter Thebens)."[9] There is thirdly the rather bold assumption of royal prerogatives by nonroyal Egyptians living under Kushite rule: self-presentations from this period regularly described the building activity of nonroyal individuals in a phraseology that had previously been reserved for kings, and in at least two cases the high steward Harwa dared to depict himself holding the crook and flail upon his own ushabtis (Fig. 11.2).[10] Finally, it is at least noteworthy that nonroyal acknowledgments of the Kushite royal house declined following their initial expulsion from Egypt by the Assyrians; this is hardly unexpected but has been taken to validate the use of nonroyal inscriptions as a measure of Kushite control in Egypt.[11]

While the theory of intentional disregard is easily supported, it must nevertheless be tempered with other considerations—among them the possibility that nonroyals were separated from the Kushite regime less by open rebellion than by social distance. Unlike the Libyans before them and the Saites who came after, the Kushite kings all seem to have been raised to adulthood outside of Egypt, and their domain stretched at least 1,400 kilometers beyond the country's borders; as a result, they could very well have had less familial relationship to and personal contact with most Egyptian elites. In

11.2. Fragmentary ushabti of Harwa, Dynasty 25, 760–660 BC, serpentinite, 12x7.6cm, Hay Collection, Gift of C. Granville Way, 72.745 (photograph © 2019 Museum of Fine Arts, Boston)

this regard, it may be more than coincidence that the few nonroyals who did name Kushite pharaohs upon their own nonroyal statuary were simultaneously rare exceptions to this social distance: Montuemhat was married to a granddaughter of Pi(ankh)y; Ity served in Pi(ankh)y's funerary cult; and Pesdimen was the son of a presumed Kushite named Pakash.[12] Reference to individual Kushite kings was naturally more common among the functionaries of the God's Wife of Amun, but even for this group the kings' names appear almost exclusively within statements of the God's Wife's royal filiation—not as expressions of direct personal connection between a nonroyal official and the Kushite king.[13] Theban officials boasted of their favor with the God's Wife far more than they did of their favor with the king. An unusual degree of social distance between Kushite pharaohs and the nonroyal populace is equally suggested by the latter's consistent absence from royal monuments in Egypt; as Exell and Naunton have observed, "decorum dictated that it was only the pharaoh and the Divine Adoratrices who could be shown in association with the gods on such monuments."[14] Indeed, there seems to have been a mutual silence at work: nonroyal individuals were seldom named and even less frequently pictured upon royal monuments, just as the Kushite kings were rarely named upon nonroyal statuary.

A still more compelling explanation for the omission of Kushite royal names upon nonroyal statuary would attribute this pattern to changes in the stylistic conventions of self-presentation. In previous epochs, mention of the king by name had been an occasional feature of the *Laufbahnbiographie*, but this subgenre is seldom attested under Kushite rule, giving way to the *Idealbiographie* and its emphasis upon moral action and eulogistic personal epithets.[15] Most significantly, Vittmann observes that this catalog of epithets now revived the old title of 'royal acquaintance' (*rḫ-nsw*) during the Twenty-fifth Dynasty[16]—paradoxically at the very same time that royal names had all but disappeared from nonroyal statuary. It would therefore seem that the vague and formulaic language of the increasingly popular *Idealbiographie*, along with the extended social distance between the Kushite pharaoh and his Egyptian subjects, had combined to veil the royal name in virtual anonymity upon nonroyal statues: kings were left unnamed, both because the subgenre no longer prioritized their explicit identification and because the status of royal acquaintance entailed only a generalized service to the larger royal house, not necessarily a close personal relationship with the pharaoh himself.

An illustrative case in point is provided by the Abydene stela of a woman named Taniy, whose lunette and first line only are shown here as figure 11.3. The biographical section presents the *rḫ-nsw mꜣꜥ* Taniy through a series of moralistic epithets highlighting her value to an unspecified royal house:

11.3. Stela of Taniy, Kunsthistorisches Museum Vienna AE 192

I am a possessor of character,
foremost among people,
honored, praised by my lord,
one perfect in that which comes forth from the mouth,
esteemed by the king for her rectitude,
whom he rewarded with gifts every day.
I entered with praises
and went forth beloved,
one whose mouth made her excellence,
who spoke and things were done for her,
one honored before the great royal wife, the crowned one, the true royal acquaintance, Taniy, the honored one, justified with the great god, lord of the West.[17]

So dense is the text's syntactic arrangement of participial and nominal relative statements that de Meulenaere initially mistook the whole for a Middle Kingdom stela.[18] Temporal specificity is conveyed only by certain phraseological, palaeographic, and iconographic features (on which see further below) that betray its creation during the Twenty-fifth Dynasty: royalty is invoked in the text as a standard of moral value, but never as chronological reference point.[19]

The formulaic turn in Twenty-fifth Dynasty self-presentation should, therefore, caution against any supposition of widespread and intentional disregard for the Kushite regime, and it also suggests important qualifications to other theories. Gnirs has suggested that biographies of the Kushite and Saite eras relied on archaic "formal and phraseological elements" so that "actual political circumstances such as usurpations or foreign occupation could be handled with delicacy and put into a broader historical context."[20] In some respects, this reading is entirely justified: Montuemhat, survivor of the Assyrian occupation, alluded to that traumatic event only euphemistically as "the raging of the hill-countries," and the widespread imitation of First Intermediate Period self-presentations during this era was reasonably interpreted by Otto as an attempt to put contemporary political circumstances into the broader historical context of Egypt's earlier periods of fragmentation.[21] Nevertheless, Gnirs's interpretation is most apt in reference to the *late* Twenty-fifth Dynasty and subsequent Twenty-sixth; by contrast, there is little indication in the surviving records that the first eighty years of Kushite suzerainty and occupation would have been perceived by the Egyptian populace as usurpation or national trauma. In fact, Otto observed that "[d]ie Kämpfe der Libyer und Äthiopen wirken im Spiegel ägyptischer Quellen nicht anders als die Kämpfe *ägyptischer* Dynasten."[22] This treatment of Kushite rule is all the more remarkable because the self-presentational and other Egyptian sources made no attempt to disguise the fact that the Kushite dynasts were not, in fact, of Egyptian origin. In his so-called Crypt Inscription, Montuemhat boasted openly of *ꜥ3 n mnḫ.i ḥr* [*ib nb.i*(*?*)] *iy m rsy*, "the magnitude of my excellence in [the heart of my lord(?)] who came from the south."[23]

Self and Compatriots under Kushite Rule

Representation of the nonroyal self vis-à-vis compatriots during the Twenty-fifth Dynasty presents a similar problem for analysis. On the one hand, a great many nonroyal biographies placed heavy emphasis upon family pedigree across the Third Intermediate and Late Periods, often listing several generations of ancestors.[24] On the other hand, Vittmann has lamented the "frequent" and "bewildering . . . lack of information on parentage and family relations" in the inscriptions of nonroyal individuals living in Egypt who bore Kushite names during the Twenty-fifth Dynasty.[25] Here we may offer a ranking of two provisional explanations.

The absence of pedigrees for Kushite individuals in Egypt might conceivably be attributed to an Egyptian popular stigma against immigrant ancestry and a resultant Kushite reticence to celebrate it, but this theory would not accord well with the iconographic evidence. Markers of Kushite ancestry are well attested in relief and statuary during the Twenty-fifth Dynasty, not only for the king and his family, but equally upon the monuments commissioned by nonroyal immigrants—particularly by Kushite women. The lunette of Taniy's aforementioned stela (Fig. 11.3) provides an illustrative example, depicting her with what Lichtheim described as a "broad flat nose and a strong chin" framing "thick lips" on a "large head" with either "short cropped hair or a tightly fitting cap"—in sum, "Nubian traits as depicted in sculpture and relief of the Twenty-fifth Dynasty."[26] Elsewhere in the corpus, Kushite women are equally characterized by unusual attire and coiffure, including such elements as a "curiously raised" hairstyle, tasseled frontlets, and a wide cape, often with a fringe and apparent tail.[27] The Kushite image cannot reasonably be interpreted as a stigmatized topos during the Twenty-fifth Dynasty, for its distinctive features influenced even the representation of certain Egyptian officials. The head of Ity (Fig. 11.1) exemplifies this trend, with its "emphasis on the nostrils, with the small folds of flesh to the sides . . . and the crisply outlined, pleasantly set mouth."[28] The manner in which Kushite features were represented and imitated in the iconographic evidence from this period offers no simple answer as to why nonroyal Kushites of the same era would have omitted information about their parentage and family relations.

To gain better purchase on this question, it is worth examining more closely those Egyptians who did include pedigrees when their Kushite counterparts did not. In the inscription upon his aforementioned statue, Ity provided the names and titles of his paternal ancestors for the preceding six generations, each of them connected to either or both of the Theban cults of Amun and Khonsu in which Ity himself was priest.[29] This example fits well with the larger observation that pedigree functioned in biographical inscriptions primarily as a legitimation of one's succession to office, a priority equally suggested by the centrality of the hometown in biographies of this era and also by their frequent reliance upon the didactic model of the paternal instruction.[30] The omission of pedigrees from the biographies of Kushite individuals in Egypt cannot be rationalized as their disinterest in heredity, because Kushite royal inscriptions over the next several decades quite frequently invoked the importance of hereditary succession for nonroyal officials *in Nubia*.[31] Consequently, the dearth of Kushite familial data in Egypt must be explained by other means. Here Vittmann has made a useful intervention, observing that, not only Kushite immigrants, but also the Egyptians Harwa, Akhamenru, and Pedamenope, had provided surprisingly little information about their parentage and family relations.[32] This pattern might be explained by the fact that each of these men was something of a parvenu, having risen to an office and evident wealth that his ancestors do not appear to have possessed.[33] It would therefore seem reasonable to conclude that officials were most likely to enumerate several generations of ancestors if that line of succession could justify their current office; for Kushite immigrants in Egypt, pedigree seldom offered such an advantage, so it was not included in their self-presentation.

Self-Presentation in Nubia

In 1990 Wolf attributed a self-presentational stela found at Semna to the famed mayor of Thebes, Montuemhat, and for the next two decades this interpretation became popular across the literature on the Twenty-fifth Dynasty.[34] Yet Wolf's attribution seems to have been a red herring: subsequent analysis of the archaeological context, iconography, palaeography, prosopography, technical vocabulary, grammar, phraseology, and expressed cultural values of that stela indicate that it more likely belonged to a general named Montuemhat during the Middle Kingdom.[35] Examination of the larger geographic and historical context of that monument simultaneously exposed a remarkable pattern: no nonroyal biographies or nonroyal statues contemporaneous with the Twenty-fifth Dynasty have yet been found in the whole of Nubia.[36] At a time when personal piety yielded a relative profusion of nonroyal religious testimonials in Egypt, Nubia appears to have been wholly bereft of textual self-presentation by nonroyal individuals. This contrast between the Egyptian and Nubian halves of the Double Kingdom may be explained either as a shortage of native officials to commission such monuments in Nubia, as a royal prohibition against nonroyal self-presentation in Nubia, or instead as a shortage of craftsmen in Nubia trained in lapidary inscription and sculpture.

An earlier generation of Egyptologists imagined the administration of Nubia during the Twenty-fifth Dynasty as a cadre staffed mostly, if not entirely, by Egyptians—men whose monuments of self-presentation were better sought back home in Thebes.[37] Yet this interpretation has been considerably undermined in recent decades by our improved understanding of Kushite onomastics. Just two generations after the Kushite withdrawal from Egypt, royal stelae of Aspelta mention a total of thirty-two nonroyal officials, of whom *only seven* bear clearly recognizable Egyptian names.[38] Among the remaining twenty-five names, several exhibit one or more of the elementary graphemes most typical of group writing, as used for non-Egyptian names; the names of these twenty-five officials are perhaps to be seen as linguistically Meroitic, particularly as several include specific phonemic sequences that would later recur in names transcribed in the Meroitic script.[39] In the case of at least one of these officials (Malowiamani), the attribution of his name to the Meroitic language would appear certain from the inclusion of a recognizably Meroitic lexeme (*wi* "travel" or "arrive") that is elsewhere followed by a combination of unvocalized Egyptian determinatives 𓂾𓂻 to clarify its Meroitic meaning.[40] Kushite inscriptions of the same era repeatedly invoke the principle of hereditary succession for nonroyal officials, so it would seem logical to conclude that some of the Kushite officials who held office under Aspelta were descended from earlier Kushites who held office in Nubia during the Twenty-fifth Dynasty.[41] There is consequently little reason to believe that the dearth of nonroyal self-presentation in Nubia would have resulted from a shortage of native officials to commission such monuments there.

A seemingly more plausible explanation would attribute this dearth to a royal prohibition against nonroyal self-presentation in Nubia. For instance, Török has observed that, south of the First Cataract,

> [p]ersonal piety existed only within the framework of the god-king relationship, viz., in the form of the cult of the colossal royal statues. . . . It follows from this that the types of private representations in the round, in relief and in painting which were created in Egypt in association with temple- and mortuary cults were not adopted in Kush, even though the representation of Kushite dignitaries in Twenty-Fifth Dynasty Egypt was common.[42]

Yet Török judiciously refrains from interpreting this distribution of evidence as the result of a formalized policy, acknowledging that nonroyal persons did at least appear unnamed within temple reliefs and in the minor arts; they were not absent from Kushite iconographic and textual records, but their appearance in those corpora lacked an "independent cult significance" of the kind produced by so many examples of nonroyal self-presentation in Egypt.[43] In support of Török's interpretation, it should be noted that the Kushite royal records did not impose anonymity upon nonroyal Kushites: Pi(ankh)y's Great Triumphal Stela acknowledged a Kushite general by name, and the image of an unnamed lector priest in Taharqo's procession of officials at Kawa was singled out by later vandals for very careful and selective erasure.[44] Moreover, a private stela commissioned by a nonroyal Kushite named Pasalta is known in Nubia *after* the Twenty-fifth Dynasty, as is a bowl inscribed for the priest Penamun.[45] These examples combine to raise doubts as to whether there was any absolute censure of either visual or textual self-presentation among Kushite elites.

It would therefore seem most likely that the lack of nonroyal statues and biographies in Nubia during the Twenty-fifth Dynasty resulted instead from a shortage of available craftsmen trained in lapidary inscription and sculpture. Indeed, even statues of Kushite queens have seldom been found in Nubia: Amanimalel's statue from Gebel Barkal remains the earliest known example, but its subject lived after the Twenty-fifth Dynasty.[46] In Nubia, the de facto restriction of statuary and inscription primarily to Kushite kings may derive in large part from their reliance upon Egyptian specialists. Though found at Gebel Barkal, Pi(ankh)y's Great Triumphal Stela used the locational adverb *dy* (here) in a manner suggestive of Egyptian authorship, and the text notably closed by hailing the king as "ruler, beloved of Thebes."[47] Likewise, Taharqo famously levied the craftsmen for his Kawa temple from distant Memphis.[48] A similar case can be made for many of the ushabtis buried with Taharqo and his successors at Nuri, because Howley has astutely noted several features indicative of Egyptian manufacture: the use of distinctly Egyptian materials like serpentine and alabaster, the latter carved most easily soon after its quarry; a particularly fine variety of faience found also on contemporaneous ushabtis in Egypt; and the appearance of ushabtis with dorsal pillars, bearing only a single hoe, or with text covering only the back side—all characteristics that first emerged in Egypt during the Twenty-sixth Dynasty.[49] Kushite royals would seem to have enjoyed exclusive access to these Egyptian imports, as well as to Egyptian craftsmen experienced in large stone sculpture and inscription; they may well have exercised a monopoly on that trade of the kind that both Török and Edwards have proposed for their Meroitic royal successors—but, unlike those successors, the kings of the Twenty-fifth Dynasty do not appear to have redistributed those prestige goods in any appreciable degree among lower-level elites.[50] The native Kushite officials who served that dynasty lacked ready access to such Egyptian imports and Egyptian craftsmen, so that nonroyal biographies and statuary of the kind found in contemporaneous Egypt either did not exist in Nubia or were created in such small numbers that none has survived.

Conclusions

For the theme of self-presentation, the features that most distinguish the Kushite era from preceding and succeeding periods are three enigmatic absences: the absence of royal names upon the great majority of nonroyal monuments in Egypt; the absence of pedigrees in the records of Kushite immigrants in Egypt; and the absence of biographies and statuary for nonroyal individuals in Nubia. In response to each of these puzzles, the analysis offered here has favored practical explanations rather than grand political or ideological ones. While a hypothetical case could be made for an intentional disregard of the Kushite regime in the Egyptian nonroyal corpus, the absence of royal names in that corpus is better attributed to the formulaic language of the *Idealbiographie*, combined with the extended social distance between the Kushite pharaoh and his Egyptian subjects. Similarly, the omission of pedigrees from the biographical inscriptions of Kushites in Egypt does not appear to have resulted from Egyptian xenophobia but instead from the simple fact that foreign pedigrees did not effectively legitimate the offices of first- and second-generation immigrant parvenus. Finally, the absence of biographies and statuary for nonroyal individuals in Nubia should not be taken to suggest that Nubia was devoid of native officials or that those officials were forbidden from self-presentation by a royal policy; the most defensible conclusion is that nonroyal officials did not have sufficient access to the (mostly Egyptian) craftsmen trained in lapidary inscription and sculpture.

None of these issues was as salient under earlier Libyan and later Saite rule. Even though the dynasties of Bubastis, Leontopolis, and Sais were descended from Libyan forebears, those ancestors had long been Egyptian residents, and the domestic governance of those dynasties did not draw their kings far beyond the borders of Egypt itself; as a result, there would seem to have been no exceptional social distance between those royal houses and the populace over whom each ruled. Most of the nonroyal Libyans who served those dynasties were likewise descended from Egyptian residents, so that their pedigrees could justify current offices in Egypt by impressive lines of hereditary succession. Lastly, the Libyan and Saite regimes do not appear to have had any significant cadre of officials permanently residing far from Egypt's borders and ateliers, so there would seem to be no adequate parallel in those epochs to the nonroyal Kushite officialdom of the Double Kingdom's Nubian half. The effects of these problems upon the biographical corpus during the Twenty-fifth Dynasty consequently differentiate that era within the long history of Egyptian self-presentation. In most other respects, the period of Kushite rule fits seamlessly between the Third Intermediate and Late Periods, so that these few peculiarities of biography form the weft drawn across the more continuous warp of foreign rule, immigration, archaism, personal piety, and self-presentation during the first millennium BC.

Notes

1 G. Vittmann, "A Question of Names, Titles, and Iconography: Kushites in Priestly, Administrative and Other Positions from Dynasties 25 to 26," *MSGB* 18 (2007), 139–61; J. Winnicki, *Late Egypt and Her Neighbours: Foreign Population in Egypt in the First Millennium BC* (Warsaw, 2009), 145–371, 379–495.

2 J. Heise, *Erinnern und Gedenken: Aspekte der biographischen Inschriften der ägyptischen Spätzeit* (Göttingen, 2007), 362.

3 C. Price, review of *Inschriften der Spätzeit*, III: *Die 25. Dynastie*, by K. Jansen-Winkeln, *Orientalistische Literaturzeitung* 107.2 (2012), 147. E.g., Osorkon I, II, and III are commonly named upon nonroyal statuary: K. Jansen-Winkeln, *Inschriften der Spätzeit*, II: *22.-24. Dynastie* (Wiesbaden, 2007), 63, 65, 67, 126, 134–35, 139, 148, 152–53, 301, 304, 306, 309–10.

4 K. Jansen-Winkeln, *Inschriften der Spätzeit*, III: *Die 25. Dynastie* (Wiesbaden, 2009); cf. K. Jansen-Winkeln, *Inschriften der Spätzeit*, IV: *Die 26. Dynastie, 1–2* (Wiesbaden, 2014).

5 Jansen-Winkeln, *Inschriften der Spätzeit*, III, 30, 204.

6 E.g., Jansen-Winkeln, *Inschriften der Spätzeit*, III, 28–30, 34, 36–37, 53, 194–96, 209, 212, 216–17, 220, 225, 227.

7 For the sizable corpus of nonroyal monuments even beyond Thebes and Abydos, see: Jansen-Winkeln, *Inschriften der Spätzeit*, III, 364–95, 564.

8 For a nonroyal statue bearing the name of Psusennes I, see K. Jansen-Winkeln, *Inschriften der Spätzeit*, I: *Die 21. Dynastie* (Wiesbaden, 2007), 69–70.

9 U. Rößler-Köhler, *Individuelle Haltungen zum ägyptischen Königtum der Spätzeit* (Wiesbaden, 1991), 147.

10 Heise, *Erinnern und Gedenken*, 344; Rößler-Köhler, *Individuelle Haltungen*, 72; F. Tiradritti, "Three Years of Research in the Tomb of Harwa," *EA* 13 (1998), 6; see, also, HRW 1997 R 200 in S. Einaudi and F. Tiradritti, eds., *L'enigma di Harwa: Alla scoperta di un capolavoro del Rinascimento Egizio* (Milan, 2004), 196 fig. 43; Boston MFA 72.745 in C. Pérez Die, *Nubia: Los reinos del Nilo en Sudán* (Barcelona, 2003), 165, no. 76; cf. M. Ayad, "The Funerary Texts of Amenirdis I: Analysis of Their Layout and Purpose" (PhD diss., Brown Univ., 2003), 34, n. 146.

11 Rößler-Köhler, *Individuelle Haltungen*, 365.

12 See n. 5 above, as well as: E. Russmann, "Mentuemhat's Kushite Wife (Further Remarks on the Decoration of the Tomb of Mentuemhat, 2)," *JARCE* 34 (1997), 24; P. Barguet, Z. Goneim, and J. Leclant, "Les tables d'offrandes de la grande cour de la tombe de Montouemhât," *ASAE* 51 (1951), 493–94, pl. 2; London BM 24429, lls. 5–6, in J. Leclant, *Enquêtes sur les sacerdoces et les sanctuaires égyptiens à l'époque dite "éthiopienne"* (Cairo, 1954), 17, 21–22, pl. 5; Vittmann, "Question of Names, Titles, and Iconography," 152.

13 One unusual case in which the king is named as living regent and not ancestor: Cairo JE 37346 in Jansen-Winkeln, *Inschriften der Spätzeit*, III, 248–49.

14 K. Exell and C. Naunton, "Administration," in T. Wilkinson, ed., *The Egyptian World* (London, 2007), 104.
15 Heise, *Erinnern und Gedenken*, 287, 289, 291; cf. K. Jansen-Winkeln, "Zu den biographischen Inschriften der 25. und 26. Dynastie," *Die Welt des Orients* 38 (2008), 171–72.
16 Vittmann, "Question of Names, Titles, and Iconography," 146.
17 See Cairo CG 20564, lls. 6–10, in M. Lichtheim, "The Stela of Taniy, CG 20564: Its Date and Its Character," *SAK* 16 (1989), Taf. 2.
18 H. de Meulenaere, "Retrouvaille de la dame Taniy," in J. Baines, T.G.H. James, A. Leahy, eds., *Pyramid Studies and Other Essays Presented to I.E.S. Edwards* (London, 1988), 68–72.
19 A. Leahy, "Taniy: A Seventh Century Lady (Cairo CG 20564 and Vienna 192)," *GM* 108 (1989), 45–56; Lichtheim, "Stela of Taniy."
20 A. Gnirs, "Biographies," in D. Redford, ed., *The Oxford Encyclopedia of Ancient Egypt*, I (Oxford, 2001), 188.
21 Cairo CG 42241 (=JE 37176), sixth col. from viewer's left below lunette, in J. Leclant, *Montouemhat, quatrième prophète d'Amon, prince de la ville* (Cairo, 1961), 84, pl. 22; E. Otto, *Die biographischen Inschriften der ägyptischen Spätzeit: ihre geistesgeschichtliche und literarische Bedeutung* (Leiden, 1954), 78. See also Heise, *Erinnern und Gedenken*, 350–57, but cf. Jansen-Winkeln, "Zu den biographischen Inschriften der 25. und 26. Dynastie," 167–68.
22 Otto, *Biographischen Inschriften der ägyptischen Spätzeit*, 114 [original emphasis]. See also: K. Jansen-Winkeln, "Die Fremdherrschaft in Ägypten im 1. Jahrtausend v. Chr.," *Orientalia* 69 (2000), 13–16, 19–20; J. Assmann, *Ägypten: Eine Sinngeschichte* (Munich, 1996), 319; D. O'Connor "New Kingdom and Third Intermediate Period," in B. Trigger, B. Kemp, D. O'Connor, A.B. Lloyd, eds., *Ancient Egypt: A Social History* (Cambridge, 1983), 195.
23 Text B, North Lateral Wall, col. 12, in Leclant, *Montouemhat*, pl. 68; R. Ritner, *The Libyan Anarchy: Inscriptions from Egypt's Third Intermediate Period* (Atlanta, 2009), 559–60.
24 Price, review of *Inschriften der Spätzeit*, III, 146.
25 Vittmann, "Question of Names, Titles, and Iconography," 146.
26 Lichtheim, "Stela of Taniy," 207–208; see also, Leahy, "Taniy," 46–47.
27 Russmann, "Mentuemhat's Kushite Wife," 25–27; A. Lohwasser, "Die Darstellung der Tracht der Kuschitinnen der 25. Dynastie," in S. Wenig, ed., *Studien zum antiken Sudan* (Wiesbaden, 1999), 586–603; A. Lohwasser, *Die königlichen Frauen im antiken Reich von Kusch* (Wiesbaden, 2001), 210–25; A. Lohwasser, "Ein archäologischer Beleg für einen kuschitischen Kopfschmuck," *MSGB* 17 (2006), 121–25; L. Habachi, "Mentuhotp, the Vizier and Son-in-Law of Taharqa," in E. Endesfelder, K.-H. Priese, W.-F. Reineke, S. Wenig, eds., *Ägypten und Kusch* (Berlin, 1977), 169 and first two unnumbered pls.; F. Griffith, "Scenes from a Destroyed Temple at Napata," *JEA* 15, no. 1.2 (1929), 26–28, pl. 5. For the vestiture of Kushite men, see A.

Hallmann, "The 'Kushite Cloak' of Pekartror and Iriketakana: Novelty or Tradition?" *JARCE* 43 (2007), 15–27, to which may now be added A. Leahy, "Kushites at Abydos: The Royal Family and Beyond," in E. Pischikova, J. Budka, and K. Griffin, eds., *Thebes in the First Millennium* BC (Newcastle upon Tyne, 2014), 61–95, esp. 67–68.

28 E. Russmann, *Eternal Egypt: Masterworks of Ancient Art from the British Museum* (London, 2001), 227.

29 Leclant, *Enquêtes sur les sacerdoces*, 17.

30 Price, review of *Inschriften der Spätzeit*, III, 146; Heise, *Erinnern und Gedenken*, 261, 289, 302–306.

31 Ny Carlsberg Glyptotek Æ.I.N. 1708, l. 10, in M. Macadam, *The Temples of Kawa*, I (Oxford, 1949), pls. 15–16; Louvre C 257, lls. 14–16, 18, in H. Schäfer, "Die aethiopische Königsinschrift des Louvre," *ZÄS* 33 (1895), Taf. 4–5; and D. Valbelle, *Les stèles de l'an 3 d'Aspelta* (Cairo, 2012), pls. 4A–4B; Cairo JE 48865, l. 10, in N.-C. Grimal, *Quatre stèles napatéennes au Musée du Caire* (Cairo, 1981), pls. 9a-9.

32 Vittmann, "Question of Names, Titles, and Iconography," 146.

33 Cairo JE 37377 in Jansen-Winkeln, *Inschriften der Spätzeit*, III, 280; pBrooklyn 47.218.3, col. 5, l. 5, in R. Parker, *A Saite Oracle Papyrus from Thebes in the Brooklyn Museum* (Providence, RI, 1962), 16, Nr.6/6a, pl. 4; J. Leclant, "La prêtre Pekiry et son fils le Grand Majordome Akhamenrou," *JNES* 13.3 (1954), 154–84; Leclant, *Enquêtes sur les sacerdoces*, 3–12; G. Vittmann, *Priester und Beamte im Theben der Spätzeit: Genealogische und prosopographische Untersuchungen zum thebanischen Priester- und Beamtentum der 25. und 26. Dynastie* (Vienna, 1978), 102–103; R. Bianchi, "Petamenophis," *LÄ* IV (1982), 991–992.

34 P. Wolf, "Die archäologischen Quellen der Taharqozeit im nubischen Niltal" (PhD diss., Humboldt-Uni. Berlin, 1990), 34, 113; L. Török, *The Kingdom of Kush: Handbook of the Napatan-Meroitic Civilization* (Leiden, Boston, 1997), 250; K. Dallibor, *Taharqo: Pharao aus Kusch: Ein Beitrag zur Geschichte und Kultur der 25. Dynastie* (Berlin, 2005), 230; L. Török, *Between Two Worlds: The Frontier Region between Ancient Nubia and Egypt 3700* BC*–500* AD (Leiden, Boston, 2009), 344–45.

35 J. Pope, *The Double Kingdom under Taharqo: Studies in the History of Kush and Egypt c. 690–664* BC (Leiden, Boston, 2014), 154–74.

36 Erratum: Pope, *Double Kingdom under Taharqo*, 173, where it is misleadingly implied that some *nonroyal* biographical texts are known from Upper Nubia during the Twenty-fifth Dynasty.

37 H. Brugsch, *Egypt under the Pharaohs: A History Derived Entirely from the Monuments* (London, 1891), 387; J. Breasted, *A History of Egypt: From the Earliest Times to the Persian Conquest* (New York, 1905), 537–38; G. Reisner, "Excavations at Napata, the Capital of Ethiopia," *BMFA* 15 (1917), 26.

38 For chronology, see J. Pope, "Shepenwepet II and the Kingdom of Kush," in K. Cooney and R. Jasnow, eds., *Joyful in Thebes: Egyptological Studies in Honor*

of Betsy Bryan (Atlanta, 2015), 356–57. For a list of these nonroyal officials, see Pope, *Double Kingdom under Taharqo*, 146–48. As members of the royal family, Henuttakhebi and Madiqen are both excluded from the present discussion of nonroyal officials.

39 For *s-k-n*, see: Valbelle, *Les stèles de l'an 3 d'Aspelta*, 43, 78–83; K.-H. Priese, "Das meroitische Sprachmaterial in den ägyptischen Inschriften des Reiches von Kusch" (PhD diss., Humboldt-Uni. Berlin, 1965), 127; N.-C. Grimal, *La stèle triomphale de Pi('ankh)y au Musée du Caire* (Cairo, 1981), pls. 1, 5; Vittmann, *Priester und Beamte*, 96, 99, 100, 171; Nu. 36 in D. Dunham, *Royal Cemeteries of Kush*, II, *Nuri* (Boston, 1955), 19–24 fig. 12, 198, 204 no. 5, pl. 141 no. 1; T. Eide, T. Hägg, R.H. Pierce, L. Török, eds., *Fontes Historiae Nubiorum*, I (Bergen, 1994), 211–14.

40 Valbelle, *Les stèles de l'an 3 d'Aspelta*, 84–86, pls. 3A–3B.

41 See n. 31 above.

42 Török, *Kingdom of Kush*, 403–404.

43 Török, *Kingdom of Kush*, 404.

44 Cairo JE 48862, l. 8, in Grimal, *La stèle triomphale de Pi('ankh)y*, pls. 1, 5; T. Kendall, *Gebel Barkal Epigraphic Survey 1986: Preliminary Report of First Season's Activity* (Boston, 1986), 23 n. 35; on the Kushite name *Lemerskeny*, see n. 39 above. For the erased priest, see Macadam, *Temples of Kawa*, II, pl. 15 b.

45 For Pasalta, see Boston MFA 21–2–101 in: D. Dunham, *The Royal Cemeteries of Kush*, V, *The West and South Cemeteries at Meroe* (Boston, 1963), 395, 397 fig. 220; R. Leprohon, *Corpus Antiquitatum Aegyptiacarum: Museum of Fine Arts Boston*, fasc. 3, *Stelae II: The New Kingdom to the Coptic Period* (Mainz, 1991), 131–34. For Penamun, see: C. Bonnet and D. Valbelle, "Un prêtre d'Amon de Pnoubs enterré à Kerma," *BIFAO* 80 (1980), 8, pls. 1–4.

46 Khartoum SNM 1843 in R. Morkot, "A Kushite Royal Woman, perhaps a God's Wife of Amun," in K. Sowada, ed., *Egyptian Art in the Nicholson Museum, Sydney* (Sydney, 2006), 155–56, n. 4.

47 Cairo JE 48862, lls. 26–27, 159, in Grimal, *La stèle triomphale de Pi('ankh)y*, pls. 1, 4B, 6, 12.

48 Khartoum SNM 2678 (= Merowe Museum 52), l. 21, in Macadam, *Temples of Kawa*, I, pls. 7–8.

49 K. Howley, "Imports or Influence? Tracing the Origin of Royal Tomb Assemblages from Nuri" (Paper presented at the annual meeting of the American Schools of Oriental Research, San Diego, California, November 20, 2014). Some ushabtis were nevertheless fashioned in Upper Nubia, as ushabti molds were found at Sanam: F. Griffith, "Oxford Excavations in Nubia VIII–XVII: Napata, Sanam Temple, Treasury and Town," *LAAA* 9 (1922), 75, 81, 85, 87–89, pl. 17.

50 D. Edwards, *The Archaeology of the Meroitic State: New Perspectives on its Social and Political Organisation* (Oxford, 1996), 29, 47; L. Török, "Kush and the External World," in S. Donadoni and S. Wenig, eds., *Studia Meroitica, 1984* (Berlin, 1989), 49–215, 365–79.

12

Self-Presentation in the Late Dynastic Period

Damien Agut-Labordère

The first Persian domination (525–404 BC), corresponding to the Manethonian Twenty-seventh Dynasty, constitutes a deep rupture in the political and cultural history of Egypt: for the first time, the pharaonic crown was confiscated by a foreign imperial power for a long time.[1] During more than a century, Egypt was governed from Persia. For five generations, the Egyptian elites were kept out of the highest level of the power that was confiscated by the Persians headed by the satrap based in Memphis.[2] This chapter aims primarily to study how these two centuries of profound transformation have marked the discourse by which the Egyptian elites presented themselves in their self-presentation.

Egyptian Nonroyal Self in the First Persian Domination (525-404 BC)

The history of self-presentation during the first Persian domination can be divided into two distinct phases. A first one corresponds to the reigns of Cambyses (525–522 BC) and Darius I (522–486 BC). Despite some notable changes, this period saw the continuation of trends attested at the end of the Saite Period. The second phase began with the reign of Xerxes I (486–465 BC) and ended in 404 BC with the beginning of the rule of the last 'indigenous dynasties.' This last phase is characterized by an unprecedented scarcity or even disappearance of individual inscriptions in hieroglyphs.

From Cambyses to Darius I: Continuity of Saite Traditions (525-486 BC)

Since the pioneering work of G. Posener, the figure of Udjahorresnet has dominated the historiography of the Egyptian elite under Persian domination. The cursus of the high official is first known thanks to a long hieroglyphic inscription engraved on a fine statue in the Museo Egizio Vaticano.[3] Because Udjahorresnet holds in his hands a naos containing a statue of Osiris-hemag, one supposed that this statue was placed in the temple of this god in Sais. The gesture is explained by the inscription: "O Osiris, Lord of eternity! The chief doctor Udjahorresnet wraps you with his arms in protection" (l. 3–4). The cenotaph of Udjahorresnet in the Abusir cemetery was excavated by the University of Prague.[4] The inscriptions on the walls and on the sarcophagus found in situ complete the self-presentation on his naophorus statue. Under Amasis and Psametik III, Udjahorresnet occupied very important military positions: chief of the Hau-Nebu mercenaries and overseer of the royal *kbnwt*-vessels. Like his father, he also played a central role in royal administration and court. The variety and importance of his titles denote a man whose career took place in the higher sphere of Saite state. With the Persians, Udjahorresnet loses his military and financial titles. His political role then seems to have been limited to counseling the great kings on Egyptian affairs.

The figure of Udjahorresnet is at the center of the discussions concerning the way in which Cambyses installed his power in Egypt.[5] Generally, the inscription of the Vatican statue was read through the prism of what M.J. Versluys calls "methodological nationalism," which attributes to the whole of humanity the same national feelings as those of Europeans of the nineteenth and twentieth centuries.[6] According to this paradigm, the Egyptian elites should have spontaneously rejected Persian domination because of its foreign origin. In this perspective, the itinerary followed by Udjahorresnet is perceived as that of a traitor, a *collaborateur* who tried to justify his betrayal in his inscriptions.[7] It is nothing of this sort. In the inscription of the *Naoforo vaticano*, the coming to the service of the Persians is presented with sobriety: "His Majesty assigned me the function of chief physician, he made me live with him as companion and director of the palace and compose his royal titulature, his name of king of Upper and Lower Egypt: The-offspring-of-Re" (Text B: 12–13). If Udjahorresnet mentions a catastrophe (*nšn*; Text B: 40–42) and describes the intrusion of soldiers into the sacred enclosure of the temple of Sais, it is only to slip into the classic role of the pious notable, that of restorer of the temples of the city he patronizes.[8] Udjahorresnet suggests that the good deeds accomplished by Cambyses and Darius I for the temples of Sais were the result of his influence on the Persian kings. The self-presentation on the Vatican statue is not a statement on Cambyses's general policy in Egypt but a demonstration proving that Udjahorresnet is the best intermediary between the priests of Sais and the Persian power. The enumeration of Cambyses's benefits is only to serve the glory of Udjahorresnet: "His Majesty (Cambyses) did this because I had made His Majesty know Her Majesty's (Neith's) greatness." Restorer of the cults, intermediary between the local populations and the king, the self-presentation of Udjahorresnet is in line with those of the former Saite elite.

The fact that Udjahorresnet has received such sustained scrutiny by historians has cast into the shadows the other inscriptions concerning Egyptians who served the first Achaemenid kings. Their careers have been situated in very precise sectors of the state: the financial administration and the management of precious metals. We do not know exactly which Persian king, Cambyses or Darius I, the Egyptian Ptahhotep served, as overseer of the Treasury, attested by a schist statue in particular.[9] A second example of such royal administrator is given by the statue of Psamtiksaneith, chief of all craftsmen of the king in gold and silver.[10] The same clichés concerning the good notable protecting the local gods appear on Saite self-presentation carved on the Ptahhotep statue at the Brooklyn Museum: "I protected their shrines by taking care of them at all times and providing their altars with food. I have increased their sacrificial tables, I have equipped their temples abundantly with all things, I have done great things (?) in the tem[ple of Ptah]." It is vain to see in this passage the evocation of the destruction of temples by the Persians. There is no element to authorize such an interpretation. It is more probably a way to present the self as restorer of cults.[11]

The search for signs of rupture on nonroyal statues has led to the overestimation of the historical meaning of some sculptural elements. The best example of such misinterpretation is provided by the so-called Persian wrap, a garment with one knotted strap which gives to the lower part of a statue a cylindrical form "covering the legs, so that the subject resembles a pillar or column."[12] It was for a long time considered as typical of the Persian Period, but it is now clear that it is attested at least from late Twenty-sixth Dynasty through the Roman Period.[13] Malaise pointed out that this cloth was associated with the presence of a naos.[14] Its presence could, therefore, attest that the notable had the right to carry a divine statue in procession.[15] Another sculptural feature interpreted as a sign of Persianism is what is called the 'Persian gesture,' which refers to the fact that the right hand of the subject is folded over his left wrist. Attested in Egyptian nonroyal statuary up to Roman times, the origin of this gesture has not been established with certainty. In the present state of our knowledge, we have to consider that it is only 'Persian' in name.[16] If the analysis of the clothes or postures proves somewhat unsatisfactory, it is not the same for that of the jewels in 'Persian style' on statues. As we know that Persian kings offered necklaces and bracelets as reward to favorites, the exhibition of this type of object on the statues could attest to a close link with the Achaemenid power.[17]

The most important and remarkable fact lies in that the elements that bind the Egyptian elite to the Persians are nonverbal. This link is expressed first in a sculptural way on the statue, not in the text. It is as if, in the absence of physical presence of the Persian kings in Egypt, the relationship between the notables and the Persian kings had become impossible to describe through language. If the elite exhibit their rewards, they never tell the acts that brought them. The first fundamental change between the self-presentations of the Persian Period and those of the Saite Period is the absence of the king.[18] This situation is verified by the disappearance of titles expressing a close relationship with the king as "king's acquaintance" (*rḫ nsw*).[19] Just as significantly, the title of "overseer of the antechamber" (*i͗my-r rwt*), held by those who were responsible for organizing the royal hearings, also falls into disuse. The only Egyptian to mention Cambyses then Darius I in one of his inscriptions is Udjahorresnet; he is the only one that we are sure met two Persian kings in person because he was one of their physicians. Here lies the origin of the dating problem posed by Persian Period statues of nonroyal individuals; without explicit mention of a royal name, specialists are obliged to rely first on stylistic criteria, hence the importance taken by sculptural criteria in the study of statuary from the Persian Period.

Among the sculptural features, more or less relevant, attached to the Persian Period is the emergence of what Bothmer called the "true portraiture." Derived from his work on the already mentioned statue of Psamtiksaneith, Bothmer notes the realistic character of the face on it. He points out that "the Period of Persian domination shows portrait-like features which follow no given formula, but seem to have been taken directly from the living model."[20] Relying on the statue of Psamtiksaneith, he clarifies his purpose: "The quizzical expression seems to reflect the face as the sculptor saw it, unconventional and portrait-like." Moreover, a few statue heads were modeled in the course of the fifth century BC, which must be regarded as true portraiture since they rendered the individual features of definite persons, presenting not only the structure and outer form of a man's head, but something of the inner personality as well.[21] One may then wonder whether this novelty is due to a change in aesthetic sensitivity or may be considered as an indication of a change in the relationship between the sculptor and his model. The realism of the heads of the Persian Period statues could, therefore, testify to a greater proximity between the artist and the notable. It is, therefore, possible that many Persian Period statues were entirely financed by the notables themselves without any support from the crown. This situation could explain the desire to seek a physical resemblance between the head of the statue and its model.

The Dark Age of Egyptian Self-Presentation (486-404 BC)

With the reign of Xerxes (486–465 BC) begins a unique period in the millennial history of Egyptian self-presentation characterized by a complete absence of inscription and even statues. No statue can be dated with certainty from a period that extends from the 480s until the dawn of the fourth century BC. Some commentators argue that this absence is due to chance of discovery and conservation hazards. However, this argument runs up against the fact that there is no such period of absence during the second and the first millennia BC. Due to this, four or five generations of members of the Egyptian elite are plunged into darkness.

The same phenomenon is observed concerning the funerary material. D. Aston has convincingly argued that the scarcity of Persian Period funerary artifacts (sarcophagi, coffins, shabti figures, canopic jars, stelae, Ptah-Sokar-Osiris figures, funerary papyri, amulets, bead nets, etc.) may be due to the difficulty in dating the material from the period.[22] Aston concludes that these findings concerning funerary stelae and Ptah-Sokar-Osiris figures could be extended to almost all funerary material: "It is probable that a number of so-called Thirtieth Dynasty examples are a little earlier, and so-called Twenty-Sixth Dynasty examples a little later." Even if the methodological bias pointed out by him is correct, it is nevertheless not enough to explain the fact that during the Persian Period, and especially from the 480s onwards, the same problem arises for *all* Egyptian type of material: statues, stelae, funeral artifacts, demotic papyrus, etc. The Egyptian documentation, as a whole, becomes rarefied. The typological problems highlighted by Aston most certainly have their origin in the poverty of documentation: given the small number of documents available, it is difficult to establish typologies for artifacts dated to the period of 480–404 BC.

How to explain this deletion? Arguing only the loss of political power of the Egyptian elite leads to circular reasoning. Indeed, to the extent that statues constitute one of the main sources concerning the role played by Egyptians in the satrapy of Egypt, their disappearance forbids us any conclusion regarding the reality of the political power held by the Egyptian elites during the period 480–404 BC. This little 'Dark Age' of self-presen-

Table 12.1. Statues of Egyptian elites from the reign of Amasis to the end of the first Persian domination (570–c.400 BC)

Amasis (570–526 BC) 44 years	Cambyses and Darius I (525–486 BC) 50 years	From Xerxes to the end of the first Persian domination (486–404 BC) 82 years
30 statues	*12 statues*	*0 statues*
CG 672 [185]	Baltimore, WAM 11.208	
Louvre A.91 [189]	Brooklyn Mus. 37.353 [Ptahhotep]	
Cairo JE 34043 [190]	Brooklyn Mus. 71.139 [Ptahhotep]	
JE 34044 [191]	Caire, coll. Michaelidès [Udjahorresnet]	
[192]	Carthage, MC 883.1 [statue base]	
[193]	Cleveland, CMA 1920.1978 [Horudja, son of Tefnakht]	
[194]	Florence MA 11900	
CG 679 [195]	Unknown (seen in 1828–1829 by Rosselini) [Udjahorresnet]	
Bologne 1820 [196]	Unknown (seen in Basel in 1972)	
JE 34045 [197]	Karlsruhe, BLM H.350	
CG 677 [198]	Seattle WA, SAM 47.63	
Firenze 1522 [199]	Vatican, MGE 22690 (196) [Udjahorresnet]	
[200]		
BM 134 [204]		
Firenze 1784 (1523) [205]		
[206]		
Louvre E.1310 [208]		
Berlin 1048 [210]		
Cairo TN 27/11/58/8 [211]		
Philadelphia 42–9–1 [212]		
CG 1279 + Musée de Roanne [213]		
E.2.1865 [214]		
Alexandria 402 [215]		
Alexandria 26532 [216]		
[217]		
Alexandria 435 [220]		
Storehouse Sakkara [239]		
CG 666 [261]		
[262]		
[263]		

Sources:
Col.1: list of statues based on K. Jansen-Winkeln, *Inschriften der Spätzeit*, IV/1, Wiesbaden, 2014; numbers in square brackets refer to this work.
Col.2: my gratitude goes to S. Qaheri-Paquette, who completed the list of statues from the Persian Period.

tation may be explained by economic factors, namely by a general impoverishment of the Egyptian elite throughout the fifth century BC. We must indeed not forget the very basic fact that the existence of the self-presentational inscriptions presupposes that the notables had access to hard stones extracted most often from remote regions of the Nile. For the Saite Period, we know that some statues were made in royal workshops and offered to the deserving royal officials.[23] One must also keep in mind a passage of the petition of Peteise relating the moment when Peteise I, under the reign of Psamtik I (664–610 BC), took advantage of an inspection to obtain stones intended to build the monuments that he promised himself to install in the temple of Teudjoi: "He went then in the South country in inspection. He came to Elephantine and to make a stele in Elephantine stone and blocks for two stone statues, and brought them to Teudjoi" (P. Rylands IX 7:15). The disappearance of the Saite state and the creation of a satrapy dominated by Persian elites, certainly, deprived the Egyptian elites of charges in the royal administration and of remunerative advantages leading to a general impoverishment.[24] This could explain the disappearance of nonroyal inscriptions and statues and the scarcity of the funerary furniture during the period 480–404 BC. This, added with the reduction in royal donations to Egyptian temples, attested by the decree of Cambyses, had to affect the incomes connected with sacerdotal prebends.[25]

Period of Independence (404–343 BC): A Return to Tradition?

Unsurprisingly, the return to independence from 404 BC to 343 BC, corresponding to the Twenty-eighth through Thirtieth Dynasties, saw a resurgence of classic, that is, Saite form of self-presentation. This resilience, after eighty years of silence, is the clear sign of the importance of such self-presentational texts for the Egyptian elite. However, if the reappearance of self-presentation is marked by the resumption of many characteristics attested in Saite inscriptions, the self-presentation texts of the fourth century BC present also some unique features.

Reconnecting with Interrupted Tradition

The evocation of relationships between the notables and the king makes its return in the inscriptions, in particular with the Thirtieth Dynasty.[26] Not surprisingly this reappearance of the royal person in the self-presentation is accompanied by that of aulic titles fallen into disuse during the first Persian domination such as 'king's acquaintance' or 'overseer of the antechamber.' Even more significantly, Djedhor, son of Wennefer and Diamuntjau, who bears the title of *ḫtmty-bity* (royal seal-bearer; Mexico City, Private

Collection), vaunts himself as the one "who served his lord in private" (*šms nb.f m wʿʿ.w*; l. 1) enjoying private audiences with an unnamed king.[27]

As under the Saites, the self-presentation of the independence period is dominated by the above-mentioned cliché of the notable restorer of one or more local temples. An inscription of Djed-Hor, known as 'the Savior' (Cairo 4/6/9/1), who lived during the second half of the fourth century BC, gives a good overview of the qualities that must be possessed by the good local potentate who has "to protect the weak from the strong, [Djed-Hor is] the leader from the whole multitude, who does justice in all things, his task is to annihilate iniquity, who repels the plunderer."[28] The identity of these looters, mentioned in other inscriptions from the second half of the first millennium BC, is a matter of debate. They have often been assimilated with Persians. But, in a general way, no inscription explicitly refers to Persian domination. The formula "who repels the opponents" (*ḫsf šnʿw*), which is attested elsewhere, remains too vague to be interpreted.[29] Only the statue MMA 1996.91 provides a more precise mention. It belonged to a notable who had carried out restoration work on the temple of Abydos. In the part of the inscription devoted to the description of its benefits, he mentions "the anguish which the foreigners had caused" (l. 4).[30] In this specific case, it is possible that reference is made to the Persian or Macedonian troops.

The same indifference toward the Persians appears in the remarkable self-presentation preserved in the Naples Stela, a statue base belonging to the chief priest of Sakhmet Somtutefnakht.[31] Due to his advanced medical knowledge, Somtutefnakht was taken to the Achaemenid court in Persia, and later, sometime around Alexander's conquest, fled back to his Egyptian home town of Herakleopolis after seeing his god Herishef in an oracular dream.[32] In all cases, whether the self-presentation was engraved on statues placed in temples or in funeral self-presentation inscribed in tombs, we find the same expressing that the decisions taken by the subject were encouraged by deities: Herishef in the case of Somtutefnakht, and Isis for the son of Nektanebo II.[33]

The same absence of qualms concerning the collaboration with foreign authority prevails in the tomb of Wennefer at Saqqara, who mentions being arrested under suspicion of a conspiracy by the "Superior" (*ḫrp*) who governed Egypt. Cleared of guilt, Wennefer was sent to the "Lord of the Two Lands" who was at the "country of Su[sa]" (the toponym is damaged). The absence of a proper name in the narrative has led historians to multiple hypotheses about the identity of the "Superior" and, above all, of the "Lord of the Two Lands." According to von Kaenel, this episode took place in the late 360s or 350 BC, when the Egyptian king Tachos (Djed-Hor), on campaign against the Achaemenid Empire,[34] was driven from power by a coup d'état and found refuge in Susa. Following this hypothesis, the "Lord of the Two Lands" would be the king Tachos in exile.[35] Ladynin pointed out the inconsistency of this hypothesis. Indeed, at the time when Tachos was in Susa he had lost all authority in Egypt, making incomprehensible the absolution he would have given to Wennefer, especially since it was accompanied by an exhortation to return to live in a country of which he was no longer king. Ladynin proposes to identify the "Lord of the Two Lands" as Alexander the Great and the "Superior" as Cleomene of Naucratis.[36]

Emergence of the Figure of the Wise Priest in the Fourth Century BC

Insisting on a close link uniting the subject and his god is not a new thing. However, in the self-presentation of the fourth century BC, this element took on a new nuance. The Egyptian notables of this period present themselves not only as pious men, but—and this is a novelty—as able to protect the local gods themselves, as expressed by Klotz in the conclusion of the important study he devoted to naophorous statues: "the peculiar form of standing naophoroi popular in the 4th century B.C., where dedicants would hold the shrines unnaturally between their hands without pillar or support. By assuming this impossible posture, sculptors drew attention to the artificiality of the naophorous conceit, the notion that a human could carry or protect a god."[37] In the same perspective, Gorre has shown that the notables of the fourth century BC insist on their role of priests, putting forward their religious titles.[38] They present themselves as with clean-shaven heads, expressing their ritual purity, ready to perform worship.[39] The insistence on priestly functions is coupled with an emphasis on the wisdom expressed by various epithets as *wr m rḫ* (great of knowledge), well attested in the sarcophagi of the Thirtieth Dynasty,[40] or *dns ib* (heavy of mind).[41]

Showing the extent of one's knowledge is one of the main features of the self-presentation of this period. This could probably explain the taste for cryptography and for complex graphic/hieroglyphic puns observed on several statues and texts. The fascinating Brooklyn Green Head (Brooklyn Museum acc. No. 55–175 + Cairo JE 38064 K586) constitutes a masterpiece of this emerging trend. Dated from about 360–340 BC, it represents a priest of Monthu. Meulenaere assumed that the curious image engraved at the top of the pillar showing the god Osiris sitting with a *wr*–bird could be an encrypted form of the name of the priest: *Wsir-wr*.[42] A similar kind of rebus was already being decrypted by Yoyotte in the falcon statues representing Nektanebo II (*Nḫt-Ḥr-Ḥbyt*; Strong is Horus of Hebyt) in which the king holding a sword (*nḫt*) and a jubilee pavilion (*ḥb*) is placed between the legs of Horus (*Ḥr*).[43]

Besides these scholarly games, some self-presentations of the independence period[44] are written with an alphabetic spelling very similar to those attested on the two royal stelae from Naukratis and Thonis.[45] Combining alphabetic orthographies using hieroglyphic signs and graphic puns, this script avoids the determinatives and some of the phonetic markers. The use of such kind of writing, in nonroyal but also in royal inscriptions, forgetting three millennia of Egyptian scribal tradition, could be interpreted as the sign of the transformation of the traditional Egyptian scribal culture. After a long period of absence, the hieroglyphic writing could have been invested with a higher cultural value while, paradoxically, the Egyptian scribes, more peculiarly in the Delta and the royal entourage, became less and less proficient in it. Therefore, the scholarly games of the scribes of the Thirtieth Dynasty could be considered as a form of preciosity typical of small groups of scholars aware of being part of an intellectual elite. Whereas the scribes excluded from these circles could have been tempted to imitate, less formally, hieroglyphic writing without, however, being able to follow its graphic and orthographic rules. Anyway, this kind of erudite and distant relationship to hieroglyphic script foreshadows the Ptolemaic writing system. The reappropriation of the self-presentation and the hieroglyphic script in the fourth century BC are part of the same reinvention of Egyptian traditions after at least one century of political, economic, and cultural weakening of the Egyptian elite.

Conclusions

From Cambyses to the end of the fifth century BC, for the first time in the millennial history of Pharaonic Egypt, the Egyptian elite lose control of the state. It is important to note that no self-presentational inscription insists on the apocalyptic aspect of this invasion. None was, strictly speaking, anti-Persian. In a very striking and puzzling contrast with the Assyrian invasions of seventh century BC, which deeply impacted the collective memory of the Egyptians,[46] the Persian domination only had a very limited echo in the Egyptian cultural memory.[47] Despite this, Persian domination induced a profound rupture in the whole Egyptian society, leading to a redefinition of the role of the elite expressed in their self-presentations. The inscription of Udjahorresnet was the last one providing so many details concerning the actions accomplished by a notable in the service of pharaohs. In the fourth century BC, the service of the local god largely replaced that of the king. This led the elites to emphasize their religious functions and to present themselves first as priests. This is not a complete novelty, but after the

Persian domination of the fifth century BC, the religious aspect monopolized the narrative space in the self-presentation. This evolution was accompanied by the promotion of erudition in the field of Egyptian high culture. Contrasting with the Saite period during which dignitaries presented themselves as pious men of power, close to the king and protected by their gods, the Egyptian elite of the Persian Period, deprived of position (and income) in the high administration of the satrapy, withdrew to the priestly functions. Excepting the sixty years of independence, from 400 to 342 BC, Egyptian culture ceased definitely to be shared by the rulers who dominate Egypt; it takes refuge in temples, kept in the hearts and minds of Egyptian priests.

Notes

1 The political situation created by three Assyrian invasions during the first part of the seventh century BC is in no way comparable with the thirteen decades of the first Persian domination.

2 D. Agut-Labordère, "Administrating Egypt under the First Persian Period: The Empire as Visible in the Demotic Sources," in B. Jacobs, W.F.M. Henkelman, and M. Stolper, eds., *Administration in the Achaemenid Empire* (Wiesbaden, 2017), 685–689.

3 For the translation of the text see G. Farina, "La politica religiosa di Cambise in Egitto," *Bilychnis* 18.1 (1929), 449–57; G. Posener, *La première domination perse* en *Egypte. Recueil d'inscriptions hiéroglyphiques* (Cairo, 1936), 3–25; G. Botti and P. Romanelli, *Le sculture del Museo Gregoriano Egizio* (Rome, 1952), 36–41; E. Otto, *Die biographischen Inschriften der ägyptischen Spätzeit: Ihre geistesgeschichtliche und literarische Bedeutung* (Leiden, 1954), 169–73; M. Lichtheim, *Ancient Egyptian Literature*, III: *The Late Period* (Berkeley, 1980), 36–41; U. Rößler-Köhler, "Zur Textkomposition der naophoren Statue des Udjahorresnet/Vatikan Inv. Nr. 196," *GM* 85 (1985), 43–54; J. Baines, "On the Composition and Inscriptions of the Vatican Statue of Udjahorresnet," in P.D. Manuelian, ed., *Studies in Honor of William Kelly Simpson*, I (Boston, 1996), 83–92; L. Bareš, *The Shaft Tomb of Udjahorresnet at Abusir. With a Chapter on Pottery by Květa Smoláriková and an Appendix by E. Strouhal* (Prague, 1999), 32–35; A. Kuhrt, *The Persian Empire: A Corpus of Sources from the Achaemenid Period*, I (London, 2007), 117–22 (who follows Posener 1936); H. Sternberg el-Hotabi, *Ägypter und Perser: Eine Begegnung zwischen Anpassung und Widerstand* (Rahden, 2017), 21–30.

4 L. Bareš, *The Shaft Tomb of Udjahorresnet at Abusir*.

5 P. Briant, *From Cyrus to Alexander: A History of the Persian Empire* (Winona Lake, IN, 2002), 57–61.

6 M. Pitts and M.J. Versluys, "Globalisation and the Roman World: Perspectives and Opportunities," in M. Pitts and M.J. Versluys, *Globalisation and the Roman World World: History, Connectivity and Material Culture* (Cambridge, 2015), 7.

7 See, for example, G.B. Gray, "The Foundation and Extension of the Persian Empire," in J.B. Bury, ed., *Cambridge Ancient History*, IV (Cambridge, 1964), 19. Udjahorresnet was a traitor who would have kept the fleet out of the battle. G. Godron, "Notes sur l'histoire de la médecine et l'occupation perse en Égypte," in *Hommages à François Daumas*, I (Montpellier, 1986), 285–97, which identifies Udjahorresnet as the ophthalmologist of the king Cyrus.

8 C. Thiers, "Civils et militaires dans les temples. Occupation illicite et expulsion," *BIFAO* 95 (1995), 493–516.

9 Brooklyn Museum 37.353.

10 Cairo CG 726 (=JE 31335), Bothmer, *Egyptian Sculpture of the Late Period 700 B.C. to A.D. 100* (New York, 1960), 78–79 no. 65 and pls. 61–62. J.A. Josephson, "An Enigmatic Egyptian Portrait in the British Museum (EA 37883)," *GM* 184 (2001), 16–17, suggested the fourth century BC to date this statue on stylistic criteria. This proposition is rejected by G. Vittmann, "Rupture and Continuity: On Priests and Officials in Egypt during the Persian Period," in P. Briant and M. Chauveau, eds., *Organisation des pouvoirs et contacts culturels dans les pays de l'empire achéménide* (Paris, 2009), 98.

11 On this kind of inscription which does not make reference to a specific event, see H. Bassir, *Image and Voice in Saite Egypt: Self-Presentations of Neshor Named Psamtikmenkhib and Payeftjauemawyneith* (Tucson, AZ, 2014), 3.

12 Bothmer, *Egyptian Sculpture of the Late Period*, 89–90, pl. 68 (San Francisco de Young Museum 54664); D. Klotz, "Replicas of Shu: On the Theological Significance of Theophorus and Naophorus Statues," *BIFAO* 114.2 (2014), 298–99.

13 G. Vittmann, "Continuity and Rupture," 97–98 n. 37.

14 Malaise, "Les hypostoles: Un titre isiaque, sa signification et sa traduction iconographique," *CdE* 82 (2007), 316–18; Klotz, "Replicas of Shu," 298.

15 As an example, see, I. Guermeur, "Les monuments d'Ounnefer, fils de Djedbastetiouefânkh, contemporain de Nectanébo Ier," in I. Regen and F. Servajean, eds., *Verba Manent: Recueil d'études dédiées à Dimitri Meeks par ses collègues et amis* (Montpellier, 2009), 177–99.

16 J.D. Cooney, "*The Portrait of an Egyptian Collaborator*," *BBM* 15 (1953), 1–16; J.D. Cooney, "Persian Influence in Late Egyptian Art," *JARCE* 4 (1965), 44–46; C. de Wit, "Some Remarks Concerning the So-Called 'Isis' in the Museum Vleeshuis, Antwerp," *CdÉ* 39 77/79 (1964), 61–66 ; B. Rantz, "A propos de l'Égyptien au geste 'perse'," *Revue belge de Philologie et d'Histoire* 67 (1989), pl. IIIb (Paponot statue), IVb (JE 52523).

17 M. Wasmuth, "Reflexion und Repräsentation kultureller Interaktion: Ägypten und die Achämeniden" (PhD diss., Basel, 2009), 268–70; S. Qaheri, "Recherches sur la cour royale égyptienne à l'époque saïte (664–525 av. J.-C.)" (Phd diss., Lyon, 2014), 163–96; M. Wasmuth, "Persika in der Repräsentation der ägyptischen Elite," *JEA* (2018), 241–50.

18 Otto, *Die biographischen Inschriften des ägyptischen Spätzeit*, 116–17.

19 As noted by Vittmann, "Rupture and Continuity," 97–98.

20 B. Bothmer, *Egyptian Art* (New York, 2004), 151–52.
21 Bothmer, *Egyptian Art*, 150, fig. 9.7.
22 D. Aston, "Dynasty 26, Dynasty 30, or Dynasty 27? In Search of the Funerary Archaeology of the Persian Period," in A. Leahy and J. Tait, eds., *Studies on Ancient Egypt in Honour of H. S. Smith* (London, 1999), 17–22.
23 Qaheri, "Recherches sur la cour royale égyptienne à l'époque saïte," 163–65.
24 The "distinct lack of new tomb constructions" and the fact that most burials dated from the Persian period were placed in shallow surface graves or intruded within ancient tombs (see, D. Aston, "In Search of the Funerary Archaeology," 22) could be another indicator of this impoverishment.
25 D. Agut-Labordère, "Beyond the Persian Tolerance Policy: Great Kings and Egyptian Gods during the Achaemenid Period," in D. Edelman, A. Fitzpatrick-McKinley, and P. Guillaume, *Religion in the Achaemenid Persian Empire* (Tübingen, 2016), 320.
26 Klotz, "Replicas of Shu," 308.
27 Klotz, "Replicas of Shu," 306, n. e.
28 P. Vernus, *Athribis Textes et documents relatifs à la géographie, aux cultes et à l'histoire d'une ville du delta égyptien à l'époque pharaonique* (Cairo, 1978), 193–95 [doc. 161].
29 D. Klotz, "Two Studies on Late Period Temples at Abydos," *BIFAO* 110 (2010), 144, n. m.
30 G. Gorre, *Les relations du clergé égyptien et des Lagides d'après les sources privées* (Leuven, 2008), 198–209; Klotz, "Two Studies," 147.
31 O. Perdu, "Le monument de Samtoutefnakht à Naples," *RdÉ* 36 (1985), 89–113.
32 G. Burkard, "Medizin et Politik: Altägyptische Heilkunst am persischen Königshof," *SAK* 21 (1994), 39–40.
33 J.J. Clère, "Une statuette du fils aîné du roi Nectanabô," *RdÉ* 6 (1951), 135–56, pl. I.
34 Briant, *From Cyrus to Alexander*, 663.
35 F. von Känel, "Les mésaventures du conjurateur de Serket Onnophris et de son tombeau," *BSFE* 87–88 (1980), 31–45; F. von Känel, *Les prêtres-ouâb de Sekhmet et les conjurateurs de Serket* (Paris, 1984), 198–201.
36 I. Ladynin, "An Egyptian Prince at Alexander's Court at Asia? A New Interpretation for the Evidence of the Statuette of the Son of Nectanebo II," in K. Nawotka and A. Wojciechowska eds, *Alexander the Great and the East: History, Art, Tradition*. (Wiesbaden, 2016), 9–18.
37 Klotz, "Replicas of Shu," 328.
38 Gorre, *Les relations du clergé égyptien et des Lagides.*
39 Klotz, "Replicas of Shu," 300. For a different interpretation of these statues, see B. Bothmer and H. de Meulenaere, "The Brooklyn Statue of Hor, Son of Pawen," in L.H. Lesko, ed., *Egyptological Studies in Honor of Richard A. Parker Presented on the Occasion of His 78th Birthday December 10, 1983* (Hanover, NH, London, 1986), 10–15.

40 Klotz "Two Studies," 140–41.
41 Klotz, "Replicas of Shu," 307.
42 Bothmer, *Egyptian Art*, 164–65.
43 J. Yoyotte, "Nectanebo II comme faucon divin?" *Kêmi* 15 (1959), 70–74.
44 For other references on the Naples Stela, Louvre A 94, and the Mexico City statue of Djedhor son of Wennefer and Diamuntjau, see Å. Engsheden, "On the Verge of Ptolemaic Egyptian: Graphical Trends in the 30th Dynasty," *Abgadiyat* 1 (2006), 35–41.
45 Klotz, "Replicas of Shu," 301 (with references). A.S. von Bomhard, *The Decree of Saïs: The Stelae of Thonis-Heracleion and Naukratis* (Oxford, 2012).
46 The Assyrian invasion generated an abundant epic literature centered, in particular, on the figure of Inaros; see K. Ryholt, "The Assyrian Invasion of Egypt in Egyptian Literary Tradition," in J.G. Dercksen, ed., *Assyria and Beyond: Studies Presented to Mogens Trolle Larsen* (Leiden, 2004), 484–90; I. Rutherford, "The Earliest Cross-Cultural Reception of Homer? The Inaros-Narratives of Greco-Roman Egypt," in T. Rutherford, ed., *Greco-Egyptian Interactions. Literature, Translation, and Culture 500 BCE–300 BCE* (Oxford, 2016), 83–106.
47 D. Agut-Labordère, "From Cultural to Political Persianism: The Use and Abuse of the Memory concerning the Looting of the Egyptian Temples during the Ptolemaic Period," in R. Strootman and M.J. Versluys, eds., *Persianism in Antiquity* (Stuttgart, 2017), 147–62.

13

Women's Self-Presentation in Pharaonic Egypt

Mariam Ayad

When considering Egyptian culture and society, expressions of self-presentation are often hidden under layers of intermediaries. For men, we are dealing with one layer: the artist/scribe composer of the text or relief, who had to interpret the preferences of the "order-giving self."[1] For women, an added layer of male relatives comes between us and women's self-presentation in art and text. Nearly all surviving textual and iconographic representations of women were commissioned by their male relatives: a husband, a father, or a son.[2] The image that emerges from these textual and artistic representations is, thus, mostly mediated by a double male perspective: that of the male relatives who commissioned the work, as well as that of the scribes and artists who produced the work. The resulting representations and expressions are thus often reflective of this male perspective.[3] Still, some information may be gleaned from women's titles and epithets—how they developed, shifted, and evolved over time—and a few examples of women's biographical texts. Despite the dearth of the latter, closer examination of these exceptional examples will help us achieve a more nuanced understanding of how ancient Egyptian women chose to present themselves for their peers and for all posterity.

The Old Kingdom and First Intermediate Period

Egyptian self-presentational inscriptions from the Old Kingdom are attested in a funerary context. The earliest self-expressions are found on epitaphs inscribed in nonroyal tombs. This is true for both men and women's self-presentations.[4] But whereas men's self-presentations focused on the professional progression of their careers and their 'moral personality,' women's self-presentational inscriptions consisted mainly of their honorary or priestly titles, and only occasionally, contained some genealogical information.[5] Possibly because women were mostly confined to the private realm, their self-presentational inscriptions were more limited than men's.[6]

The earliest attestations of women's self-presentational epithets, dating to the Fourth Dynasty, belong to priestesses associated with the cult of Hathor.[7] Priestesses of Hathor were drawn from the ranks of elite women, including royal princesses such as Hemetre (also called Hemi), whose tomb inscription identifies her as the "bodily daughter" of King Unas of the Fifth Dynasty.[8] Whether the priestly titles of these women were honorific or reflected actual duty in the cultic service of Hathor has been the subject of some debate. But enough evidence survives to suggest that they earned some income, possibly in connection with their priestly duties.[9]

A priestess of Hathor, Nedjetempet, had her own separate tomb in the Teti cemetery in Saqqara, just a few meters to the northeast of the tomb of the vizier Mereruka, her son.[10] Her false door is among the largest false doors solely dedicated to a woman.[11] Nedjetempet's inscriptions include:

> An offering which the Great God gives
> That she may travel the perfect ways of the West
> And that she may be followed by her *ka*s.
> Having grown old most perfectly.
> The royal acquaintance, priestess of Hathor lady of the sycamore, priestess of Neith north of her wall, priestess of Wepwawet, the *imakhu* in the sight of Anubis, Nedjetempet, whose perfect name is Iteti.[12]

Similar prayers are found on a group of First Intermediate Period funerary stelae from Naga al-Dayr. On the stela of Hedwi, a priestess of Hathor and "Sole Royal Ornament," a prayer reads:[13]

> May she land and cross the heaven
> May her hand be taken by the great god, Lord of the Sky, that he may lead (her) to his pure places

At their core, such (simple) prayers reflect the deceased's desire for an afterlife.[14]

Slightly more substantial self-presentational information may be gleaned from a dedicatory inscription at al-Qasr wa-l-Sayed. Dating to the reign of Pepi II, the text is inscribed above a tomb shaft dedicated by one Idu Seneni to his "beloved wife Asenkai." After detailing the exact measurements of the shaft he had constructed for his wife, Idu Seneni threatens action against anyone who attempts to take the shaft away from her.[15] In his rather lengthy text, Idu Seneni declares that he is the legal owner of the tomb and proceeds to praise his wife, writing that "She has not uttered a sentence which has repulsed my heart; she was not angry while she was alive."[16] The text concludes with the speech by Asenkai, in which she says:

> I am a priestess of Hathor, beloved of her whole town.
> In respect of any person who shall take this shaft from me,
> I shall be judged with them by the Great God.[17]

Naga al-Dayr stelae depicting women sitting alone before an offering table may have been similarly dedicated by husbands, desiring to have their wives join them in the afterlife.[18]

An example from Akhmim (CG 1613) dating to the end of the Old Kingdom, or possibly later,[19] reads:

> An offering which the king and which Anubis, who is on his mountain, who is in his wrappings, give that invocation of offerings be made for the royal acquaintance, priestess of Hathor, Iret
> It was her husband who made these inscriptions, the royal document scribe Bawy.[20]

Highlighting a wife's concern for her husband's approval and blessing, the inscription of Nebet, a priestess of Hathor, ends with the phrase "one honored before her husband, his beloved, the praised one of her mother, Nebet, whose beautiful name is Iby" *(im3ḫt ḫr ḥi.s mrt.f ḥsyt mwt.s Nbt rn.s nfr Iby)*.[21] In her inscription, Nebet replaces a deceased's favorite god with a reference to her husband. Paralleling the standard balanced sentence construction of male biographies, Nebet declares that she was "beloved of her husband, praised of her children,"[22] once more substituting "husband" for "father" and "children" for "mother," respectively. Similar substitutions may also be seen in the funerary inscriptions of Khamerernebty, another priestess of Hathor.[23] The same desire for approval is echoed in a stela from Naga al-Dayr, dedicated to the "Royal ornament, noblewoman, royal acquaintance, the priestess of Hathor, Ankhnes-Pepy, whose good name was Neni," who was also "praised of her husband" because of her "excellent character" *(nfr ḳd)*.[24]

Economically independent women, from the Old Kingdom onwards, could find their voice and express themselves. For instance, Khentit-ka, a priestess of Hathor, recites the threat formula on her son's stela. She says: "As for any man who will do anything ill to this, there will be judgement with him because of it by the Great God."[25] Typically, the tomb owner uttered this familiar threat. In this instance, Khentit-ka's recitation of the threat formula may indicate that she provided for the burial of her son, Wer-ka, a metal worker. A mother's provision for her son's burial is also indicated on an inscription on a fragmentary false door recovered from Giza mastaba tomb 7766.[26] On a stela dating to the Heracleopolitan Period, a son clearly declares that the source of his wealth was his mother, who appears seated next to him.[27] That may have also been the reason why the son of a provincial governor names his mother on his false door, referring to himself as the "son of Khenet."[28]

The source of these women's wealth could be hereditary or an array of administrative positions that women could hold during the Old Kingdom, including positions relating to stewardship or oversight and ones associated with the funerary service, such as "steward," "overseer of department of stores," "inspector of the treasure," "treasurer," and "overseer of funerary priests," among others.[29]

An Abydos stela (CG 1578) depicts one such woman: Nebet, who stands opposite a man, Khui, presumably her husband, from whose tomb the stela was recovered. Khui held title of overseer of the pyramid city. But it is Nebet's titles that dominate the stela.[30] On it, she is identified as a "Judge" and a "Vizier." Perhaps because this is the only known attestation of a female vizier of the Old Kingdom,[31] Nebet's titles have been dismissed as honorific. Fischer suggested that it was actually her husband Khui who "performed the functions of vizier."[32] Her exceptionally high status was also attributed to her close connection to King Pepy I of the Sixth Dynasty, who married two of her daughters, with the titles bestowed upon Nebet in "an attempt to enhance the otherwise commonplace background of a woman who became the grandmother of a king."[33] The stela would have been erected as "a late commemoration for Nebet."[34]

Nebet's self-presentational inscription, though, contains certain phrases borrowed directly from the standard male self-presentation, but modified to reflect her gender. Such phrases include "praised of *her* mother," who had "a caring heart for the orphan" (*smt-ib m nmḥw*).[35] In asserting her generosity to the less fortunate, Nebet claimed one of the essential (male) attributes of the moral character.[36] But her assertion may also reflect her economic autonomy or independence.

Other women also borrowed 'stock' phrases from the typical male self-presentation, such as "one whom people praise" and "whom all her town loved."[37] While Fischer maintains that these late Sixth Dynasty self-presentational epithets are "isolated examples,"[38] such moral assertions reflect the women's desire to emphasize their moral character and may be linked to their economic self-sufficiency. These assertions may thus be reflective of these women's agency and their possible autonomy.

Similar phrases were also engraved on limestone blocks that once stood in the decorated tomb chapel of lady Djehutinakht at Barsha, dating to the late Eleventh Dynasty. The blocks, which were discovered in 2014 above her burial shaft, bear two epithets of Djehutinakht's: *im3ḫt* (revered one) and *iry-pꜥt m3wt*. The adjective *m3wt* (new) placed after *iry-pꜥt* (hereditary noble woman) suggests that Djehutinakht's titles had been recently acquired, possibly as a sign of royal favor. Stock phrases commonly found in the self-presentational inscriptions of men, including "I gave bread to the hungry, water to the thirsty, clothes to the naked," were inscribed for Djehutinakht.[39] While assertions such as Djehutinakht's are commonly found in male autobiographies dating to the First Intermediate Period and the Middle Kingdom, they are rarely inscribed for women. Indeed, there does not seem to be any evidence for female self-presentations in the Middle Kingdom.[40]

The Middle Kingdom and Second Intermediate Period

Although no self-presentational texts of women survive from the Middle Kingdoms and the Second Intermediate Period, there are other modes of self-expression that survive: titles as well as visual media, particularly statuary. Statuary often provided the context for inscriptions.[41] But even when devoid of inscriptions, the decisions involved in carving and placing a statue are quite telling.

A title that first appears in the Eleventh Dynasty, *nbt pr* (mistress of the house), becomes quite popular by the mid-Twelfth Dynasty.[42] Initially, the title *nbt pr* was held by the wives of the provincial elite. But by the end of the Middle Kingdom, women associated with the royal court could also self-identify as *nbt pr*.[43]

The duties of a *nbt pr* revolved around overseeing household staff. In larger, better-off households, her duties also included supervising weavers and potters and anyone else responsible for the production of household items and food preparation.[44] While confining women's role to the domestic realm, this title gave women power, economic and otherwise, over the household.[45]

That this is so is evident from the case of the overseer of the Eastern Desert, Khenumhotep (II), who seems to have had two wives: Khety, who held the title of *nbt pr* and Tjat, who, initially held the title of *sḏ3wtyt/ ḫtmtyt* (sealer). Ward suggested that holders of this title "may have been in charge of household stores or perhaps the personal belongings of aristocratic women."[46] Tjat was thus a member of Khenumhotep's household staff. The distinction in status between Khety and Tjat is very clear on the south wall of the main chamber of Khenumhotep's tomb.[47] There, Khety is depicted on the western end of that wall, seated at an offering table. She sits facing left on a low-backed chair with feline legs and a piece of cloth folded on its back. She extends one hand toward the offering table, while in the other she holds a lotus flower to her nose.[48] Behind Khety, five women are depicted standing: three of her daughters; Tjat, who is accompanied by two children, a boy and a girl; and at the end of the procession, a *mnꜥt* (wet nurse).[49] There, Tjat is labeled as a "sealer" (*sḏ3wtyt/ḫtmtyt*). Elsewhere in the tomb, Tjat holds that title, even when she appears next to Khenumhotep. Her presence in his boat in one of the fishing scenes implies that she was his second wife.[50] But while Khety lived, Tjat seems to have held a secondary, or unofficial, status. Whenever they appear together, only Khety is labeled as a *nbt pr*.[51] Khety was also a daughter of a count (*s3t ḥ3ty-ꜥ*), a countess (*ḥ3tyt-ꜥ*), a priestess of Hathor (*ḥmt nṯr ḥwt-ḥr*), and a priestess of Pakhet (*ḥmt-nṯr p3ḫt*).[52] But of all her titles, it is *nbt pr* that immediately precedes her name.

Several nomarchs' wives seemed to prefer the title *nbt pr* over other titles, including the somewhat more prestigious title *ḥmt-ḥḳ3* (wife of a ruler). One such woman was Sat-ip, the wife of the nomarch Khenumhotep I, who appears next to her husband in his Beni Hassan tomb.[53]

A *nbt pr* could occupy a prominent position on the walls of her husband's tomb. For example, on the south wall of her husband's tomb, the *nbt pr* Hetepet, who was also a daughter of a count (*s3t ḥ3ty-ꜥ*), a priestess of Hathor, a priestess of Pachet, and a true royal acquaintance (*rḫ nsw m3ꜥt*), is depicted seated before her offering table, while six registers of household staff prepare and present her with food offerings.[54]

Occasionally, a *nbt pr* could have her own funerary stela, statue, and even her own tomb. In the Late Middle Kingdom site of Harageh, near Fayoum, the wealthiest burial belongs to the *nbt pr* Iytenhab.[55] Although plundered in antiquity, the tomb yielded several pieces of inlaid jewelry, including two silver pectorals, a cowry belt of shells, three mirrors, two cosmetic spoons, and several scarabs.[56] That Iytenhab was the sole owner of this tomb is clear from a stela recovered from it. The stela may have once stood in a chapel constructed above the tomb shaft, but it was misplaced and discovered inside the tomb.[57] The rectangular stela is decorated with a cavetto cornice and bears three lines of inscriptions that feature Anubis as the guarantor of funerary offerings in the *ḥtp di nsw* formula. The offerings are made for the *kꜣ n imꜣḫyt ḫr inpw iit-n-ḥb tn mꜣꜥt ḫrw msyt n ḥḏ mꜣꜥt ḫrw nbt imꜣḫ* ("the *ka*-spirit of the one revered before Anubis, this Iytenhab, justified, born of Hedjemaat, the justified, mistress of reverence"). No other person is mentioned on the stela. The only title included for Iyetenhab is *nbt pr*. Only her mother, with no titles, is named by way of filiation.[58] Represented on the left, Iytenhab faces right and is seated on a fine, low-backed, lion-legged chair with papyrus decoration, a piece of cloth folded on its low back. Iytenhab dons a long sheath dress and a tripartite wig as she extends a hand toward an offering table piled with three rows of offerings. On the other side of the offering table, an older woman sits on the ground holding a young boy on her lap.[59] This older lady may have been a grandmother, or a wet nurse hired to take care of the child.[60]

A tomb (TT 60) located in the cemetery of Sheikh Abd el-Qurna on the Theban western bank seems to belong to the *nbt pr* Senet. The tomb was initially thought to belong to Antefiqer, a vizier under Senwosret I.[61] Senet features prominently in that tomb, including on the false door, and often appears alone when receiving offerings from attendants.[62] She was initially identified as Antefiqer's wife, but seems to have been his mother. A seated statue of Senet, and fragments of another, were recovered from the tomb.[63] Inscriptions on either side of Senet's legs include a *ḥtp di nsw* formula that invokes Osiris "the Lord of Abydos, who is in the midst of the western hills" and identifies Senet as "a priestess of Hathor" and "a revered one before the great god, the lord of the sky" (*imꜣḫyt ḫr nṯr ꜥꜣ nb pt*).[64] Oddly, the figure of the vizier is either erased from scenes where he normally would have been represented, or is "completely obliterated by red ink."[65] The reasons for these erasures remain obscure. But it is possible that they were motivated by a need to make room for the tomb's new occupant.[66]

A granite, 64-cm-high statue dating to the Thirteenth Dynasty depicts the *nbt pr* Henutpu seated on a cubic chair, her hands resting on her thighs (CG 42035).[67] Recovered as part of the Karnak cachette,[68] and presumably commissioned by her son, the vizier Ankhu, this statue was placed near the sanctuary of Amun-Re at Karnak along with two other statues, also commissioned by Ankhu, commemorating himself and his father. On her statue, Henutpu is only identified as a *nbt pr*.[69] But the inscriptions on her son's granite statue further identify her as a vizier's wife, a king's daughter, and—surprisingly—a *t3tyt* (female vizier).[70] It has been suggested that Henutpu's importance may be attributed to her status as the wife of a vizier and the mother of another.[71] But if taken literally, the title of *t3tyt* (female vizier) may account for the placement of her statue at Karnak, an honor not accorded any other woman of her time.[72] Only three other statues depicting private women were placed in the precinct of Amun-Re at Karnak prior to the Late Period, all of which post-date the statue of Henutpu.[73]

A Thirteenth Dynasty bronze statue represents a woman sitting in an asymmetrical squat, one foot tucked under her, while the other is solidly anchored on the ground in front of her. Her upright leg and knee support a naked boy to whom she offers her right nipple, which she holds between her thumb and index finger. The boy, whose youth is indicated by a sidelock, wears a uraeus at his forehead, and may thus have been a royal prince. Another uraeus appears atop the woman's tripartite wig, prompting speculation that she may have been a royal princess herself.[74] Of unknown provenance, the 10.5-cm-high statue is currently in the Brooklyn Museum. A crudely incised text inscribed on the statue's base identifies the woman as "the hereditary noblewoman Sobek-nakht." While no other titles appear on the statue, she may have been the same Sobek-nakht mentioned on a stela from Edfu. There, she is identified as "king's daughter" in addition to being a "hereditary noblewoman."[75] It is not clear whether Sobek-nakht's statue was a votive offering evoking Isis, commissioned in the hopes of bearing a child of her own, or whether the statue represents her while nursing her own son or a royal prince.[76]

Statues representing wet nurses holding their nurslings are extremely rare, even in the New Kingdom, when royal nurses appear on funerary stelae and in the Theban tombs of their husbands and sons, holding their royal nursling.[77] In fact, only the New Kingdom statue of Satre holding Hatshepsut as king on her lap survives from that period.[78]

The New Kingdom and Third Intermediate Period

Satre's life-sized sandstone statue (Cairo JE 56264), which once stood in Hatshepsut's funerary temple at Deir el-Bahri, seems to have been smashed in antiquity.[79] Hieroglyphic inscriptions on the statue identify Satre as *mnʿt wrt šdt nbt t3wy* (chief nurse, who nurtured the Mistress of the Two Lands).[80] Satre is represented seated on a high-backed block chair, holding Hatshepsut on her lap.[81] Hatshepsut, who faces right, is depicted here as a miniature adult king in a manner reminiscent in composition and iconography of the Old Kingdom statue of Pepi II seated on his mother's lap (Brooklyn 39.119).[82] The placement of Satre's statue in the temple and its life-sized scale sets it apart from other New Kingdom, and particularly Eighteenth Dynasty, statues depicting women and may indicate that Hatshepsut herself commissioned it as a sign of her high esteem for Satre.[83] Satre's statue seems to be not only the earliest sculptural representation of a (nonroyal) wet nurse holding a royal child in that particular pose, but also "the earliest extant representation in any artistic medium of a nurse/tutor in a nurturing pose with a royal child."[84]

In tomb representations, the earliest attestation of this motif of a royal nurse holding a child on her lap seems to occur in the tomb of Kenamun (TT 93), where his mother is shown holding the smaller figure of King Amenhotep II on her lap. She is depicted facing left, while the king wearing his royal regalia is orientated toward the right, his hand extended to touch her, while his feet rest on the backs of nine bound captives who are represented on the side of the chair. She extends her right arm around his back, as her hand supports his head. She is labeled as *mnꜥt wrt šdt nṯr* (chief nurse, who nurtured the god). Standing opposite the king and his nurse are Kenamun and Pehsukher, presenting them with offerings.[85]

In Saqqara, the tomb of Maya, the *mnꜥt nsw* (royal nurse) of Tutankhamun is one of the most elaborate tombs dedicated to a woman in the New Kingdom. The tomb, which was discovered in 1996 by the French mission working in Saqqara, is dominated by representations of Maya, who is shown with Tutankhamun sitting on her lap.[86] On the east wall of chamber 1, Maya is depicted enthroned, facing left, and donning an elaborate wig held in place by a floral band and topped by a perfume cone and a lotus blossom. Facing her is Tutankhamun, who sits on her lap wearing his royal kilt and the blue crown, a coiled cobra at his brow. Maya places a lotus blossom at Tutankhamun's nose. Behind Maya are two registers of high officials. Two kneeling men occupy the top register, while four men wearing long kilts and holding various scepters appear on the lower register. The small scale of these officials is rather remarkable. They only come up to the lower part of the chair's back.[87] Elsewhere in the tomb, Maya is shown at a larger scale than other individuals represented in the tomb. While this is typical for male tomb owners, the representations of Maya remain strikingly exceptional.[88]

In belonging solely to her, and not to her husband, Maya's tomb is unique. Other royal nurses of the Eighteenth Dynasty appear prominently in the tombs of their husbands or sons, but do not have their own tombs in the Theban necropolis.[89]

One such woman is Hunay, the royal nurse of Amenhotep II, whose name is known from the tombs of her son Mery (TT 95 and TT 84), who served as high priest of Amun during the reign of Amenhotep II. In both tombs, she appears next to her son in scenes where one might expect the wife. In the traverse hall of TT 95, whether standing behind Mery as both make offerings to Amun-Re, Ra-Horakhty, and Amenhotep II (on the pillars), or seated next to him as recipients of funerary offerings (on the left wall), Hunay is depicted at the same scale as her son. The inscriptions identify her as *mnˁt wrt n nb tȝwy* (chief nurse of the Lord of the Two Lands), a title that indicates that she served a prince who later became a king.[90] In TT 84, a tomb partly usurped by Mery, Hunay's name is engraved where the name of the previous tomb owner's wife once stood, and the older inscription is changed to indicate that Hunay is Mery's mother, not his wife (*snt.f* changed to *mwt.f*). But Hunay's titles as royal nurse are not included in TT 84, possibly because of its earlier date to the reign of Thutmose III, whom Hunay had not served in this particular capacity.[91]

Another royal nurse, or *mnˁt nsw*, of Amenhotep II, Senetnay, appears in the tomb of her husband, Sennefer (TT 96) and is mentioned on his funerary cones. Her name is included next to his on stone vessels recovered from the Valley of the Kings (KV 42), and she is represented next to her husband in the tomb of the vizier Amenemopet (TT 29). In both TT 96 and TT 29, the epithet *šdt ḥˁw nṯr* (the one who nurtured the body of god) appears next to her name. Senetnay appears seated next to her husband on a statue that once stood at the temple of Amun at Karnak and is currently housed in the Egyptian Museum, Cairo (CG 42126). The half-life-size statue depicts Senetnay seated to the left of her husband, her arm wrapped around his waist. Shown at the same scale as her husband, she wears a simple wig and a sheath dress. In all identifying inscriptions on this pair statue, she is clearly identified as a *mnˁt nsw*.[92]

In the tombs of Mery (TT 84), Kenamun (TT 93), Sennefer (TT 96), and Amenemopet (TT 29), scribal equipment is depicted underneath the seats of women.[93] While the names of some of these women no longer survive, so that it is not clear whether they were the royal nurses discussed above or their sisters or daughters-in law, the presence of these scribal kits indicate that at least some women in these rarefied social circles were literate.[94] Remarkably, four of the five women depicted with scribal kits and included in Bryan's study held the title of *šmˁyt* (chantress) in the service of Amun-Re, Mut, Monthu and other gods.[95]

Although a few women held the title of *šmˁyt* prior to the New Kingdom, the title becomes commonplace during the New Kingdom and Third

Intermediate Period, particularly from the Nineteenth to the Twenty-first Dynasties.[96] Stelae depicting women alone abound in the New Kingdom and Third Intermediate Period. While many of the women continue to identify as *nbt pr* (mistress of the house), a substantial number were *šmꜥyt* (chantress). Although of diverse social status and geographic origin, the *šmꜥyt* were women with access to wealth.[97]

Four self-presentational inscriptions belonging to women survive from the Libyan Period (Twenty-first through Twenty-third Dynasties).[98] But despite the dearth of evidence, a few patterns may be discerned in these biographies. One of the earliest examples of that period dates to the reign of Pinudjem I of the mid-Twenty-first Dynasty and belongs to Tawdjatra (*tꜣ-wḏꜣt-rꜥ*), a chantress of Amen-Re.[99] Two self-presentational sections are included in her funerary papyrus (Cairo SR VII 11498/ JE 34033).[100] In addition to her role in the cult of Amen-Re, Tawdjatra was a chantress in the "Pure Foundation of Ptah" (*šmꜥyt n pꜣ grg wꜥb n Ptḥ*)[101] and a singer in the cult of Mut, where her titles included "great singer in the chamber of Mut, mistress of heaven" (*ḥsyt ꜥꜣt ꜥ n Mwt nbt pt*) and "singer in the chamber of Mut" (*ḥsyt n pꜣ ꜥ n Mwt*).[102] That latter title is found frequently in Theban tombs dating to the Twenty-first Dynasty, and is also attested in Memphis.[103] Tawdjatra's inscriptions include the rather enigmatic assertion "I served the King of my time,"[104] possibly indicating that she was a royal appointee or that she served the king directly.

Dating to the Twenty-second Dynasty, the self-presentational text of Shebensopdet (*šb-n-spdt*), daughter of Nimlot C and granddaughter of Osorkon II, appears on both sides of her seated statue at the Egyptian Museum, Cairo (CG 42228), and continues on the back of the statue.[105] An inscription running down the front of the statue and framing the legs of her seated figure indicates that the statue was dedicated by her husband Hor.[106] Shebensopdet was the daughter of Nimlot C, the son of Osorkon II by a minor wife. Nimlot C was the high priest, first in Heracleopolis and, later, in Thebes.[107] Shebensopdet's marriage to Hor, a "Royal Secretary of the South" who hailed from a distinguished Theban family of high officials, served to consolidate her father's Theban ties and helped him establish his position as high priest at Thebes. Hor's dedication of this statue for his wife may be taken as a sign of his high regard and affection toward her. It may also account for why information regarding him and their children were included in her inscriptions. Additionally, the self-presentational statements in Shebensopdet's inscription emphasize her personal charm. Such 'feminine' themes occur in the earliest attested female self-presentations.[108] Exceptionally, though, her inscriptions include the following lines:

On the left side:[109]

iḳrt mitt.i špst rḫ r.s
sꜣt nsw iḳr-biꜣ wꜥb-ꜥ.wy m ḫt nb
One virtuous like me, a noble lady who knows her speech,
King's daughter, who is good-natured, and pure-handed in everything.

And, on the back of her seat:

iḳr-mdw ḫnmw.s iry m ꜥntyw[110]
Skilled in speech whose fragrance is myrrh

and

wnn.i ḥm ḥr tp tꜣ wd<.i> mꜣꜥ n bw nb[111]
While I dwelled on earth I spoke truth to all.

Referring to Maat was an honor normally reserved for royal women.[112] That Shebensopdet included the statement that she "spoke truthfully (*wd.i mꜣꜥ*) to everyone," with its reference to Maat, may be reflective of her high status: in addition to being a royal granddaughter, she also became the mother-in-law of "the future vizier Nekhefmut C."[113] Crucially though, Shebensopdet's marriage to Hor established an important link between the Theban elite and the Tanite ruling house.

The self-presentational inscription of Nesi-khonsu-pakhered (*Ns-ḫnsw-pꜣ-ḫrd*), a granddaughter of Sheshonq I, is inscribed on a statue of her son Djed-Djehuti-ankh (CG 42206).[114] Like Shebensopdet, Nesi-khonsu-pakhered may have served as a pawn in the ruling house's policy of establishing marriage alliances with prominent Theban dignitaries. She came from a similar background and, like Shebensopdet, married into an established Theban priestly family. Nesi-khonsu-pakhered's father Iuput was appointed high priest of Amun at Thebes by his own father, King Sheshonq I, and was also granted the title of "army leader" (*ḥꜣwty*). Later, Iuput's monuments refer to him as governor of Upper Egypt.[115] Sometime during the reign of Sheshonq I, Nesi-khonsu-pakhered married Djed-Khons-ef-ankh, a descendant of an ancient Theban family of dignitaries (eleven earlier generations of Djed-Khons-ef-ankh's family are known).[116]

Much like Shebensopdet's, Nesi-khonsu-pakhered's biographical inscription combines elements emphasizing personal charm with information regarding her husband and children. Remarkably though, Nesi-khonsu-pakhered's inscription ends with a statement declaring her desire to establish her heirs in the temple of Mut, and considers her ability to secure those positions for them as the ultimate achievement for which she would be remembered. The text reads, in part: *pꜣ sḫꜣ n mnḫt mi ḳd ṯs iwꜥ.i m pr.s* (it is the remembrance of my own ability that my heirs flourish in her [Mut's] house).[117] This kind of expressed desire to pass on official and priestly positions to one's descendants is often seen in male self-presentational inscriptions. But it is very rarely seen on monuments belonging to women, since, normally, most women had no power to transmit any official positions. A similar declaration survives on a block statue belonging to a woman whose name does not survive. Dating to the reign of Sheshonq I, the inscription details how she buried her son, established his funerary cult, and secured her son's position for his child, her grandson.[118] Similar statements are often found in the self-presentational inscriptions of men, where the emphasis is on the burial of the father so that the son could succeed him in office, but are only rarely attested for women.

Dating to the reign of Osorkon II, similar family zeal may also be found in the inscriptions engraved on two statues of the fourth priest of Amun, Nakhtefmut. In addition to Nakhtefmut's own biographical statements, the statues bear prayers by Nakhtefmut's mother, wife, and daughter. While the mother boasts of her "noble descent," both mother and daughter express their emotional desire not to be separated from Nakhtefmut and to see him again, while the daughter declares her intention to protect the property her father had granted her.[119] The wife further beseeches Amun to protect their daughter, praying:[120]

> We here wish to dwell together
> God not separating us!
> As you live for me, I leave you not!
> Let your heart not grieve!
> Rather sit at ease each day,
> There is no evil coming!
> Let us not go to the land of eternity,
> That our names not be forgotten!
> Worth more is a moment of seeing sun-rays
> Than lasting lordship of death-land![121]

While the wife's prayer is not strictly biographical, it illustrates her closeness to her husband.

The Nubian, Saite, and Late Periods

A few more biographical inscriptions are attested from the Twenty-fifth and Twenty-sixth Dynasties and later. Self-presentational inscriptions are found on two statues of Amenirdis I (CG 565 and CG 42198).[122] A royal daughter and sister, Amenirdis was the daughter of Kashta and the sister of Pi(ankh) ye. She was also the first Nubian woman to become a God's Wife of Amun. Her appointment as God's Wife in Thebes probably helped consolidate Nubian power in the Theban region, making their subsequent conquest easier. [123] In her life-size alabaster statue (CG 565), Amenirdis I is represented standing, left foot slightly forward, wearing a tight sheath dress, anklets, and wide-cuff bracelets. In her hands Amenirdis hold a *menat*-necklace and a lily scepter, which she holds across her chest. A *modius* crown of cobras rests atop her tripartite wig and vulture headdress.[124] On the statue's back pillar, three long columns of text are inscribed. The second column reads, in part:

> I am a God's Wife, efficient (*mnḫ*) for her town,
> pleasant/friendly to her district/nome,
> I gave bread to the hungry, water to the thirsty, clothes to the naked
> (because) I knew what the god of my city loves.[125]

These lines echo standard phrases found in male autobiographies and are similarly found on her seated gray granite statue (CG 42198),[126] where we read:

> I have come from my city
> I have descended from my nome,
> I have done what people love and the gods praise:
> I gave bread to the hungry, clothing to the naked.[127]

These expressions are typical of male self-presentations.[128]

Similarly, typically male phraseology is found on the fragmentary stela of Taniy, a (female) royal acquaintance (*rḫt nsw*). Found in Abydos, the bottom part of the stela is currently in Cairo (CG 20564), while the top part is in Vienna (Wien 192).[129] The two parts were (virtually) joined by Meulenaere, who initially assigned a Twelfth Dynasty date to the stela.[130] But both Lichtheim and Leahy later demonstrated that the stela dates to late Twenty-fifth Dynasty and seems to be contemporaneous with Mentuemhat.[131] Taniy's inscriptions read in part:

> I was a person of character
> foremost among people,
> Honored and praised by my Lord;
> One perfect in her pronouncements,
> Esteemed by the king because of her righteousness,

whom he rewarded with gifts daily.
I entered in favor and went out beloved,
One whose mouth made her excellence,
One who spoke and things were done for her;
One honored by the great queen, the crowned one,
The true royal acquaintance Taniy, the honored one,
Justified before the great god, lord of the west.[132]

Although it is known from the Old Kingdom onward, Leahy suggested that the title *rḫ nsw mꜣʿ* (true royal acquaintance) had become honorific by the late Twenty-fifth Dynasty, when it is attested for three wives of Mentuemhat, as well as for Irtierou and Mutirdis.[133]

Mutirdis was a member of the entourage of the God's Wife of Amun during the early Twenty-sixth Dynasty.[134] Mutirdis boasted of her closeness to the God's Wife of Amun through the frequent use of epithets such as the "one to whom the God's Wife spoke (privately)"[135] and "the eyes of the Divine Worshiper, the ears [of the god's wife]" (*i͗rti dwꜣt- nṯr ʿnḫwj [n ḥmt-nṯr]*).[136] Mutirdis further describes the easy access she enjoyed to the God's Wife by claiming that she was one "who freely moved around in the house of her mistress"[137] and "the first to enter and the last to come out."[138] Similar self-presentational statements and assertions of beneficence are found throughout her tomb in the Assasif cemetery.[139] Her statements bear striking resemblance to the phraseology of male self-presentations and include such stock statements as:

[I gave] bread to the hungry, water to the thirsty and clothing to the naked. [140]

And

[I was . . .] a refuge for the inhabitants of her city,
a protector of her fellow citizens;
I gave bread to <the> hungry, water to <the> thirsty.[141]

When an attempt was made to compose an epithet that reflected Mutirdis's femininity, we get a statement such as "[I was] a nurse, rich in milk, from whom everyone sucked" (*mnʿt ʿšꜣt i͗rtt i͗w s nb snḳ i͗m.s*),[142] a statement that Jansen-Winkeln has characterized as a particularly unfortunate choice of words.[143] It is, however, one that may harken back to the high-ranking New Kingdom women who held the title of *mnʿt nsw* (royal nurse).

Self-presentational inscriptions are also engraved on a 70-cm-high statue of the Saite God's Wife Ankhnesneferibre (CG 42205). Ankhnesneferibre was the daughter of Psametik II and became God's Wife in the summer of 595 BC.[144] The statue shows her as a voluptuous woman, standing, a lily scepter in her right hand.[145] Further emphasizing her femininity are the biographical statements engraved on the statue. There, she is labeled as someone who is "beautiful of eyes to behold" (*nfr irty ḥr gmḥw*), a "mistress of all that the Aten encircles," (*ḥnwt m šn nb n itn*), someone who is "pure of hands, carrying the sistrum, with whose voice Amun-Re is pleased" (*wʿb ʿwy ḫr sššty ḥr sḥtp Ỉmn m ḫrw.s*).[146] More details of Ankhnesneferibre's titles can also be gleaned from her 'adoption' stela (JE 39907). There, she is identified as the "great songstress in the residence of Amun" and the "high priest(ess) of Amun."[147] The latter title was an honor that had not been accorded a woman previously.[148] The stela details not only the ascension of Ankhnesneferibre to the position of God's Wife of Amun, but also her performance of every proper rite for her predecessor, Nitocris, during her interment. Carrying out the funerary rites of Nitocris legitimated Ankhnesneferibre's position as the rightful successor.[149]

On his Serapeum stela, a priest named Hor (Louvre C137) provides us with the names and titles of his mother and sister(s).[150] His sister, Nitiqrt, is "praised of the god of her city, venerated one before her father, praised of her mother, gracious to her siblings," (*i3m ib n snw.s* = lit. "kind-hearted to her brothers"),[151] while *her* sister, Shebensopdet, is characterized as being "of good character to everybody" (*nfrt m bi3 ḫr-ḥr s nb*).[152] By affiliating herself directly to her sister, the emphasis is placed on Nitiqrit rather than on Hor, the owner of the stela.

Conclusions

From these representative examples of women's self-presentation in ancient Egypt, certain patterns seem to emerge. From the Old Kingdom onwards, women of means could afford a burial. The evidence that these burials yield—tomb decoration, stelae, false doors, grave goods—and their locations point to the possibility that at least some women enjoyed a degree of financial independence.

In the Old Kingdom and First Intermediate Period, texts associated with women's burials mostly listed the deceased's titles, epithets, and, occasionally, some information on her descent (Nedjetempet, Hedwi). That these short self-presentational statements are often found on monuments dedicated to or commissioned by a woman's husband (Asenkai) suggests that the husbands wanted to include their wives in their afterlife. Similarly, women appropriating the format of the ideal (male) self-presentation, but adapting the phraseology to mention their husbands and children where men would include references to the gods, implies that these women thought their husbands' approval and praise were indispensable for an afterlife. In this context, some women preferred to highlight their husbands' attachment to them (Nebet, Khamerernebty). For some elite women, being able to assist others on their way to the afterlife allowed them to say things about themselves that most women could not (Khentit-ka).

Whatever the sources of a woman's wealth, having the means to sponsor another person's burial (typically, a son) may have justified for such a woman the appropriation of the same kind of 'moral character' expressed in the typical male self-presentation. One could thus remark, for example, on how her resources were judiciously used to help the less fortunate (for example, "a caring heart for the orphan"—Nebet, Sixth Dynasty). This is a particularly telling development, as it stresses the woman's activity, agency, and autonomy. It may also reflect a deeper (religious) shift toward a more self-reliant approach to the afterlife. Whereas, previously, a woman (Ankhnes-Pepy) had needed to insinuate that her husband's love had to do with her good character, she would now be entering the afterlife with a more open, self-assertive approach to self-presentation.

In the First Intermediate Period, a time of social upheaval and upward social mobility, the 'newly minted' noblewoman Djehutinakht could appropriate stock phrases from male autobiographies. "I gave bread to the hungry, water to the thirsty, clothes to the naked," she says in her Eleventh Dynasty inscription at Dayr al-Barsha. Choosing to emphasize that her elite status was recently acquired, she simultaneously boasted of her new position in life while indicating that she had both the economic means and moral character to carry out the moral obligations of such a position. Here, for the first time, we see two of the most important demonstrations of male power and agency appropriated by women: resources and morality. Later, in the Third Intermediate Period, this tendency becomes even more pronounced. Women of means could now indicate their concern with the appointments of heirs (Nesi-khonsu-pakhered) and could claim the typically male characteristics of being "efficient," "praised by," "a protector" (Amenirdis, Djehutinakht, Taniy, Mutirdis), or "truthful" ("speaking Maat"—Shebensopdet). Emphasizing their character, individual ability, and prowess, these character traits point to the deceased's agency and self-sufficiency in achieving success in this life as well as in the afterlife.

On the other hand, a more limited use of self-aggrandizing phrases seems to be linked to periods of political stability. Such statements are virtually absent from the Middle and New Kingdom evidence, where the emphasis is typically on a woman's family connections and/or her roles in the household (*nbt pr*), in the temple (*ẖnr, ḥsyt, šmꜥyt*), or at court (*ẖḳrt nsw, mnꜥt nsw*). The latter title is particularly significant, as its holders are often prominently depicted in their husbands' and sons' tombs, or on their own with the king shown as a nursling sitting on their lap (Satre, Maya). Some of these New Kingdom women, particularly those with the title *šmꜥyt*, chose to emphasize their elite status by having scribal kits depicted under their seats in tomb art, possibly also pointing to their literacy.

The emphasis placed on a woman's more passive characteristics, such as beauty, personality, and family-informed self-presentations, seem to be associated with periods of relative stability (Ankhnesneferibre, second half of the Saite Period). During less stable times, women seem to have enjoyed a broader ability to boast more openly about their own abilities and agency.

Notes

1 J. Assmann, "Preservation and Presentation of Self in Ancient Egyptian Portraiture," in P.D. Manuelian, ed., *Studies in Honor of William Kelly Simpson*, I (Boston, 1996), 55.

2 See, for example, M. Lichtheim, *Ancient Egyptian Autobiographies Chiefly of the Middle Kingdom: A Study and an Anthology* (Freiburg, Göttingen, 1988), 37; K. Jansen-Winkeln, "Bemerkungen zu den Frauenbiographien der Spätzeit," *Altorientalische Forschungen* 31. 2 (2004), 373.

3 Also pointed out in G. Robins, "Ancient Egyptian Sexuality," *DE* 11 (1988), 61–73; G. Robins, "Some Images of Women in New Kingdom Art and Literature," in B.S. Lesko, ed., *Women's Earliest Records from Ancient Egypt and Western Asia: Proceedings of the Conference on Women in the Ancient Near East, Brown University, Providence, Rhode Island, November 5–7, 1987* (Atlanta, 1989), 105–16.

4 Lichtheim, *Egyptian Autobiographies*, 1–2, 5; N. Kloth, *Die (auto-)biographischen Inschriften der ägyptischen Alten Reiches: Untersuchungen Zu Phraseologie und Entwicklung* (Hamburg, 2002). Fischer attributes the dearth in evidence for female administrative titles to the fact that these titles are known mostly from funerary contexts in H.G. Fischer, "Administrative Titles of Women in the Old and Middle Kingdom," in *Egyptian Studies: Varia* I (New York, 1976), 73.

5 Lichtheim, *Egyptian Autobiographies*, 5–6; M. Galvin, "The Hereditary Status of the Titles of the Cult of Hathor," *JEA* 70 (1984), 42.

6 Lichtheim, *Egyptian Autobiographies*, 37; H.G. Fischer, "Women in the Old Kingdom and the Heracleopolitan Period," in B.S. Lesko, ed. *Women's Earliest Records from Ancient Egypt and Western Asia: Proceedings of the Conference on Women in the Ancient Near East, Brown University, Providence, Rhode Island, November 5–7, 1987* (Atlanta, 1989), 5.

7 Galvin, "The Cult of Hathor"; R. Gillam, "The Priestesses of Hathor: Their Function, Decline, and Disappearance," *JARCE* 22 (1995), 211–237.

8 N. Strudwick, *Texts from the Pyramid Age* (Atlanta, 2005), 386–87, no. 283.

9 Gillam, "The Priestesses of Hathor," 212–14.

10 PM III.2, plan LII; N. Kanawati and A. Hassan, *The Teti Cemetery at Saqqara: The Tombs of Nedjet-Em-Pet, Ka-Aper, and Others*, I (Sydney, 1996), 11–30, pls. 3–12; Strudwick, *Texts from the Pyramid Age*, 396.

11 Strudwick, *Texts from the Pyramid Age*, 396; Kanawati and Hassan, *The Teti Cemetery*, I, pl. 5.

12 Strudwick, *Texts from the Pyramid Age*, 396. Similar expressions are cited in Lichtheim, *Egyptian Autobiographies*, 37–38.

13 D. Dunham, *Nag-Ed-Dêr Stelae of the First Intermediate Period* (London, 1937), 35–36, pls XII, 1 (Dunham no. 21); Lichtheim, *Egyptian Autobiographies*, 37–38.

14 Lichtheim, *Egyptian Autobiographies*, 37.

15 Strudwick, *Texts from the Pyramid Age*, 188–89.

16 Strudwick, *Texts from the Pyramid Age*, 189.

17 E. Edel, *Hieroglyphische Inschriften des Alten Reiches* (Leipzig, 1981), fig. 4; Strudwick, *Texts from the Pyramid Age*, 189; Fischer, "Women in the Old Kingdom and the Heracleopolitan Period," 5.

18 Dunham, *Nag-Ed-Dêr Stelae*, 35–36, 65–66, and 107–108, pls. XII, 1–2, XVI, 1, XXXIV, nos. 21, 22, 53, 87; Lichtheim, *Egyptian Autobiographies*, 38.

19 Strudwick, *Texts from the Pyramid Age*, 394.

20 L. Borchardt, *Denkmäler des Alten Reiches (ausser den Statuen) im Museum von Kairo: Text und Tafeln zu nr. 1542–1808*, II (Cairo, 1964), 85, pl. 82; Strudwick, *Texts from the Pyramid Age*, 394, no. 293.

21 É. Drioton, "Description Sommaire des Chapelles Funéraires de la VIe Dynastie: Récemment Découvertes Derrière le Mastaba de Mérérouka à Saqqara," *ASAÉ* 43 (1943), 496.

22 Drioton, "Chapelles Funéraires de la VIe Dynastie," 496.

23 Strudwick, *Texts from the Pyramid Age*, 231, no. 144 (4–5).

24 Dunham, *Nag-Ed-Dêr Stelae*, 65–66, pl. XVI, 1; Lichtheim, *Egyptian Autobiographies*, 38.

25 Fischer, "Women in the Old Kingdom and the Heracleopolitan Period," 9, and fig 2 on p. 13. The slab is currently in the Musée d'Ethnographie, Neuchâtel, Eg 323, cf. PM 3.2, 568.

26 MFA, Boston neg. B 6873, see Fischer, "Women in the Old Kingdom and the Heracleopolitan Period," 9, n. 30; H.G. Fischer, *Egyptian Women of the Old Kingdom and of the Heracleopolitan Period* (New York, 2000), 59, n. 43.

27 Berlin 24032, see Fischer, "Women in the Old Kingdom and the Heracleopolitan Period," 9–10; and H.G. Fischer "The Nubian Mercenaries at Gebelein during the First Intermediate Period," *Kush* 9 (1961), 44–80, on p. 64, fig. 1, pl. 10.

28 Fischer, "Women in the Old Kingdom and the Heracleopolitan Period," 10; H.G. Fischer "Four Provincial Administrators at the Memphite cemeteries," *JAOS* 74 (1961), 26–29, at 28.

29 Some of these positions could also be held by men. See Fischer, "Administrative Titles of Women in the Old and Middle Kingdom," 70–71, 73.

30 Borchardt, *Denkmäler des Alten Reiches*, II, 59–60; Strudwick, *Texts from the Pyramid Age*, 395, no. 295; Fischer, "Administrative Titles of Women in the Old and Middle Kingdom," 74–5.

31 B.M. Bryan, "In Women Good and Bad Fortune Are on Earth: Status and Roles of Women in Egyptian Culture," in A.K. Capel and G.E. Markoe, eds., *Mistress of the House, Mistress of Heaven* (New York, 1996), 39.

32 Fischer, "Administrative Titles of Women in the Old and Middle Kingdom," 74.

33 Strudwick, *Texts from the Pyramid Age*, 395; Fischer, "Administrative Titles of Women in the Old and Middle Kingdom," 75.

34 Bryan, "Status and Roles of Women in Egyptian Culture," no. 109, on pp. 190–91.

35 Drioton, "Chapelles Funéraires de la VIe Dynastie," 495–96; Fischer, "Women in the Old Kingdom and the Heracleopolitan Period," 5.

36 M. Lichtheim, *Maat in Egyptian Autobiographies and Related Studies* (Freiburg, Göttingen, 1992), 14–15.

37 Fischer, "Women in the Old Kingdom and the Heracleopolitan Period," 5; Z.Y. Saad, "A Preliminary Report on the Excavations at Saqqara 1939–1940," *ASAE* 40 (1940), 681, fig. 72; Edel, *Hieroglyphische Inschriften*, fig. 4.

38 Fischer, "Women in the Old Kingdom and the Heracleopolitan Period," 5–6.

39 H. Willems, *Historical and Archaeological Aspects of Egyptian Funerary Culture: Religious Ideas and Ritual Practice in Middle Kingdom Elite Cemeteries* (Leiden, Boston, 2014), 74–75.

40 For example, R. Landgráfová, *It Is My Good Name That You Should Remember: Egyptian Biographical Texts on Middle Kingdom Stelae* (Prague, 2011); S. Kubisch, *Lebenbilder Der 2. Zwischenzeit: Biographische Inschriften Der 13.–17. Dynastie* (Berlin, New York, 2008), do not contain any examples for women's self-presentations.

41 Particularly pertinent in this context are Baines's remarks on the need to integrate the textual and visual material. See, for example, Baines, "Egyptian Elite Self-Representation in the Context of Ptolemaic Rule," in W.V. Harris and G. Ruffini, eds., *Ancient Alexandria: Between Egypt and Greece* (Leiden, Boston, 2004), 33–61, at 34–35.

42 For the earlier attestations of the title of *nbt pr*, see Fischer, "Administrative Titles of Women in the Old and Middle Kingdom," 76, n. 42, and P.E. Newberry, *Beni Hasan*, I (London, 1893), 14, 82, pls. 12, 18, 46. Contra W. Grajetzki, *Court Officials of the Egyptian Middle Kingdom* (London, 2009), 158, who is of the opinion that the title first appears in the middle of the Twelfth Dynasty. In that Grajetzki follows the chronology of the title first suggested by K. Pflüger in "Private Stelae of the Middle Kingdom," *JAOS* 67 (1947), 127–35, at 129.

43 Grajetzki, *Officials of the Egyptian Middle Kingdom*, 158.

44 D. Stefanovic, "The Non-Royal Women of the Middle Kingdom – I *mnat*," *GM* 216 (2008), 79; Grajetzki, *Officials of the Egyptian Middle Kingdom*, 161.

45 W.A. Ward, *Essays on Feminine Titles of the Middle Kingdom and Related Subjects* (Beirut, 1986), 8.

46 Ward, *Essays on Feminine Titles*, 17.
47 Newberry, *Beni Hasan*, I, pl. 35.
48 J. Kamrin, *The Cosmos of Khnumhotep II at Beni Hasan* (London, 1999), 125–26.
49 Newberry, *Beni Hasan*, I, 43, pl. 35.
50 W.A. Ward, "The Case of Mrs Tchat and her Sons at Beni Hassan," *GM* 71 (1984): 59; Grajetzki, *Officials of the Egyptian Middle Kingdom*, 160–61.
51 See, for example, Newberry, *Beni Hasan*, I, pls. 32, 35.
52 Newberry, *Beni Hasan*, I, 43, pl. 35; Kamrin, *The Cosmos of Khnumhotep II*, 126, n. 367. For *ḥ3tyt-ʿ*, *ḥmt-nṯr P3ḫt*, and *ḥmt-nṯr ḥwt-ḥr*, see Ward, *Essays on Feminine Titles*, 10.
53 Newberry, *Beni Hasan*, I, pl. 46.
54 Newberry, *Beni Hasan*, I, pl. 18.
55 W. Grajetzki, *Harageh, an Egyptian burial ground for the rich around 1800 BC* (London, 2004), 31; H. Ranke, *Die Ägyptischen Personennamen*, I (Glückstadt, 1935), 11, nos. 13, 14.
56 R. Engelback, *Harageh* (London, 1923), 15–16; Grajetzki, *Harageh*, 31–32.
57 Grajetzki, *Harageh*, 31.
58 Engelback, *Harageh*, pl. 73; The stela is currently in Copenhagen (AEIN 1664); AEIN 1664, see L. Manniche, *Egyptian Art in Denmark* (Copenhagen, 2004), fig. 40 on p. 96; O. Koefoed-Petersen, *Les stèles égyptiennes* (Copenhagen, 1948), no. 13, 12–13, pl. XX.
59 Engelback, *Harageh*, pl. 73; Manniche, *Egyptian Art in Denmark*, fig. 40 on p. 96; Koefoed-Petersen, *Les stèles égyptiennes*, no. 13, 12–13, pl. XX.
60 Manniche, *Egyptian Art in Denmark*, 97.
61 Antefiqer held office as vizier between the years 17 and 20 of Senwosret I, see N. Davies, *The Tomb of Antefoker, Vizier of Sesostris I and of his Wife, Senet (no. 60)* (London, 1920); PM I.1, 121–23; J.P. Allen, "The High Officials of the Early *Middle Kingdom*," *in* N. Strudwick and J.H. Taylor, eds., *The Theban Necropolis: Past, Present and Future* (London, 2003), 14–29; Grajetzki, *Officials of the Egyptian Middle Kingdom*, 157, 162–63; R. Soliman, *Old and Middle Kingdom Theban Tombs* (London, 2009), 131–33.
62 Davies, *The Tomb of Antefoker*, 25–26, pls. XXX, XXXIII, XXXIV.
63 PM I.1, 123; Davies, *The Tomb of Antefoker*, 26, pls. XXXVIII, XXXIX; Soliman, *Old and Middle Kingdom Theban Tombs*, 132.
64 Davies, *The Tomb of Antefoker*, 2.
65 Davies, *The Tomb of Antefoker*, 6, 22, pls. III, XIV, XXIII, XXV.
66 Davies, *The Tomb of Antefoker*, 4, 5–7; Soliman, *Old and Middle Kingdom Theban Tombs*, 132–33.
67 A. Verbovsek, *"Als Geunsterweis des Königs in den Tempel gegeben ..." Private Tempelstatuen des Alten und Mittleren Reiches* (Wiesbaden, 2004), 96, 99–100, 104, pl. 9 (d).
68 Grajetzki, *Officials of the Egyptian Middle Kingdom*, 165; A. Verbovsek, "Befund oder Spekulation? Der Standort privater Statuen in Tempeln des

Alten und Mittleren Reiches," in B. Haring and A. Klug, eds., *Ägyptologische Tempeltagung: Funktion und Gebrauch altägyptischer Tempelräume. Leiden 4.–7. September 2002* (Wiesbaden, 2007), 260; G. Legrain, *Catalogue Général des Antiquités égyptiennes du Musée du Caire. Statues et Statuettes de Rois et de Particuliers: Nos. 42001–42138* (Cairo, 1906), 21.

69 Legrain, *Statues et Statuettes*, 21; Verbovsek, *Private Tempelstatuen*, 418.

70 CG 42034, line 3 on the right side, published in Legrain, *Statues et Statuettes*, 20, pl. XXI; Verbovsek, *Private Tempelstatuen*, 96, 437.

71 Verbovsek, "Befund oder Spekulation?," 260.

72 Grajetzki, *Officials of the Egyptian Middle Kingdom*, 165; cf. the tables in Verbovsek, *Private Tempelstatuen*, 94–97.

73 Capel and Markoe, *Mistress of the House, Mistress of Heaven*, 58, n. 9. The other statues are CG 42134, CG 42135, and CG 42228. Three additional statues depict women in family groupings. These are CG 42118, CG 42126, and CG 42133, see Legrain, *Statues et Statuettes*, I, 21, 67–68, 86–57, pls LXIX, LXXV, LXXIX; *Id.*, *Statues et Statuettes*, III, 67–70, pl. XXXV.

74 Brooklyn 43.137, published in Capel and Markoe, *Mistress of the House, Mistress of Heaven*, 60–66. A scarab (Cairo JE 75039) dating to the Thirteenth Dynasty and bearing the same title and name as this bronze statue helps date it to the Thirteenth Dynasty. For the scarab, see Martin, *Egyptian Administrative and Private Name Seals* (Oxford, 1971), 109, no. 1409, pl. 19.1.

75 Capel and Markoe, *Mistress of the House, Mistress of Heaven*, 60. For the stela Cairo CG 20537, see O. Lange and H Schäfer, *Catalogue Général des antiquités égyptiennes du Musée du Caire: Grab- und Denksteine des Mittleren Reichs. Nos. 20001–20780*, II: *Nos. 20400–20780* (Berlin, 1908), 144–45.

76 Capel and Markoe, *Mistress of the House, Mistress of Heaven*, 60.

77 C.H. Roehrig, "The Eighteenth Dynasty Titles Royal Nurse (*mnꜥt nswt*), Royal Tutor (*mnꜥ nswt*), and Foster Brother/Sister of the Lord of the Two Lands (*sn/snt mnꜥ n nb tꜣwy*)" (PhD diss., Univ. of California, Berkeley, 1990), 3–4.

78 Roehrig, "The Eighteenth Dynasty Titles Royal Nurse (*mnꜥt nswt*)," 3–4.

79 Fragments of the statue were discovered by the Metropolitan Museum expedition to Deir al-Bahri during the 1927 and 1931 excavations seasons. See H.E. Winlock, "The Egyptian Expedition 1927–1928: The Museum's Excavations at Thebes," *MMAB* 23.12 (1928), 3–28, at 14 and 20; H.E. Winlock, "The Museum's Excavations at Thebes," *MMAB* 27.3, Pt 2 (1932), 1, 4–37, at 10, fig. 6; C.H. Roehrig, "The Statue of the Royal Nurse Sitre with her Nursling Maatkare Hatshepsut," in M. Eldamaty and M. Trad, eds., *Egyptian Museum Collections Around the World. Studies for the Centennial of the Egyptian Museum, Cairo*, II (Cairo, 2003), 1003–1010, pls. I–II.

80 Roehrig, "The Eighteenth Dynasty Titles Royal Nurse (*mnꜥt nswt*)," 272.

81 Winlock, "The Museum's Excavations at Thebes," 10, fig. 6; Roehrig, "The Eighteenth Dynasty Titles Royal Nurse (*mnꜥt nswt*)," 272; Roehrig, "The Statue of the Royal Nurse Sitre with her Nursling Maatkare Hatshepsut," 1006, pls. I–II.

82 Roehrig, "The Eighteenth Dynasty Titles Royal Nurse (*mnʿt nswt*)," 273–74, 276, n. 12. For the Brooklyn Museum 39.119 statue, see R.A. Fazzini, *Ancient Egyptian Art in the Brooklyn Museum* (New York, 1989), #15.

83 Roehrig, "The Statue of the Royal Nurse Sitre with her Nursling Maatkare Hatshepsut," 1008; Roehrig, "The Eighteenth Dynasty Titles Royal Nurse (*mnʿt nswt*)," 275–76.

84 Roehrig, "The Eighteenth Dynasty Titles Royal Nurse (*mnʿt nswt*)," 272, 276.

85 N. de Garis Davies, *The Tomb of Kenamun at Thebes* I (New York, 1930), pl. IX; N. de Garis Davies, *The Tomb of Kenamun at Thebes* II (New York, 1930), pl. IX.A; Roehrig, "The Eighteenth Dynasty Titles Royal Nurse (*mnʿt nswt*)," 294–95; Roehrig, "The Statue of the Royal Nurse Sitre with her Nursling Maatkare Hatshepsut," 1007.

86 A. Zivie, *La Tombe de Maïa Mère Nourricière du Roi Toutânkhamon et Grande du Harem. Les Tombes du Bubasteion à Saqqara*, I (Toulouse, 2009).

87 Zivie, *La Tombe de Maïa*, pl. 21.

88 See, for example, Zivie, *La Tombe de Maïa*, pls. 29–33, 44.

89 Roehrig, "The Eighteenth Dynasty Titles Royal Nurse (*mnʿt nswt*)," passim.

90 Roehrig, "The Eighteenth Dynasty Titles Royal Nurse (*mnʿt nswt*)," 137–39, 142.

91 Roehrig, "The Eighteenth Dynasty Titles Royal Nurse (*mnʿt nswt*)," 140–41, particularly n. 449 on p. 140.

92 Roehrig, "The Eighteenth Dynasty Titles Royal Nurse (*mnʿt nswt*)," 143–49, 151–55.

93 B. Bryan, "Evidence for Female Literacy from Theban Tombs of the New Kingdom," *BES* 6 (1985), 17–32, at 20–22.

94 B. Bryan, "Evidence for Female Literacy from Theban Tombs," 24.

95 S.L. Onstine, *The Role of the Chantress (šmʿyt) in Ancient Egypt* (Oxford, 2005), 23.

96 Onstine, *The Role of the Chantress*, 25.

97 Onstine, *The Role of the Chantress*, 20, 24–5.

98 Jansen-Winkeln, "Frauenbiographien der Spätzeit," 364.

99 Jansen-Winkeln, "Frauenbiographien der Spätzeit," 358 and 361. The Chantress Tawdjatre appears as no. 149 in the database compiled by Onstine, *The Role of the Chantress*. For her sarcophagus (Cairo JE 29737), see G. Daressy, "Les Cercueils des Prêtres d'Ammon (deuxième Trouvaille de Deir El-Bahari)," *ASAE* 8 (1907), 13; A. Niwiński, *21st Dynasty Coffins from Thebes: Chronological and Typological Studies* (Mainz, 1988), 131, no. 143.

100 Jansen-Winkeln, "Frauenbiographien Der Spätzeit," 361; A. Niwiński, *Studies on the Illustrated Theban Funerary Papyri of the 11th and 10th Centuries* B.C. (Freiburg-Göttingen, 1989), 295, 297.

101 Onstine, *The Role of the Chantress*, 72; Jansen-Winkeln, "Frauenbiographien der Spätzeit," 359–61; Niwiński, *Illustrated Theban Funerary Papyri*, 297.

102 Onstine, *The Role of the Chantress*, 72; Niwiński, *21st Dynasty Coffins*, 131, no. 143.

103 K.A. Kitchen, *Ramesside Inscriptions: Historical and Biographical*, V (Oxford, 1983), 250.

104 Jansen-Winkeln, "Frauenbiographien der Spätzeit," 361.

105 G. Legrain, *Catalogue Général des Antiquités égyptiennes du Musée du Caire. Statues et Statuettes de Rois et de Particuliers* (Cairo, 1914), 67–70, pl. xxxv; Jansen-Winkeln, "Frauenbiographien der Spätzeit," 364; K. Jansen-Winkeln, *Ägyptische Biographien der 22. und 23. Dynastie* (Wiesbaden, 1985), 156–167; 520–24, pls. 37–40.

106 Jansen-Winkeln, *Biographien der 22. und 23. Dynastie*, 520–21, pl. 37; Legrain, *Statues et Statuettes de Rois*, 67–70; Jansen-Winkeln, "Frauenbiographien der Spätzeit," 364; Lichtheim, *Maat in Egyptian Autobiographies*, 84–85.

107 K.A. Kitchen, *The Third Intermediate Period in Egypt (1100–650 B.C.)* (Warminster, 1995), 322.

108 Jansen-Winkeln, "Frauenbiographien der Spätzeit," 364.

109 Legrain, *Statues et Statuettes de Rois*, 69; Jansen-Winkeln, *Biographien der 22. und 23. Dynastie*, 159, 522, col. 9, pl. 38; Lichtheim, *Maat in Egyptian Autobiographies*, 84.

110 Legrain, *Statues et Statuettes de Rois*, 69, line 4; Jansen-Winkeln, *Biographien der 22. und 23. Dynastie*, 524, line 4 and pl. 40; Lichtheim, *Maat in Egyptian Autobiographies*, 84–85.

111 Legrain, *Statues et Statuettes de Rois*, 70, col. 6; Jansen-Winkeln, *Biographien der 22. und 23. Dynastie*, 524, coll.5–6, pl. 40; Lichtheim, *Maat in Egyptian Autobiographies*, 84–85.

112 Lichtheim, *Maat in Egyptian Autobiographies*, 84–85.

113 Kitchen, *Third Intermediate Period*, 328.

114 Legrain, *Statues et Statuettes de Rois*, 15–17; Jansen-Winkeln, *Biographien der 22. und 23. Dynastie*, 25–34, 443, pl. 6.

115 Kitchen, *Third Intermediate Period*, 288–99.

116 Kitchen, *Third Intermediate Period*, 289, no. 263.

117 Legrain, *Statues et Statuettes de Rois*, 17; Jansen-Winkeln, *Biographien der 22. und 23. Dynastie*, 443, coll. 4–6, pl. 6; Jansen-Winkeln, "Frauenbiographien der Spätzeit," 364.

118 Jansen-Winkeln, "Frauenbiographien der Spätzeit," 365.

119 Lichtheim, *Moral Values*, 62.

120 Lichtheim, *Moral Values*, 62–63.

121 Lichtheim, *Moral Values*, 63.

122 Legrain, *Statues et Statuettes de Rois*, 6–8, pl. VI; O. Perdu, "L'avertissement d'Aménirdis Ière sur sa statue Caire JE 3420 (= CG 565)," *RdE* 47 (1996), 43–44; Jansen-Winkeln, "Frauenbiographien der Spätzeit," 365–66.

123 Kitchen, *The Third Intermediate Period in Egypt*, 150–51, 359–60; M.F. Ayad, *God's Wife, God's Servant: The God's Wife of Amun (c. 740–525 BC)* (London, 2009), 16.

124 Perdu, "L'avertissement d'Aménirdis," 43; A good image of the statue may be found in F. Tiradritti, ed., *Egyptian Treasures from the Egyptian Museum in Cairo* (New York, 1999), 278.

125 Perdu, "L'avertissement d'Aménirdis," 45 and 55; Jansen-Winkeln, "Frauenbiographien der Spätzeit," 365.
126 Legrain, *Statues et Statuettes de Rois*, VII, pl. VI; Capel and Markoe, *Mistress of the House, Mistress of Heaven: Women in Ancient Egypt*, 115–17.
127 Legrain, *Statues et Statuettes de Rois*, VII; Jansen-Winkeln, "Frauenbiographien der Spätzeit," 366.
128 Lichtheim, *Maat in Egyptian Autobiographies*, 25, 32.
129 Jansen-Winkeln, "Frauenbiographien der Spätzeit," 365; H. De Meulenaere, "Retrouvaille de la Dame Taniy," in T.G.H. James, A. Leahy, and A.F. Shore, eds., *Pyramid Studies and Other Essays Presented to I.E.S. Edwards* (London, 1988), 68–72.
130 Meulenaere, "Retrouvaille de La Dame Taniy."
131 M. Lichtheim, "The Stela of Taniy, CG 20564: Its Date and Its Character," *SAK* 16 (1989), 203–15; A. Leahy, "Taniy: A Seventh Century Lady (Cairo CG 20564 and Vienna 192)," *GM* 108 (1989), 45–56.
132 Meulenaere, "Retrouvaille de la Dame Taniy," 69; Leahy, "Taniy," 55; Lichtheim, "The Stela of Taniy," 211.
133 Leahy, "Taniy," 49.
134 E. Graefe, *Untersuchungen zur Verwaltung und Geschichte der Institution der Gottesgemahlin des Amun vom Beginn des neuen Reiches bis zur Spätzeit*. I: *Katalog und Materialsammlung* (Wiesbaden, 1981), 94–96.
135 J. Assmann, *Grabung im Asasif 1963–1970* VI: *Das Grab der Mutirdis* (Mainz, 1977), 18, 55; Jansen-Winkeln, "Frauenbiographien der Spätzeit," 366.
136 Assmann, *Mutirdis*, 49; Jansen-Winkeln, "Frauenbiographien der Spätzeit," 366.
137 Assmann, *Mutirdis*, 55.
138 Assmann, *Mutirdis*, 51, fr. 71.
139 Jansen-Winkeln, "Frauenbiographien der Spätzeit," 366; Assmann, *Mutirdis*, passim.
140 Assmann, *Mutirdis*, 18, 23 (frag. 6–8; lls. 3–4); Jansen-Winkeln, "Frauenbiographien der Spätzeit," 366.
141 Assmann, *Mutirdis*, 18, 25, pl. 6 (b); Jansen-Winkeln, "Frauenbiographien der Spätzeit," 366.
142 Assmann, *Mutirdis*, 18, 25; Jansen-Winkeln, "Frauenbiographien der Spätzeit," 366.
143 Jansen-Winkeln, "Frauenbiographien der Spätzeit," 367.
144 A. Leahy, "The Adoption of Ankhnesneferibre at Karnak," *JEA* 82 (1996), 145–65, on p. 157; Ayad, *God's Wife, God's Servant*, 27–28.
145 Legrain, *Statues et Statuettes de Rois*, 13–14, pl. XII; G.A. Gaballa and W.A. Osman, *Nubia Museum* (Cairo, 2003), 114–15.
146 Legrain, *Statues et Statuettes de Rois*, 14; Jansen-Winkeln, "Frauenbiographien der Spätzeit," 367; L. Troy, *Patterns of Queenship in Ancient Egyptian Myth and History* (Uppsala, 1986), 178, 190.

147 Leahy, "The Adoption of Ankhnesneferibre," fig. 1 on p. 146 (lls. 4–5), 148, 158.
148 Ayad, *God's Wife, God's Servant*, 116; Leahy, "The Adoption of Ankhnesneferibre," 158.
149 Ayad, *God's Wife, God's Servant*, 140–41.
150 É. Chassinat, "Textes provenant du Sérapéum de Memphis (suite)," *RT* 25 (1903), 50–62, especially pp. 52–53; Jansen-Winkeln, "Frauenbiographien der Spätzeit," 367.
151 Chassinat, "Textes provenant du Sérapéum," 53, l. 13; Jansen-Winkeln, "Frauenbiographien der Spätzeit," 367. For *im3-ib* as "gracious," see Lichtheim, *Moral Values*, 82–83.
152 Chassinat, "Textes provenant du Sérapéum," 53, l. 14; Jansen-Winkeln, "Frauenbiographien der Spätzeit," 367.

14

Traditions of Egyptian Self-Presentation

Hussein Bassir

The writing of the nonroyal self,[1] or life-writing,[2] is one of the most ancient literary practices through which individuals wished to express identity and leave their fingerprints on time to avoid being forgotten and ensure survival.[3] This genre of writing started early on in ancient Egypt.[4] The traditions of Egyptian self-presentations were deeply rooted in ancient Egypt since the early Dynastic period, and they differed in aspect, composition, and themes from the beginning of Egyptian history to the late Dynastic period.

Self-presentation was the most ancient and crucial component of Egyptian high culture. Members of the nonroyal elite presented themselves through language and art within the setting made by the history and antiquities of their periods. The elements of self-presentation varied with their protagonists in titles, reign, professions, and overall background, and they all concentrate on the meanings and history of self in the telling of a life story.

The power of artworks and texts to reshape as well as to reflect history and cultural identity may be seen through self-presentation of ancient Egyptian individuals. Text (language) and image (art)[5] represent major components of constructing and reshaping the overall self-presentation of such individuals.[6]

Documenting nonroyal life saw many attempts to identify the patterns used by individuals when describing their lives. The first definitions include history, life events, and life. Such autobiographies mainly state the life events of the subject of the biography in the first person, while there are, also, biographies indicating the life events of other people mainly written in the third person.

Ancient Egyptian self-presentations were written during the lifetimes or after the deaths of the protagonists. Moreover, the subjects of the self-presentations concerned may have participated in or even dictated the actual context of their self-presentation, though that is not certain. Autobiography was differently used in ancient Egypt, with there being no reference or linkage to our contemporary understanding of it. Hence, the term *biography* would be more appropriate to use when referring to ancient Egyptian self-presentations, since it covers a wider spectrum of the type of relationship between the text and its subject.

The majority of ancient Egyptian self-presentations are written in the first person, which is why they are called 'autobiographies' by scholars who have believed that the author of such self-presentations is the protagonist. Based upon such misunderstandings or assumptions, both titles are commonly used: 'autobiography,' though we may not be sure of the real author of the literary work, and 'biography.' Ancient Egyptian self-presentations were inscribed on statues, stelae, tomb and temple walls, and coffins starting from the Old Kingdom and going right through to the Greco-Roman Period.

Histories of the Self

The roots of such self-presentations go back to the beginnings of Egyptian history, maybe starting from the First Dynasty[7] and including the Third Dynasty wooden panels of Hesy-Re (Fig. 14.1), which are on display in the Egyptian Museum in Cairo, and the self-presentations of Metjen that date back to the early Fourth Dynasty and handle some legal issues and property inheritances.[8] The titles of Prince Rehotep and his wife Nofret on their statues represent early examples of self-presentations (Fig. 14.2). The first self-presentations that include a fictional tone include that of Debehen dating back to the end of the Fourth Dynasty (Fig. 14.3) .[9] This text records the construction of the tomb of this nonroyal elite member as a favor from King Menkaure.[10] In his self-presentation, Debehen confirms that:

> With regard to this tomb of mine,
> it was the king of Upper and Lower Egypt,
> Menkaure [may he live forever] who gave me its place,
> while he happened to be on the way to the pyramid plateau
> to inspect the work being done on the pyramid of Menkaure.[11]

14.1. Wooden panel of Hesy-Re, Egyptian Museum, Cairo (photograph by Sameh Abdel Mohsen/Egyptian Museum, Cairo)

During the Fifth Dynasty, the protagonists of such self-presentations tell us much about themselves, and the self-presentations can be categorized into two main genres: ideal self-presentations that agree with the moral concept of *maat* and present their subjects in long-form sentences to show them as ideal; and event self-presentations that demonstrate the experiences of the subject and the events he or she witnessed, specifically those concerning the professional career, from which dates can be deduced.

Starting from the end of the Fifth Dynasty, ancient Egyptian self-presentations begin stating the careers of their subjects in detail, including the

14.2. Statues of Prince Rehotep and his wife Nofret, Egyptian Museum, Cairo (photograph by Sandro Vannini/Laboratoriorosso)

regnal periods and the circumstances of the kings who were being served. These are called 'career' or 'professional' self-presentations, and they continued through the Sixth Dynasty. The self-presentations of the Fifth Dynasty display the reactive relationship between the king and the elite member concerned, the subject of the self-presentation. The self-presentations of the Sixth Dynasty reflect the achievements of their protagonists, and they are related to the introduction of the self-presentations of the First Intermediate Period, such as that of Qar at Edfu.

14.3. The tomb of Debehen and the top of the Pyramid of King Menkaure at Giza (photograph by author)

Self-presentations of the First Intermediate Period reflect the political fragmentation that Egypt passed through during that time. The rulers of Egypt's competing principalities adjusted self-presentation production to meet their need to appear as good rulers of the country: They showed their ability and communal responsibilities by enhancing explicit statements that dismissed the well-established traditions of the previous central court culture in the capital, and by replacing the ideal image of the former 'official' with that of the current effective 'townsman.' Those self-presentations combined historical and reflective themes by presenting the successful career of the protagonist without any blames. Self-presentations of the period refer to living difficulties, scarcities, civil war, and other factors that had huge impacts on politics of the period. In order to justify their claim to power, the protagonists, who were the protégés of deities,[12] claimed in their self-presentations that they protected and nourished the populations, restored and built temples, and guaranteed the performance of the cult.[13] In his well-known self-presentation, the Upper Egyptian nomarch of El-Moalla, Ankhtifi, claimed that:

> Horus brought me to the nome of Edfu for life, prosperity, health, to reestablish it, and I did (it). For Horus wished it to be reestablished, because he brought me to it to reestablish it. I found the House of Khuu inundated like a marsh, abandoned by him who belonged to it, in the grip of a rebel, under the control of a wretch. I made a man embrace the slayer of his father, the slayer of his brother, so as to reestablish the nome of Edfu.[14]

During the Middle Kingdom, a new trend of self-presentation appeared based upon moral values.[15] With the reunification of the country in the Middle Kingdom, self-presentational discourse changed, giving birth to a new type, the 'encomiastic autobiography.' This new type introduced the ideals and needs of the social class of new officials who had returned Egypt to monarchy. Loyalty to the king remained a crucial theme in presenting nonroyal elite members who played an important role in the state's consolidation. The image of the ideal official and his position in various social and professional media are elaborately reshaped.[16]

The Second Intermediate Period was a period of social, political, and economic crisis, related to the Hyksos invasion. The self-presentations of the period allude to this crisis where the protagonists appear independent and self-confident, reflecting the weakness of the central administration of the country. Many nomarchs appeared as local powerful authorities, however not competing with each or with the king as the situation was in the First Intermediate Period. Kamose and Ahmose I were able to depend on those loyal and strong provincial officials in the unification of Egypt, bringing the local powers into a single force under the authority of only one king of Egypt.[17]

The self-presentations from the New Kingdom include a range of historical events due to Egypt's expeditions into Asia and Africa at the time,[18] though self-presentations from the Amarna Period are scarce.[19] The self-presentations from the Ramesside Period[20] show a great respect for funerary beliefs, and this trend continued throughout the Third Intermediate Period and the Late Period. During the Third Intermediate Period, self-presentational production reached another peak, further developing the concept of personal piety and religious performance.[21] During the Twenty-fifth Dynasty,[22] the social and thematic variety of the self-presentation expanded again, assembling themes created in earlier periods with more new developments. Self-presentations applied several formal and phraseological components produced in earlier periods, especially in the First Intermediate Period, the Middle Kingdom, and the New Kingdom.[23]

Saite Egypt witnessed a political shift in which the nonroyal elite members elevated themselves to a rank normally restricted to royalty in earlier centralized periods. As a consequence of this rise in power, the nonroyal elite promoted themselves through image and text. This self-presentation reveals a rise of individualism, a characteristic of the Saite Period.[24] These special cases of self-presentation represent votive objects, clearly designed to be placed in temples, but leave little room to narrate an entire lifetime, so they typically focus on events closely related to the local temple, especially since the texts usually address the local divinity or clergy, asking for protection and veneration. Individuals, not kings, take credit for temple construction more often in the Late Period.[25] This could be a Saite phenomenon. Tombs of individuals have walls containing more detailed self-presentational texts.[26] Most of the famous narrative self-presentations from other periods also come from tombs (Harkhuf, Ahmose, son of Abana, and Petosiris), not from temple statues. Saite individuals, and by extension other Egyptians, were not trying to record complete biographies in the modern, or even the ancient Greek and Roman, sense, nor were they recording political history. Rather, by their choice of specific sculptural forms, combination of classic and innovative epithets, and selection of titles for each monument, they aimed to present idealized representations of themselves only to local divinities and clergy. The narrative life-event elements are tailored to this specific context and aim, but they should not be confused with full self-presentations. Study of self-presentations generally reveals many differences between real and ideal images. Yet their self-presentations are more personalized than those of earlier periods, revealing the uniqueness of protagonists in their religious beliefs, careers, ideas, and professions. These components combine to create their overall images. However, they do not record the chronological stages in their lives and careers; rather, they are commemorative, making a specific event the focal point of the self-presentation for which the statue was sculpted to be placed in the sacred space of the temple. Saite self-presentations differed from the norms of self-presentation in previous Egyptian periods in many ways. Among the most remarkable characteristics of their self-presentations is that theirs were not 'transformative,' meaning they did not reveal their entire lives and careers or turning points. In other words, the self-presentations do not present the career development of their owners. Individuals do not tell the story of their entire lives and careers from the beginning to the end as do several self-presentations such as that of Weni (Fig. 14.4).[27] These self-presentations are commemorative in that their main concern was to commemorate specific moments or events in the individuals' lives and careers. Another important feature of their self-presentations

14.4. Stela of Weni the Elder, Egyptian Museum, Cairo (photograph by Ahmed Amin/ Egyptian Museum, Cairo)

is that they are composed of more than biography. Although each of their self-presentations has its own scope, it constitutes part of its protagonist's life and career. Their self-presentations are votive with the same goal to commemorate on a statue a single event and show their personal piety toward the deities. Although Saite self-presentations add to their images, they do not completely encompass them. Through exploring this, it will be clear how rich and distinctive Saite self-presentations are in comparison with their counterparts from other Egyptian periods.[28]

Egyptian self-presentations were written in a form that fused together literary genres such as narrative, wisdom literature, funerary literature, and wishes for the afterlife. Such self-presentations highlighted the milestones and prominent situations of their protagonists' careers. A huge number of ancient Egyptian officials recorded such self-presentations, including priests, artists, physicians, court officials, civil and military officials of different ranks, as well as the administrative officials who supervised the royal court, the Egyptian borders, and Nubia. There were many different ranks in ancient Egypt that included first-class officials in addition to officials from the lower ranks. However, all the self-presentations that have come down to us relate to only the first rank of officials, and self-presentations of commoners and women were not documented until the Late Period.[29]

Self-Presentational Themes

The main theme of such self-presentations was to represent their subject in accordance with the beliefs of the elite class, and the main idea was to highlight the pious devotion of the protagonist before his or her deities, family, community, and future generations so he or she would remain commemorated.

It was important that his or her record of achievements should be remembered and venerated and that the family should enjoy the privileges that had come from it. They should enjoy what he or she had enjoyed during their lifetime and should rejoice in the eternal afterlife through the supply of physical offerings of food and beverages that should continue to be left in the tomb.

Within these self-presentations the subjects were represented as a reflection of the cultural and social lives that existed in ancient Egypt. Through these self-presentations, light is thus shed on the social, political, and economic life of ancient Egypt.[30] They present individuals in moral, social, and cultural contexts that are totally different from our contemporary understanding of self-presentation. The broad style of writing typical of ancient Egyptian literature, specifically that relating to the funerary context, represents the deceased as an ideal image and as a mediator to allow him or her to go on to paradise.[31]

In general, these self-presentations depend on patterns that contain the titles and attributes of the protagonist, his or her genealogy and appeal to the living, quotations from wisdom literature, and wishes for the afterlife. If the deceased did not receive the expected offerings, they would call on the living passing by their tomb to pray for them in a prayer such as the following:

> O, you who live upon earth,
> Who shall pass by this tomb
> Going north or going south,
> Who shall say, 'a thousand loaves and beer jugs'
> For the owner of this tomb,
> I shall watch over them in the necropolis.[32]

A later evolution of such appeals to the living is known as a 'verbal speech' in which the deceased assures the living that he needs nothing from them, rather than repeating a call to them, highlighting that this call is more important than the offerings themselves.[33] The formula can be found in the following text:

> A thousand types of bread and beer, oxen and fowl, ointment and clothing, incense, unguent and all kinds of herbs, all kinds of offerings on which a god lives, for the *ka* of the revered prince, count, royal seal-bearer, beloved of his lord, favored sole companion, deputy chief seal-bearer, Sehetep-ib-re, the justified, son of Dedet-Nekhbet, the justified.[34]

The context inscribed on the tomb walls of the deceased also highlights the high rank of the owner, expressing and framing it in a manner different from the images portrayed on the walls. Such verbal formulas include traditional phrases that refer to the origins and social status of the deceased, as well as his or her moral beliefs and contributions to society. For example:

> I have come here from my city,
> I have descended from my nome.[35]

Or:

> I gave bread to the hungry,
> clothing to the naked,
> I brought the boatless to land.[36]

The self-presentation of the Sixth Dynasty official Harkhuf is inscribed on the facade of his tomb at Aswan and is considered to be one of the best and most important examples of self-presentations from the Old Kingdom. It is rich in detail, excitement, and suspense, displaying life outside Egypt and its external role toward Nubia by the end of the Old Kingdom. Most probably the most elaborate element in this self-presentation is the part in which the child-king Pepi II sends a message to Harkhuf recommending him to take care of a dwarf he has brought. The phenomenon of enclosing messages from the king within the self-presentations of officials is a new trend during the Old Kingdom. Moreover, this self-presentation demonstrates the development of the genre. The traditional introduction includes "an offering which the king gives and Osiris," as well as the name and titles of the deceased:

> I have come here from my city,
> I have descended from my nome;
> I have built a house, set up (its) doors,
> I have dug a pool, planted sycamores.
> The king praised me,

My father made a will for me.
I was one worthy . . .
One beloved of his father,
Praised by his mother,
Whom all his brothers loved.[37]

Later Self-Presentations

From the Middle Kingdom, one can refer to a segment of the Twelfth Dynasty self-presentation of Ikhernofret inscribed on his stela, number 1204, in the Egyptian Museum in Berlin (Fig. 14.5). In this self-presentation, Ikhernofret describes the mission he was ordered by King Senwosret III to undertake from his royal court at Lisht in northern Upper Egypt to Abydos in Upper Egypt to restore a statue of the god Osiris and other statues related to him.[38] In addition, Ikhernofret brought the materials necessary for the rituals and accomplished the procedures requested to finish them at Abydos. He says:

14.5. Stela of Ikhernofret, Ägyptisches Museum, Berlin, ÄM 1204 (photograph by Sandra Steiß)

> I did all that his majesty commanded in executing my lord's command for his father, Osiris, Foremost-of-the-Westerners, lord of Abydos, great power in the nome of This. I acted as 'his beloved son' for Osiris, Foremost-of-the-Westerners. I furnished his great bark, the eternal everlasting one. I made for him the portable shrine that carries the beauty of the Foremost-of-the-Westerners, of gold, silver, lapis lazuli, amethyst,[39] *ssnḏm*-wood, and cedar wood. The gods who attend him were fashioned, their shrines were made anew. I made the hour-priests [be diligent] at their tasks I made them know the rituals of every day and the feasts of the beginnings of the seasons.[40]

The Eighteenth Dynasty self-presentations are remarkable (Fig. 14.6). The self-presentation of Ahmose, son of Abana, is considered to be one of the best among them. It is inscribed in his tomb at El Kab in Upper Egypt. The importance of this self-presentation is that it is a historical document relating the history of the expulsion of the Hyksos from Egypt from an Egyptian point of view in which the subject was an eyewitness and participated in contending against the Hyksos. Ahmose, son of Abana, says in this regard:

> Now when I had established a household, I was taken to the ship 'Northern' because I was brave. I followed the sovereign on foot when he rode about on his chariot. When the town of Avaris was besieged, I fought bravely on foot in his majesty's presence. Thereupon I was appointed to the ship 'Rising in Memphis.' Then there was fighting on the water in the 'Pjedku' of Avaris. I made a seizure and carried off a hand. When it was reported to the royal herald gold of valor was given to me.[41]

14.6. Statue of Amenhotep Son of Hapu, Egyptian Museum, Cairo (photograph by Sandro Vannini/Laboratoriorosso)

14.7. Statue of Bakenkhons, Staatliches Museum Ägyptischer Kunst, Munich (photograph by Marianne Franke)

The Nineteenth Dynasty self-presentation of Bakenkhons is inscribed on his block statue at the Egyptian Museum in Munich and was originally at the Karnak Temple in modern-day Luxor (Fig. 14.7). Bakenkhons was the highest priest of the god Amun for almost twenty years starting from the third decade of the reign of Ramesses II. He says:

I am one truly silent, effective for his god,
who trusts himself to his every action . . .
For [I am a humble man] whose hands are together upon the steering rope,
acting as a helmsman in life.
For I am happier (*nfr*) today than yesterday,
at dawn he will increase my happiness.[42]

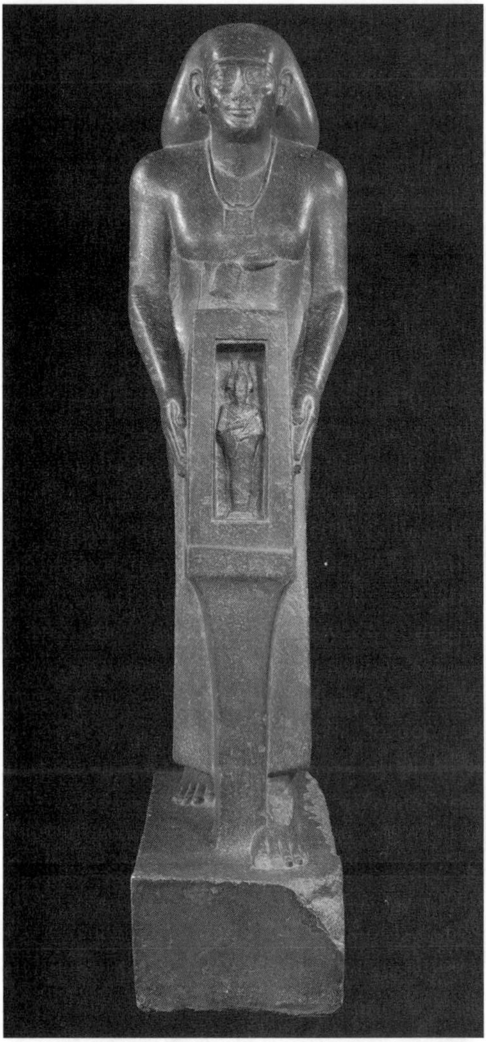

14.8. Statue of Payeftjauemawyneith, Musée du Louvre 93A (dist. RMN-Grand Palais/Georges Poncet)

The Saite Twenty-sixth Dynasty self-presentation of Payeftjauemawyneith displays the activities of restoration and heritage management of the ancestors which were practiced during the Twenty-sixth Dynasty. At the end of the Saite Period, Payeftjauemawyneith came from Lower Egypt on a royal mission to restore and rebuild the temple of the god at Abydos and Thinis in Upper Egypt. This self-presentation is inscribed on his block statue (A93) now on display at the Louvre Museum in Paris (Fig. 14.8). At the end of his self-presentation Payeftjauemawyneith mentions that:

His majesty praised me for what I had done.
May he give life to his son, Amasis son of Neith,
May he give me favors from the king,
And reveredness before the great god!
O priest, praise god for me!
You who come from the temple of the blessed, say:
May the high steward Peftuaneith,
Born of Nanesbastet, be in the god's bark,
May he receive eternal bread at the head of the blessed![43]

The Saite self-presentation of Neshor named Psamtikmenkhib on his statue Louvre A90 (Fig. 14.9). is very remarkable and sheds light on some unknown affairs taking place in the south. In this self-presentation, Neshor named Psamtikmenkhib says:

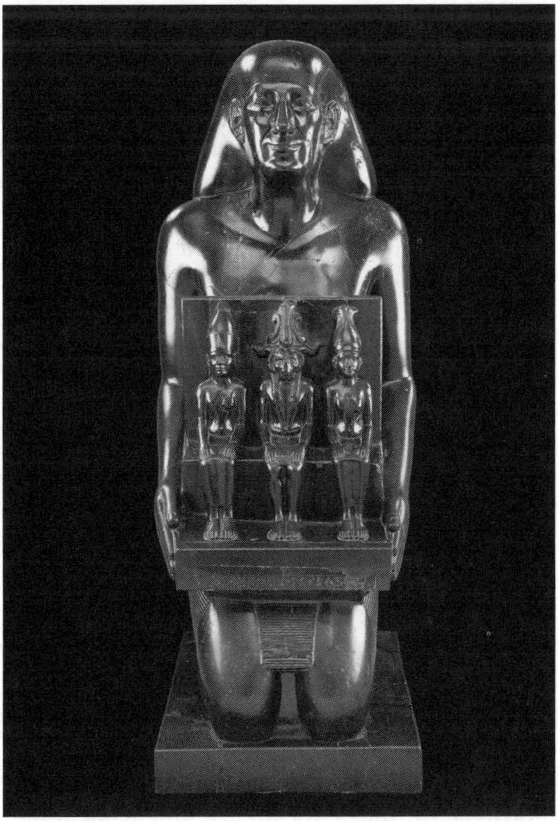

14.9. Statue of Neshor named Psamtikmenkhib, Musée du Louvre A 90 (dist. RMN-Grand Palais/ Georges Poncet)

> According as you saved me from a difficulty at the hands of the Bowmen, Bedouins, Greeks, Asiatics, and the rebels, who had put [plan]s into their heart(s) to go flee to Shais-Heret, being afraid of his majesty on account of the wretched act which they had done. I calmed their hearts with my actions, I did not allow them to go over to Nubia, but I made them go before the place where his majesty was. What his majesty did was their massacre (?).[44]

Furthermore, Late Period self-presentations focused on historical details of conquest, new ruling dynasties revealing changes in the state, and political attitudes toward the new administration.[45] The well-known self-presentation on the statue of the priest of Sais and chief physician Udjahorresnet in the Museo Egizio Vaticano is a good example of an Egyptian who collaborated with Cambyses, the Persian invader of Egypt. Udjahorresnet tried to demonstrate perfection in his ethical and political conduct.[46] In this context Udjahorresnet says:

> The Great Chief of all foreign lands, Cambyses came to Egypt, and the foreign peoples of every foreign land were with him. When he had conquered this land in its entirety, they established themselves in it, and he was Great Ruler of Egypt and Great Chief of all foreign lands. His majesty assigned to me the office of chief physician. He made me live at his side as companion and administrator of the palace.[47]

Conclusions

The traditions of Egyptian self-presentations were deeply rooted in ancient Egypt since the early Dynastic period, and they differed in aspect, composition, and themes from the beginning of Egyptian history to the late Dynastic period. Self-presentations display the lives of the elites and vividly represent their beliefs, culture, and expectations for the afterlife. Those texts also display their wish to be remembered and not to be forgotten after death. They reveal their eagerness to be commemorated by the living to avoid the possibility of a miserable afterlife.

The principal aim of writing self-presentations—or self-portraiture in words, similar to that in sculpture and relief—was to elaborately present the distinctive characteristics of individuals in a very positive way, showing their virtues and worthiness to enjoy eternity in the afterlife and in the eyes of future generations.[48] The relationship between royalty and nobility in self-presentations was changeable. In some periods, individuals witnessed a highly independent spirit, very visible in their self-presentations, when the power of elite members increased; and many cases reveal their king-like manner. Several examples reveal the rising power of the elite members. These actions of these nonroyal elite members are clear evidence for the prerogatives these officials probably received due to their rising power. Thus, Egyptian self-presentations were a reflection of kingship and a good indicator for the relationship between the king and his high officials.[49] Nonroyal elite members showed appreciation to the ruling king, and as a result, the king appeared in an outstanding position in their texts when he was very strong. If the king was weak, some nonroyal elite members expressed themselves in a kingly manner and, in some cases, ignored the ruling king or mentioned him briefly in a remote place that lacked appreciation, revealing an increased sense of individualism of the nobles. For example, the name of King Amasis is inscribed in a remote place toward the end of the self-presentation of Payeftjauemawyneith on his statue Louvre A93 (Fig. 14.10).[50]

The self-presentations and monuments of elite members preserve scattered specific events concerned with public and moments in their lives and careers, and not the entire process of their 'self-fashioning.' Thus, the content of the self-presentations are more personalized. Elite members represent the different aspects of Egyptian administration of the country. Some officials chose to narrate what they considered significant in their whole lives and careers, exploring self through their achievements. Self-presentations display different tones of individualism and reflect the person's formal achievements, spiritual thoughts and beliefs, and their hopes for the afterlife.

In order to reconstruct nonroyal individuals' lives and careers, we should, of course, know as much as possible about the individuals from birth to death. However, if we have little information about Egyptian individuals, it is not easy to fill in the gaps of their lives and careers, unlike the case with many modern (auto)biographies. Each self-presentation reveals its own method and composes part of the person's total self-presentations. Each one is a separate unit with a distinctive identity within the whole domain of each individual's self-presentation. This genre can be called fragmentary biography, as opposed to the lengthy traditional ancient Egyptian biography, due to the limited space of the monuments on which they are placed. Some self-presentations are short and commemorative and do not contain several topics. Moreover, some individuals have many self-presentations, probably for two reasons: to commemorate an achievement, and to record a new office that they reached in their careers.

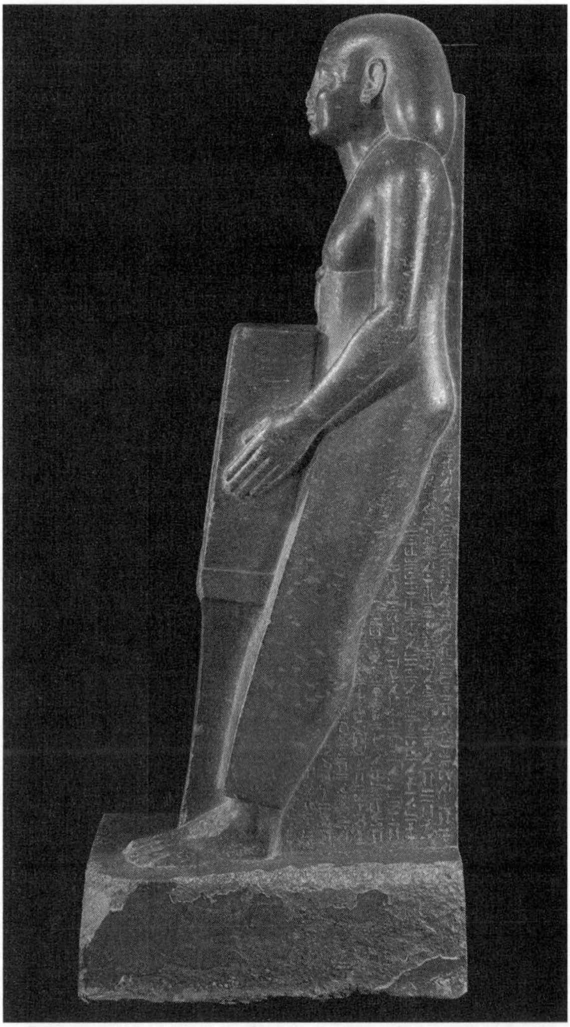

14.10. Statue of Payeftjauemawyneith, left, Musée du Louvre 93A (dist. RMN-Grand Palais/Georges Poncet)

Individuals' presence is very rich, especially when interacting with the formal presence of royalty. Therefore, the relationship between royalty and nobility in self-presentations is unique and helps us to understand the periods and the circumstances which produced nonroyal self-presentations. The role of the individual within the formal sphere of the political realm is much increased. The presences of individuality—the individual's presence, the deity's presence, and the king's presence—interact in the individuals' life, career, and the afterlife. Individuals' concepts of themselves, the deities, and the king are intertwined in their self-presentations.

There is an interplay of image and text in presenting the life and career of individuals' identities. The interdependency of literature and history through self-presentations is clear.[51] The self-presentations and monuments of nonroyal individuals help us to understand the individuals' selves in any period. The cultural and political practices that formed the history of any period are patronage, representations of authority, nobility, and royalty. The shaping force of history on the status of individuals is revealed through self-presentations that constitute as well as reflect history. The cultural and political practices of any period highlight the distinctive characteristics of self-presentation, and place each text and its owner within the broad context of Egyptian self-presentation traditions. The well-documented self-presentations of elite members are among the most remarkable of their times.

Notes

1 The self can be best defined, according to B.N. Olshen, "The Self," in M. Jolly, ed., *Encyclopedia of Life Writing: Autobiographical and Biographical Forms*, II (London, Chicago, 2001), 799, "as a kind of subjective structure – that is, one belonging entirely to the subject, to the individual who experiences, who is conscious, who has an 'inner life' and a point of view." Olshen, "The Self," 800, further states that "Instead of a concept of self, Stern suggests that we think in terms of the '*sense* of self', by which is intended something that encompasses more, something that extends further back in personal history, than a *concept* of self."

2 For more on the term life-writing, see D.J. Winslow, *Life-Writing: A Glossary of Terms in Biography, Autobiography, and Related Form* (Honolulu HI, 1980), 24, who points out that the inclusive term *life-writing*, which has been introduced since the eighteenth century AD, can mean biography in the narrow sense, and in general autobiography. See, also, M. Jolly, "Editor's Note," in M. Jolly, ed., *Encyclopedia of Life Writing: Autobiographical and Biographical Forms*, I (London, Chicago, 2001), ix, who states that the term *life-writing* refers to "openness and inclusiveness across genre" and "encompasses the writing of one's own or another's life." See, further, J. Baines, "Egyptian Elite Self-Presentation in the Context of Ptolemaic Rule," in W.V. Harris and G. Ruffini, eds., *Ancient Alexandria between Egypt and Greece* (Leiden, 2004), 34–35.

3 For more on survival and life writing tradition, see D.L. Ames, "Survival and Life Writing," in M. Jolly, ed., *Encyclopedia of Life Writing: Autobiographical and Biographical Forms*, II (London, Chicago, 2001), 854–856.

4 For more on the history and origin of this literary form in ancient Egypt, see G. Misch, *A History of Autobiography in Antiquity* (Cambridge, 1951 [1950]), 20–46. For an overview and historical survey from the Old Kingdom to the Late Period on this genre in ancient Egyptian literature, see A.M. Gnirs, "Die ägyptische Autobiographie," in Antonio Loprieno, ed. *Ancient Egyptian Literature: History and Forms* (Leiden, 1996), 191–241; A.M. Gnirs, "Biographies," in D. Redford, ed., *The Oxford Encyclopedia of Ancient Egypt*, I (New York, 2001), 184–89; O. Perdu, "Ancient Egyptian Autobiographies," in J.M. Sasson, ed., *Civilizations of the Ancient Near East* (New York, 2000 [1995]), 243–54; S. Kubisch, *Lebensbilder der 2. Zwischenzeit. Biographische Inschriften der 13.–17. Dynastie* (Berlin, New York, 2008); E. Frood, "Self-Presentation in Ramessid Egypt," PhD diss., University of Oxford, 2004; E. Frood, *Biographical Texts from Ramessid Egypt* (Atlanta, 2007); E. Frood, "Review of Kubisch, Sabine. 2008. *Lebensbilder der 2. Zwischenzeit. Biographische Inschriften der 13.–17. Dynastie*. Sonderschrift, Deutsches Archäologisches Institut, Abteilung Kairo 34, Berlin, New York: Walter de Gruyter," *Bryn Mawr Classical Review* 2011.03.79, 1; H. Bassir, *Image and Voice in Saite Egypt: Self-Presentation of Neshor Named Psamtikmenkhib and Payeftjauemawyneith* (Tucson, AZ, 2014). See, also, K. Jansen-Winkeln, "Lebenslehre und Biographie," *ZÄS* 131 (2004), 59–72; J. Assmann, "Schrift, Tod und Identität: Das Grab als Vorschule der Literatur im alten Ägypten," in A. Assmann, J. Assmann, and C. Hardmeier, eds., *Schrift und Gedächtnis: Beiträge zur Archäologie der literarischen Kommunikation* (Munich, 1983), 64–93; L.D. Morenz, "Tomb Inscriptions: The Case of the I versus Autobiography in Ancient Egypt," *Human Affairs* 13 (2003), 179–96; J. Stauder-Porchet, *Les autobiographies de l'Ancien Empire égyptien: étude sur la naissance d'un genre* (Leuven, 2017); N. Kloth, *Autobiographien des Alten Reichs und der Ersten Zwischenzeit* (Munster, 2018).

5 On this, one could also cite lately R.J. Leprohon, "Ideology and Propaganda," in M.K. Hartwig, ed., *A Companion to Ancient Egyptian Art* (Oxford, 2015), 309–27.

6 For more on self-presentation in ancient Egypt, see B. van de Walle, "Biographie," in *LÄ*, I, 815–22; M. Lichtheim, *Ancient Egyptian Autobiographies Chiefly of the Middle Kingdom: A Study and an Anthology* (Göttingen, 1988); M. Lichtheim, "Autobiography as Self-Exploration," in J. Leclant, ed., *Sesto Congresso internazionale di egittologia, Atti*, I (Turin, 1992), 409–14; P. Vernus, *Essai sur la conscience de l'histoire dans l'Égypte pharaonique* (Paris, 1995); S.-A. Naguib, "Mémoire de soi: Autobiographie et identité en ancienne Égypte," in E. Wardini, ed., *Built on Solid Rock: Studies in Honour of Professor Ebbe Egede Knudsen on the Occasion of His 65th Birthday, April 11th 1997* (Oslo, 1997), 216–25.

7 For more on the representation of the early kingship of royal women, see S. Roth, "Königin, Regentin oder weiblicher König? zum Verhältnis von Königsideologie und 'female sovereignty' in der Frühzeit," in R. Gundlach and C. Raedler, eds., *Selbstverständnis und Realität: Akten des Symposiums zur ägyptischen Königsideologie in Mainz 15.-17.6.1995* (Wiesbaden, 1997), 99–123.

8 For more, see J. Baines, "Forerunners of Narrative Biographies," in A. Leahy and J. Tait, eds., *Studies on Ancient Egypt in Honour of H. S. Smith* (London, 1999), 23–37; E. Edel, "Untersuchungen zur Phraseologie der ägyptischen Inschriften des Alten Reiches," *MDAIK* 13 (1944), 1–90.

9 For more on the king in the Old Kingdom, see J. Baines, "Kingship before Literature: The World of the King in the Old Kingdom," in R. Gundlach and C. Raedler, eds., *Selbstverständnis und Realität: Akten des Symposiums zur ägyptischen Königsideologie in Mainz 15.–17.6.1995* (Wiesbaden, 1997), 125–74.

10 However, N. Kloth, *Die (auto-)biographischen Inschriften des ägyptischen Alten Reiches: Untersuchungen zu Phraseologie und Entwicklung* (Hamburg, 2002), 38–39, puts this text not before the middle Fifth Dynasty, suggesting that various features of the decoration and the type of the self-presentation might indicate that the scenes were executed posthumously by his son.

11 N.C. Strudwick, *Texts from the Pyramid Age*, Atlanta 2005, 271.

12 See D. Franke, "First Intermediate Period," in D.B. Redford, ed., *The Oxford Encyclopedia of Ancient Egypt* (New York, 2001), I, 530.

13 See J. Clère and J. Vandier, *Textes de la Première Période Intermédiaire et de la XI Dynastie* (Brussels, 1948); Gnirs, "Biographies," 186; Perdu, "Ancient Egyptian Autobiographies," 2249.

14 See M. Lichtheim, *Ancient Egyptian Literature: A Book of Readings*, I, *The Old and Middle Kingdoms* (Berkeley, Los Angeles, London, 2006 [1973]), 85–86.

15 See J.M.A. Janssen, *De traditioneele egyptische Autobiografie vóór het nieuwe Rijk*, 2 vols. (Leiden, 1946); M. Lichtheim, *Maat in Egyptian Autobiographies and Related Studies* (Fribourg, Göttingen, 1992); See, also, Perdu, "Ancient Egyptian Autobiographies," 2249. For more on the king's image in the Middle Kingdom, see D. Franke, "'Schöpfer, Schützer, Guter Hirte': zum Königsbild des Mittleren Reiches," in R. Gundlach and C. Raedler, eds., *Selbstverständnis und Realität: Akten des Symposiums zur ägyptischen Königsideologie in Mainz 15.–17.6.1995* (Wiesbaden, 1997), 175–209.

16 Gnirs, "Biographies," 187.

17 For more on Second Intermediate Period self-presentations, see S. Kubisch, "Biographies of the Thirteenth to Seventeenth Dynasties," in M. Marée, ed., *The Second Intermediate Period (Thirteenth–Seventeenth Dynasties): Current Research, Future Prospects* (Leuven, 2010), 313–27, esp. 325; S. Kubisch, *Lebensbilder der 2. Zwischenzeit: biographische Inschriften der 13.-17. Dynastie*, passim.

18 See E. Rickal, "Les Épithètes dans les autobiographies de particuliers du Nouvel Empire égyptien," 2 vols. (Doctoral Diss., Université Paris IV–Sorbonne, Paris, 2005); E.B. Simmance, "Amenhotep Son of Hapu: Self-Presentation through Statues and Their Texts in Pursuit of Semi-Divine Intermediary Status" (MA Diss., University of Birmingham, Birmingham, 2014); Perdu, "Ancient Egyptian Autobiographies," 2251. See H. Guksch, *Königsdienst: Zur Selbstdarstellung der Beamten in der 18 Dynastie* (Heidelberg, 1994); A. Hermann, *Die Stelen der thebanischen Felsgräber der 18. Dynastie* (Glückstadt, 1940); also M. Schade-Busch, "Bemerkungen zum Königsbild Thutmosis' III. in Nubien," in R. Gundlach and C. Raedler, eds., *Selbstverständnis und Realität: Akten des Symposiums zur ägyptischen Königsideologie in Mainz 15.–17.6.1995* (Wiesbaden, 1997), 211–23; C. Maderna-Sieben, "Der König als Kriegsherr und oberster Heerführer in den Eulogien der frühen Ramessidenzeit," in R. Gundlach and C. Raedler, eds., *Selbstverständnis und Realität: Akten des Symposiums zur ägyptischen Königsideologie in Mainz 15.–17.6.1995* (Wiesbaden, 1997), 49–79.

19 See M. Sandman, *Texts from the Time of Akhenaten* (Brussels, 1938); Gnirs, "Biographies," 187; see also W.J. Murnane, *Texts from the Amarna Period in Egypt* (Atlanta, 1995); Gnirs, "Die Ägyptische Autobiographie," 230–33; Guksch, *Königsdienst*, 29–39, 62–65, 73–77.

20 For more see, Frood, *Biographical Texts from Ramessid Egypt*, passim.

21 See Perdu, "Ancient Egyptian Autobiographies," 2252. For the recent and full publication of Third Intermediate Period self-presentations, see K. Jansen-Winkeln, *Inschriften der Spätzeit I: die 21. Dynastie* (Wiesbaden, 2007); K. Jansen-Winkeln, *Inschriften der Spätzeit, II: die 22.–24. Dynastie* (Wiesbaden, 2007). See, also, E. Frood, "Sensuous Experience, Performance, and Presence in Third Intermediate Period Biography," in R. Enmarch and V.M. Lepper, eds., *Ancient Egyptian Literature: Theory and Practice* (Oxford, 2013), 153–84.

22 K. Jansen-Winkeln, *Inschriften der Spätzeit, III: die 25. Dynastie* (Wiesbaden, 2009). For more on the concept of kingship in the Kushite Twenty-fifth Dynasty, see K. Zibelius-Chen, "Theorie und Realität im Königtum der 25. Dynastie," in R. Gundlach and C. Raedler, eds., *Selbstverständnis und Realität: Akten des Symposiums zur ägyptischen Königsideologie in Mainz 15.–17.6.1995* (Wiesbaden, 1997), 81–95.

23 Gnirs, "Biographies," 187–88.

24 See Perdu, "Ancient Egyptian Autobiographies," 252–53. For the recent and full publication of Saite self-presentations, see K. Jansen-Winkeln, *Inschriften der Spätzeit, IV: Die 26. Dynastie*, 2 vols. (Wiesbaden, 2014). See also, U. Rößler-Köhler, *Individuelle Haltungen zum ägyptischen Königtum der Spätzeit: Private Quellen und ihre Königswertung im Spannungsfeld zwischen Erwartung und Erfahrung* (Wiesbaden, 1991).

25 See N. Spencer, *A Naos of Nekhthorheb from Bubastis: Religious Iconography and Temple Building in the 30th Dynasty* (London, 2006); N. Spencer, "Sustaining Egyptian Culture? Nonroyal Initiatives in Late Period Temple Building," in L. Bareš, F. Coppens, and K. Smoláriková, eds., *Egypt in Transition: Social and Religious Development of Egypt in the First Millennium BCE, Proceedings of an International Conference, Prague, September 1–4, 2009* (Prague, 2010), 441–90.

26 For example, the Saite tomb self-presentation of Ibi, see PM I.1.2, 63 ff.; K.P. Kuhlmann and W. Schenkel, "Vorbericht über die Aufnahmearbeiten im Grab des Jbj (Theben Nr. 36)," *MDAIK* 28 (1972), 201–11; K.P. Kuhlmann, "Eine Beschreibung der Grabdekoration mit der Aufforderung zu kopieren und zum Hinterlassen von Besucherinschriften aus saitischer Zeit," *MDAIK* 29 (1973), 205–13; K.P. Kuhlmann and W. Schenkel, *Das Grab des Ibi: Obergutsverwalters der Gottesgemahlin des Amun, Thebanisches Grab Nr. 36*, I, *Beschreibung der unterirdischen Kult- und Bestattungsanlage* (Mainz, 1983), 71–74, pls. 23–25; E. Graefe, *Untersuchungen zur Verwaltung und Geschichte der Institution der Gottesgemahlin des Amun vom Beginn des Neuen Reiches bis zur Spätzeit* (Wiesbaden, 1981), 21 ff.; J. Heise, *Erinnern und Gedenken: Aspekte der biographischen Inschriften der ägyptischen Spätzeit* (Fribourg, Göttingen, 2007), 116–26 (II.1); Rößler-Köhler, *Individuelle Haltungen zum ägyptischen Königtum der Spätzeit*, 216–18 (53 a). For his other self-presentation, see E. Graefe, "Die vermeintliche unterägyptische Herkunft des Ibi, Obermajordomus der Nitokris," *SAK* 1 (1974), 201–206; Heise, *Erinnern und Gedenken*, 127–32 (II.2).

27 For more on his tomb, see J. Richards, "The Archeology of Excavations and the Role of Context," in Z.A. Hawass and J. Richards, eds., *The Archaeology and Art of Ancient Egypt: Essays in Honor of David B. O'Connor*, II (Cairo, 2007), 327–33.

28 For more see, Bassir, *Image and Voice in Saite Egypt*, passim; Heise, *Erinnern und Gedenken*, passim.

29 For more on women's self-presentations, see Chapter 13 in this volume, and K. Jansen-Winkeln, "Bemerkungen zu den Frauenbiographien der Spätzeit," *Altorientalische Forschungen* 31.2 (2004), 358–73. One of the well-known women's self-presentations is the late Ptolemaic self-presentation of Taimhotep (on stela British Museum EA 147), wife of a high priest of Ptah in Memphis named Psherenptah. For more on her text, see J. Baines, "Stela of Taimhotep, 42 BCE," in M. Puchner, S. Akbari, W. Denecke, V. Dharwadker, B. Fuchs, C. Levine, P. Lewis, and E. Wilson, eds., *The Norton Anthology of World Literature*, A (New York, London, 2012), 92–94; M. Panov, "Die Stele der Taimhotep," *Lin. Aeg.* 18 (2010), 169–91; M. Lichtheim, *Ancient Egyptian Literature: A Book of Readings*, III, *The Late Period* (Berkeley, Los Angeles, London, 2006 [1980]), 59–65.

30 For examples from different periods, see K. Sethe, *Urkunden des ägyptischen Altertums: Urkunden des Alten Reiches* (Leipzig, 1932–1933); A. Roccati, *La littérature historique sous l'Ancien Empire Égyptien* (Paris, 1982); W. Schenkel, *Memphis Herakleopolis Theben: Die epigraphischen Zeugnisse der 7.–11. Dynastie Ägyptens* (Wiesbaden, 1965); K. Sethe, *Ägyptische Lesestücke zum Gebrauch im akademischen Unterricht: Texte des Mittleren Reiches* (Leipzig, 1928); K. Sethe, *Urkunden des ägyptischen Altertums: 7 Abt. (recto) Historisch-biographische Urkunden des Mittleren Reiches* (Leipzig, 1935); M. Lichtheim, *Ancient Egyptian Autobiographies Chiefly of the Middle Kingdom* (Fribourg, Göttingen, 1988); W. Helck, *Historisch-biographische Texte der 2. Zwischenzeit und des frühen Neuen Reiches* (Wiesbaden, 1983); K. Sethe and W. Helck, *Urkunden des ägyptischen Altertums: 4 Abt. (recto) Urkunden der 18. Dynastie, Fasc. 1–22* (Berlin, 1903–1958); K.A. Kitchen, *Ramesside Inscriptions: Historical and Biographical*, 8 vols. (Oxford, 1968–1990); K.A. Kitchen, *Ramesside Inscriptions Translated and Annotated: Translations*, I (Cambridge, 1993); K. Jansen-Wilkeln, *Ägyptische Biographien der 22. und 23. Dynastie* (Wiesbaden, 1985); E. Otto, *Die biographischen Inschriften der ägyptischen Spätzeit: Ihre geistesgeschichtliche und literarische Bedeutung* (Leiden, 1954).

31 See J. Assmann, "Schrift, Tod und Identität: das Grab als Vorschule der Literatur im alten Ägypten," in A. Assmann, J. Assmann, and C. Hardmeier, eds., *Schrift und Gedächtnis: Beiträge zur Archäologie der literarischen Kommunikation* (Munich, 1983), 64–93; J. Assmann, "Sepulkrale Selbstthematisierung im Alten Ägypten," in A. Hahn and V. Kapp, eds., *Selbstthematisierung und Selbstzeugnis: Bekenntnis und Geständnis* (Frankfurt, 1987), 208–32.

32 See Lichtheim, *Ancient Egyptian Literature*, I, 24.

33 For this formula, see P. Vernus, "La formule 'Le Souffle de la Bouche' au Moyen Empire," *RdE* 28 (1976), 139–45. That is really where we find "more important to the offerer than the deceased" texts.

34 See Lichtheim, *Ancient Egyptian Literature*, I, 129.

35 See Lichtheim, *Ancient Egyptian Literature*, I, 24.

36 See Lichtheim, *Ancient Egyptian Literature*, I, 24.

37 See Lichtheim, *Ancient Egyptian Literature*, I, 24.

38 For more on the image of Middle Kingdom kings, see Franke, "'Schöpfer, Schützer, Guter Hirte,'" 175–209; and esp. on Senwosret III, see L. Gestermann, "Sesostris III.: König und Nomarch," in R. Gundlach and C. Raedler, eds., *Selbstverständnis und Realität: Akten des Symposiums zur ägyptischen Königsideologie in Mainz 15.–17.6.1995* (Wiesbaden, 1997), 37–47.

39 See K. Yamamoto, "The Materials of Iykhernofret's Portable Shrine: An Alternative Translation of Berlin 1204, Lines 11–12," *GM* 191 (2002), 101–106. This then gives us a perfectly symmetrical list that consists of two kinds of metals, two semi-precious stones, and two kinds of wood.

40 See Lichtheim, *Ancient Egyptian Literature*, I, 124.

41 See M. Lichtheim, *Ancient Egyptian Literature: A Book of Readings*, II, *The New Kingdom* (Berkeley, Los Angeles, London, 2006 [1976]), 12

42 See Frood, "Self-Presentation in Ramessid Egypt," 97.

43 See Lichtheim, *Ancient Egyptian Literature*, III, 35. For more on this self-presentation, see H. Bassir, "On the Historical Implications of Payeftjauemawyneith's Self-Presentation on Louvre A 93," in R. Jasnow and K.M. Cooney, eds., *Joyful in Thebes: Egyptological Studies in Honor of Betsy M. Bryan* (Atlanta, 2015), 21–35.

44 See Bassir, *Image & Voice in Saite Egypt*, 38. For more on this self-presentation and the discussion of its content, see H. Bassir, "Neshor at Elephantine in Late Saite Egypt," *JEH* 9.1 (2016), 66–95.

45 See Gnirs, "Biographies," 188.

46 See Gnirs, "Biographies," 188. For more on Udjahorresnet, see M. Wasmuth, "Persika in der Repräsentation der ägyptischen Elite," *JEA* 103.2 (2018), 241–50; L. Bareš, "Offering Lists in the Large Late Period Shaft Tombs at Abusir," in K.A. Kóthay, ed., *Burial and Mortuary Practices in Late Period and Graeco-Roman Egypt: Proceedings of the International Conference Held at Museum of Fine Arts, Budapest, 17–19 July 2014* (Budapest, 2017), 47–52; K. Smoláriková, "Udjahorresnet: The Founder of the Saite-Persian Cemetery at Abusir and His Engagement as Leading Political Person during the Troubled Years at the Beginning of the Twenty-Seventh Dynasty," in J.M. Silverman and C. Waerzeggers, eds., *Political Memory in and after the Persian Empire* (Atlanta, 2015), 151–64; B. Menu, "L'apport des autobiographies hiéroglyphiques à l'histoire des deux dominations Perses," *Transeuphratène* 35 (2008), 143–63; J. Baines, "On the Composition and Inscriptions of the Vatican Statue of Udjahorresne," in P.D. Manuelian, ed., *Studies in Honor of William Kelly Simpson*, I (Boston, 83–92); U. Rößler-Köhler, "Zur Textkomposition der naophoren Statue des Udjahorresnet/Vatikan Inv.-Nr. 196", *GM* 85 (1985), 43–54; A.B. Lloyd, "The Inscription of Udjaḥorresnet: A Collaborator's Testament," *JEA* 68 (1982), 166–80.

47 Lichtheim, *Ancient Egyptian Literature*, III, 37.

48 Lichtheim, *Ancient Egyptian Literature*, I, 4.

49 On kingship in ancient Egypt, see, for example, J. Baines, "Kingship, Definition of Culture, and Legitimation," in D. O'Connor and D.P. Silverman, eds., *Ancient Egyptian Kingship* (Leiden, 1995), 3–47; J. Baines, "Origins of Egyptian Kingship," in D. O'Connor and D.P. Silverman, eds., *Ancient Egyptian Kingship* (Leiden, 1995), 95–156; R.J. Leprohon, "Royal Ideology and State Administration in Pharaonic Egypt," in J.M. Sasson, ed., *Civilizations of the Ancient Near East*, I (New York, 2000 [1995]), 273–87; R.

Gundlach, "Zu Inhalt und Bedeutung der ägyptischen Königsideologie," in R. Gundlach and C. Raedler, eds., *Selbstverständnis und Realität: Akten des Symposiums zur ägyptischen Königsideologie in Mainz 15.–17.6.1995* (Wiesbaden, 1997), 1–8; R. Gundlach, "Die Legitimationen des ägyptischen Königs: Versuch einer Systematisierung," in R. Gundlach and C. Raedler, eds., *Selbstverständnis und Realität: Akten des Symposiums zur ägyptischen Königsideologie in Mainz 15.–17.6.1995* (Wiesbaden, 1997), 11–20; R. Gundlach, *Der Pharao und sein Staat: die Grundlegung der ägyptischen Königsideologie im 4. und 3. Jahrtausend* (Darmstadt, 1998).

50 See Bassir, "On the Historical Implications of Payeftjauemawyneith's Self-Presentation on Louvre A 93," 24, 28–29, 31, 35.

51 For more, see C. Eyre, "The Semna Stela: Quotation, Genre, and Functions of Literature," in S. Israelit-Groll, ed., *Studies in Egyptology Presented to Miriam Lichtheim*, I (Jerusalem, 1990), 134–65; C. Eyre, "Is Egyptian Historical Literature 'Historical' or 'Literary'?," in A. Loprieno, ed., *Ancient Egyptian Literature: History and Forms* (Leiden, 1996), 415–33; M.A. Korostovtsev, "À propos du genre 'historique' dans la littérature de l'Ancienne Égypte," in J. Assmann, E. Feucht, and R. Grieshammer, eds., *Fragen an die altägyptische Literatur: Studien zum Gedenken an Eberhard Otto* (Wiesbaden, 1977), 315–24.